Free Market Economics, Third Edition

Free Market Economics, Third Edition

An Introduction for the General Reader

Steven Kates

Associate Professor of Economics, School of Economics, Finance and Marketing, RMIT University, Melbourne, Australia

Edward Elgar
PUBLISHING

Cheltenham, UK • Northampton, MA, USA

Published by
Edward Elgar Publishing Limited
The Lypiatts
15 Lansdown Road
Cheltenham
Glos GL50 2JA
UK

Edward Elgar Publishing, Inc.
William Pratt House
9 Dewey Court
Northampton
Massachusetts 01060
USA

A catalogue record for this book
is available from the British Library

Library of Congress Control Number: 2016962580

Printed on elemental chlorine free (ECF)
recycled paper containing 30% Post-Consumer Waste

ISBN 978 1 78643 138 7 (cased)
ISBN 978 1 78643 140 0 (paperback)
ISBN 978 1 78643 139 4 (eBook)

Typeset by Servis Filmsetting Ltd, Stockport, Cheshire
Printed and bound in the USA

Contents

Preface to the second edition   vii
Preface to the third edition   xi

Introduction   1

Definitions   8

1   The axioms and underlying principles of a free market economy   32

2   The economics of the free market   54

3   Value added   82

4   Governments and the market   93

5   Factors of production, finance, innovation and the role
    of the entrepreneur   108

6   Supply and demand   129

7   Supply and demand: beyond equilibrium   153

8   Marginal analysis   176

9   Measuring the economy   206

10 An interlude on the history of economics   240

11 The Keynesian Revolution and Say's Law   266

12 The basic Keynesian macroeconomic model   281

13 Aggregate demand and aggregate supply   309

14 The classical theory of the business cycle   329

15 The classical theory of growth and recession   353

16 Cyclical activity and governments   368

17 Savings and the financial system   385

18 Controlling inflation   416

Afterword   434

References   436
Index   439

Preface to the second edition

I wrote my *Free Market Economics: An Introduction for the General Reader* in early 2009, just as the various stimulus programmes were being put into place across the world to deal with the economic consequences of the Global Financial Crisis; it was written in white heat between February and May as the text for the course I was teaching in Economic Analysis for Business. What drove the book to completion was my dismay at the return of Keynesian theory and policy as the guide to recovery. My assumption at the time was that my book would be one of many such texts written in response to the devastation that would inevitably be brought on by the stimulus. What is to me quite astonishing is that this book, even in this second edition, remains the only book of its kind. I fear that, given the years of teaching nothing other than Keynesian theory, most economists can no longer see what the problem with modern macroeconomics is and why a Keynesian demand-side stimulus could not possibly have worked.

What makes this book different is that the macroeconomics is not just pre-Keynesian and not just un-Keynesian but actively anti-Keynesian. The book also explains Keynesian theory, of course, since it is impossible to teach economics without discussing modern macroeconomics as it is currently taught. Nevertheless, anyone interested in understanding the classical pre-Keynesian theory of the cycle, which focused on a very different explanation for recessions and an equally different path to return an economy to rapid rates of growth and low unemployment, will find no other introductory book to guide them in what I think is the right direction. Let me merely note that free market does not mean *laissez-faire*.

On the macroeconomics side, the core concept is what has come to be known as Say's Law, which few understand unless they have personally read the narrow and specialist literature on this fundamental concept. The one person, moreover, from whom one cannot find out its meaning is Keynes. Keynes made it his business to demonstrate that Say's Law is wrong; the original name of Say's Law, it might be noted, having been the Law of Markets. Keynes went about his work firstly by setting up his straw man version of Say's Law and then by refuting a proposition no one had ever supported. Indeed, it is utterly fantastic that Keynes was ever able to convince anyone that classical economists had always assumed full employment was assured even when they were discussing recession, but that he did. This has now entered into the mythology of economic theory, which is one of the reasons few economists look back at the economic theories that preceded the publication of *The General Theory*.

Since the very point of Say's Law was to deny absolutely that demand deficiency could have been the cause of recessions, even while recognizing that recessions were frequent and often devastating, it can be seen how different a non-Keynesian theory of the cycle is from virtually all versions of macroeconomics today. What this book does is provide a guide to the pre-Keynesian theory of the cycle which makes clear not only what does cause economic crises, but also why using Keynesian policy to attempt to restore growth through increasing aggregate demand is doomed to failure. Since these Keynesian policies have unquestionably failed, asking why that is ought to have become the main order of business across the economics world. Thus far, however, such concerns have been near invisible while the teaching of introductory theory remains largely undisturbed.

But the book does more than recast macroeconomics in its classical form. The microeconomic sections of the book also provide a different perspective on the nature of the market, the role of the entrepreneur and the unparalleled importance of uncertainty, whose significance in economic analysis cannot be exaggerated. The text wages a battle against the other major innovation of the 1930s, the diagrams associated with marginal revenue and marginal cost. Anyone who has studied economic theory has been dragged through a set of diagrams that show how the prices of individual products are determined according to where the additional cost of producing one more unit of output is equal to the additional revenue that would be received by producing that one extra unit of output. Maddeningly complex while simultaneously shallow, this will leave an economist almost completely unequipped to deal with the genuine questions an economy poses to policy.

This analysis, at the centre of what is called 'the theory of the firm', has distracted economists from focusing on what is most important about entrepreneurial decision making by making it appear that profit maximization is about getting marginal revenue (MR) to equal marginal costs (MC) by doing not much more than adjust prices and the number of units sold. The reality of business, however, is that the future is an absolute unknown; economic decisions are seldom about single products and never about whether one more unit of anything ought to be produced. Instead, virtually all economic decisions are based on conjectures built on the past and projected ahead into the future, about which nothing can ever be known with certainty, and the more distantly into the future decision makers project, the less they are likely to get right.

This, then, is how marginal analysis needs to be explained. Decision making occurs as the expected costs associated with some decision (their marginal cost) are weighed against the expected return (their marginal revenue). Such decision making has nothing to do with deciding whether to produce one more unit of output. It is about making decisions that often put millions on the line and involve years of pre-planning. The free market succeeds because there are many different projections being made by people who venture their own money and who therefore have the most intense interest imaginable in getting it right, and then correcting their errors when things go wrong, as they inevitably do. That is what marginal analysis is actually about.

The book is my update for the twenty-first century of two of economic theory's great classics: John Stuart Mill's *Principles of Political Economy* published in 1848, and Henry Clay's *Economics: An Introduction for the General Reader* published in 1916 and from which I adopted the title. They knew nothing of Keynesian economics other than its being a common but at the time unnamed fallacy that economists had to refute continuously. Keynesian economics is now, however, the mainstream. If you would like to understand what is wrong with Keynesian theory and much else, as well as understanding how to view the economy and economic issues from a classical perspective, this book is the place to start.

This will also explain the meaning of the cover, which shows a water mill made of clay which I chose precisely because the two most important influences on me have been John Stuart Mill and Henry Clay. I therefore looked for something fitting that description, a mill made of clay, and my wife found just such a combination up for sale. I therefore bought the plaque, which has a nicely archaic look, photographed it, and now the clay representation of a mill is on the cover. I also like it because it is both nineteenth century as well as being a representation of the productive apparatus of an economy. And it further fits in with my understanding of Jean-Baptiste Say, whose own factory was powered by a water mill of this type. Finally, I just think it is beautiful.

Let me also add how delighted I am that this second edition is being published in association with the Institute of Economic Affairs. There has been no organization more influential on my way of thinking about economic issues than the IEA, which almost alone stood up for free markets and free enterprise in those dark days of the 1970s and early 1980s. It was the IEA, which brought to wider public attention authors such as Milton

Friedman, Friedrich Hayek and James Buchanan. The points they made have to be continually reiterated, as ideas with a less impressive academic provenance, not to mention frequently disastrous economic results, continually take hold in public policy debates.

Preface to the third edition

The major change made in this third edition is to introduce a model of an economy that explains the difference between the modern theory of recession on the one hand, and the classical theory of the business cycle on the other. Mainstream theory continues to revolve around demand deficiency with the resulting policies to return an economy to rapid growth and full employment dependent on increases in aggregate demand. The theory has maintained its place in spite of the failure of increased public spending to achieve a recovery anywhere in the world at any time in history. Aggregate demand will eventually disappear from economics, although when that will be is hard to say. Bad theory does seem to persist for an unconscionably long period of time.

The model introduced in a new Chapter 15 explains the causes of recession in relation to distortions in the structure of supply through the use of a simple graphical model. Although the explanation in this new chapter provides greater clarity, it is only a summary statement of the arguments that were already present in the first and second editions. The model is based on the economics of John Stuart Mill and Henry Clay, as is almost the entire book and as were both the first and second editions, which is why the cover for this new edition continues to display a water mill made of clay.

Introduction

This is a book about the market economy.

A market economy is one in which overwhelmingly the largest part of economic activity is organized by private individuals, entrepreneurs, for personal profit. Such entrepreneurs are private citizens, not government employees. They make decisions for themselves on what to produce, who to hire, what inputs to buy, which machinery to install and what prices to charge.

There are, of course, in every nation state legislative barriers put in place by governments which limit every one of these decisions. No market is or ever has been even remotely laissez-faire. Entrepreneurial decisions are circumscribed by the laws, rules and regulations that surround each and every such decision.

And in every economy there are various areas of production undertaken by governments to a greater or lesser degree. There is no economy without government production of various kinds.

But in a market economy, although governments impose their will on the market process and engage in production themselves, it is the individual entrepreneurs who make the ultimate decisions on the largest part of what is produced, how it is produced and the prices that are to be paid.

It is from these activities that entrepreneurs earn their incomes. It is how they earn the money they spend. It is through their value-adding activities that their own purchasing power is created, and not only their own but the purchasing power of their employees as well. Indeed, since governments live off tax revenues, a government's own ability to spend on what it buys is largely dependent on that same entrepreneurial success.

SHARING THE WEALTH

There are, of course, other ways of claiming a share of the output of an economy. Theft, charity, welfare, government grants of various kinds all provide an opportunity to receive some part of what has been produced.

But while each of these has economic consequences, they are not forms of market activity. Providing charity is an individual choice that will have as much if not more to do with the surrounding culture than it has to do with the nature of the economic system.

The provision of welfare by governments is a political decision that is generally unrelated to the economic system, except to the extent that welfare is more likely to be provided in strong economies than in weaker.

Government grants – the receipt of income through political decisions rather than through the market – is a major industry in itself. Governments are prevailed upon at every turn to hand out money, usually but not always with some stated social purpose attached.

Many such projects do not even achieve the social purposes that their advocates have promised, but whatever may be the outcome, the decision is made by those with political power for political reasons. Not all decisions to direct money in some particular direction are intended to strengthen the economy, and even where it is the intent, governments are often poor judges of the economic benefits of what they do.

But this at least can be said. The ability of governments to make such grants is ever-dependent on the underlying strength of the economy from which the expenditure must be funded. There is therefore always at least some interest in governments to see the community prosper. It is well that there is.

Because it is here that the market comes into its own. It is only in market activity that those who receive incomes give something back in return, and by the nature of the system give back at least as much in value if not more than what was received. It is only through market activity that those who receive do so because they have also produced.

It is therefore only through the market that wealth and prosperity can be achieved. It is upon the market-based exchange economy, one of the greatest social discoveries ever made, that our living standards depend.

THE NATURE OF MARKET ACTIVITY

Market activity is about earning an income of one's own by creating goods and services for others to buy. It is a natural part of human life in the complex societies in which we live.

But to speak of a market economy is to speak of an abstraction. By focusing on production, exchange and the enjoyment of the produce of economic activity, it seems to remove the processes involved in earning a living from the day-to-day lives of people. It seems to suggest that there is economic activity over here, and then over there is something else which makes up the rest of life somewhere else.

One of the greatest English economists, Alfred Marshall, defined economics in this way. 'Political economy', he wrote on the very first page of his book first published in 1890, 'is a study of mankind in the ordinary business of life' (Marshall [1920] 1947: 1). There is a great deal of compartmentalization that often goes on when economics is discussed formally. There is a sealing off of economics from the everyday world when it is, in fact, seamlessly connected.

Contrasting economic activity with the study of economics is quite instructive. Economic activity is, as Marshall said, about getting on with life itself. The study of economics is about trying to understand the processes involved.

Economic activity is about people doing things that make them materially better off. The study of economics is about putting together formal analytical structures that neatly wall off such activities from everything else. Economic activity is about doing things. The study of economics is about explaining things.

What is important, therefore, in thinking about economics is that it is understood that outside the text and the theory are just people going about their lives, producing things for others and trying to earn incomes for themselves. In burying oneself in the formal study of economics, strangely enough it is possible to forget that for most people economics is just about getting on with the ordinary business of living.

There is also a notion that exists in some areas that the economics of the market and markets themselves ignore such problems as poverty, disadvantage or economic harm. That the attitude of a 'market' economist is to leave the economy to sort things out and let the chips fall where they may.

An economy is part of a community's political structure. There are innumerable ways that the political process will deal with various economic concerns.

Economic theory does not pretend to provide answers for all of life's problems, not even for all of our economic problems. No matter how an economy is run, there will be differences of income, differences in wealth, differences in power and ultimately differences in outcomes.

But what economics does do is let you understand the trade-offs that are intrinsically involved in making decisions. You cannot have everything, economists point out. You have to choose, sometimes between two goods and sometimes between two bads to work out which is the least worst.

And no matter what you do, from time to time there will be recessions and unemployment. There will be disappointment and failure.

But as history has so amply shown, the one and only road to improving the living standards of a community is through putting in place institutional structures that encourage entrepreneurial activity, continuous innovation and market-driven change.

FREE MARKETS AND POLITICAL FREEDOM

And then there is this. The free market is the only economic system consistent with personal freedom. It thus not only provides the basis for the greatest improvement in living standards, it also provides the basis for remaining free of political control over our lives.

The only other way to organize an economy is through central control and centrally determined collective action. There is a belief held by many that it is only possible to coordinate the required actions of an economy through some form of government planning and direction. With no government to coordinate activity, it is said, there is no basis for individuals working together.

It is, in fact, the opposite which is true. It is the market, and market-based activity, that is irreplaceable as the means to foster cooperative action, to encourage people to work together. And it encourages such cooperative activity because it harnesses the self-directed interests of individuals.

But it is only where such individuals are free to make decisions on their own without reference to anything other than the law of the land – where the law is itself designed to allow individuals the widest scope for making such decisions on their own – that the most productive economic decisions are made that raise, over time, the living standards of all.

ECONOMICS IS POLITICAL ECONOMY

Economics is, moreover, a branch of politics. No economic decision is ever made by economists unless the authority to make that decision has been given by those who hold political power.

Economics is also a branch of philosophy. Economists think about the good life and how to get it. There has never been an economics tract of any consequence that did not outline how its author believed the lives of individuals could be improved by organizing the economy in one way rather than another.

Economics is also by nature a guide to action. It sketches out the contours of the economic system, explains how the various bits and pieces are related to each other, and brings the lot together in such a way that those who make economic decisions are able to understand how to achieve the political ends they seek.

When all is said and done, it is those who hold the political levers of the state who decide about many if not most of what will determine the ability of a nation's economic system to perform to its potential. And overlaying all of the economic considerations will be the political demands placed upon an economy by those with political power who, in an ideal system, are responsive to the individuals in whose interests they govern.

The ancient name of economics was 'political economy'. This was in many ways more accurate as a description of the subject matter of this area of study. Politics dominates. There is no economic system anywhere that is now or ever was that has not been profoundly shaped by the political world in which it is found.

It is why books on economics are so frequently designed as manuals for government.

But there are still many reasons for the rest of us to understand how economies work. We each have to make our own way in the world based on our own assessments of what is going on. Having an understanding of economic matters is amongst the most useful areas of knowledge one can have.

By studying the economy we can judge, assess and see the consequences of the many events that will affect our own lives. It helps to explain the world we live in and can help in making decisions in the face of the uncertainties we face.

It is also useful to understand what governments are doing even when there is nothing we can do to change it. Government economic blunders of the most expensive kind are common. A knowledge of economics provides the necessary insight for a ringside seat in what is often the most intensely contested area of political debate. As with any sport, only if one knows the rules can one genuinely follow the game.

HOW THIS BOOK IS DIFFERENT

This book describes itself as being about free market economics. How, it might be wondered, does this approach differ from any other? There are a number of ways, but a few stand out.

To begin with, this book is about the entrepreneur. At the very centre of economic activity are those individuals who decide for themselves to earn their incomes by owning and running a business. Other texts seem to take a cosmic approach where things just happen without identifying the role that specific individuals have played. Ignoring the role of individuals ignores everything important about how a market economy works, indeed about how any economy works.

And then there is this. The book embeds uncertainty at every step. Much of economics is taught as if not knowing what the future will bring is just one of those things that have no effect on how economies are managed or on how economics should be taught. In reality, the fact that the future is unknown, that tomorrow may bring the most profound forms of change, means that economics and economic management must be approached in a very particular way. Uncertainty means that an economy can never be managed from the centre, that it must always be managed in as decentralized a way as possible.

To think that governments or public servants or any central body can know and understand anything other than the most minute part of what needs to be known is to be blind to the ultimate reality of economic life.

Thirdly, this book more than just dispenses with an innovation introduced into economic theory in 1936, which is the concept of aggregate demand; it attempts to demonstrate at every turn just how fallacious and misguided it is. There is now virtually no text on the economics of output, employment and growth that does not start from the notion that variations in the level of demand are needed to account for variations in the level of activity. It is the argument of this work that this is not just a poor way of thinking about such issues, it is positively wrong and guaranteed to mislead.

But because aggregate demand is now the bedrock foundation of the branch of economic theory dealing with the economy as a whole, the theory of aggregate demand is explained in this book in exactly the same way as it might be found in any normal work of economic theory. It is essential to understand the frame of reference in which decision makers are making their decisions.

The largest revolution in economic theory during the twentieth century was brought about by the English economist John Maynard Keynes who published his *General Theory of Employment, Interest and Money* in 1936. It was he who introduced aggregate demand into economic theory by rejecting a principle that had until then been part of the very foundations of economic theory.

That principle, known as Say's Law, denied in absolute terms the validity of the theory of aggregate demand. No discussion of economic theory in general since 1936 has attempted to return Say's Law to the central position it had previously held. This book does.

The full name of Say's Law was Say's Law of Markets. It is the essence of market-based economics. Without the clarity that the Law of Markets brings, economic theory has lost its moorings and the irreplaceable value of leaving things to the market in directing economic activity cannot be understood.

And because this book looks back at economic theories that had flourished before Keynes wrote his *General Theory*, it presents the classical theory of the business cycle which since 1936 has all but disappeared from economic discourse. The theory of the cycle, however, has the ability to penetrate into the darkness left by Keynesian theory in understanding the causes of recession and the steps that are needed to bring recovery about.

Finally, the book looks at the nature of the money market and uses pre-Keynesian forms of analysis to understand the nature of the inflationary process. No one can promise to settle for all time the theory of money and inflation, but what this book at least does is examine and explain theories of inflation that were common before Keynesian economics swept the field. These are market-based theories that still make logical coherent sense and shed light on what remains one of the most difficult areas of economic thought.

Definitions

Before venturing into the full text before you, it is useful to have a few definitions in your mind. The language of economics is entirely made up of words that have ordinary meanings in everyday life. But these words, when they cross over into economics, suddenly take on very specific meanings that can cause someone to lose the thread during an economic discussion. I therefore provide a series of definitions of the specialized words used in the text. Having at least a preliminary grasp of these words and their more technical meaning will also in itself provide a grounding in the nature of the economic theory you will meet in the rest of the book.

Economics often looks easy because everyone already thinks they understand what is going on in an economy without even having to study. Not true at all. For an economist it is painful to hear the mistakes that those who have not studied economics to at least a reasonable depth constantly make. But there are also major differences in the conclusions different economists reach, and these are often at a very deep level that no lay person could possibly resolve.

This text will teach you everything you will find in studying economics in a normal, usual way. But it also provides a second perspective that has been taken from the economic theories that were dominant from the mid-nineteenth century through until the 1930s. Unlike with the natural sciences, economic theory does not progress to higher planes and then remain there. Economic theory is infused with the hopes and wishes of policy makers and of those who study the subject who are predisposed to some particular point of view. People just wish the world was one way, when the way things are turns out to be something else again, and their wishes cause them to accept economic theories that are not properly grounded in the way the world actually is.

The definitions found here are already pointing in a particular direction. The very first definition is 'entrepreneur'. These are the people who run our businesses and often, if they are successful, become very wealthy as a result. As this book will explain, entrepreneurially managed firms are the foundation for wealth and prosperity for an entire community but also for personal freedom and independence from government. Economic attitudes are often determined by one's reactions to entrepreneurs running our firms.

Some people do not agree that we should allow people to run firms any way they like as long as they follow the law. Some people think that governments should run our businesses, or at least our major businesses. Or if they do not run them, should have a major say in what they do.

These are, of course, philosophical and political issues that are absolutely part of economics when thought about in the widest sense, but are not part of what gets taught at the introductory level when starting out on economic theory. Yet this is the foundational point. Economics, as we teach it and learn it today, assumes that most of what is produced is produced by businesses independent of governments and run by entrepreneurs for a profit. These businesses sell goods and services in a market, where they are bought by consumers with money they have for the most part earned by providing either their own labour or some other input into the production of some other good or service. How this process works in detail is what the study of economic theory is about.

The following list of definitions is not in alphabetical order but in a logical thematic order, so that in reading through the list from beginning to end, an overview of the economic theory presented in the text is provided in summary. Each of these concepts is expanded on in much greater detail in the text itself.

Entrepreneur

At the very centre of the economic process in a market economy is the entrepreneur, the person at the very top of a business. Entrepreneurs in a market economy are a self-selected group who earn their living by running businesses. No government appoints them. No government chooses them. They are people who rise up the hierarchy of large businesses or often simply start their own small businesses. Whichever route to the top they have followed, the entrepreneur in each firm is the final authority in deciding what to produce, how to produce, who to hire, how much to borrow, which capital to use, which innovations to attempt. Most economic theory seems to assume there are impersonal forces that cause whatever it is that happens. The reality is that there are actual people who make the decisions that set the entire process in motion. A market economy operates through entrepreneurs making specific decisions. It is these decisions that determine the direction in which an economy will travel and the more successful entrepreneurs are in the decisions they make, the more successful an economy will be.

Market economy

A market economy is one in which most of the production decisions are made by entrepreneurs running their own businesses. Most of what is bought is bought using incomes that have been earned by helping to produce something else. It is called a 'market' economy because virtually everything is bought using the money one has earned in producing these other products. There is no predetermined set of goods and services that will be produced, and no already worked out way describing how what is produced should be produced. A market economy is, instead, a free-flowing set of arrangements in which everyone makes decisions for themselves about what to produce and for whom to work. The singular characteristic is the existence of decentralized decision making in which individuals make their own decisions based on the opportunities they recognize, and then use either their own money or the money they have borrowed to put their own plans into operation in the best way they are able to do.

Microeconomics
Microeconomics is the part of economic theory that deals with individual decision making. It looks into consumer behaviour, production decisions, price setting, resource allocation and the theory of the firm. It asks why particular decisions are made and tries to explain how the entire economy knits together, looking at the incentives, options and contributions of individuals acting both on their own and collectively within the economy.

Values
Economic theory presupposes that the world is populated by people who are rational, self-interested and moral. The assumption made is that individuals, in trying to feed, clothe and house themselves, will think about the best way to achieve their ends (that is, they are rational), that their focus will be on themselves, their families, their friends and their communities (that is, they are self-interested), and they will act according to their own traditions and personal values (that is, they will behave morally). The market economy is not driven by greed and dishonest practice. The market economy provides an organizational structure that combines the maximum possible personal freedom with an ability to achieve the highest possible standard of living.

Value
The desirability of various goods and services in economics is subjective, personal. But value as discussed in economics is not entirely a first person concept. Value is determined by what other people will offer in exchange for some good or service and is usually given as a sum of money where that money could have been used to buy other things. And while there are other objectives in life besides having more goods and services, when value

is discussed in economics it is a discussion of economic goods, those goods and services that are produced for sale to others. Their value is determined according to the sum of money that one is prepared to pay. If one object costs twice as much as something else, then it is twice as valuable. The relative value in terms of price is what value ultimately means in economic discussion.

Value added

No concept may be more important than value added, not only in understanding how an economy works but also for making sound judgements about public policy. Every good or service sold on the market has value, and this obviously includes goods and services used as inputs in producing something else. Producing just about anything requires a combination of labour time, raw material inputs, capital equipment, along with whatever else was required to bring the product to completion. Each of these inputs had value. The final product also has value. Value added has occurred only if the value of the output is greater than the value of the inputs that were used in its production. Economies will only grow if in aggregate the value of products produced has been greater than the value of the products that were used up.

Macroeconomics

Macroeconomics is the study of economic aggregates. Unlike microeconomics, which looks at the individual units that make up the economy, macroeconomics looks at the various totals which are seen to somehow interact with each other. It examines consumer and investment behaviour, the effect of government spending or international trade on an economy. It takes the entire economy looked at as a whole as its province for study but often without sufficient regard for its individual constituent units.

Keynesian economics

At the centre of macroeconomic theory, going back to the publication by John Maynard Keynes of his *General Theory of Employment, Interest and Money* in 1936, is the belief that the buying of things creates economic growth irrespective of whether what has been produced is value adding in and of itself. The driving force in Keynesian economics is the level of demand. That is why a government stimulus during recession is often the policy of choice. The assumption is that no matter what the money is spent on, by increasing the level of demand such spending will get the productive ball rolling by encouraging higher levels of production and employment. Irrespective of whether a stimulus has been itself value adding, those who spend the stimulus money received will themselves create value by encouraging the production of goods and services they seek for themselves. This entirely ignores the importance of the structure of production in understanding how an economy functions.

Structure of production
The structure of production refers to the way in which an economy as a whole fits together. Every output has their inputs, and each of those inputs has inputs of their own, and so on throughout the whole of the economy. There are literally an unquantifiable number of individual units of capital, workers and potential workers each of every kind who collectively possess a vast array of skills and abilities, along with resources of every kind found in different places undertaking particular roles. All of these inputs must be fit together to produce the output that is part of a process that eventually brings to us the goods and services we consume. Keynesian economics thinks in terms of aggregates, entire blocks of buyers and producers. Economic theory properly conceived instead looks at the atomic structure of the economy, at each of the individual productive components separately to understand how they can all be made to work together in a productive way. Moreover, Keynesian economics focuses almost entirely on final demand and ignores the actual structure of the economy, which it treats as irrelevant. Pre-Keynesian classical theory, on the other hand, thought of the structure as the crucial issue. They focused on whether the structure of production was synchronized with what buyers were spending their money on. For classical economics, it was whether the structure of supply could rapidly conform to the structure of demand that was the matter of first importance in understanding how well an economy worked. The Pre-Keynesian theory of recession was based on explaining why the structure of supply and the structure of demand might no longer be in harmony. Policy during recessions was therefore directed towards restoring this balance by hastening, as best a government could, the readjustment of the economy until the structure of supply and demand were in conformity once again. You will never understand anything worth knowing about an economy if you do not understand its structure of production and how it is made to work.

Economic growth
An economy can only be said to be growing if value added across all productive activities taken together is positive. That is, an economy grows only if the value of output in total is greater than the value of all of the resources that were used up during production. One of the greatest of all economic fallacies is the belief that it is the using up of resources that creates growth, which is the concept behind Keynesian economic theory.

But it is not using resources in 'any which way' that is value adding. Only if there were more value at the end of the process than existed at the beginning could it be said that genuine value-adding activity has occurred and the economy has grown.

Innovation

It is innovation that drives an economy towards a higher standard of living. Innovation consists of new products, improved products, improved technologies, more efficient use of labour and improved labour market skills. Most innovation is not about doing the same things as before but in a better way. It is more often about doing new things in a completely different way. People have been using a device called a telephone since the late nineteenth century but the telephone of today cannot be compared with the telephone back then other than in the most primitive way. The succession of innovations between that time and this has made this device, for all practical purposes, into an entirely different product. Almost all innovation in an economy is driven by private sector entrepreneurs without whom almost no innovations would ever reach the market.

Knowledge

What makes the world we are in so extraordinarily productive is that we dwell in what might be called the 'knowledge economy'. It is the commercialization of scientific knowledge and technological advance that makes the difference in living standards today. It is not improved efficiency in the narrow sense that matters, it is not just doing the same things but in a better way that matters, but that we have created entirely new products that were inconceivable to earlier generations. It is our ability to harness such knowledge that is now the single most important driver of economic change. It is the extensive use of entrepreneurial decision making that make possible the systematic acquisition and implementation of this knowledge.

Stocks

Stocks in an economic sense are not company shares sold on the stock exchange. Nor are stocks merely the inventories kept by retailers and manufacturers. When an economist discusses stocks what is being discussed is the accumulation of past production that remains in the present. Stocks are the inheritance from the past, whether for an individual firm or for the economy as a whole. Indeed, almost the entire productiveness of a national economy is based on the vast accumulation of what has already been produced, the buildings, factories, roads and productive facilities. And not only these, but also the knowledge embodied in individual people, the skills they have, their know-how and abilities. It is these which differentiate one economy from another or the same economy in different periods of time. It is this inheritance, this stock of accumulated assets and knowledge that, more than anything else, distinguishes one economy from another.

Flows
Flows are the net increments added to existing stocks during some period of time. Stocks and flows are related terms, with the traditional definition of a flow as the change in the level of stocks. In thinking about the economy in general, it is the stock of existing productive assets, including human capabilities, that determines how much additional output, the flow of goods and services, can be produced in any period of time. Most measures of economic activity in an economy are flow measures. There are almost no measures of stock. Our concentration on flow unfortunately obscures what may be the more important of the two in terms of how well we live.

Production possibility curve
The production possibility curve is the best diagram in economics. If properly understood, it is the only diagram that is unlikely to mislead you in understanding what it is intended to explain. It is very simple: two axes and a semi-circular arc bowed out from the origin are all there is. An economy whose level of production is represented as being on the arc is producing as much as it possibly can. It is using all of its productive resources as efficiently as possible in producing some particular array of output, say consumer goods and capital. After that, if the economy is on that arc, there are no other resources available in that economy to produce anything else. The diagram therefore reminds you that an economy has limits, that even the largest economy cannot produce everything that would satisfy everyone's desires, and that a community must have some mechanism for deciding what gets produced and who gets what. It also reminds you that if we want more of something, until the economy has grown, more of one good can only be produced by having less of something else. And if an economy is producing less in total than it might have, it is either because its resources, especially its labour, are not fully employed, or even if its resources are fully employed, they are being used in a wasteful way.

Opportunity cost
What does something cost? In economics, the core idea is that the cost of something is what has to be given up in order to get it. Nothing in an

economy comes without an associated cost. Everything requires choices to be made. Opportunity cost emphasizes what has been given up in order to receive whatever one has received. To have more of one product means, given the limitation of resources, there must be less of something else. And it is a reminder that what limits how much anyone can receive is not the amount of money but the productiveness of the economy, that is, how much it is able to produce.

Factors of production

Productive inputs, the factors of production, are classified into a number of broad categories. These factors of production are the basic types of inputs whose presence is required to allow productive activity to occur. The traditional factors of production are *land, labour* and *capital*, to which the essential role of the *entrepreneur* is sometimes added, although more often it is not. But even these four are not enough, so added to these is *finance*, without which most forms of productive activity could never occur. And there is a sixth discussed in the text which is the *knowledge, skills, know-how and abilities* possessed by labour as well as the *technological sophistication* of the capital. It is not merely more labour and capital that make an economy grow, but improvements in their productiveness, especially in what capital is capable of achieving. And finally, although seldom discussed, *time* is itself a factor. The time required for a process such as fermenting wine or growing timber must be included as a separate component in production since reducing the time required to complete some process is, of itself and separately from the others, an important way to increase the amount of output an economy can produce.

Capital

Capital in common usage refers to finance, credit, money. And while occasionally that is the meaning it can have in economics, that is not what it properly means when discussing the operation of an economy. Probably we should make the distinction between 'financial capital' which is money and credit, and the 'capital stock' which is the actual implements used in production. When we talk about capital in economics, we are almost invariably talking about physical inputs into the production process that have themselves been created by the production process. It is improvements in capital in its widest sense that cause economic growth, not just the amount of capital but the technical capabilities as well. An economy grows, in large part, not just because it has more capital but also because capital has become more productive through innovation and technological changes.

Capitalist system

It is sometimes said that a market economy is a 'capitalist' economy, as if capital were the actual difference that mattered. Every economy requires capital, and improvement in the capital stock does lead to improvement in living standards. But it is not the existence of capital or owners of capital that make the difference, but the role of the entrepreneur. When someone discusses 'capitalism' what they really mean is an economy where its direction comes from private sector entrepreneurs. The owners of capital are often also entrepreneurs, but unless they run businesses, the owners of capital are not the people who make the economy what it is.

Consumption

The final end of all economic activity is to satisfy the needs and wants of the population. The term that has come into use within economics, to describe the purchase of goods and services by the community, is 'consumption'. When the term is used today, that is what is meant, buying things for final personal use. In earlier periods in economics, consumption meant using up. A new product might have emerged, but the labour time, raw materials, capital equipment or whatever had been devoted to some particular use, had been consumed, that is, had been diverted into this particular endeavour with some of the inputs, such as the flour that went into the baking of the bread, gone entirely. The modern meaning of consumption is the purchase of goods and services by their final consumers. But its alternative, earlier meaning, should also be kept in the back of your mind since it points in the direction of a more profound understanding of the ways in which economies work.

Investment

Investment is value-adding activity which draws down on resources in the present to enlarge the productive capabilities of the economy in the future. The word when used in economics must never be confused with investment in the share market or any other kind of financial investment of money to earn more money. Investment in economics is a form of production. Most economic activity is the use of resources to produce goods and services for final use by consumers. Investment is the use of resources to build an economy's productive strength. Consumption and investment are thus alternative uses of a nation's resources. In both cases the resource base is drawn down. With consumption the resources are gone and nothing has replaced them. With investment, in place of the resources that were used are various forms of capital allowing the economy to produce more than it had before.

Saving

Saving is a word you are guaranteed to misunderstand unless you make the effort to see the point. Saving in everyone's mind is about individuals putting money in the bank or keeping a store of money in some financial institution for later use. Thinking only in that way will ensure that you never understand how economies work. Unlike an individual, a nation cannot save by putting money in the bank or keeping a store of cash and credit on hand. National saving, the only kind of saving that is of interest if we are discussing the national economy, is the use of a nation's resources in productive ways. In an economy, the resources available can be used to produce consumption goods or they can be used to produce investment goods. A nation saves when it is investing and not when it is consuming.

Price

In a market economy, everything comes at a price which is almost invariably denominated as so many units of the local currency. The price of such products is decided by the sellers, although in saying this it must be understood that there are an immense number of constraints on sellers that narrow their pricing options. A seller cannot choose just any price and cannot raise (or lower) prices without significant consequences. There may be a best price from the seller's point of view but it is very hard for the seller to know what that price is. A price, in a market economy, does more than indicate the number of units that have to be paid to a seller. The price is also a reflection of scarcity on the one hand, and the intensity of demand amongst those who wish to purchase the good or service on the other.

Supply and demand

Supply and demand is the way in which production and sale are discussed within economic theory. For everything that is bought there had to have been a seller and a price. Where many units are sold to many different people, there are usually many sellers and a large number of units sold. Supply and demand analysis is the way economists discuss how individual prices are determined by the market and what causes those prices to change. Also part of supply and demand analysis is an explanation of how the volume of sales is determined in the market and how the number of units bought and sold changes over time.

Supply and demand analysis

Supply and demand has become something of a formalized clichéd expression which refers to the standard explanation given by economists for how prices are set and volumes determined for any single product. In the standard analysis, we are dealing with a single product because the aim is to conceptualize how individual prices are determined and what causes the number of units to be sold to be whatever it is. One might use this kind of analysis with cars and cameras in a superficial way, but since every model of car or camera may have a different price, this standard approach is clearly meant to be taken as metaphorical rather than actual, not a genuine description of the operation of a market. Cars and cameras do not collectively have a single price. There may be a price for a particular car model at a particular time or place, but there cannot be a price for all cars in general.

Ceteris paribus

In an actual economy everything is going on at one and the same time. It would not be going too far to say that everything is related to every-thing else, so that cause and effect are often very difficult to isolate. Why did some price change? In the buzz of events, it is hard to know what in particular made the difference. For this reason, within economic analysis the approach is to look at the effects of particular circumstances one by one. Formally, it is said that *all other things being equal* the effect of a change in some specific particular circumstance on some specific event has been such and such. We know that other things were happening at the same time, but if we wish to look at the effect of one particular cause on outcomes, then we say that 'all other things being equal' – that is, the effect of this one particular change – will have these consequences. The Latin phrase for 'all other things being equal' is *ceteris paribus*, which is a phrase often used by economists. For economists, having a factory across the road from a house will, all other things being equal, tend to lower the value of the house, irrespective of whatever other features the house may have.

Market

There are literally millions of products sold today, from paperclips to ocean liners, and for each one there is a separate market, that is, a sepa-rate set of circumstances that determines how many units are produced and the prices that are charged for each unit put up for sale. The market in general is the process by which all goods and services are sold, while particular markets refer to the purchase and sale of individual products. The notion of a market is a hangover from the use of supply and demand curves in showing how prices are determined for single products. Because supply and demand relate to the purchase and sale of individual products, the focus has been given to individual products on their own rather than to the structure of production in which each product sold is recognized as just one microscopic part of a much larger whole.

Competition

A market economy is designed to encourage competition between sellers with the aim being to encourage each to perform at their highest level. This is a process that is good for those who buy, since the competition between sellers ensures that prices are held down, products are continually improved and innovation is a continuous process. It is often said that such competition is an obstacle to cooperative behaviour amongst producers, but this is untrue. A market economy, because of the competition for buyers, ensures that there is large-scale cooperation across the economy between producers and their suppliers. The market economy and the price system are, in fact, specifically designed to encourage as much cooperative activity as possible.

Supply

Supply is not an amount but an invisible barrier whose whereabouts is never known by anyone. In every market during any period of time there is a maximum amount of each product that sellers in aggregate would be willing to sell at each price. Individual sellers may know how much they would individually be willing to sell (although they probably do not), but in relation to the market as a whole no one can possibly know how many units in total all sellers taken together would be willing to sell at different prices. Supply curves, as drawn by economists, are thus a useful fiction providing information that is never known by any market participant, but they set out, in abstract, the forces that exist in every market that help to determine how many units of each good or service will be produced and what their price will be.

Demand

Like supply, demand is also an invisible barrier whose whereabouts is never known to anyone. In every market during any period of time there is a maximum amount of each product that buyers, in aggregate, would be willing to buy at each price. Individual buyers may know how much they would individually be willing to buy but in relation to the market as a whole no one can possibly know how many units in total all buyers taken together would be willing to buy. Demand curves, like the supply curves drawn by economists, are a useful fiction providing information that is never known by any market participant, but which set out in abstract the forces that exist in every market that help to determine how many units would be bought at different possible prices.

Price determination

Goods and services are sold in a market economy at a price that is somehow, in some way, determined by the forces of supply and demand.

Those with a product to sell make decisions about what price they should charge, the most important constraints typically being their own production costs and the prices being charged by others for similar products. But into these pricing calculations go many other considerations, both long term and short, that are matters of judgement. Supply and demand is the theoretical answer, but since no one setting a price has any idea where these curves are, nor could they even pretend to do the kind of analysis that somehow equates the quantity produced with the quantity bought across the entire market, given the multitude of products a typical business sells, there is more of a trial-and-error approach to pricing than any kind of science.

Equilibrium

Equilibrium in economics is a condition where all of the forces in play are balanced in such a way that whatever the situation happens to be, it would be expected to continue into the future without change if there were no outside disturbance to cause change to occur. With supply and demand, the price and volume set would be expected to continue as far as the eye can see unless there were a change in underlying *ceteris paribus* conditions. Similarly with an economy taken as a whole. Things would be expected to continue without change unless something occurred to shift those forces which till then were in balance. But here is the reality. Nothing in an economy is ever in equilibrium. It is a condition that is never met because no economy nor any part of it is ever in a situation where the factors affecting current conditions are stable. Thinking about economies and equilibrium brings together two notions that really have nothing to do with each other. Economies are always shifting, sometimes experiencing more turbulence than other times, but they are always shifting. There is no equilibrium. The best definition of equilibrium is a condition where all expectations are met. This is obviously a condition that could never exist in the real world.

Uncertainty

The absence of sure knowledge about the future is the province in which all economic activity takes place. No one knows what is coming next. The analogy used in the text is of someone in a foreign land where they have never been before, sitting on a train with their back to the engine. All they know about what is ahead is based on what they see out of the window. They can make conjectures about what is ahead but they cannot know. This is the world in which businesses must make their own decisions. And not just businesses. Everyone must make their own economic decisions based on their own best estimates of what is ahead and how best to prepare themselves for what is coming. But no one can really know, so the possibility of error is large and therefore so too is the possibility of large-scale loss.

Risk
Because there is uncertainty in the nature of things, there are risks in every decision made. There is an approach to risk that contrasts it with uncertainty by arguing that risk is probabilistic. But this is a distinction that makes no real advance. Since economic activity is about making a single throw of the dice and not about repeatable events, it all falls back to uncertainty. And given how many facets there are to virtually every economic decision, with so many complex elements that can go wrong with major consequences, the traditional distinction between risk and uncertainty is of little practical value. In the end, every decision comes with risk because the future is uncertain and therefore outcomes will be different, sometimes very different, from how they were originally expected to be.

Economic decision making
At the centre of economic decision making – really at the centre of any decision making – is the recognition that decisions are made in the present before the consequences of those decisions are known. And because decisions are made before the consequences are known, those decisions may turn out to be wrong. Had they known then what they know now, they would not have done what they did. But they did not know then what they know now, so they made the decision and paid the price. A market economy is designed around a recognition that decision makers need to take responsibility for their mistakes. With that kind of pressure on them, those who make such decisions are, firstly, less likely to make mistakes but, secondly, are also more likely to try to repair what has gone wrong and adjust to accommodate the situation as it actually turned out to be.

Marginal analysis (traditional)
The word 'marginal' in standard economic theory means 'extra' or 'additional'. The marginal benefit from some decision is the extra or additional benefit that is gained from taking usually a single step in a particular direction, which is then compared with the addition to costs. Decision making thus involves doing whatever adds more to benefits than it does to costs. It is seen as the core of economic decision making where, it must again be emphasized, the concept deals with the effect of small adjustments on single entities producing a single product.

Marginal analysis (this text)

In the text, marginal analysis is recognized as the core of economic decision making, but the discussion is not talking about incremental change in one variable compared with its effect on some other variable. Decision making is almost always about making a decision about some complex action taken in the present where costs are borne in the expectation of an even greater return in the future. All decisions are made in what, at the time the decision was made, was the present. All decisions are made *now*, at some particular moment in time. In making these decisions, there is what is already known about the past, or at least what someone thinks they know about the past, which is mixed with the conjectures one has about the future. A decision is essentially a step into the dark. But almost every important decision is accompanied by a very deliberate weighing up of all of the possibilities. Marginal analysis is the process in which these possibilities are weighed up and a conclusion reached where the positives from making some decision are weighed up against the negatives.

Marginal revenue

The benefits of making a decision are usually classified as the revenue that will accrue from having made the particular decision. It is too narrow a measure and even when revenue is the operative word, the reality is that it is the benefits in the widest possible sense, including additional revenue, that are being assessed. Marginal revenue (MR), as discussed within economics, is the extra or additional revenue one expects to receive as the result of making a particular decision over and above the revenues one is already receiving. The expected effect on revenue is the marginal revenue. It is the additional benefit that comes from making some decision and, as noted, is more than just revenue, although in economic analysis it is almost always restricted to the monetary return.

Marginal cost

Nothing in economics comes without cost. When one makes a decision to do something, there are always costs involved. In making some decision, the extra or additional costs that are incurred because of that decision is the marginal cost (MC). It is the negative side of making some decision. These are the outlays paid that allow the revenues to be eventually earned. Note that the costs must almost inevitably come before the compensating revenues are earned.

Cost–benefit analysis

The proper basis for understanding economic decision making and marginal analysis is to recognize that when decisions are being made on whether or not to undertake some project, a project that might cost millions and take years to complete, the marginal revenue (MR) is compared against the marginal cost (MC). That is, at the moment that the decision is made, the *expected* additions to revenues are compared with the *expected* additions to costs. If the expectation is that there will be a greater addition to revenue than the addition to costs, then the decision to go ahead with the project will be taken. If, however, the expected addition to costs is greater than the expected addition to revenue, then whatever the project might have been will be rejected. Importantly, part of the cost is the opportunity cost which are projects which might otherwise have been undertaken instead. If more than one project has a potentially positive return, the choice must then be made between which will provide the best option from the perspective of those who are making the decision.

Profit maximization
Businesses can only survive if their revenues are greater than their costs, and the greater the excess of revenue over costs, the greater the profit will be. But costs must be borne before revenues are earned. Moreover, decision making must be focused on different time horizons: sometimes the immediate present, sometimes the distant future and sometimes somewhere in between. The actions of a business must be arranged in such a way that bills are paid on time and revenues cover costs, so that eventually the business has been profitable for its owners. Profit maximization cannot be summarized as any particular description of what any business will do. Profit maximization must instead be seen as a guiding principle in the management of a business since only if revenues are greater than costs will the firm survive. Beyond that, so long as costs are being met, the profitability of the firm remains something that will be determined by market outcomes.

$MR = MC$
You are warned to keep away from the following analysis which argues that profits are maximized where $MR = MC$. This is an approach that is exceptionally complex and yet will leave you with almost no understanding of what takes place in business or how decisions are actually made. This explanation of profit maximization looks at only a single product but is nevertheless often described as 'the theory of the firm'. It argues that profits are maximized for the sale of single products when marginal revenue and marginal cost are equal. It is based on adding or subtracting single units of output to see what happens to revenue and costs as more is produced and sold. If the effect of lowering price to increase sales causes the *addition* to revenue to exceed the *addition* to costs (that is, $MR > MC$),

then the advice would be to continue until adding one more unit of output leads to an increase in revenue equal to the increase in costs (that is, where $MR = MC$). At this level of output, profits are said to be at their maximum.

Money

Money is the generally accepted medium of exchange, that is, a token of purchasing power recognized by all participants in an economy. Few goods can be used as a generally accepted medium of exchange. Unlike with the possession of money, for example, it is all but impossible to exchange a basket of apples for some other good or service. But if the apples are first exchanged for a sum of money, the money can then be exchanged for other goods and services almost at will. It is this exchangeability that makes money so crucial to the smooth running of an economy. But money also has another function, which is as a *store of value*. One will only accept money for one's apples if the purchasing power of the money received remains intact for a reasonable period of time. If the value of the money rapidly diminishes, its usefulness also diminishes since the money is no longer in itself a place where value can be stored. There is also a third very important role for money, which is as a *unit of account*. People who use a particular currency are familiar with what it will buy and how difficult say a thousand units of the currency are to get. Money prices therefore provide some idea of the relative value of different products, which is very important for both consumers and businesses in making decisions about what to do.

Relative prices

A price is just a number with almost no meaning in itself until it is related to the difficulty required to get the number of units of currency required to pay the price attached to some good or service. But more importantly, so far as the economy is concerned, it is *relative* prices that are of first-rank importance. Buyers can make judgements on the qualities of the products they wish to buy and compare how much they have to pay for one product rather than another. In the same way, producers are able to use the relative prices of possible inputs to work out the lowest-cost means to produce. This not only ensures that prices are kept as low as possible but also means that production across the economy is driven to its highest level of efficiency.

Finance

Few firms are able to pay for all of their inputs from revenues already earned. Virtually all firms depend on finance, which is essentially borrowed savings that come as money in one form or another. But the actual resources that are used in production must always be kept in mind as the actual reality behind the money borrowed. It is to secure use of these resources that the money is borrowed. That is what finance does and is for.

Credit and debt

Expenditure in business typically occurs before sufficiently high revenues to cover the costs are earned. Businesses must therefore be built by using the money that has been saved by others to purchase the needed inputs so that production can take place while the cost of inputs, such as the wages paid to labour, is being met. What is borrowed comes in the form of money, or much more commonly as a credit entry in a financial institution. The funds borrowed are then used to pay for the resources used during production, which are only available because others have chosen to save.

Interest rates

Interest rates are the price of borrowed money, but seen more deeply and from the perspective of the entrepreneur, are the price paid to gain access to the available savings for use in production. There are two associated concepts that must be kept straight since both are crucial to understand the nature of investment and economic growth, the money rate of interest and the natural rate of interest. These are discussed in turn below.

Money rate of interest

The money rate of interest is the price of money and credit. The money and credit received, usually from financial institutions, can be used to buy the resources needed for production, but are not themselves those resources. Interest rates are determined by the supply and demand for such funds. Interest rates are influenced by the risks associated with lending the funds to particular users, by the current rate of inflation, by the call on funds by governments, and by any other factor that influences either the willingness to lend by those with funds or the willingness to borrow by those without. That is, interest rates are determined by the supply and demand for money and credit.

Natural rate of interest

The natural rate of interest is the price of the real savings available in an economy. Real savings is an aggregate concept which embodies all of the resources available for investment purposes. While the supply of money and credit can be increased almost at will, increments to the amount of resources available can only take place very slowly. In equilibrium, the money rate of interest and the natural rate are the same. If, however, they are different there are then a number of consequences for the economy. Good economic policy will try to keep the two rates aligned by letting the market determine the money rate of interest. Most importantly, if the money rate is lower than the natural rate, there are fewer resources available for use in investment project than there is money and credit. The result is slower growth, misdirected resources and a higher price level. Artificially low money rates of interest can do great damage to an economy.

Monetary policy
Monetary policy is the use of variations in the money supply and interest rates, usually with the intention of influencing the rate of economic growth, unemployment or the inflation rate. There are a number of techniques used by governments and central banks to raise and lower interest rates and the money supply. The two most important are *open market operations*, in which the money supply is increased by buying bonds from the public (that is, the public has more money in its hands but fewer bonds), and *adjusting the reserve ratio* which sets the proportion of the deposits that a bank must hold and not lend out (that is, the higher the reserve ratio, the more money a bank must keep in its vault and the less it can lend out).

Recession and depression
An economy is an extraordinarily complex network of production and sale, with most of the production devoted to producing inputs into the production of other inputs with only a very small proportion, less than 10 per cent of all economic activity, devoted to actually selling goods and services directly to consumers. Because an economy can make use of every value-adding form of production, a well-managed economy is structured to ensure that all of its resources are being used in the most productive way the economy can make use of them. But on occasion the complex network of relationships will become unbalanced so that the economy does not perform at its peak level. The most important characteristics at such times are the slowdown in economic activity and widespread loss of jobs.

Recovery
An economy in recession is not an inert mass where everyone simply stops working and lets fate take its course. In a market economy, everyone must make their own efforts to find work and employ their capital. While governments can take useful actions, most of the adjustment is undertaken by individuals assessing their own circumstances and accommodating

themselves to the new situation. This adjustment is taken on by every-one: by entrepreneurs, by workers, and by the owners of capital, build-ings and land. Eventually as these adjustments take place, the economy turns upwards and a full-scale recovery begins. That is, it will do so if the recovery process is not impeded by inappropriate actions taken by gov-ernments, the most typical of these being attempts to generate recovery through higher levels of non-value-adding public spending.

GDP

Gross Domestic Product, GDP, is the most significant measure of pro-duction in an economy. It is published as part of the most comprehen-sive set of data on an economy in a publication that is referred to as the *National Accounts*. It is the measure of economic growth used universally to determine the level of output. The methodology used in the expenditure approach, which is the most intuitive of the three ways GDP is measured, is shown in this identity:

$$Y \equiv (C + I + G + X) - M$$

Here Y stands for GDP while $(C + I + G + X)$ represents everything bought within the country by consumers (C), investors (I), the government (G) and by those living in other countries (X as in eXports). If what was imported, M, is subtracted from the total of everything that was bought, the remainder must as a matter of logic be the amount of output produced in the domestic economy.

Unemployment

Unemployment, as it is commonly understood, is where someone wants a job but is unable to find one. But unemployment is difficult to measure since the unemployed are often hidden away out of sight, which is why unemployment is measured using a statistical survey by national statistical agencies in every country. The unemployed, so far as the official statisti-cal measure is concerned, are those individuals who are old enough to work, want to work, are actively looking for work, could take a job if one were offered, but have not worked for even so much as an hour during the survey week. This convoluted definition is a useful reminder of how difficult economic concepts often are to measure.

Unemployment rate

The unemployment rate is the measure of unemployment used in most economies. It is the proportion of the entire labour force who are officially measured as being unemployed. The labour force is the total of those who are employed plus those who are unemployed, according to the labour force survey.

Nominal

In measuring an economic variable such as GDP, the means chosen to esti-mate the level of production between two years is to add up all of the pur-chases in each of the two years and then calculate the growth rate between the first year and the second. And that would be a perfectly reasonable approach if the price level has not risen (or sometimes fallen) between the two periods. Estimates made in the *original prices* are called nominal or money estimates. Comparisons between two periods are described as the nominal increase or the money increase in the variable. One might, for example, discuss the nominal growth in GDP or the nominal growth in consumption, but no one ever does. For almost every purpose in economics, nominal estimates are of little use.

Real

For most economic variables, there is an adjustment made to remove the effects of price movements between two periods. A nominal series is made up of a quantity of some sort, Q, and the price at which each unit was sold, P. The total amount sold is thus P times Q, that is, PQ. So if in one period the total amount sold is Q_1 and the average price at which these were sold is P_1, then the total amount is P_1Q_1. If in a second period, the quantity was Q_2 and the average price was P_2, the total would be P_2Q_2. Clearly, P_2Q_2 may be bigger than P_1Q_1 either because the quantity was larger or the prices were higher, or some combination of the two. When one is interested in the real growth, the interest is in what happened to the quantity, in this case how much larger (or smaller) Q_2 is compared with Q_1. This requires the removal of prices so that the real difference, the volume difference, may be calculated. How this is normally done is to decide arbitrarily that one year is the base year and then calculate the total level of sales at that base year price level in both years (or in terms of most statistical data, every year's figures are calculated at base year prices). In this example, if the first year were the base year, then the volumes in year two would be calculated using the first-year prices. Thus P_1Q_2. Not at all an easy thing to do, but the cal-culation of the real growth rate would then be P_1Q_2 relative to P_1Q_1 and when the prices are cancelled out, we are left with the *real* rate of growth.

Consumer Price Index

The most common measure of inflation in just about every economy is the Consumer Price Index (the CPI). There is a list of items bought by con-sumers, which is referred to as a 'basket of goods', and the actual cost of buying these items in retail outlets is estimated by the national statistical bureau on a regular basis. The series is not, however, published showing the actual total cost of the items, but as an index. If prices grow by *x* percent, the index grows by *x* percent. The rate of growth in the price level between any two time periods is determined by calculating the growth rate in the index between these time periods.

Seasonal adjustment

Most statistical series, such as GDP or unemployment, are published not just annually but on a quarterly and sometimes even monthly basis. These data are therefore often affected by seasonal variations, such as the upturn in both GDP and employment in the period before a holiday period and the lower level of activity that typically follows afterward. Statistical data are therefore adjusted for these seasonal variations so that the underlying movements are not affected by these regular and expected variations that are known and can be expected to occur.

Inflation

Inflation is the term used to describe the situation when the exchange value of money in relation to what each unit of currency will buy decreases. The purchasing power of a unit of currency falls so that what once could be bought with say ten units now requires a payment of 12. When inflation occurs, the usefulness of money as a store of value diminishes. Decision making during inflationary periods becomes more difficult since it is hard to judge what future costs of production will be. Much effort is also made to find alternative stores of value which can divert economic activity away from value-adding activities to those in which money will hold its value even if the assets bought, such as gold, are not productive in themselves.

Keynesian policy

A Keynesian policy is one that is based on increasing the level of demand across the economy as the means to hasten the rate of growth and keep unemployment as low as possible. It is the foundation for understanding macroeconomic behaviour, and based on belief that economies are pulled along by their level of demand. It is demand that comes first. The more demand there is in aggregate, the faster the economy will grow. But what is most important is that, according to Keynesian theory, the faster an economy grows, which means the greater the level of demand, the more employment there will be. Keynesian policies are typically introduced during recessions to hasten the return to faster growth and lower unemployment.

Aggregate demand

Aggregate demand is the single most important element in modern macroeconomic theory. The fundamental equation for Keynesian policies is based on aggregate demand and is similar to the equation for calculating expenditure-based growth in GDP but the brackets are put in a different place and it is an equality rather than an identity:

$$Y = C + I + G + (X - M)$$

Aggregate demand, Y, is made up of the sum of everything bought by consumers (C), plus everything bought by business investors (I), plus everything bought by governments (G), plus net exports which are exports minus imports ($X - M$). If you can raise Y, according to Keynesian theory, you can raise employment. In recession, therefore, government policy is designed to raise its own expenditure, and as G rises, so too, according to this theory, will Y and therefore so too will the level of employment. Although this has been the basic framework for macroeconomic policy since 1936, there has not been a single instance in all that time in which an economy has moved from recession to full recovery using a Keynesian expenditure policy.

Say's Law

Say's Law was the core proposition of the pre-Keynesian theory of recession. According to Say's Law, demand deficiency is never the cause of recessions and an increase in demand by governments will never lead to an economic recovery since demand deficiency is not the problem that must be fixed. The phrase associated today with Say's Law is the phrase used by Keynes, 'supply creates its own demand'. According to Keynes, and as a result just about every other economist since that time, the meaning of 'supply creates its own demand' was that everything produced would always be sold. No economist would ever have been so lacking in understanding of how an economy actually operated to have ever believed that this was true. What Say's Law did mean – and it is crucial to understand in framing policy during recessions – is that only if the increase in demand is based on an increase in value-adding forms of production could that increase in demand lead to a sustained increase in employment. Most economists before the publication of *The General Theory* assumed that no government would be able to achieve an increase in aggregate demand of this kind, and on the experience since that time they have been shown to have been correct in their judgement.

Aggregate supply

Aggregate supply was grafted onto Keynesian theory in the 1970s when it became obvious that economies could and did go into recession because of problems that occurred on the supply side of the economy. A fall in aggregate supply would therefore lead to a fall in output and employment. But even with the addition of aggregate supply, aggregate demand remained the actual driver of activity and employment.

Classical theory of the cycle

Prior to the coming of Keynesian economics, the theory of recession that was held by economists was described as the theory of the cycle. Economies were expected during some periods to perform better than in other periods. There would be periods of prosperity followed by periods of recession which were, in turn, followed by periods of prosperity. The theory of the cycle was developed to explain these cyclical movements. At the centre of the classical theory of recession were explanations why the *structure* of supply would diverge from the *structure* of demand which were based on explaining why entrepreneurial decisions had turned out badly. Such explanations centred on understanding what had taken place in an economy that had caused such decisions to have been mistaken, with changed credit conditions often but not always the most important reason. Recessions are a recurring problem for which there is still no solution. They are certain to occur from time to time, no matter what policies are pursued.

Classical policy in recession

Pre-Keynesian policies to promote recovery were based on taking actions that would assist entrepreneurs to adjust in the face of large-scale changes in the economic environment. This could include lowering business taxes, lowering interest rates, removing regulations that impeded the adjustment process, allowing real wages to adjust to encourage employment and taking steps to lower unproductive forms of spending. Recovery was seen to mean recovery of the private sector, which was the approach taken by pre-Keynesian economists and policy makers. But most of what needed to be done had to be done by individuals within the economy – the owners of the factors of production which included not just entrepreneurs but the owners of capital and their employees as well – as they tried to work out where safety lay. When recessions commence, during what is called a *crisis*, there is a subsequent period of about 3–6 months that is typically a period where it is difficult to know what to do, but as time goes by and resources shift to where they can again earn a positive return, recovery occurs, the economy picks up strength and unemployment falls.

1. The axioms and underlying principles of a free market economy

Before taking a single step into the formalities of economic theory, there are some things that have to be understood about the nature of the world if one is to understand how market economies work or even why they exist. Call these the basic axioms of a market economy:

- Nobody knows the future.
- Everything is always in the process of change.
- Commercially useful knowledge is diffused everywhere across an economy.
- Without market prices no one can tell what anything costs.
- In the commercial world, everyone does what is best for themselves.

What we have here are statements about the world that are the bedrock foundations for understanding why a free market economy is the only kind of economy that can deal with the world as it actually is. The opposite of each of these cannot be entertained. No one can genuinely argue on behalf of any of the following:

- that the future is known and knowable;
- that change either never happens or takes place so slowly that it makes no difference;
- that there is someone or some group who knows everything about the economy that needs to be known to run the economy from the centre;
- that it is possible to tell what something costs without prices that reflect scarcity and demand; or
- that individuals within an economic environment can realistically be expected to act in the best interests of total strangers rather than themselves.

Because these axioms are true statements about the nature of the world, we need an economic system able to cope with things as they actually are. Let us look at these axioms one by one.

NOBODY KNOWS THE FUTURE

If the future were known, or even knowable, there would hardly be a need for markets or market adjustment. It is because the future is invisible, except as inferences from what we see in the present and what we have learned from the past, that economic decision making is so difficult. The possibility of error is always present in every decision, and the farther into the future a return is expected, the greater is the risk of loss.

This is the most basic fact about economies: all decisions are made about the future before the future becomes known. There is therefore a need to find institutional arrangements that reward good decisions and punish those decisions which turn out to have been wrong. No one may be at fault, but unless those who run a business understand that it is their own responsibility to make that business succeed, the kinds of incentive to get things as right as possible will not be present.

And the reason that some decisions are rewarded while others are punished is because only in this way can we guide the economy in the direction of creating more net value than is used up in production. Bad decisions are wasteful. They take an economy in the wrong direction. They cause the production of things for which others do not wish to pay the full costs of production. People across the community end up less wealthy and less prosperous. Their living standards are lower. The aim of setting up our institutions as best we can is to limit as much as humanly possible the damage that such bad decisions can cause.

And because the future is invisible, it is amongst the most difficult tasks to decide in the present which forms of investment made today will produce a profitable outcome. For every successful enterprise there are many others which have fallen by the way.

There are, in fact, no guarantees of success.

All economic decisions aside from the most trivial are about the future. Economic decisions are built around individuals in the present trying to work out what the future will be like. And because the future is always different from how it was imagined, economic decisions often turn out to have been mistaken.

This is the way of the economic world in which by the nature of circumstance we will always be forced to live. It is therefore imperative that the economic system provides as much incentive as possible for decision makers to get it right the first time or to rapidly adjust to change, and that we remove from decision-making roles as quickly as possible those decision makers whose judgements are for whatever reason habitually wrong or who are unable to accommodate new circumstances as they arise.

EVERYTHING IS ALWAYS IN THE PROCESS OF CHANGE

In an economy, as with just about everything else, the processes of change never come to a halt. Some of these changes are visible to all and some are virtually invisible. Indeed, some changes are unknown to anyone although they will ultimately affect everyone; think of an impending natural disaster or an invention that will be made one year from today.

There are major economic and political events that no one can predict. Economies expand and contract. New regulations are regularly introduced. Governments come and go. Wars are declared and peace resumes.

There are new products, new technologies, new ways of doing things, and many of these have commercial possibilities that will completely upset the best-laid plans of those who are already in the market.

Amongst the most important features of an economy is that it be designed to cope with change. The phrase 'creative destruction' captures the way a modern economy adjusts. The new does not arrive and then live side by side with the old. The old is instead driven from the field, and unless adjustments are made, what was there before ceases to exist.

There was a time when the only way to cross the oceans was to go by sea, but now virtually no one does. The businesses who built and sailed the world's ocean liners were some of the largest businesses of their times. These businesses have now almost entirely disappeared and have been replaced by aircraft and airlines.

But there are also many changes that are quite trivial except in the particular workplaces they affect. A change in the price of an important input, or in the prices charged by some competitor, can come as a bolt from the blue but with devastating consequences.

The cancellation of orders from a major customer or an illness for one of the key personnel in an enterprise can create major difficulties impossible to accommodate.

This business about change being a constant has all the force of any cliché, except that like many clichés it expresses one of the profound truths about the economic world.

No economic system, nor the businesses contained within it, can survive without the means of accommodating change. The better they are at adapting themselves to new circumstances as they arrive, the more successful they will be.

A market system, which means an economy in which its producers are almost entirely private entrepreneurs, is the only kind of economic system that is specifically designed to cope with change. Each entrepreneur is looking after the interests of the businesses they run. As circumstances change, they are able to respond individually and directly, whether to new possibilities or new problems. A government-directed centrally planned economy cannot do this; only a market economy can.

COMMERCIALLY USEFUL KNOWLEDGE IS DIFFUSED EVERYWHERE ACROSS AN ECONOMY

The knowledge needed to run an economy is dispersed everywhere. No one has anything other than an infinitesimal amount of the knowledge required to keep an economy working.

Useful knowledge is contained within actual people, embedded within the individuals of whom the society is composed. This is not knowledge contained in books, but the active knowledge held by actual people who are personally capable of applying that knowledge in a real world workplace.

No one knows everything commercially useful to know. Virtually everyone has specialist knowledge that is economically useful, some with knowledge more valuable than the knowledge held by others, but each with something to contribute towards a final outcome. One of the major purposes in structuring an economy is to put that knowledge to work as efficiently as possible.

Even the most knowledgeable people have only a smattering of the relevant knowledge in any society. Most commercially useful knowledge is of quite a basic character (Where are the paint brushes usually kept? What is the quickest way to get to Major Street?) yet it is essential for making an economy work efficiently.

Getting the knowledge that is at hand into the most commercially useful places is one of the great and difficult tasks an economy is forced to solve.

Beyond that, the sum total of all the knowledge in existence is continually growing and changing shape. Things that were known on one day (where the brushes are kept) may be different the day after. A price that was charged on one day may be different a day later. A new innovation or invention may have just been released on the market or an old product removed.

Relevant knowledge is scattered everywhere. How to increase the knowledge base of a society and then coordinate and focus such knowledge towards economically useful and productive ends is the single greatest challenge an economy must face. How well or poorly it is done will determine the prosperity of an entire community.

And here again, it is the decentralized market economy, with its 'agents' known as entrepreneurs making commercial decisions, which is able to bring together into a single enterprise just those individuals who have just those skills that can be directed at producing whatever is being produced. A commercial enterprise is not a state of nature. It is the sum total of all of the decisions that have gone into making it what it has become.

WITHOUT MARKET PRICES NO ONE CAN TELL WHAT ANYTHING COSTS

The more any individual product costs, the less of everything else that can be produced. That is, the more resources the production of any particular good or services uses up, the fewer resources are left over to produce other things. Some mechanism is therefore needed in any complex society to allow consumers and producers to work out how to satisfy their wants at the lowest possible cost to the economy.

The centre, the absolute centre, of a properly functioning market economy is therefore based around the price mechanism. It is almost impossible to emphasize enough just how important to an economy the generation of *market* prices is.

Market prices reflect the intensity of demand on the one side and the relative scarcity of the good or service on the other. Prices instruct economic agents (that is, buyers and sellers) on how to economize.

In very simple terms, the price mechanism identifies which products, services or resources are the least abundant relative to demand. Prices therefore guide producers to use relatively more abundant resources and smaller amounts of relatively less abundant resources.

Without prices set in the market no business can make economically rational decisions on what to produce since there is no actual information available to producers about what others want to buy. (They want shirts, you say – then tell me what colour, what size or what style?)

And even if businesses knew in detail which final products to produce for consumers, which they never would, there would be no means whatsoever to determine which production techniques and which inputs would keep costs to a minimum.

Businesses would never know, without market prices to tell them, whether they were using scarce inputs which were relatively hard to find and expensive to produce. It would be impossible to determine what proportion of the entire productive potential of an economy was being used up to produce any particular array of goods and services.

Without prices to guide them, businesses could not know what forms of production will earn a profit since they could not know how much each input cost. Without a realistic set of prices to indicate the relative scarcity of inputs, no business would have the foggiest notion which set of factors of production would keep costs to a minimum.

Prices also connect the present to the future, at least to the limited extent we can ever know the future. What we know we know today, and part of what we think we know today, is what is *believed* about the future. Market prices therefore adjust as assessments about the future shift.

Change in the economy is also automatically reflected in movements in market prices. Irrespective of what happens, if it comes to the attention of either those who sell and set prices or those who wish to buy, forces are put into play which move prices in the direction to reflect either increased or diminished scarcity or an increased or diminished willingness to buy the product.

The thread that connects all parts of the economy together is the price mechanism. It allows what could never otherwise be done, by bringing together inputs from all over the world to produce goods and services sold all over the world; it allows activities to be coordinated which could not be coordinated in any other way.

The crucial point is this. Without the information provided by market prices, which can only be produced in a market economy, no complex economic decision could ever be made.

IN THE COMMERCIAL WORLD, EVERYONE DOES WHAT IS BEST FOR THEMSELVES

The way this is traditionally stated in economics is to say that individuals act in their own self-interest.

Since everyone has their own perspective on the world, everyone acts in the way they think is best based on their own morality, background and personal circumstance. Cultural traditions are often of immense importance, overriding almost every other consideration. Everyone does what they believe will be, given their own perspective, the 'best' thing to do.

Moreover, everyone acts as a moral agent in trying to do what they see is the right thing to do, but the only perspective from which anyone can see the world is from their own. To point out that we all do what is best for ourselves does not mean we are acting in a selfish way. It means that even when we try to help others, we are acting in this way because we personally believe that is the right thing to do. To follow one's own self-interest does not conflict with someone acting in what they consider a morally appropriate way. Moral choices are by definition self-interested choices.

A mother looking after her children, someone giving money to a charity, others doing what they can to help the poor, are all examples of acting in ways that each of these people believe will be best.

But moving away from such intense personal circumstances, virtually all economic activity is undertaken between strangers, frequently between people who live in different countries and often on entirely different continents.

Market-based activity is not a personal relationship between people. Economic activity is not a form of charity. The different individuals who participate in the making of an item of clothing, for example, whether harvesting the cotton, spinning the yarn, weaving the cloth or cutting and sewing the fabric, are undertaken far from the person who will eventually buy the shirt.

Producing goods and services that others wish to buy should therefore be seen as actions intended to serve consumers by allowing sellers to achieve ends of their own. People undertake those various productive activities for a variety of reasons, but to believe that the reasons are ever independent of their own personal interests will make understanding the nature of the economic world impossible.

There are personal relationships and then there are commercial relationships, and sometimes, but not very often, they are the same. An economy is run on self-interest, in which the central aim for all, whether the owner of the firm, the workers employed or the lenders from whom funds are borrowed, is to earn an income.

The greatest protection for a buyer is that the self-interest of any firm which intends to stay in business lies in producing quality products at the lowest possible price. In a commercial competitive environment, self-interest works for those who wish to buy and not against them.

THE FUNDAMENTAL PRINCIPLES OF A MARKET ECONOMY

These are the basic axioms, not of a market economy but of any economy beyond the absolutely primitive. If even only one of these axioms were true, the need for a market would be proven. That all five are true, and obviously true, makes market-based economies an imperative.

Economics is not, however, merely designed to satisfy our curiosity. It is designed as a guide to policy, to instruct decision makers on what they should do, and what they should not do. From the above axioms are derived the basic policy blueprint for understanding the management of a market economy. It is a framework that is also almost entirely invisible in spite of being everywhere before your eyes. Yet they represent the fundamental background conception one needs to have to understand the economics of the industrialised world.

These are also important because governments frequently try to override these rules with consequences that often turn out very badly. Where they are not followed, where any of these is not permitted to be among the operating principles in the functioning of an economy, that economy will experience slower growth and lower incomes than it would otherwise have achieved. Think of these as ideals against which the management of an economy may be judged.

To the extent to which these are not the operating principles of an economy, to that extent the economy cannot be expected to succeed. The more these principles of economic management are ignored, the more poorly an economy can be expected to run.

The five axioms represent the reality that every economy must face not just a market economy. They outline an economic world that is, by necessity, continuously undergoing changes that no one can predict and whose consequences no one can know. Every business can therefore find itself no longer viable because of the changes that have gone on around it that they could never have foreseen. The market economy is a free form exercise in which everyone does what they can to earn an income and where the economy tries to encourage productive effort from those who wish to share in its output. It is founded on free institutions and individual decision making, where the past is no more than a guide and for which there are no predetermined rules.

Some societies are entirely traditional, where almost everything done in the present is the same as what was done in the past. But given the rapid movements in technologies, the modern world now assumes everything can be done better than it is being done already and almost everywhere has incorporated large elements of the market economy into the way things are done. The largest difference between economies is the extent to which taxation, government spending and regulation affect the structure of the economy and the consequent economic outcomes. As a general rule, the greater the intrusion of governments beyond a necessary minimum – and there is a necessary minimum – the less prosperous the economy will be.

The dynamics of a market economy are based on private individuals working out for themselves how to make a living by producing and selling to others. The role of governments is to provide an institutional and legislative environment that allows each individual to earn an income, either in running a business or as wage earners working for others.

These are the basic conceptual essentials needed to understand how a market economy works and what is needed so that it can be made to function successfully. These are what you must understand if you are to understand the economic world in which you live. Some of it may seem obvious, but these are nevertheless essential parts of how a modern economy works.

These then are the fundamental principles of a free market economy.

1. No One Runs a Market Economy, it Runs Itself

A market economy is designed so that the personal decisions of producers and consumers shape the economic environment in which they live. Laws and regulations determine the decisions that can be legally made and limit the commercial possibilities that businesses can pursue. But within the law, the decisions made are personal and private.

The shape and structure of a market economy have been designed by no one. It is just the outcome of millions upon millions of individual decisions, including decisions by governments.

On the production side, the driving force is profit. On the consumption side the driving force is personal satisfaction, often referred to as 'utility'. Businesses make decisions that are expected to bring them the greatest excess of revenue over cost, which they can do only by providing buyers with the goods and services they want.

The belief that some form of central planning can replace the market is a dangerous fallacy. An economy cannot be managed from the centre. The knowledge required to know what resources are available, the need to be aware of changing demands and supply across the entire range of productive inputs while simultaneously keeping track of the shifting wishes of consumers is an impossibility that cannot ever be undertaken successfully by any government agency.

Beyond that, only in a market economy will innovation occur since only in a market economy no one has to ask anyone's permission or receive funding from the government to attempt forms of production that have never been attempted before. Every major innovation since the eighteenth century, with only a handful of exceptions, has been developed and commercialized by private sector firms.

Any attempt to run an economy from the centre is certain to plunge a population into poverty. The only successful form of economic structure is a market economy since only a market economy encourages innovation, contains production costs and raises the standard of living.

2.   Only an Economy in which Private Sector Entrepreneurs Make Most of the Production Decisions can Succeed

To repeat, no one runs a market economy, it runs itself. There is no single person, no government agency, no decision making body of any kind, working out what, where and how to produce that vast flow of output we find made available for us to buy. Yet our economies move along in an orderly way, goods and services get produced, new and better products come onto the market, and there is never any reason to believe that we will be unable to buy tomorrow what we need in the same way we were able to buy these goods and services today.

And the reason our economies work so well is because we find those individual entrepreneurs who run our businesses making all of the necessary decisions on their own without any guidance from anyone other than those they choose to consult. These businesses produce not only what final consumers buy, but the inputs that go into the production of everything across the economy. No one tells these entrepreneurs what is needed, no one tells them what is demanded, no one tells them how to find the cheapest inputs, no one provides them with new technologies and new processes. These must all be worked out for themselves by themselves on their own.

Central planning does not work because it cannot work. It is not possible for a government to know what individuals wish to buy, but as crucial as this is, that is the least of the problems. More importantly, it is not possible for producers, even if they know what buyers want, to find the lowest cost means of production without the trial-and-error processes of the market. A price is not some arbitrary number plucked from the air. A price is an essential piece of information that tells every business what some product or service costs to produce. It tells those businesses what they must pay out of their own revenue streams to have access to those inputs. If the prices of some of their inputs begin to rise, other ways of doing things are sought so that production costs can be kept to a minimum. Unless those costs are met, these inputs will not be produced, or if they are produced, will not be produced for long.

The role of the entrepreneur in a market economy is moreover not to decide at some moment that this is what will be done and then let events unfold. The role is, instead, to be there, on hand, monitoring and adjusting every aspect of the business as the economic environment in which it operates changes. The entrepreneur must be able to adjust what is done as the demand for the products sold changes, as input costs go up, as skilled labour becomes more expensive, as government regulations change, as taxes rise, as interest rates or exchange rates go up, as the supply chain breaks down, as new competition enters the market, as new innovations are introduced, as key personnel find other jobs, as machinery breaks down, and as any number of other problems come up.

Entrepreneurs are not only right there and on the spot, personally involved with every aspect of their own businesses, they also have a personal financial interest in ensuring that things go as well as they possibly can. No one else without this kind of incentive will take the same detailed interest, and certainly no government employee, administering a central plan, will ever be as personally concerned with the success of an enterprise as those who own and manage their own businesses themselves.

3. The Consequences of Economic Decisions can Never be Known in Advance

Some business ventures are successful and others are not. Many of the decisions made would not have been made had those who made them known then what they later found out for themselves. A business decision is a step into the unknown. The aim is to produce goods and services whose production will repay their costs with a profitable return to the owner. Without the prospect of profit, no such venture will even be commenced. Without such ventures, the goods and services we buy will not be produced.

Yet no venture can be commenced, nor can any change or innovation be introduced, without understanding that the outlays made in setting things up may never eventuate in a positive return that repays all of the costs involved while providing a profitable return to the producer.

Uncertainty is at the heart of economic decision making. Not to understand that the future is profoundly unknowable, which never turns out as one had expected, means one has not understood the first and most fundamental element about the operation of an economy. Every business venture is a step into the dark. No business venture is certain of success.

Such ventures that are undertaken by private sector entrepreneurs are undertaken by individuals whose own money is at risk, or if not their own money, then the money lent out by those who have helped finance the expenditure. In complete contrast, ventures undertaken by governments are financed and underwritten by taxpayers who are compelled to provide the finance whether they wish to or not. As a result, such forms of government expenditures are less likely to succeed than private sector investments, will cost more to complete than a similar venture undertaken in the private sector and are much less likely to set out in a new, more innovative direction.

To complain about the profits made by successful firms is to complain that a business has discovered a means to satisfy its buyers' wishes more completely than others have done. They have either provided a better product or lower prices than anyone else. They have done so in a jungle of competing businesses, many of which have as an aim to take their customers for themselves, which they can only do by providing an even better product or by selling at an even lower price.

And as every owner of every firm understands, even if they are able to earn profits this year, there is no certainty about the year to follow, or the year to follow after that. Nothing is guaranteed. Every business has had to cover its set up and running costs, which it can do only if it can sell what it has put up for sale. The risks are enormous since uncertainty about what will happen next to the environment in which they operate can never be known in advance. Our economies move forward only because entrepreneurs are willing to take such risks, and these risks can be seen in the many many businesses that find themselves forced to close every year because they misjudged the future and what they would be able to sell while covering all of their costs.

4.   Only Value Adding Forms of Production Create Growth and Prosperity

Production only adds to the total amount of goods and services available if the value of what is produced is greater than the value of the resources used up. Production requires inputs all of which have a value of their own. Only if the value of what is produced has greater value than the value of the resources that were used as inputs will an economy grow.

This is what economic growth means. This is why the word 'added' is so important in understanding value added. Value already exists across an economy, embodied in its capital goods, skilled workers, buildings, resources and technology. These can be used in many different ways, but whichever way they are used, some of the resources disappear forever while some end up being used in some ways instead of others. Growth occurs when, and only when, the resources are used in ways that leave behind an even larger economy than existed at the start.

This does not mean that every project must be value adding. Many are not because those who set these projects in motion miscalculated about the potential return. Nor will these projects even begin to offer a return until they are actually producing and earning an income. But the net effect of value adding activity is that the economy, over time, increases its ability to produce and there is more for the entire community to share.

It should also be clear that only investment can create value. Only outlays that are not only intended to create value but actually have done so create growth. Spending of itself does not create growth. All expenditure draws down on the economy's resource base. Some of that expenditure is pure consumer demand, the final outlays on the goods and services that are the final intended purpose of economic activity. These may be valuable, but they are not value adding. They may improve a person's welfare but they do not improve an economy's ability to produce. Being able to purchase a greater flow of goods and services may be the result of improved economic productivity, but it is not the cause.

There is no greater fallacy in all of economics than to believe that demand drives an economy forward. Buying things does not create value. Buying does not make an economy grow. As obvious as it must sound, only production causes growth; it is only production that causes workers to be employed. Demand determines what gets produced but is not itself production. Production requires someone to have come to the belief that there would be demand for some good or service if it were produced who is then prepared to outlay money to produce whatever it is they believe can be sold at a profit. Only then does production take place and workers are hired. An economy is driven from the supply side and never by demand.

5. The Price Mechanism Must be Left to Itself to Determine Relative Prices

Entrepreneurs decide not only what products to produce but also the prices these goods and services are to be sold at. Entrepreneurially-determined prices are not just a bi-product of a market economy but are indispensable in allowing a modern economy to function at all. Without market prices, it is impossible to measure production costs. If production costs cannot be measured, there is no means for businesses to work out the least costly way to produce any particular unit of output. Unless the importance of keeping costs down is understood, how an economy works cannot be understood. Not just a market economy, moreover, but any economy.

Why are water pipes not made of gold? And if they are not made from gold, what should they be made from? Iron? Steel? Plastic? Bronze? Copper? Lead? Glass? Clay? What is done is to make them from the cheapest material that will do what we want done. So here is what must be understood. Without input prices that reflect scarcity and production costs, no one can work out which is the cheapest way to produce. And even then, the question of knowing 'what we want done' is often determined by what can be afforded. There are many things someone might wish water pipes to do, such as lasting a hundred years before they need to be replaced. But the costs involved in building hundred-year pipes may be much higher than forty-year pipes. This is why costs matter since such decisions have to be made.

And that is the simplest of examples. Humans have been building water pipes since civilization began. Choose anything more complex and the ways they might be put together becomes more complex. There are many ways to cook a restaurant meal, each using different combinations of capital, labour and ingredients. Most restaurants care about the prices they put on menus because most of their customers also care.

But going further still, the reason that production costs matter is that the cheaper each product is, the fewer resources needed to produce whatever it is. And the fewer resources needed to produce each individual product, the more products in total we are able to produce. Only if we have a means to work out, even roughly, which is the least costly way to produce the goods and services we produce, can we raise the average standard of living. Without the price mechanism, there is no possible way to work these things out.

Everyone makes decisions based on price. But unless the prices their decisions have been based on represent the underlying relative costs of production, fiddling with the price mechanism through gadgets like price ceilings and price supports will only distort the information decision-makers base their decisions on. It may be politically popular but it is economics at its worst.

6.   The Most Important Economic Role of Government is to Create a Productive Economic Environment

Properly structured laws and regulations allow businesses and individuals to coordinate the economic activities that take place amongst themselves as productively as possible. But in any area where individuals must deal with each other, it is essential that the rules of engagement are clearly spelled out. This is the role of governments, who must decide on how the market mechanism will operate.

There is always potential for conflict, especially where money is at stake. Conflicts can occur between two businesses, a business and its customers, a business and its suppliers, a business and its employees, between different customers, and between all of them and financial institutions. There are also no end of conflicts between the government and the governed. Moreover, the business environment is always changing as new ways of doing things conflict with what had till then been in place.

Only a government that understands that economic prosperity depends on successful entrepreneurial activity, undertaken by individuals who are neither agents of the government nor financed through the public sector, will be able to put in place an institutional structure that allows productivity to grow. Success in business often looks so effortless from the outside that others think it is a fluke, that anyone could do it if only they tried. The reality is that there is little that is as difficult as sustaining a successful business over a number of years and the consequences of running an unsuccessful business are large. A government that truly wishes to raise the living standards of wage earners and of the public in general must know in its very bones that the only way it can be done is by encouraging private sector businesses to grow.

7.   Economies are Driven from the Supply Side and Not by Demand

It is obvious that a community can demand only what it has first produced. Less obvious, but equally true, is that it is production itself that allows buyers to demand. Demand is constituted by supply. An increase in demand across an economy can only occur if there has been an increase in production. If you seek to encourage an increase in the community's ability to demand, you must first work out what is needed to encourage the members of that same community to produce. And not just to produce, but to produce what others wish to buy.

Demand has no reality until something is purchased. Supply, however, is represented by the incredible array of goods and services available for sale. All of it has been produced in anticipation that there would be enough buyers who will each pay enough so that all of the production costs are covered by the sale receipts. Production must therefore inevitably come before the sale. Demand has no concrete reality in driving an economy forward. It is only the beliefs held by entrepreneurs that cause production to occur.

Even goods made to order, or services not rendered until they are sought, are not driven by demand, but only by anticipation of demand. In virtually every case, there are businesses that have already been set up to sell as demand arises, such as construction firms which exist so that someone wishing to build a house has someone to ask to build it. An airline must already be in business before someone can seek to travel to some foreign destination. There is demand, but until something is bought, demand has no concrete reality.

Moreover, the number of units demanded of any product will depend on the price it is sold for. Demand is thus not even an amount, but an entirely abstract concept relating different prices to the different amounts that would be bought at each price. Economists may choose to draw demand curves showing the amounts that would be bought at different prices, but since only a single price will ever exist at any one time, everything about that demand curve is pure conjecture. Exactly the same may be said about the amount supplied, which for every product will be at different levels depending on the prices sellers expect to receive.

Equilibrium is therefore a notion that is preserved for the textbook, and not the real world. The real world is constantly undergoing change. Equilibrium has no actual existence in an economy as it actually is.

Beyond the notion of demand for individual products there is the concept of aggregate demand, the total demand by everyone for everything. And again, there is an actual outcome that can be measured at the end of some period of time, so that one can say that the total level of purchases across an economy during the last year, let us say, was some particular amount.

But what cannot be said, although it is said, and said often, is that the demand for output was the cause of the production. Undoubtedly what was bought validated the decisions of the sellers who sold what was bought, along with the distributors who dispersed the products through various transport networks, the manufacturers who produced the products as well as the inputs that went into those products, plus those who had made available the energy that was used in the production process, plus the farmers, miners and drillers who had made the various raw materials available so that they could be processed, almost all of which had occurred well before the final sale was made.

Buying some product at a retail outlet is merely the end of a long and intricate economic structure that lies behind everything that ends up available to buy. It is the structure of production – the long series of purchase and sale as products are brought together through time and effort – that allows something to be bought. To look only at demand, when it is the structure of supply that matters, is to ignore almost everything that matters and to concentrate on what hardly matters at all.

The belief that governments can make an economy grow more rapidly, or create more employment, by raising the level of aggregate demand is a fallacy. Government spending, unless it is properly targeted and value adding, will slow an economy, reduce living standards, and can even lead to a fall in the total number of jobs available. The straightforward fact, as history has shown time and again, is that economic growth is not raised by increasing demand, but only by increasing the economy's ability to produce.

Governments have neither the knowledge nor the expertise to make business decisions. Neither do the public servants who work in public administration. Their knowledge of the commercial realities that face business is extremely limited. They are seldom if ever in a position to second-guess productively the decisions made by firms.

8. Commercializing Innovation is How Living Standards are Raised

Most of what causes our living standards to improve comes from innovation. New products, new technologies, new industrial processes, and new discoveries are the elements that remake our economic structures. Innovation is, moreover, overwhelmingly a product of the private sector, of entrepreneurially-managed business firms.

Commercializing new ideas is what a market economy does best. Entrepreneurs test the waters with different possibilities and focus in on product innovations that find favour with those who buy. There are always constraining forces that attempt to slow and sometimes stop such innovation. It is the private sector that continuously brings forward these new ways of doing things, some of which become generally accepted even with the barriers they might confront.

Improved productivity is only minimally the result of doing the same things in a cheaper way. Most economic improvement is the result of innovation that lead to formerly entirely unthought-of products as well as ways of doing things.

A car and a phone are, of course, related to products of the same name that existed a hundred years ago. But what you find today and what you might have found then are virtually discontinuous. However you might wish to classify such changes, they are the result of entrepreneurially driven commercialization of innovations in products, technologies, industrial processes, know-how and design.

9. Recessions are the Result of Dislocations in the Structure of Supply

An economy is an intricate network of businesses, most of which produce inputs for other businesses. The link between businesses occurs through the price mechanism where each firm does what it can to keep its costs to a minimum while producing the best product it can at the price. But behind the scenes, nothing is standing still. There is also an on-going series of innovations that continuously affect what is produced and how it is produced. The price of inputs, their supply and availability, are always in flux. Beyond that, governments are forever changing the rules under which businesses operate. There are international shifts taking place at every moment. Credit conditions never stand still.

What is remarkable is not that there are recessions from time to time, but that the entire system works as well as it does. Yet recessions do occur, with the most important consequence being that many more workers than usual find themselves unemployed.

The most remarkable fact about a market economy is how well it adjusts over time. There are changes taking place at every moment. What we produce and how we produce changes relentlessly. It is not the fact that change takes place that causes recession even though the impact on individuals can be large. Change means that some jobs will disappear. Businesses close, or move, or reduce their size of operation. What must be understood, however, is that at the same time, other businesses are opening or increasing their size of operation. No business will ever remain as it began, nor will it last forever. No job is a job for life. Every worker must understand that whatever job they are in is unlikely to last forever. Unless we are going to freeze an economy in whatever structure it now is, there will be changes going on that mean those who are employed will have to find alternate ways to earn their living.

Recessions, however, are different. They are periods of time when the economy slows, many firms close or contract, and much larger numbers of workers than usual become unemployed at the same time. And the reason it happens is that there have been various events of some kind that have brought a sudden slowdown in production in some parts of the economy, and this slowdown has been transmitted through market processes to others. The problem is structural imbalances. The problem is not deficiency of demand or an excessive level of saving.

Knowing what causes recessions is crucial to understanding what should be done to bring recessions to an end while bringing the unemployment rate back to normal. If it is believed that recessions are caused by there not being enough demand, then the solution is to increase the level of demand. If instead the problem is seen as structural, then the solution is to allow the economy to readjust as fast as it can so that the imbalances can be righted.

And if the problem is structural, increasing the level of public spending will not only fail to bring about recovery, it will make the problem worse than it already is.

10.   Equality is Not an Economic Principle

Equality is not an economic principle. An economy is not managed so that everyone can come out the same. It is, instead, managed so that each of us can pursue our own destinies, which mean that we must each end up with different levels of income and a different command over the world's goods and services. This is all part of what it means to live in a free society.

Individuals tend to receive the value of the output they produce. The market tends to reward individuals with their own contribution to value adding production, with the value of a product determined by how much others are willing to pay. If people wish to pay large amounts to see their football team win, the best players in the world will earn very large amounts of money. Each of us takes out of the economy more or less what one has put in, with the value of our contributions determined by the market. There are relative adjustments made through the payment of taxes and the distribution of welfare but for the most part, the highest incomes are paid to those whose services are in greatest demand relative to supply.

The aim of economic 'equality' is the wish of those whose contribution to total output is lower than the amount of money they would like to spend. This is a different concept from assisting the poor, the sick, the aged, or anyone else unable to earn a living of their own. The demand for 'equality' is a demand for a transfer of income from the more productive to the less productive. Everyone seeks to assist the disadvantaged. But the aim in providing welfare assistance is not to equalize incomes, but to help those who for one reason or another fall by the way.

Equality is a political demand. It is, moreover, a demand contrary to the ethos of a free community. The demand for equality is the demand for the state to take from the productive and transfer their incomes to the less productive, and often the non-productive.

At the very minimum, the harm done is to reduce the efforts of the productive parts of the community. If part of the income earned is to be taken away and transferred to others, there will be less incentive for the productive to continue as they have in the past. There will be an inevitable fall in the level of production among the productive. Some who have been working will choose alternative means to earn incomes by receiving transfers from governments in place of having to work.

The result is an economy less capable of producing. Fewer people are working while the incentives to remain productive among those still employed are reduced. Economic growth diminishes and living standards will not rise as rapidly as they might have, even among those who are the supposed beneficiaries of these transfers. It is even possible that the more that equality becomes a political aim, the lower real incomes will be across an economy.

The harm done is also moral. Earning one's own living is to live as a free individual. To live off the state is a form of servitude. The dignity of work is replaced with an attitude that the world owes one a living. Earning an income becomes disassociated with any contribution to the common good. One is a taker, the recipient of hand-outs, rather than a contributor who is taking out from the common stock the value of what one has put in.

The special case of the public sector also needs to be considered. For those in the private sector, the proof that one is contributing to communal wealth is shown by the very fact that one is employed by profitable firms. For government employees, the evidence is less clear cut. Some of what governments do is necessary, some is productive, but some is not. Large swathes of public sector activity are undertaken for political purposes without genuine evidence that the value of what is produced is greater than the value of the resources used up.

In times when governments were obliged to balance budgets in every year, there were fewer dangers that government waste would grow to excessive levels. But since Keynesian economic theory became dominant, there have been two important changes in attitude. The first has been to assume that economies are driven by increases in aggregate demand. Economists had previously understood that economies are driven from the supply side. With Keynesian theory, the general belief is that it is demand that is the all-important variable. The result is that governments believe they are doing good when they spend, irrespective of what they spend their money on. This has created major diversions of resources away from the private sector and into non-productive public sector projects where resources are used up but no positive return occurs, or if there is a positive return, it is well below the level the private sector might have achieved.

The second has been the acceptance of budget deficits as a near-perennial feature of public finance. This has led to large increases in undisciplined levels of public spending, which have not been anchored in value adding activities. This process has been furthered through government control of the money creation process since governments are able to create the money they then immediately spend rather than needing to depend on taxation. The massive growth in public debt has vastly weakened economies in which such undisciplined spending has occurred without improving the equity of the income distribution. Instead, the main beneficiaries have been government employees and firms in direct receipt of additional public outlays.

Providing governments with the licence and ability to spend increased proportions of a nation's wealth has only constrained living standards generally, reduced growth rates within their economies and has often made income distribution even more inequitable than it had previously been.

SOME QUALIFICATIONS

These are the principles of a market economy in which individual entrepreneurs determine the overall direction of economic activity through making choices for themselves on what to do and how to do it.

But no one lives in anything even remotely resembling a laissez-faire economy where the decisions of businesses are the last word. Business decision making is hemmed in at every turn by government regulation and control. It is the government that is the final arbiter of what can and cannot be legally done.

Economics is a branch of politics.

An economy runs itself but will only do so productively if the proper legal and institutional structures have first been put in place. It requires a government to understand what is required and to legislate to ensure proper structures exist. This, in turn, requires governments to understand the tremendous productive powers of private sector activity, and to appreciate what is required to make individual decision making work.

Institutional arrangements must be designed to accommodate the needs of private decision making. Meaning what? Meaning this: that governments must stand almost completely apart from the business decision making going on across the economy.

There is also a role for governments to set limits on permissible actions. Commercial activity is not a system of anything goes. It is a system in which custom and law separate the permissible from what is not allowed. These rules and regulations will almost as often specify what individuals and businesses must do (for example, pay their taxes) as it will decree what is forbidden (pouring waste products into the nearest river).

Government is also responsible for administering the justice system. Courts to adjudicate and a legal system to enforce are necessities.

Governments will almost always provide a safety net for those whose incomes do not reach some socially determined minimum standard, and assist those who might otherwise fall by the wayside.

But when all is said and done, the success of a government will be judged on how well it is able to put in place a framework that permits the private sector to get on with producing without government involvement. The certainty is that rules of one kind or another will be put in place by governments. But if the aim is economic success, the rules should be designed so that governments are almost never directly involved in the decision making processes of firms.

GOVERNMENTS ARE SOCIAL INSTITUTIONS RUN BY INDIVIDUALS

Government involvement is everywhere, often by popular demand. But you would not want to get too carried away with the notion that governments are some kind of noble institution that anyone can depend on for their health, happiness and general welfare.

There is no 'social' in the sense that there is some benevolent collective entity that watches over what individual decision makers do. The collective is itself made up of other individuals who have different economic functions but are human beings all the same, with all of the limits that being human brings.

Decisions made by governments are decisions made by individuals on behalf of the entire community. But simply because they are made on behalf of the entire community does not guarantee that they will be good decisions either in intent or consequence. They are still decisions made by individuals who have their own motivations and purposes clearly in mind.

Governments often have a will of their own that produce outcomes that sometimes benefit the community and sometimes harm the community, but in all cases benefit the governments that make those decisions, or at least attempt to.

Governments should never be thought of as doing things with a benevolent purpose in mind. Self-sacrifice is not in the nature of government action.

Only a government over which a population has some control can be expected to act in the interests of the community it represents. Representative government, where the representatives must frequently renew their mandate with the population at large, is the least-worst form of government if the interests of the community at large are a prime consideration.

2. The economics of the free market

This is a book for those whose intention is to understand economic issues. It is for those who wish to follow policy discussions with some insight, read a newspaper with some clarity and discuss economic questions within a solid frame of reference. It is designed for those who wish to have familiarity with the underlying concepts and theory without being overwhelmed with the detail. It is for those who would like to know how those in decision-making roles think and the kinds of analysis they apply when those decisions are being made.

It is foremost for those who want a good working knowledge of how economies work so that they can understand economic events as they unfold. The aim is thus to make you an informed follower of public discourse. It should allow you to understand what policy makers and professional economists are saying to each other and to the public. It should provide you with the tools needed to make sense of the decisions made by governments and various economic agencies. It should allow you to make sense of economic events, to have some personal idea of the complexities of such events and to be able to make your own judgements on how such events might unfold.

The aim of this book is to allow you to follow the policy debates that inevitably find their way into the media and which are played out within governments. You should then be able to make your own judgements on the policy actions being taken, since the intent is to provide you with a framework from which such judgements can be made.

WHAT THE STUDY OF ECONOMICS IS FOR

The first question, though, is this: why bother? Why take the trouble to know anything at all about how economies work?

At the most basic, the aim is to understand how communities become prosperous, how the individual members who make up the community can themselves become prosperous and, still within the same framework, to understand how economic theory can provide guidance to decision makers to help them devise appropriate economic institutions to create the sought-after prosperity.

Economics is a policy science. Its aim is to inform decision makers on the different consequences that can be expected to follow from the different decisions they might be asked to make in attempting to solve the economic problems that come before them. In dealing with economic questions, there are seldom choices that do not require some kind of balancing between different sets of outcomes.

Some of the costs associated with some decisions may come early but lead to improvements later. On other occasions the good bits come first but are followed by harsher medicine. There is often a necessity to choose between one thing or another in which both would be desirable but where only one is possible at a time.

In economics, having it all is never an option. Having to choose is the only option ever available.

DEFINITION OF ECONOMICS

Economics, as Adam Smith in the first great work in the subject stated in his very title, is *An Inquiry into The Nature and the Causes of the Wealth of Nations*. This is the classical conception written in 1776. It was the way of thinking about the subject matter of economic theory that lay behind economic thinking for a hundred years.

It is the right definition. Economics is about the national economy and how a nation and its citizens can become more prosperous.

Economics is the study of what it takes to provide material well-being not just to a community but to the individual members of that community as well.

And beyond that, the study of economics explains how that same community and the individuals within it should be able to live with a continuous expectation that, over time, their material well-being will continue to improve.

And finally, economics explains why economic conditions can and often do deteriorate, and provides remedies to halt and reverse such deterioration when it occurs.

Economics is about making people individually and collectively better off. In some ways, it might be thought of as an abstract science, like astronomy, in which the subject matter is looked at without any means or intention of becoming involved in changing how it performs. Knowledge for knowledge's sake.

That, however, is not what economics as a science does, nor why it is studied. It is an area of study because an understanding of how an economy works is the start of a process towards making our economic arrangements work to our own benefit to a greater extent. That is what it is for and that is what economists do.

The most common definition of economics nowadays is somewhat different. It comes from the economist Lionel Robbins, who in the 1930s defined economics as:

> The science which studies human behaviour as a relationship between ends and scarce means that have alternative uses. (Robbins, [1935] 1945)

This is a different kind of definition. There is much merit in this definition, which is why it is so commonly used. It draws attention to the major problem in all economies, which is to try to satisfy the almost infinite demands of a population with the very finite amount of resources available. In this definition scarcity is at its very core.

But as a definition of so vast a subject as economics it is not quite right. It is technical. It narrows the focus from outcomes to process.

In this definition, there are people who have numerous ends they want to achieve and only limited means with which to achieve whichever amongst those ends they choose to pursue.

This is, of course, the human dilemma of economics. So much to do, but so little to do it with. The nature of economics is therefore, according to this way of thinking, an investigation into the ways in which such choices are made with the aim being to improve the decision-making process.

But while economics often involves having to choose, that is by no means the whole story. Economics is about all aspects of how economies work with the focus on how they bring food to our tables and put shelter above our heads. It undoubtedly involves scarcity of means and limitless human ends. But it is more. Any definition that fails to recognize what that more is, does not describe what most people who choose to study economics are there to find out.

SOCIAL CONDITIONS

There are also many aspects of what make an economy succeed that are not themselves intrinsically economic in nature. The surrounding moral, ethical and institutional environment is crucial. You cannot make a community prosperous where the population does not regularly act in a moral or ethical way. If the members of a community cannot trust each other or its government, a lasting prosperity will never be achieved.

Rule of Law

Amongst the most important aspects of the social arrangements needed to create prosperity is the rule of law. The rule of law, a phrase hardly found in the normal economics text, is as important a component in the creation of a successful economy as one can possibly find.

The rule of law means that we are governed by pre-existing rules that everyone is aware of so that they know what is and what is not permitted. And most importantly, once the laws are in place, no one will be subject to the arbitrary decisions of governments. When business decisions are made, the ground rules are already known.

The most fundamental point is this. Economies will never be productive if the legal system does not protect the incomes and the property of those who produce a nation's wealth. The people who run businesses are seldom if ever the same as those who are in control of the government. Only where the civil authority is used to protect the incomes and profits earned through productive activity will that productive activity occur.

How often do those who understand nothing about the basic requirements for economic growth and prosperity act as if those who run a nation's businesses are also, and for that reason, in control of its government as well?

The order is absolutely the other way round. Business never controls the government of any country. But it is only in countries where those who run its political structures are resolute in protecting from thievery and plunder those who run their nation's businesses that prosperity can occur.

Moreover, this thievery and plunder can come just as easily, indeed more easily, from governments as it can from the community generally. The self-restraint of government in allowing businesses to succeed and thrive is the most basic requirement for an economy to succeed.

If governments are determined to take from businesses the profits that ought to have remained within the business, whether the profit is taken by governments for their own purposes or, as it is said, 'to share the wealth' with the whole community, the result is, at best, diminished prosperity, lower incomes and a slower improvement in the standard of living for the population as a whole. At its worst, it causes wealth not just to grow more slowly than it otherwise could, but to actually decrease, often leaving large segments of the population in desperate poverty.

Laws must protect commercial activity, enforce contracts and ensure fair dealing between those who buy and those who sell.

Beyond this, no society in which some are privileged by the structure of the legal system while others are kept in a subordinate position can ever hope to succeed. Within this legal structure, there should be clarity in terms of the importance of governments, and especially of the importance of the popular control of governments, in seeking to achieve particular economic outcomes.

No one is above the law. All should be subject to the law. And the laws must be designed in ways that provide impartial abstract justice so that commercial disputes are decided according to the laws of the land, not by who can bribe the most or who happens to be related to someone else.

Honesty and Character

The character of a population makes an all-important difference to its economic success. The rule of law and the role of courts are important but the personal ethics and values of a population are possibly more important still.

An exchange economy only works where those who engage in production and trade are personally honest in their dealings with others. If agreements can only be enforced through courts of law and the involvement of the civil authorities, then an economy will not work.

One cannot push this to an extreme. Dishonesty exists everywhere. With so much wealth at stake, one must accept that the commercial world will inevitably attract towards it a fairly large number of those who will be dishonest in their dealings with others who will rob and defraud them if they can.

No economic system can rid itself of such individuals. Theft occurs only where there is something to steal. In the commercial world, corrupt practices are an everyday occurrence and a normal, if regrettable, part of the ongoing activities of those who are involved in trade and finance.

That such activity occurs should not be seen as anything more than a product of human nature. But that such activities can and should be weeded out to the greatest extent possible is an imperative.

An economy works best where the population at large is disgusted by corrupt practices and refuses to accept dishonesty at any level. Those who act in a dishonest way need to be culled from the normal activities of economic life. The various forms of identifying such people – whether through credit agencies, personal references, criminal prosecution and the disgrace that comes from the publicity that can surround unfair dealing – needs to mean that there are severe penalties for dishonesty.

Where dishonest practices become the norm, especially where dishonest and corrupt government practices are common, no economy can expect to succeed. Corruption regularly drains away the potential profits of a successful business. It bleeds business dry and vastly reduces the incentives for productive economic behaviour while limiting the ability of business to finance innovation and internal growth.

An ethical honest population is a necessary part of any successful economy. Whether it is in employer–employee relations, in the dealings between one business and another, or where it is governments involved with business, honest and fair dealing is essential. Acceptance of corrupt practice as just one of those things that no one can do anything about may be facing the inevitable, but it will condemn a society to economic stagnation.

Property Rights

As important as the rule of law are the rights to property. Who owns what, and what those who own are allowed to do with the property they have, are major questions. Only where ownership is recognized, and the full weight of the legal system is designed to maintain the security of the owners of property in the possession of what they own – and in terms of entrepreneurs, in maintaining what they have built – will an economic environment be created in which prosperity can be achieved and maintained.

It is the law that defines what can be owned and the various forms of ownership. Property comes in the widest variety of forms, from actual land and structures to pieces of paper that are promises to pay certain amounts of money on certain dates, or are rights to commercialize or license some new piece of technology that one has invented oneself.

If the owners of property must continuously be on the lookout for thieves and governments – different in theory but potentially equally disastrous in their effects – the basis for wealth creation, a very patient and long-term process, will seldom be achieved. And it is the poor more than anyone else who benefit from the strong protection of property rights.

The wealthy and powerful can usually take care of themselves. It is those possessing little wealth or power who have almost no means to protect even the little they do have, and who are vulnerable to the depredations of thievery and lawless governments.

MACRO- AND MICROECONOMICS

Economics, as it is now taught, is divided into two halves, macroeconomics and microeconomics. This has become a major division in which issues are approached, but it was not always so.

Macroeconomics is more or less a study of the movements in various economic aggregates, such as the level of national output or the price level of all goods and services taken together. Microeconomics looks at the smaller units that make up an economy, such as the demand for particular products and how their prices are determined. As now taught, macro is almost totally isolated from micro since macroeconomic shifts are not seen as related to movements in the microeconomic world.

This is not how things should be or previously were. What we now refer to as macroeconomics was once built around the theory of the business cycle. And in the theory of the cycle, the overall direction of the economy, its pace of growth, the movement in prices, the generation of jobs, all were seen as a direct counterpart of the actions at the micro level. The division of economics into macroeconomics and microeconomics is part of a confusion that pervades much of economic theory to this day.

Macroeconomics

As economic theory is now constituted, *macroeconomics* looks at the entire economy as one large productive unit. The role of macroeconomic theory is to explain how a series of aggregates fit together, and in fitting together how the entire mechanism, taken as a whole, leads to increased or diminished employment, a higher or lower price level, faster or slower rates of growth and a balanced or unbalanced level of international trade.

It also looks at the financial side of economic activity. It looks at how interest rates come to be what they are and at how the financial system is interconnected with the productive parts of the economy.

And it looks at the policy actions that should be taken to achieve what are the traditional aims of economic policy:

- low rates of unemployment;
- high rates of economic growth;
- low rates of inflation; and
- stability in the balance of payments.

All of these issues are related to the material well-being of communities and all are related to questions about how to get more output from available resources.

There is a fifth aim of policy that sometimes is and sometimes is not included, and that is making an 'equitable' distribution of income one of the objectives of a sound economy. Whether it really belongs as an economic rather than a political objective is more of a philosophical question. But there can be no doubt that governments do take actions to equalize incomes through the tax and welfare systems, and such issues are frequently a major political issue in many countries.

Like it or not, questions about the distribution of wealth and income do become part of the economic debate, so that reducing disparities within populations becomes one of the tasks that economists find themselves having to examine and provide policies to achieve in ways which do not affect the achievement of the other economic objectives in the above list.

Microeconomics

Microeconomics is the part of economic theory that looks at the actions taken by individual producers and buyers. It looks at who does what and the motivations behind the economic decisions made by individuals as either consumers or producers.

An economic decision concerns itself with whatever it is that provides individuals with their material well-being: food, clothing, shelter at its most basic; the vast array of the most exotic and varied goods and services at its most expansive.

But one way or another, microeconomics is about the decisions that individuals make, as producers and buyers, that cause particular goods and services to be produced and to end up in the hands of the particular people into whose hands they find their way.

When economies run well, the entire process is invisible. No one pays much attention or lets it cross their mind for so much as a second about how they are fed, clothed and sheltered.

Although virtually every single item in any inventory of a person's possessions, and virtually every single service received from the market, was the result of an extraordinary web of decisions that have been made, some of which might have been made years before in far-off lands, this is normally taken as no more remarkable than the daily appearance of the sun in the sky.

Microeconomics is about the economic coordination between various producers who buy inputs from each other, and the further coordination between producers and those who finally buy the consumer goods and services at the end of the trail.

A shirt bought today will be made from cloth that might have been spun in the last six months from cotton that was picked in Egypt a year before. The plants from which the cotton was picked might have been put in the ground five years before that.

All of the machinery used at each stage in the preparation of the cloth might have been designed and built 25 years before the cotton was grown, and the different parts of the process might have taken place not just at different times but in different countries. And then there is the thread that finds its way into the shirt, and the buttons, not to mention the design or the marketing.

And at every stage there will be individual workers who have specialist skills in the specific tasks that have been required, from the planting to the spinning to the weaving to the sewing to the packaging, and then finally to the retailing at the very end. And each of those skills will have had to be taught and each individual will have had to decide to learn how to do just those tasks that have been required to complete everything that needed to be done.

How just the right amount of the ingredients that went into making up that shirt happened to enter the world and were brought together in just the right proportions is the mystery that microeconomics tries to explain.

THE MARKET MECHANISM, PRICE SYSTEM AND SUPPLY AND DEMAND

Here is a distinction you need to keep in mind. There is something called the market mechanism. There is then something else called the price system. And finally there are the forces of supply and demand. Knowing the difference is essential to understanding the market and how it works.

Market Mechanism

The *market mechanism* refers to a system in which individuals produce goods and services for others. Moreover, in virtually all instances, those from whom purchases are made are people generally unknown to the buyers; they are usually, in fact, total strangers. We may know the retailer, although even that is becoming less frequent, but we almost certainly do not know the identity of the persons who made the particular products we buy.

The market mechanism is the process through which each of the individual elements in the production and distribution of goods and services unfolds. And it is called the 'market' mechanism because virtually every one of the inputs which went into the production of each and every individual product were produced for sale to the market. Someone, somewhere, had to have made decisions to produce the final output, but many others in many places also had to have made their own decisions to produce each of the inputs, price them and put them up for sale.

As an example of the market mechanism in action, in 1900 there was not a single cinema in the United Kingdom principally because at the time there were no films being made, but by 1914 there were 5000 (Davis, 2007: 357). Where did these cinemas come from, as well as the films they showed? Where, in fact, did cameras, film and everything else needed to make these movies come from, and how was it all organized?

It was the market, which is another way of saying it was individual entrepreneurs making decisions on what to produce because they saw a potential market, and then bought the required inputs from other entrepreneurs who had made separate decisions on what to produce because they too saw a potential market. Governments occasionally become involved, but almost invariably, just as it was with the film industry, the goods and services you see have made their way to you because of entrepreneurial decisions made by private individuals who saw opportunities for personal gain by providing others with the goods and services they seek and want.

It is this process that is the market mechanism.

Price System

At the core of the market mechanism is the *price system.* To understand how the market works it is necessary to understand the role of the price system. But understanding the price mechanism and how it works is different from understanding supply and demand.

Supply and demand is a description of how an individual good or service ends up with a particular price. Knowing how prices become attached to particular things is important, but it is not as important as understanding that it is *relative* prices that matter most.

What is a price? It is a number; a number stating how many units of currency have to be paid in exchange for some object or service.

For buyers, that number only has relevance when looked at against all of the other prices in that economy, the incomes being earned and the alternative ways that their income might be spent.

For a business buying an input, the number of units an item costs has to be looked at against the prices of other possible inputs and, most importantly, against the backdrop of how many units of currency the products being produced will themselves attract when put up for sale.

The market mechanism should therefore be seen as a continuous process in which every good and service competes with every other good and service to find buyers, with prices of every item offered to the market under ongoing and relentless pressure to fit into the entire framework of purchase and sale.

Every product must pay its own way. Each purchase must satisfy some need. But since costs are always changing in the same way that the needs, wants and desires of buyers are always changing, prices are in constant flux, shifting relative to each other to reflect the costs of production on the one hand and the willingness of buyers to pay the price on the other.

From the sellers' perspective, each and every producer, of both inputs and final goods, not only decides what to put on the market but also decides what prices to charge. There are many constraints on these prices, some based on the cost of inputs and some determined by how much buyers are prepared to pay. But every product in a market economy has a price, although for some goods the reserve price, below which the product will not be sold, is known only to the seller.

Putting prices on products is a crucial part of how an economy works. High prices relative to costs encourage production. But high prices also encourage others to enter the market, while lower prices tend to keep others out. High prices also encourage innovation by competitors that allows products to be sold at lower prices and in greater volume. Low prices also, of course, encourage additional sales, but all other things being equal, can also lead to lower profits per unit of output sold.

But more important than the absolute price which is given as so many units of the local currency for a particular amount of the product is the *relative* price, how much one product costs in comparison with another.

The *price system* in spite of its name is not just a mechanism for putting prices on single products. What the price system crucially does is determine the *relative* prices within the market so that the prices of some goods or some inputs become relatively more expensive while others become relatively cheaper in comparison with each other. This is the crucial role of the price system. It allows buyers of both inputs and final products to be guided towards the least-cost means of satisfying their aims.

And why this is important from the perspective of the national economy is because lower costs mean fewer resources are absorbed during the production of any individual product. The fewer resources absorbed, the more resources are available to produce other goods and services. The price system is essential in guiding producers and buyers towards satisfying their economic aims in a way that allows the economy to produce more overall. That is not, of course, anyone's individual aim in being guided by relative prices, but that is the effect all the same.

Supply and Demand

Where most texts start and finish in discussing prices is with *supply and demand*. These are the separate forces that explain how the prices of single products are determined and what causes those prices to change.

With every product, the first issue is the decision to supply. Nothing is available to buy until someone has decided to sell, which means there has been a prior entrepreneurial decision to produce. The decision to produce is invariably based on the assumption that there are others who are prepared to buy if the product is put up for sale. The sellers and the buyers are the constituent elements of supply and demand.

But the underlying forces that determine market supply and demand, although they most certainly exist and prod economic decisions in one direction or another, are nevertheless invisible to any individual and are never known by anyone in any market. We draw curves to represent these two forces but they are a pale and distant portrayal of what is actually taking place. The reality is that both forces are invisible constraints on both producers and buyers.

For producers, because the time between making a decision to produce and the moment when the product is finally brought to market is an important consideration, decisions to supply are surrounded by endless issues. There are production costs, competition, the possibilities of innovation, the behaviour of buyers and the deep uncertainties of the future to consider that make it very difficult to decide what to produce, how many to produce and what prices to charge.

And while we may know after the fact about some market – how many units were supplied at what price – we never know how many might have been supplied had the price been different, since every other possible price is only hypothetical. The very premise of a supply curve, which shows the amounts that would be supplied at every price, is nothing more than an abstract conjecture with no real-world existence.

Similarly with the demand curve. It, too, shows how many of any particular product would be bought at different prices. But only one of those prices will ever exist and the answer to the question of how many units buyers would buy, will be known, even for that particular price, only when the period has finally passed.

Stocks and Flows

There is one further complication that needs to be taken on board when discussing markets, which is the difference between the market for products which can be easily reproduced and those where the supply is more or less fixed.

If we think only about the very short run, in most markets most of the time, there is only a particular number of units of any product available for sale. More are subsequently brought to market during successive periods of time and production is generally paced at a rate that will comfortably satisfy existing demand. Supply is not then a *stock*, a fixed amount, but a *flow* of output to the market. Prices in competitive markets are therefore more or less based on production costs rather than on the intensity of demand, since the flow of the product to market is expected to continue at the same rate as the level of demand.

If, however, there is some obstacle to receiving the normal flow of some particular product – food, let us say – the effect is suddenly to cause the intensity of demand to become the most important determinant of price. In normal times the price would almost certainly be lower, but if the usual amount supplied is stopped, then other considerations are brought to bear. Then it is the demand for the stock of available product, which might be no different from the stock that was available at a lower price when normal supplies were stopped, that becomes the most important determinant of the price.

Other examples of how the stock determines prices occurs with antiques, for example. The price of a 100-year-old vase is not determined by its production costs. There are only so many available, the amount cannot be increased, so the price is decided by those who seek to buy.

If, on the other hand, such vases were in production at the time of sale, while demand would still be a factor, since it is the *expected* demand for the product that will limit how many are produced, production costs in a competitive market would be the more important determinant of the price.

Given the level of demand, the price will be determined according to the production costs that must be paid by the highest-cost producer, which is why supply curves usually slope upwards. The more units demanded, the higher the average price will usually be.

Ultimately prices paid must cover the costs of production not only in the firm producing the product, but in each of the firms supplying inputs into the production process as well. Loss-making firms cease producing.

MARKET COOPERATION AND COORDINATION

Although seldom ever asked, even though we see the process in front of us every day, the central question that surrounds economic activity is: how are the actions of consumer and producers, and of producers with other producers, coordinated across the untold millions of transactions that take place every day?

More difficult still is the question of how this coordination ends up working so well that there is virtually no interruption in the flow of the innumerable varieties of every imaginable commodity and service found in the world today.

Yet the fact that it does so is unmistakable as it seamlessly coordinates the commercial, productive and economic actions of total strangers and allows them to cooperate with each other as a matter of course. Whether these are total strangers from across the world or best friends from across the street, the market mechanism coordinates what they do, so that a business in Cairo and a buyer in Saigon can make rational decisions about what to produce and which inputs to use.

Because of the nature of the market, in a well-ordered economy everything that commercially exists, with only trifling exceptions, has an owner, is someone's property. The owner may be a government, but in a properly functioning economy, for the most part most of what exists in the commercial world is owned by private individuals or the businesses these individuals own.

This is not just a description of the way things are. This is a statement of how matters must be arranged if a nation's resources are to be used in the most productive ways. Private property is an essential part of the foundation of any prosperous economy. Without a legal system dedicated to the protection of individual property rights, no economy can prosper.

In that same properly functioning economy, there must also be clearly understood rules for how the rights associated with any single item of property – from an apple to an orchard – can be transferred from one person to another.

Most things produced are produced for others. Most things owned will one day be owned by someone else. The orderly transfer of goods and services from one person to another, or from one business to another, is an essential part of the operation of an economy.

OBSTRUCTING MARKET FORCES

Getting in the way of the price mechanism to prevent prices from showing the relative costs of putting things onto the market will inevitably lead to economic problems that will not go away until prices are again allowed to reflect relative scarcity. Price controls of various sorts are often seen as the answer to various economic problems. They never are. They only add to problems in the longer run and economically speaking solve nothing.

The basic units of analysis for the market mechanism are the forces of supply and demand. Supply and demand explain how an individual price for an individual product ends up being set.

It is a process that starts from the decisions by sellers to produce something for sale to others with the intention of making a profit. It then turns to examine the actions of buyers who, once the various goods or services are offered up for sale, will buy more at lower prices and less at higher prices.

And finally, it points out that somewhere there exists a price at which the amount that the sellers wish to sell and the amount that buyers want to buy will be the same. This point of convergence is known as the point of equilibrium, where the number of units in total that will be sold and the price at which those sales will take place are simultaneously determined.

It shows how the market, if left to its own devices, will satisfy the demands of all those willing to cover costs through the prices they pay. It shows how prices change and why allowing prices to follow the movements of supply and demand is essential if an economy is to prosper. It points out how the emergence of equilibrium prices ensures that neither shortages nor surpluses persist, even if they occur.

But perhaps most importantly, it tells governments and other would-be regulators the consequences of trying to set prices against the market. Any other price but the market-determined price will leave either buyers or sellers unsatisfied, and often both.

Most often the price is kept below what the market would have led to; that is, below the price at which sellers would have been willing to produce the number of units buyers wished to buy. The result may be lower prices, although if black markets spring up prices may even end up being higher, but the certainty will be that fewer units are produced.

DECISION MAKING AT THE MARGIN

At the core of economic analysis is the assumption that individuals making their own decisions about their own economic circumstances will lead to the best outcomes for themselves. No one else can ever know what a person truly desires. Therefore no one else can make decisions that will create as much personal satisfaction as those that are made by individuals acting on their own behalf.

Each person is therefore recognized as weighing up all of the alternatives they have before them and making decisions based on their own judgement of what is best. No one else is seen to be better placed to decide than individuals on their own who are given both the freedom and the responsibility to make their own decisions within their own lives.

This same freedom to apply one's own judgement is bestowed upon the production side of the economy as well. Incomes are earned largely by selling to the market what one has to offer, whether it is a manufactured good, a personal service or one's labour market skills. All producers must decide for themselves what they will offer up for sale in order to earn the incomes they will spend, which in turn means they must make whatever prior efforts are required to allow them to provide those products, services or skills to others.

And here too there is a balancing act required:

- There needs to be an understanding of the role that decision making at the margin plays in economic analysis – why economists put such emphasis on the relationship between costs, properly understood, and benefits, properly understood.
- Some idea of the nature of the market mechanism is needed so that there is at least an appreciation of the relationship between the market in full and the actions of individual producers.
- Also needed is some idea of market structure; that there are different possible outcomes depending on the relative number of sellers and the size of their firms compared with the total level of sales.
- There should be some idea of the crucial role of innovation and change in the development of economies.
- Also required is some idea of the difference between the short and the long run and how such considerations temper almost every economic decision.
- Finally, there is a need to understand the nature of market failure why it is impossible to leave all economic outcomes to the market – which is supplemented with an appreciation that not all failures that take place in the market are forms of market failure.

Being *marginal* means that the moment of calculation is *now*, in the present. The past is unalterable and must be taken as a given. It is what it is. The present is merely the baggage that has been deposited by everything that has come before.

This inheritance from the past includes the stock of all machines and forms of capital, and not just what they are but where they are. It includes all of the labour with all of the skills that the labour force might possess. It includes all of the technical knowledge available at the time, either embodied within the workforce and capital stock in ways that can be put to use (because if they are not there when they are needed, so far as an economy is concerned, they might as well not even exist at all). This inheritance also includes the cultural, historical and ethical values of the population. It includes the abilities of its entrepreneurs and of its politicians and public servants.

In essence, the legacy from the past includes everything there is.

From that initial point, any decision is expected to bring with it benefits (which are all of the reasons, financial or otherwise, why the decision might be made) and costs (which are the reasons why that same decision might not be made). If the expected benefits exceed the expected costs – that is, if taking some action is expected to provide a net improvement in one's circumstances – then the decision is taken.

These net benefits may or may not be calculated in terms of money, which is why the notion of 'utility' was introduced into economics. Only when the change is expected to add to one's satisfactions, one's total 'utility', will an action be taken.

These additional benefits, when seen in terms of production decisions, are usually referred to as *marginal revenue*, that is, the extra revenue that comes about because of the decision. These additional costs are referred to as *marginal costs*, referring to the extra costs that the decision will lead to. A decision to do something will be made, it is said, when the marginal revenue exceeds the marginal cost because that will mean more money comes in than goes out.

At the end of the day, everyone is seen as the captain of their own ship, the decision maker in their own lives. Each person is expected to make decisions that, at least in their own opinion, will make the greatest positive difference to themselves.

What other people think, what their family thinks, what society in general thinks, all of these are important considerations that will weigh in on every decision. But when all is said and done, in a free society it is each individual alone who is given the right to choose what actions to take that will lead to the highest possible level of personal 'utility', so far as they are able to determine this for themselves.

THE ENTREPRENEUR

The single most important element in the unfolding drama of economic activity, growth and prosperity is the entrepreneur. Who is the entrepreneur? The entrepreneur is the ultimate authority and decision maker in a business. The entrepreneur guides an enterprise in whichever direction it is to go. The entrepreneur runs the show. All decisions are ultimately determined by this one person who carries the responsibility for the success of the entire enterprise.

Entrepreneurs are people who have the following characteristics:

- they run and often personally own private sector firms;
- they make decisions on what to produce, how to produce and where to produce;
- they are dependent on the success of the businesses they run for their own personal livelihood.

It is entrepreneurs, taken collectively but acting individually, who assess community needs, introduce innovation, secure finance, buy or rent premises, put capital in place, hire labour, buy inputs and pay the bills.

They are a self-selected group of people who have decided to make their living by operating a firm. No one in a market economy chooses who will run our businesses. They choose to do so themselves, either by starting a firm on their own, or by being employed by an already existing business and rising to the top of the management structure.

It is from the willingness of such people to take on the risks associated with the management and ownership of firms that we have our dynamic growth, the improvements in our standard of living, the real increases in the level of earnings and the continuous and ongoing innovation in the products from which we can choose.

It is the embedding of the entrepreneur within the market economy that causes the economy to become as productive as it is. Without the entrepreneur, we are left with the government to decide what should be produced and the way in which production should take place. It is a recipe for poverty.

UNCERTAINTY AND RISK

At the centre of the unfolding of economic events is the existence of uncertainty and the risks such uncertainty creates. The entire economy is wrapped in an impenetrable shroud of unknowing. No one can know the future, the very time frame towards which all economic activity is directed.

Other than for the most trivial examples, production and investment decisions are made in the present but are expected to provide their returns at some later date, often a date many years ahead. All production and investment are done in anticipation of future returns on productive activity that will take place then. Yet, even while such decisions are being made, the fact that no one can and does know what will happen next makes such decision making extraordinarily difficult.

Think of the world in this way. You are riding on a train in some foreign land with your back to the engine. All that you know about what is coming up ahead, you know only from what you can see by looking out of the window. And what you can see is only what has already gone by. From what is seen, inferences can be made, but there is no certainty that what will come next will be similar to what has already gone past. What is up ahead may be entirely different but this will not be known until reaching each point along the track. And no matter how much has already been seen, there is always the possibility – the likelihood – that what is ahead is vastly different from what has already gone by.

This is the meaning of uncertainty. The future is invisible and unknown. Yet all decisions of any significance are decisions that must be made in relation to that unknown future.

Business decisions often go wrong because the future did not turn out as expected when those decisions were made. And this uncertainty must be distinguished from risk. Uncertainty pertains to the state of the world. Risk is the potential loss borne by every decision maker in making a decision about what to do.

Because uncertainty is pervasive and continuous, risk is therefore a fact of life for everyone making decisions. Since the future cannot be known, every decision carries with it various consequences for having been wrong. These are the risks, and in the commercial world they are often enormous. Those who make decisions in an uncertain world are taking on risks in which money, reputation and self-esteem are at stake.

DECISION MAKING AND UNCERTAINTY

Because of the nature of uncertainty, which forces us to make inferences about the future based on what we know from the past, there are risks involved in every decision. There are no facts about the future. Everything is a matter of judgement as different possibilities are assessed. There are no probability tables available as there would be for tossing a coin, since the past can only be an imperfect guide to what will happen next. And even then, low-probability outcomes do turn up, often with devastating consequences. It is all judgement about how things will be in a future that has not yet arrived.

A business deciding whether to take on some investment that might take five years to construct and be expected to repay its costs over the subsequent ten years is in many ways taking a leap of faith, since there is no method of knowing the state of the world 15 years ahead.

There is, in fact, no way of knowing the state of the world one day ahead, but the farther out a decision's implications will reach, the less that can be known.

The economist Frank Knight published one of the great works on this issue in 1921. In his *Risk, Uncertainty and Profit* he discussed the impossibility of calculating too far into the future. He wrote:

> Business decisions . . . deal with situations which are far too unique, generally speaking, for any sort of statistical tabulation to have any value for guidance.

The conception of an objectively measurable probability or chance is simply inapplicable. (Knight, [1921] 1933)

Each decision is one decision amongst endless other such decisions that are made day after day. Each decision is dependent for its success on the state of the world, the actions of other businesses, legislative and other changes made by governments, the desires of buyers, the discovery of new inventions and innovations, the prices of inputs, and so on and so on. How little anyone knows even of what is taking place right now in the present as a decision is being made, never mind what will happen in the future about which nothing concrete is known at all.

The relative calm in economies is deceptive. Moment by moment the actual circumstances faced by any business are shifting. Each day decisions must be made, some small, some momentous. But each such decision changes the character of the firm and either makes it better able to compete with its rivals or takes it closer to its own demise. Firms that have been around even for a hundred years or more may one day just go under through the relentless competition of the marketplace.

No one has a crystal ball, there is no map of the future that can eliminate the need for making decisions in the darkness of the unknown. It is for this reason that the entrepreneur, the person whose own capital is often at stake, is the person best placed to organize our productive efforts. Because it is entrepreneurs, often with their own capital on the line, who can be expected to take into consideration as many factors as possible in assessing what to do next.

Nor do all such decisions turn out well. But what does happen is that those who make successful decisions, for whatever reason, are rewarded with profits and allowed to continue, while those who make decisions which turn out to have been wrong, often a mere matter of luck, are less likely to be entrusted with the capital needed to run another firm.

PRODUCTION IS IN ANTICIPATION OF DEMAND

Only by appreciating the existence of uncertainty and its consequences can one understand the nature of recession and the fluctuating fortunes of business.

The production of all goods and services is in *anticipation* of demand. An item bought on any particular day has become available for sale only because of a string of production decisions that go back in time, often well back.

Everything available for sale exists only because someone had formed the belief at some stage in the past that it could be sold at a price that would cover all of its production costs. This is a conclusion that is often right but frequently wrong.

A business that loses millions of dollars on some project has not done so on purpose. Money is lost because at the time the production decision was made, the way in which events would later on unfold was incorrectly foreseen.

Because decisions must be made before their consequences can be known, and because events occur that no one had foreseen, no business can be assured of a profitable outcome. Individual losses and sometimes bankruptcy occur because mistaken decisions have been made.

This, of course, happens all the time in even the strongest economies. Mistaken decisions and poor judgement are not uncommon, but looked at individually cannot be seen as the cause of recession and large-scale unemployment.

Economic decisions are made before anyone can tell whether the decision will lead to a profit or loss. The motivation is always gain, but the outcome is only sometimes profitable. It is only in understanding that some economic decisions turn out in hindsight to have been the wrong decisions that a proper theory of recession and unemployment can be built.

Recessions occur where losses are made by many firms at one and the same time. The theory of the business cycle was designed to explain why large numbers of firms have made such wrong business decisions at the same time, why so many had at one and the same time failed to anticipate correctly the demand for the products they sold.

STRUCTURE OF PRODUCTION

In thinking about an economy, time and sequence are of immeasurable importance. Recognizing at each moment what can and cannot be known is essential if one is to understand how difficult it is to coordinate all of the economic decisions that go into the production of almost anything at all.

Production is a process that takes place through time, where every stage of production must be preceded by earlier stages of production that are the necessary foundation for what comes after.

And it is important to understand such things in order to understand the consequence of poor decision making in regard to what is produced. Poor decisions in one part of the economy have consequences at many other stages of the production process.

A cotton shirt bought at a retail establishment, looking backwards into the past, has required amongst many many other things all of the following:

- the planting of cotton;
- the spinning of cotton into yarn;
- the conversion of yarn into cloth;
- the use of the cloth to make a shirt;
- the tailoring of the shirt, requiring designers, cutters, tailors;
- the construction of a building which can be used as a shop;
- the rental or purchase of a shop of which one particular purpose will be the sale of shirts to others;
- the purchase of an inventory of shirts;
- the employment of sales staff.

Each of these required an entrepreneurial decision by someone. Someone had to decide to grow the cotton, for example, while someone else had to construct the shop and employ the sales staff. All of these decisions not only had to be made well before the buyer finally bought the shirt, but they had to be made in the proper sequence by individuals who were for the most part entirely independent of each other.

This matrix is only one small part of the entire *structure of production* of an economy. How all of the necessary elements fall into place for the final production of the millions of items now sold worldwide is the basic mystery that economic analysis sets out to explain.

STRUCTURE OF DEMAND AND SUPPLY

The important consideration in understanding the dynamics of growth and recession is the *structure* of demand, not the *level* of demand. Yet it is the level of demand that in modern macroeconomic analysis is considered to be the determinant of the growth rate in output and the level of employment.

Nevertheless, it is the structure of demand relative to the structure of supply that is the central issue. Economies grow, employ and continue to prosper so long as the structure of supply – the set of goods and services put up for sale – matches the structure of demand – the goods and services that individuals wish to buy.

Now, it needs to be understood that the structure of supply continues to change because of changes on the supply side alone. Technological change by itself changes how production is undertaken. The relative costs of inputs change, new production techniques are introduced and innovation brings whole new products onto the market.

But the structure of supply must also change in response to changes in what buyers choose to buy. It is this which producers must anticipate because it is only the goods and services that others wish to buy that can be sold. Tastes can change, average incomes rise (and occasionally fall), population levels can increase, while the demographic mix can shift. But the major reason for such changes in the structure of demand comes from the introduction of new products.

No market is ever free from change. In the world as we know it, there is a continuous flow of improvement and novelty. Better versions of what has already existed join with entirely new products that have never before been seen. The result is a shifting in the pattern of what is bought, which means that there must be a continuous change in the pattern of what is produced.

Suppliers in this kind of world do not respond to what buyers wish to buy, but in fact lead buyers into whole new areas of expenditure.

Moreover, while the typical concentration is on the market for the goods and services bought by final consumers, in reality most of what is bought in an economy are the goods and services used in the production of other goods and services. And every one of these inputs is subject to the same forces of innovation, product development, cost adjustment and redundancy. Every one of these inputs has the potential to be replaced in the volatile markets of a normal economy.

In an economy nothing stands still. Any business that believes it can stand still will soon find itself out of whatever business it was originally in.

THE NATURE OF THE MACROECONOMY

An economic world seen in this way is one in which there is a continuous mutual accommodation taking place between those who buy and those who sell, remembering all the while that those who produce are both sellers of what they create and buyers of the inputs sold to them by others.

Each producer of inputs is typically selling their products to a range of buyers. Amongst those buyers are businesses that are growing larger, others that are growing smaller, but all of which may have a different level of demand for the products they buy as each day, month and year goes past.

Each and every one of these businesses must remain completely alive to the commercial world in which they are engaged. They must be aware of the prices they pay, the prices they charge, the demands of their customers, the actions of their competitors, along with having some notion of the state of the economy they are operating within.

This interlocking maze of commercial relationships constitutes the structure of production. It has emerged spontaneously, largely through entrepreneurial decision making, to accommodate the structure of demand that is itself in part determined by the structure of incomes paid out by those who produce to those who participate in the various economic activities that are ongoing across the economy.

RECESSIONS AND THE STRUCTURE OF PRODUCTION

It is when the structure of demand moves out of alignment with the structure of production that economies slow and unemployment goes up. Thinking about economies in terms of their structure, in terms of how all the parts fit together, makes it possible to understand the nature of economic activity and why it sometimes goes wrong.

To look at these issues in terms of aggregates is utterly mistaken. Although aggregate economic analysis is the standard approach in macroeconomics today, there is an older tradition that took a more microeconomic approach. It is this approach that actually sheds light on the nature of economic activity and the causes of fluctuations in economic growth and employment.

But all of this leaves out what is more to the point. It is the relationship between the various parts of the economy that makes the important difference. Understanding the macro side of the economy means understanding that it is the structure of the economy that is all important.

In following the contours of the macroeconomy, measures are needed that will allow policy makers to judge whether genuine problems actually exist in each of these areas.

Yet to repeat, while it is the structure of the economy that will determine how well an economy operates, near enough all of modern macroeconomic theory and policy is built around questions related to the *level* of activity, not the economy's *structure*.

At the centre of the modern approach to macroeconomic management is the notion of aggregate demand failure. Embedded in this approach is a set of instructions which show why the aim must be to stimulate aggregate level of demand when economic conditions slow.

The aggregates are, however, not in themselves actual components of the economy. They are a summation of actions taken by millions of individuals added together to give an overall total. These aggregates do not have an independent life of their own.

Moreover, the level of aggregation is at such a high level that almost nothing that is actually going on inside the economy is visible. No entrepreneur is visible nor are entrepreneurial decisions. None of the microeconomic elements of the economy are properly reflected in the aggregates as described. The problem of the microeconomic foundation of macroeconomics has been discussed almost since the first introduction of modern macroeconomics in the 1930s. It is a problem that has not been solved.

THE THEORY OF THE CYCLE

Prior to the revolutionary arrival of modern macroeconomics, the swings and roundabouts of economic activity were explained by the many theories of the cycle that had until then existed. Almost all such theories have disappeared into history and are seldom any longer understood or referred to.

What has remained as the last vestigial trace of this once huge body of knowledge is a diagram which is still a staple of the textbook. It shows a rhythmic wave, with the level of activity on the vertical axis and time on the horizontal axis.

There is then a low point in each wave which is called the trough. Following the trough, the wave moves upwards and is variously labelled as the recovery, upturn, expansion or whatever, with the words indicating that conditions are getting better.

There is then an upper limit reached which is typically called the peak of the cycle, or sometimes a crisis, after which there is a downward movement variously described as a recession, downturn, contraction, or again whatever else might indicate that economic conditions are worsening.

The wave-like pattern is shown recurring time after time with more or less the same period shown from peak to peak, and the exact same horizontal amplitude of each of the successive individual cycles. And with that the typical discussion of the cycle ends.

Why the cycle is by nature cyclical, why there are variations in the length of each phase, why the depth of the downturn or the height of the upturn vary in each cycle, are no longer even hinted at. Yet these are crucial issues.

The theory of the cycle was based on understanding how, in an economy where businesses produce for profit, production errors would occur across an economy. All economic activity was based on businesses being able to anticipate demand, with the theory of recession based on explaining why many businesses had at one and the same time failed to anticipate correctly the level of demand for the goods and services they produced.

Production would occur before the goods were bought. A service would be offered before others had decided to purchase. The expenditure that went with being in business – purchase of capital, hiring labour, renting premises and the rest – would occur before any actual sales took place.

In every economy, mistakes in production decisions would inevitably be made. Firms would fail to earn profits, and either contract or disappear. This is how the economic system works in taking resources out of the hands of those who are unable to use in a productive (that is, profitable) way the resources that have been entrusted to their care. Businesses are always failing. But this is not in itself a cause of recession.

Recessions are the result of systematic economy-wide errors in production decisions which are caused by factors that lead large numbers of businesses into productive activities that turn out not to have been profitable after all.

The kinds of factors that can have these effects include large and unexpected changes in interest rates, a major fall in the availability of credit, major disruptions caused by changes in government policies or large increases in input costs, such as the price of labour or the price of crude oil.

And even though such misjudgements may only initially affect a relatively small proportion of the economy, in the right set of circumstances the effects can spread farther and wider as each industry contracts and therefore reduces its own demands for the products of others.

The downturn, which might start anywhere, thus becomes cumulative and eventually affects the entire economy, with some industries harmed to a greater extent than others.

The subsequent upturn reverses the downward spiral. Some industries begin to recover and the increased production in one area leads to increased demands for the products of other industries. The slow return to better conditions continues until there is again a peak in activity, at which point the entire structure turns down once again. And so on and so on, *ad infinitum*.

EXCHANGE RATES, INTERNATIONAL TRADE AND INTERNATIONAL CAPITAL FLOWS

There is finally the nature of international economic relations. It is the part of economic theory that in many ways remains closest to the original free market concept of the classical economists, most likely because it is the most difficult area of an economy's structural relationships for a government to influence.

Not that governments do not try. At every turn there are efforts made to affect exchange rates, the level of imports, the growth in exports and the escape of financial capital from the domestic economy.

Yet the theory stubbornly refuses to move very far from what is basically a market-driven view of the world, for the most part because every intervention, especially in the modern world, has tended to reduce the economic welfare of the domestic population.

Even so, there is a large degree of misunderstanding about the importance of free trade. Everyone is a natural protectionist unless they can learn to see the harm that protectionist measures cause.

Some understanding of the importance of free trade in raising domestic incomes and evening out economic instability (the reverse of the common perception) provides a minimal requisite for understanding how markets make individuals better off.

Moreover, persistent downward movements of the exchange rate are almost invariably signs of economic mismanagement and are a useful means of keeping track of how well a government is performing in the arrangement of a nation's domestic economic affairs.

And the flight of financial capital from insecure economies towards economies showing greater stability and potential growth helps to explain why governments so frequently try to bottle up such capital flows.

Trade in goods and services encourages efficiency in the domestic economy because whatever may be the case locally, across the world there are always others who will take markets away if given the chance. Local producers are therefore much more diligent in open economies. They do what is required to keep the competition away.

COMPARATIVE ADVANTAGE IN TRADE

Trade also restructures production in every economy towards the production of what each country is better able to produce, *relative* to the production of competitor nations. It is the relative efficiency that is important. Even where one country can produce everything at a lower total cost than a second country, they will still be able to trade because other countries will have some things that they are relatively better at producing.

What does 'relatively' mean in this case? If one country can produce shirts for $5 apiece and bottles of wine for $10 each, then in that country each bottle of wine is worth two shirts. If in a second, less efficient country the costs are $10 for shirts and $50 for wine, then each bottle of wine is worth five shirts. Trade will ignore the fact that the first country can produce both items more cheaply and focus on which country is relatively cheaper at producing which product.

The first country is therefore better off buying between two and five shirts with each bottle of wine instead of continuing to produce any shirts at all. Meanwhile, the second country should give up on wine production, since each shirt can buy half a bottle of wine from the second country, while within the country itself that same shirt will only buy a fifth of a bottle. The actual exchange relationship is likely to shift under trade, but both countries end up better off, with each having more shirts and more wine.

This is known within economics as the *law of comparative advantage*. It is a theory that demonstrates what everyone already knows. Consumers are better off where international trade can take place. Where no one gets in the way of trade, trade is guaranteed to expand. It would not happen if those engaged in trade were not being made better off.

3. Value added

Possibly the most difficult area to understand about economics is one that you would think would be amongst the easiest and most commonly understood. This is the area of value and value added.

If economics were going to provide an understanding of anything, it would have to be, you would think, an understanding of what value is and where it comes from. And while economists do have such theories, they are relatively obscure and are almost never discussed at the introductory level. Value in economics is a very difficult idea.

Yet for all that, it is not possible to have a clear understanding of either economics or economic policy unless one has a reasonably clear idea about what value is and how it is created. And unless one has this reasonably clear idea about the nature of value, it is almost impossible to make judgements about almost anything done in an economy, from its very organization to the finer details of individual decisions.

That the aim of economic activity is to create value is obvious and straightforward, for all the difficulty in knowing just what value actually is. And the point is this. *Something has value to the extent that a person is better off with it than without it.* In economics we frequently say that a good or service has value if it is able to provide *utility*. Economic activity is aimed at providing individuals with increased levels of personal utility.

But it is also true that in almost all cases to produce something of value it is first necessary to use up some of our resources that also have value. Nothing comes from nothing. And this is where the notion of value needs to be further refined. A tonne of steel also has value, but not as a final good providing utility. It has value only as a productive input that can be used to produce the goods and services that do provide that utility. The value of such inputs is derived from the value of the final goods and services they can be used to produce. Which brings us to the crucial issue of value *added.*

To create value in the form of the final goods and services that provide utility is the central purpose of economic activity. In the process of creating such value, some part of the resources that exist must be used up. Value added underscores what is too often forgotten: that to add value one must also at the same time destroy value. The word 'added' is there to remind us that we have also had to subtract the resources used up in producing whatever has now been brought into existence. Value added is thus the *net* result of using up various resources which already have value, to create other products that have even more value.

It is only if the value of the products newly produced is greater than the value of the resources used up that value adding has occurred. Economic growth is the way we normally discuss value adding activities. They are one and the same. The value of output must exceed the value of the inputs used up if economic growth across an economy is to occur.

VALUE AS UTILITY

Value, as in the utility provided by goods and services, is subjective. There was a period in the early history of economics where it was thought that value was an embodied measurable quantum found in goods, such as the amount of labour that went into their production. Eventually, but only after a century of dwelling on the nature of value, was it fully appreciated that value is the personal valuation of an individual in relation to some good or service.

In exchange, this is typically quite easily seen. I want a shirt, which it can be seen is something that has value for me, and this is known precisely because I happen to want it. As I see things, having that shirt would make me in some way better off in comparison with not having it.

But to obtain that shirt I typically must hand over something in exchange, and in the world in which we live, almost invariably what is handed over is a sum of money. Buying something means that there is a valuation put on having the product or service relative to the value put on the money that is paid out. The value of the money lies, of course, in the other goods or services that I might have bought instead.

Money is the measuring rod of value. It is the medium of exchange. Individuals receive money in exchange for what they produce and they give money to others in exchange for what they wish to buy. When people freely spend their own money in buying goods and services, there is no question that in their own view they expect to be better off for having made the purchase.

But in understanding that, it is only a very small step on the way to understanding what value means within economics.

VALUE ADDED IN PRODUCTION

Creating value is not generally about buying but about producing. And it is not entirely about the payment of money, although money valuations almost always come into it. It is instead about the transformation of one set of goods and services into another set of goods and services through the production process, where the newly produced goods are expected to provide at least as much if not more value to their owners in comparison with the resources that have gone into their production.

It is an old cliché in economics to state that nothing comes free. It is the kind of statement that everyone hears as it goes in one ear and out the other. Unless one understands in one's bones what this old cliché actually means, it really is a meaningless set of words that gets you nowhere.

So to understand this principle, take a very simple example. I own wood and nails. I have a hammer, saw and some time. All of these have value. These are transformed into a table which also has value. Value has been added if the value of the table to me is greater than the value of the inputs that went into its construction.

Or take a shirt. At some stage it was nothing more than some cloth, thread and buttons. There were also sewing machines, labourers and buildings in which all of the necessary ingredients for creating a shirt were brought together.

Each of these inputs had value on its own. And each at some earlier date had in turn been a mere set of inputs into some production process. The cloth, for example, may at some stage may have been cotton growing in some field before it went through the many different stages before being turned into the piece of material ready to be turned into a shirt.

And all of these different inputs into the shirt, and the inputs into the various inputs, and so on going backwards to earlier stages of production, were all inputs that could have potentially been used for something else. All had value in that they could have been used elsewhere to make other things.

Nor should it be thought as we move to earlier stages that we are moving to less sophisticated stages. The cloth may have been shipped by air. The labour involved in building and maintaining the various forms of capital equipment might have required years of education and on-the-job skills development to reach the point of being able to undertake the technical tasks required.

THE PRODUCTION PROCESS DESTROYS VALUE WHILE IT CREATES IT

At every stage in the production process there are valuable – often highly valuable – inputs needed to produce not just the final output but also each of their inputs. In this case the entire chain of inputs was put together to produce a shirt. And clearly, that shirt could not have been produced for only a single person, but was one of possibly millions of such shirts, the sale of each contributing to the entire cost of production.

In paying for the shirts that were eventually produced, every one of the inputs used in the chain of production along the way had to be paid at least enough to cover every one of the costs involved. If their production costs are not covered, the inputs will not be produced. If the inputs are not produced, the final product can never come into existence.

But what validates the final production of those shirts, that is, what allows the entire production chain to come into existence? There is only one thing, and that is the payment of enough in total to the shirt maker to pay in full for all of the inputs into the production of those shirts.

This, then, is the meaning of value added. In the production of those shirts there was sales revenue earned. At the same time, there was the value used up in the production of those shirts by the shirtmaker and then in turn by all of the businesses in that chain of production that led up to the production of that shirt.

There is therefore the value of the output which must be compared with the value of all of the inputs.

Value added occurs when the total receipts in producing *and selling* those shirts is greater than the value of those goods and services which have been devoted to the production of that end product.

The various inputs have disappeared into the production of this shirt. Each shirt may have only been responsible for an infinitesimal part of the whole of the costs involved. But each shirt must carry its weight in generating the revenue to cover the shirt maker's costs of production.

What is true for this shirt is true for everything produced across the economy. Value is generated when the revenues earned cover all of the costs involved in creating just that structure of production that allowed this tiniest bit of the totality of economic activity to be carried on.

But in looking at the products and services at the end of the production chain it is absolutely necessary to understand that all along the way value has been destroyed so that some product can come into existence or some service be performed. That value had existed – the labour, the transport networks, the capital equipment, the factories, and the thousands of other inputs, all of which could have been used in different ways – of this there is no doubt.

That value which had existed has now disappeared – the labour involved, for example, has already been used in one particular way and in no other – of this there is also no doubt. And in the place of all of the inputs used are the products and services we see before us in the present.

Economic activity, in all of its different forms, should be recognized as attempts to create value by using up existing goods and services at one end of the production process to produce other goods and services at the other end of the production process.

VALUE ADDED AND ECONOMIC GROWTH

In an economy that wishes to remain viable, all of that previously existing value must be replaced with products at least as valuable as those that were used up.

If an economy does no more than replace the value used up, that is an economy that stays exactly where it was. If there is more value created at the end of the process than existed when it began, then we are looking at an economy that is growing. And where the amount of value created is less than the amount of value used up, then this is an economy that is less well off than it was before.

And the value used up must include not just the raw inputs but the value of the labour time applied and the value of the capital equipment that has been eroded while being used.

Yet even this does not quite get us there. Value as described is equivalent to covering the costs of production. It is the product of the purchase and sale that go on through each national economy and indeed across the world. Profitable businesses are the strongest evidence that value has been created.

But beneath even this is a hidden assumption that businesses are responding to the wishes and desires of buyers.

VALUE IS SUBJECTIVE

Value is subjective. It is a personal evaluation of the benefit that will be accrued in adding something to one's life, whether a dinner, a service or an addition to one's saving. Whatever adds to one's life satisfactions is seen to add value, that is, to provide one with *utility*.

The reason for the choice of this word was to take away the notion that everything one receives gives actual pleasure or even some kind of satisfaction. Many goods or services one might pay for – a filling in one's tooth, for example – are bought and paid for not because there is some intrinsic pleasure in the purchase but because of some necessity.

The value received is personal in that the amounts paid out are in exchange for some good or service which is chosen in preference to having the money that has been spent. There is some utility received in the purchase.

But how do we know that such utility has accrued? We assume it because individuals making free decisions to spend money in one direction rather than another are demonstrating that this is where they believe their highest level of utility can be found.

This is one of the fundamental assumptions of economics: that the individual is the best judge of what will provide utility. No one else can be a better judge than single individuals, taken on their own, making decisions for themselves about where to spend their own money.

In such an economic environment, using business profitability as the proximate measure of value added allows the commercial world to be shaped by the individual decision making of the entire community. It is only in this kind of economic structure that it can be said that the consumer is sovereign.

VALUE ADDED AND UTILITY

There are thus two forces. There are the businesses run by entrepreneurs who are constantly trying to work out what would give people utility. And there are buyers who are continuously sifting through all of the products offered for sale to determine for themselves which products will give them this utility.

These are, generally speaking, the same people looked at firstly as producers who earn incomes, and then as consumers who use their incomes to buy those goods and services that they believe will provide them with the highest possible level of utility.

What is being described here in a generally abstract manner is nothing other than the normal activity of everyone. As producers, we are trying to work out what others would be willing to buy from us. As buyers, we are continually trying to work out which purchases would provide us with the largest net satisfaction.

It is why businesses and consumers are always looking for new products, one to sell and the other to buy. The changes in the market are due overwhelmingly to the discovery of products that will provide higher levels of utility. Producers are continuously trying to put up for sale better products at lower prices, while buyers are making their own assessment of which products will more completely satisfy their needs and wants.

STRUCTURE OF PRODUCTION

It is important also to be fully aware of the phrase *structure of production*. Within an economy there is at every moment in time an actual existing deeply layered texture of economic relationships between all its different producers and all of the different buyers of everything that is being produced.

There is a shape given to an economy's productive efforts by the value-adding activities of all of its producers in combination. Each of those producers, those entrepreneurially run businesses, is making a decision about what will be bought, not in the present but in the future.

Each business, in response to its own estimate of where profitable sales activities will occur, makes decisions about what to produce, and from that initial decision flow subsequent decisions on what capital to install, which workers to hire, what buildings to rent, and all of the other decisions that have to be made before anything at all can be produced.

Beyond that, there are very few firms which actually have only a single customer. Virtually all producers sell to a wide assortment of buyers, whether final purchasers or other producers.

Cloth is produced, but not just for making shirts. The shirt makers buy cloth from suppliers who are supplying woven cotton for any number of other uses, whether fabrics for chairs or bandages to dress wounds. Each one of these uses might create higher prices in the short term, but may over the longer haul create economies of scale that tend to bring down the price for all of the cloth's users.

Moreover, each producer almost certainly produces more than a single good or service. Every firm offers a range of products. We tend to speak of supply and demand as the core concept of the microeconomy, and there should be no doubt over how centrally important it is. But in doing so, supply and demand must always be put in the context of the many other goods and services that any single business entity can be expected to produce.

So to picture an economy as it actually is, rather than seeing it merely as suppliers supplying a single product one at a time to a set of buyers buying single products one at a time, it is instead necessary to see all of the overlapping and multidirectional criss-crossing of purchase and sale that is going on.

A convenience store that sells one person a loaf of bread at eleven o'clock at night will only do that because it is selling someone else a carton of milk at 10.30. The airline that flies someone halfway round the world will only do so because it can sell other tickets to all of the other passengers on the same flight and on other flights that day, that week and that year.

In some very important sense, everything in an economy is related to everything else. The loaf of bread and the bottle of milk are trivial in their own way and each sale changes nothing.

But as you build out from all of the sales and all of the producers and all of the relationships between one firm and another, and between firms and the final demanders at the end of the process, there is a very large and intricate network in place that is difficult to picture but should be seen in its totality to grasp some idea of where the goods and services we buy originally come from.

In some sense it is a quite delicate apparatus, and in a more important sense it is quite robust. But it is a series of relationships that is forever changing under the shifts in demand that are a constant, the new products that come onto the market and the new forms of production that become routine. Innovation is never-ending.

And then there is overlaid above all of that the decisions made by government. These decisions change the regulations under which businesses work, and the taxes that are paid by everyone at every stage of the production process.

The structure of production continuously reconfigures itself almost moment by moment. Old firms disappear. New firms arrive. Existing firms change what they do and how they do it, either because they come up with some innovation themselves, or more often because the pressure of competition will pronounce a death knell on any firm that thinks it can continue into the future without change from what it did in the past.

But it is the pathways that lead both backwards and forwards from the productive environment of an economy. The connections for the production of anything are so dense that they cannot possibly be traced. No one can even remotely know how the entire organic structure of an economy fits itself together.

One business might have a list of all of its own suppliers, but who supplies those suppliers no one can possibly know. And so on throughout the whole of the economy. All of the relationships are spontaneously made by individuals and businesses who see products and prices and know generally very little else about how any of it came into existence.

WHY CENTRALLY PLANNED ECONOMIES CANNOT WORK

This is why prosperous centrally planned economies are an impossibility. For central planning to work, someone must know all of the inputs into all of the outputs, and then know where each must go. They must also know the relative prices of each of the inputs and the effect of changing prices on production costs. And all of this must be known almost instantaneously if any of the millions of adjustments that go on in an economy are to be made as circumstances change.

Central plans are made under the assumption of one set of circumstances, but those circumstances change. In a market economy, there is a shift as sales either increase or fall for some things, and there are then adjustments made with suppliers and the workforce.

In a centrally planned economy, none of that can happen because there is no mechanism for the instant response to changes in economic conditions.

How does the market respond? It responds by changing production decisions that affect conditions either in a small circle of businesses or, in some instances, across the entire economy.

An increase in the demand for shirts leads to an increase in the demand for cloth, so that perhaps there is some overtime for the workforce or new employees are hired while the prices of cloth goes up. We never think twice about such things because that is how we now expect it to happen.

Similarly, but more profoundly, if there is an increase in rates of interest, change will occur which will affect pretty well all businesses at once. There are changes which ripple through the economy as each firm accommodates itself first to the change in interest rates, and then, secondly, to the changes in all other firms that have occurred because of those changes in rates of interest. And then there are further changes as businesses react to the second set of reactions, and then so on, and so on, and so on.

The changes can be pretty drastic for something like a large increase in rates. Some firms may lower their production levels and may even shut. Other firms will find they cannot sell as much as they did and will respond in their own way to the cut in sales, and may themselves reduce the number of their employees.

EQUILIBRIUM

The notion of an equilibrium in economics is, therefore, a concept that tends to have very little relevance to an actual functioning economy.

Equilibrium is a concept that indicates that all of the forces at work more or less balance, so that as long as conditions do not change, everything will simply continue into the future as it had in the past.

When the forces of supply and demand balance, prices do not change, nor do the amounts bought and sold. In an economy taken as a whole, everything just continues along with production and employment remaining as they had previously been.

If one wishes to think of equilibrium in the sense of growth rates, then an equilibrium is said to exist when everything continues to grow in the next period at the same rate of growth as in the previous period.

One of the best definitions of equilibrium is that it is a condition in which all expectations are met.

But however one might define the concept, what is absolutely clear is that no economy, indeed almost no market within an economy, will ever be in equilibrium in any of the senses in which the term might be used.

CETERIS PARIBUS – ALL OTHER THINGS BEING EQUAL

Nothing ever stands still. Everything is always in flux. The concept of *ceteris paribus* is central to thinking about economic issues. *Ceteris paribus* is a Latin phrase which means 'all other things being equal'. It is a phrase that helps us to isolate individual factors that affect an overall outcome.

In almost all imaginable circumstances, for example, having a factory across the road will lower the value of a home. What a statement like that means is that a house across the road from a factory will tend to have a lower selling price than a house that is not across the road from a factory, if every other factor happens to be exactly the same.

All other things being equal is the condition that all of the other factors are exactly the same except for this one particular feature. Using this *ceteris paribus* condition allows you to look at the effects of particular conditions one by one.

It does not pretend that everything does stay the same. Everyone knows that the underlying conditions of every market are under constant pressure to change. Nothing stays as it was, and the longer that time goes by, the more changes one can expect.

REACTING TO CHANGE

Nothing is ever in equilibrium. Everything is always in disequilibrium. But that is not the same as chaos. It is because everyone is acting with their eyes open and is alert to change that the proper accommodation to new circumstances takes place.

There is no doubt that sometimes things happen so quickly that the ability for everyone to accommodate everything that has happened is swamped. Businesses fail, people lose jobs, the future becomes even more clouded than usual. Rather than only a small proportion of those engaged in economic activity having to work out what is taking place and needing to think through what to do next, a much larger proportion find themselves in the same boat in that same storm at the same time.

There are at such times no ready answers that can be provided by anyone, as all of those affected try to work out how to accommodate the changes. Each person will understand only a very small part of the whole. But as each of the individuals caught up in the tempest begins to work out what to do to save themselves, things become clearer, first for some and then for all. And eventually, the clouds begin to pass and economic conditions settle.

What returns is what passes for equilibrium, which is change that takes place at a relatively sedate pace. But if by equilibrium we mean everything that happens has been expected in advance, that never happens and cannot happen.

That is why private ownership of the means of production is the optimal means of organizing an economy. The owners of private firms, and usually their employees as well, have something personal at stake. They make the effort to overcome problems and achieve the best possible outcome given all of the circumstances that fate has thrown in their way.

4.   Governments and the market

Economics is a sub-branch of politics. Governments are not a 'necessary evil' as it has sometimes been said, but are simply necessary for our well-being. Historical experience has made it abundantly clear that governments can be and often are the greatest problem plaguing a population or nation state. Government economic mismanagement is only the start of the many problems that a government can cause to individuals and the societies they govern. But for all that, governments will always be with us.

The need for any community is to ensure that its government is responsive to its wishes and that the government has as little control over individual lives as possible. While this is an extraordinarily difficult task for any community to achieve, and to maintain over time even once achieved, being able to restrict the role of government is necessary if individuals outside the political class of their countries are to live in freedom and prosperity.

Economies are embedded in the political process. The identification of an independent, self-guiding process in which goods and services are produced, priced, distributed and sold without any active role of government was a momentous discovery. But an economy always finds itself in operation within some nation state and subject to the laws, rules and regulations imposed by the legal authority of the nation.

How well or how badly an economy will run is to an important extent dependent on the actions of government, but that is only the start. There are always the customs, moral beliefs, personal values, prejudices and attitudes of the population of a nation that must be considered. If the views of a population are hostile to the operation of a market economy, or if envy or ignorance drive community decision making, once again a market economy can be expected to operate poorly. Market activity will never cease totally, since production for others is part of how humans behave. But the market will not operate to its full potential and the community will be less well served by its economic activities.

FREE MARKETS AND THE 'MIXED' ECONOMY

There are, in theory, only two ways in which a highly developed and technologically sophisticated economy can be managed. One is through the market mechanism, the price system and dependence on the forces of supply and demand to determine what gets produced and prices paid.

Or an economy can be run by government from some central point, at which there are decisions made about what to produce and how to produce without reference to market-determined prices. This is referred to as central planning, often called a 'command economy'. A command economy is run through some kind of central plan in which the blueprints for the entire economy are mapped out by those in government. Entrepreneurially determined market prices play no serious role in such an economy.

It is sometimes said that we live in a 'mixed economy' in which there are elements of both market behaviour and central planning. This is almost entirely untrue. There are many activities taken on by governments in market economies but almost invariably their actions are undertaken through the market rather than through central direction.

Understanding the dangers that governments pose in the modern world is almost entirely unrelated to concerns that governments will take over major industries and try to run them by political edict and through central planning. This has been tried and it has failed. Virtually all economies are now run using self-directed enterprises of some sort to generate market prices. It is these self-directed enterprises which determine the direction in which resources will go and activity take place.

THE ACTUAL PROBLEMS OF GOVERNMENTS AND THE ECONOMY

The problem of governments is not that we live in a 'mixed' economy where governments run some things by ordering resources to be used in certain ways. The problem is now quite different. The problem now is that governments can and do spend immense amounts of money that they gather through the tax system, borrow from the public and even print up when the other options are closed.

Beyond that, governments now attempt to fix economic problems by creating regulations that may be fine as some abstract principle but are unrealistic when applied in an actual commercial setting. The lack of genuine understanding of the needs of industry that affects many governments in what are supposedly free market economies is a growing menace to prosperity.

Governments now see themselves as capable of making major expenditure decisions that direct resources into uses that are politically determined with little regard for the value-adding potential of what is produced. There are certain activities that governments are keen to associate their activities with: education, infrastructure and health being amongst the most common. Governments are also pleased to be seen as the bearers of welfare and social services of various kinds. In all of this, they seek recognition as the providers of the good things in life.

There is a case to be made for many of these but there is also an even better case for governments to leave what can be achieved through market activity to the market.

Moreover, the role of the private sector in government activity is almost always understated and underappreciated. Governments decree the construction of hospitals and schools and allocate funds to those ends. But the actual inputs – the timber, nails, paint and glass – are produced by private firms. It is only the end products that are determined by a government. The rest, made up of virtually all of the inputs, is provided by private sector firms operating through the market.

GOVERNMENTS AND MARKETS

Some of what governments do is value adding, some is not. In fact, some of what governments do is essential to the smooth running of an economy. Nor should this be thought of as some kind of throwaway line where it is market outcomes that ought to prevail with only the occasional exception.

Markets will not work without governments. But what is needed are governments attuned to the needs of the market, even when those governments are pursuing objectives other than those that businesses or consumers might have preferred. There are market outcomes that if left without government involvement would be socially undesirable. Governments play an absolutely necessary mediating role.

There are quite clearly forms of market behaviour that can endanger some and harm others. These are often best controlled by government decisions that forbid particular actions where there are larger social purposes involved.

But in no sense should this be seen as warranting some kind of open-ended government involvement in economic activity. If anything, given the abysmal record of government involvement in economic decisions and regulation, the clear rule should be that as much as possible should be left to the market. When in doubt, leave it to the market to sort things out.

That governments too often are not in doubt when they take on their regulatory role is a major problem. Governments can and often do cause much damage in taking the actions that they routinely do.

Governments acting to improve the economic well-being of a community have done more harm in ruining lives and destroying wealth than even the most destructive wars.

Government activities to improve the well-being of a population are nevertheless inevitable. You may be sure that governments will do things, and they will do things with the expressed intention of improving economic outcomes. But the fact of the matter is that unless they understand their limits, the harm they do can be almost limitless.

Understanding the role of markets and how they work may be the single most important attribute of a government if economic prosperity is the ultimate intent.

What, then, is the economic role of government?

Legal and Administrative

There is, firstly, the legal, administrative and enforcement side of what governments do. These, along with national defence, are the historic roles of government found as far back as history itself. From the smallest tribal bands to the most complex and extended empires, putting rules in place and ensuring that the rules are followed has been the primary and most necessary part of what governments do.

Anarchy is literally the opposite of government. A society without laws, courts and effective enforcement will not function. In such surroundings, wealth-creating activity will disappear. The most important contribution that governments make is to create a space for civic peace in which individuals can go about their value adding economic activities.

Beyond that, governments contribute to economic activity by its administration generally. Not just through law enforcement but through managing the community's affairs in ways that improve the economic environment. A community is an intricate social network that requires management. The general administration of a community's affairs are activities that governments, and only governments, can undertake.

Regulation

What is best for any individual in a market may not necessarily be what is best for society as a whole. Regulation of economic activity is essential if communal welfare is to reach its highest level.

Zoning laws, that prevent the construction of intrusive manufacturing plants in the midst of residential housing, are an example of a general case. Some activities, even though potentially profit making, are incompatible with personal well-being for others. Government regulation of economic activity, which attempts to reconcile the needs of the market with the health, safety and well-being of the members of the community, is essential.

It is not only essential for individuals, but it is essential for the proper operation of a market economy. Not all economic issues can be resolved through the market system and price mechanism. There are frequently 'externalities' in market transactions, where third parties beyond the buyer and seller are affected by the production and sale of goods and services (individuals affected by polluted streams due to industrial waste, for example).

Government regulation to balance the losses against the gains, to ensure that the harm caused to third parties is taken into account, is required. Getting the balance right is often difficult, but recognizing that there is a balance required, between the positive value of whatever has been produced and the cost of those externalities that affect others outside the transaction, is an essential part of the political process.

Importantly, recognizing that balance is required not because there is a market but because there is production, production which would occur in any economic system, will help decision makers in crafting regulations that provide a compromise between the harm done by particular activities and the good achieved by living in a prosperous economy.

Infrastructure

Governments also provide infrastructure. These are the capital works that are the major connecting rods of economic activity. Public transport, wharves, harbours, roads all provide economic benefits and these have been frequently, but not necessarily, supplied by governments.

In some instances infrastructure is provided by governments because no one else can be expected to undertake such projects. But where the private sector might have produced such infrastructure, it may have been little more than historical circumstance and custom that have determined that in one economy it is governments which provide the service, while in others it is the private sector.

Welfare

Governments have also taken on some of the responsibility of providing at least a minimum of welfare for the poor and indigent, going back centuries. 'Bread and circuses' might have been a catchphrase of the

Roman Empire, but it suggested that the government had taken on the task of ensuring that the population did at least have something to eat. Governments have throughout history sought ways to assist those who could not fend for themselves.

One of the biggest differences in the modern world relative to the past is the wealth now available for politically motivated redistribution. The temptations for governments are enormous, as are the political demands. But every increase in welfare payments means a loss somewhere else. Someone has to pay: someone else's income must be reduced so that welfare payments can be increased.

Taxation Levels and Structure

In undertaking all of their tasks, governments have depended on the tax revenues raised. Whether as tariffs or tolls or taxes in general, the principal source of funds for governments has been the monies collected from the populations they govern.

Taxing lightly and in ways that do least damage is important, but governments have not always been fastidious about how they raised their revenue nor about the amounts that were raised. The theory of public finance had to wait until the eighteenth century to have even its first rudimentary discussions. But in choosing how and how much to tax, governments, both then and now, have played an important role in encouraging industry and promoting value adding industry.

Government Businesses

And then beyond that there is a possible role for governments in running businesses of their own. The most common form of government business has been natural monopolies.

Natural monopolies are industries whose initial capital costs are extremely high, but the additional costs of servicing one more customer so extremely low that the first firm to enter the industry ends up being the only firm.

This is why public utilities, such as telephones, power and water, were in many places once typically owned by governments. Post offices and municipal transport are also frequently publicly owned. Whether governments are the best qualified to manage even such natural monopolies is a serious question, but given the suspicions that often attach to private monopolies, especially natural monopolies in goods and services, this arrangement was until recently generally accepted.

Schools are the other area that governments have almost universally taken on. In almost all countries, schooling, at least to a certain level, is entirely financed and managed by governments. To what level, and whether there should be competition for publicly owned schools, are matters of debate. But that governments own and run the largest part of the elementary education infrastructure is now almost universal.

In most places, medicine is to a varying extent a state-run enterprise, and for the same sorts of reasons. Something as important as health, it is sometimes said, should not be run as a profit-making enterprise and however managed, should not be allowed to price anyone out of receiving the healthcare they need. That they will 'need' more healthcare when the effective price is zero is what anyone running such a system must always expect.

There are then what is known as 'public goods'. These are products and services for which 'free-riding' is a problem. The provider of the service is unable to receive payment from all those who benefit. Once the product is in existence, everyone can receive its benefits, with the result being that it is in no one's private interest to provide the service or contribute to its revenue stream. These are rare, with national defence being the most typical example, but which anyway was never going to be part of the market economy. Radio and television signals are also potential examples.

Governments, in addition, do run other sorts of businesses. There is almost no form of business that governments have not run somewhere at some time. Marxist theory demanded that governments own and run the 'commanding' heights of the economy, and in some places there was no private sector activity of any kind whatsoever permitted.

Yet the record shows that where governments have owned and operated businesses, these businesses have seldom been managed well and have frequently run at a loss. Governments have run profitable enterprises, but usually they are public utilities of the natural monopoly variety.

And even then, as with public transportation systems, possibly because governments have imposed on themselves a public service obligation so that even unprofitable parts of the business are allowed to continue, such enterprises are not just unprofitable, but often lose substantial amounts of money. They cannot be made to pay their own way. Many techniques have been attempted to force government enterprises to operate in ways similar to private sector firms, but these have almost invariably been unsuccessful.

Governments do not have the knowledge to manage businesses successfully and their agents are public servants whose expertise is seldom related to managing firms and for whom the personal costs of failure are typically very low. Beyond that, the disciplines that a private sector firm has imposed upon it by the market are often not there with public sector firms, which can usually draw on taxpayers to make up the losses incurred.

Government enterprises have a very poor record of achieving economic success and adding value to the resources being managed.

Government Spending in Recession

But the final justification for government spending has been the advent of economic theories that suggest that public spending, especially in times of economic distress, is an appropriate counterweight to an economic downturn in the private sector. Moreover, such theories almost totally discount the need for such spending to add value. Any spending will do to start the wheels of exchange turning.

This is the use of government deficit finance to 'stimulate' the economy, to 'prime the pump'. Putting purchasing power into the hands of individuals, even if what they are doing creates no value in itself, will have them spending, and their expenditure will cause other activity and then other activity after that, in what is described as a 'multiplier' process.

It is the belief that unproductive public spending can cause overall economic growth that may be the largest fallacy in the realm of government. Unproductive spending is unproductive. It does not itself, by definition, contribute to value adding production and cannot induce value adding activity overall, since at the end of the expenditure chain no net value has been created.

SUMMING UP THE GOVERNMENT CONTRIBUTION

In sum, governments can contribute to value-adding production but just because they can do so in theory does not mean that they necessarily do. Incompetent economic management, grossly inflated expenditure on non-value-adding forms of output, along with inept and costly regulation, impede growth and prosperity rather than enhance it. But where governments improve things, they do so by providing:

1. good economic management;
2. sound public administration;
3. the development of a commercially appropriate legal system and enforcement network;
4. appropriate infrastructure (roads, harbours, airports, and so on);
5. the provision of welfare to those seen to be in need of assistance;
6. value-adding production in industries with a positive externalities that cannot be captured by the supplier and which can usually be expected

to run at a loss if a fully extensive service is to be provided (public transport, education);

7. the production of goods and services that have a naturally monopolistic industry structure (telecommunications, gas, water).

The emphasis should be put on the fact that governments *can* create value with such activities but they do not necessarily do so. Governments need to know their limits.

Sound economic management and public administration are necessary. Direct government activities are potentially value-creating but are problematic all the same. As much of such government production is not tested by the market, or in the case of natural monopolies there are no genuine forms of competition, there is also no inbuilt gauge, such as a market test, to indicate whether too much has been spent and whether what has been spent has been spent efficiently.

There is therefore a tendency for governments to pay more for such forms of output than is warranted by the value created relative to other economic activities that could have been undertaken in their stead. It is very difficult to constrain government expenditure, and in the end the main part of the restraint is provided by the community's tolerance for being taxed.

Unlike with private sector activity, buyers cannot direct their spending towards those forms of output that give them the greatest satisfaction. With political decision making, it is typically all or nothing, and usually there are many other considerations besides economic management that determine the nature of the government.

But then there is this, the last area of public activity:

8. public expenditure to lift an economy out of recession and stimulate growth.

This is, in many ways, a warrant for public sector waste. If it can be properly fitted in under any of the previous categories, then so much the better, although normally it is not.

Outlays as a means to minimize the impact of recession are generally the least well targeted, least properly based, least productivity-enhancing forms of expenditure. But because such spending is typically introduced during the down-phase of the cycle, when economic conditions are in retreat, when enterprises are closing down and job losses high, it is typically the least well monitored. The result is often a far higher level of national debt with almost nothing to show for the money that is now collectively owed.

PRODUCTION POSSIBILITY CURVE

The production possibility curve is typically drawn to provide a basic under-standing that in any economy there are limits and that choices need to be made. Although usually presented as a throwaway before getting onto the 'real' economics, the diagram instead contains an enormous storehouse of conceptual ideas needed to understand how economies work. Basic though this analysis is, it can make clear a number of issues of genuine importance.

To understand the curve properly, it must be understood that it rep-resents combinations of forms of output that *completely* exhaust the resource base of the economy. On the curve itself, the available labour and technology are not only being fully utilized, but they are also being used as efficiently as possible so that, given the existing institutional arrangements of an economy, the stock of existing capital, the skill sets and knowledge of the labour force, and the entrepreneurial and managerial skills available, only so much can be produced and no more. The crucial point is that it is not physically possible for that economy to produce more than it does. An example of such a curve is shown in Figure 4.1.

In the example, and it is only an example of one possible use of produc-tion possibility curves, an economy can either produce goods and services wanted by the private sector or it can produce goods and services sought by government. This is what is described within economics as a 'trade-off'. And if we are at some point on the curve itself (*A*, for example), then there

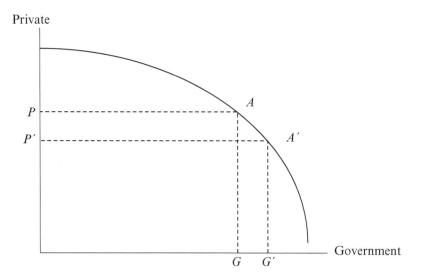

Figure 4.1   Production possibility curve

is not just a particular amount of private sector goods (*P* in this case) and a particular amount of public sector goods (here shown as *G*) that are being produced, but no more of either could be produced given the limitations of the economy's resource base.

Opportunity Cost

In a fully employed economy at some moment in time, it is only possible to produce more of one set of goods if there is less production of other goods. More public sector goods and services can only be had by having fewer private sector goods and services. The cost – referred to in economics as the *opportunity cost* – of having more of one good or service is the value of the goods and services that have to be given up so that one can have more of something else.

To produce more government goods means there must be less of everything else. The extra government use of resources in moving from *G* to *G'* means that there are fewer resources for the private sector to put to its own uses, whether as consumers or investors. The amount of output produced by the private sector falls from *P* to *P'*. The extra government use of resources comes at the expense of private sector use. There is more public spending but less private.

Economic Growth

In the longer run, as growth takes place, a community can have more of both, but the ability to have more is still constrained by the limits imposed by the economy. As shown in Figure 4.2, when growth has occurred the production possibility curve moves out, representing an increase in the productive capabilities of the economy. But however far from the origin the curve may be, it nevertheless remains as an absolute barrier. Beyond it, the levels of production remain impossible. The maximum possible amount of output that can be produced remains the various combinations found on the line itself.

Unless the economy has grown, to have more output taken up by governments means that there is less available for private individuals, as either consumers or producers. It is possible, indeed likely, that some of what is provided by governments is wanted by at least some members of the population. Where to draw the line between private and public spending is always a major political question.

Growth occurs when the economy is capable of producing more of all kinds of goods and services, and is shown in Figure 4.2 by the second production possibility curve that is further out from the origin in comparison

Private

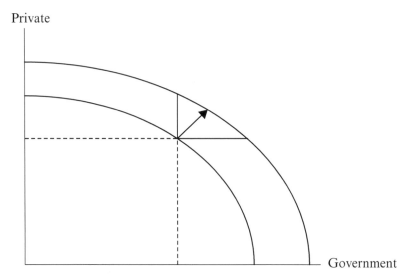

Figure 4.2   Economic growth

with the first. With growth, it is possible to have: (1) more goods and services going to the private sector without any loss of the amount going to government; or (2) more goods and service available to government without any reduction in the amount that goes to the private sector; or (3) it is possible to have more of both. The arrow between the two darker lines shows how, with growth, it is possible to have more of everything.

Unemployment and Inefficiency

Production possibility curves are also useful for explaining how economies do not reach their full potential.

The point X in Figure 4.3 represents the production of P units of private sector goods and services and G units of public sector goods and services. Because it is inside the production possibility curve, it means that more could be produced of either one or both with the available resources and technology.

Not as much as could have been produced was produced. What might the reason be?

a.   Unemployment
The most obvious and straightforward reason is due to unemployment and underemployment, usually thought of as relating to labour, but it can just

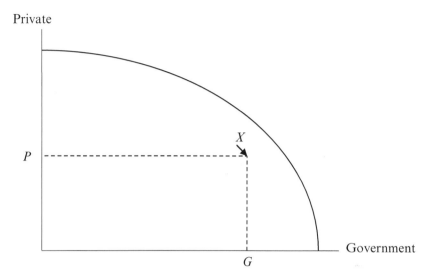

Figure 4.3 An economy not reaching its potential – unemployment and/or inefficiency

as well occur with all other kinds of resources. Some of the resources that were available were not put to work. Why this is the case would require more investigation, but it is well known that this happens. Unemployed labour is a particularly well-known social phenomenon, always one of the major issues in any economy.

For the individual, unemployment can range from being a nuisance to an absolute personal disaster. Unemployment can simply be a brief period without paid work, or in other circumstances can ruin an individual's life. Economic policy is designed to ensure that as little unemployment as possible occurs, and when it does, that the duration of unemployment is as minimal as possible.

b. Inefficiency

The second reason an economy may be inside the production possibility curve is because of the inefficient use of resources. This is a reason that may over the longer term be more important, and is often much more difficult to deal with than unemployment, as difficult as that is to deal with.

Resources are wasted when they are not used in such a way as to produce the combination of goods and services that would have created the highest level of value added within a community. They may be employed, just not employed in their most efficient way.

Efficiency is, however, related to purpose. In most cases, using an ambulance as a taxi is very inefficient since the cost of an ambulance is very high relative to the cost of a taxi. Using an ambulance in this way is, therefore, usually a misallocation of the resource base of a community.

But there are possibly instances when taxis might be urgently needed while ambulance services are not. In such circumstances, using an ambulance as a taxi turns out to be the most efficient use of resources.

Given the intent, an efficient allocation of resources takes place when, whatever the output desired might be, it is being produced at the lowest possible cost. Keeping costs to a minimum – that is, using as little of our resource base as possible to produce each of the goods and services we want so that more output in total can be produced – means that production is efficient. But where resources are being wasted on output of lower value than might otherwise have been produced, production has been carried out inefficiently. We could have had more, but because of the way our resource base was used we ended up with less.

As far as the production possibility curve is concerned, the result is that the community is producing at a point inside the curve. It is not producing as much as it might have, and if resources were better deployed, more could be had.

It is one of the most important tasks of market competition to drive resource use to the highest-valued form of utilization. Competition is designed to lower the profits of firms which are not using the resources they are buying to the maximum advantage. If another business can do it better, either by being better able to work out what buyers want, or by being better able to provide what they want at a lower cost, that firm will lose customers, and may ultimately disappear.

Market competition pushes firms towards the most efficient form of production. Because every firm in a competitive economy is driven to be as efficient as possible, it pushes the economy as a whole towards producing as much as it possibly can with the resources that it has on hand.

A NOTE ON DIAGRAMS

The final reminder about this and other diagrams drawn in economics is that they are just for instruction and are not in any way an exact representation of anything at all. They are drawn to provide an understanding of concepts, not to be seen as a scale model of some underlying actual reality which almost invariably no one ever knows. It is the concepts that are important. In this case, production possibility curve analysis shows that:

- there are always limits on how much can be produced from available resources;
- in a fully employed economy, to have more of some goods and services it is absolutely necessary to have less of others;
- not producing at the maximum possible is either due to some resources being unemployed (and unemployment here includes more than just labour) or it is due to resources not being used as efficiently as they might have been;
- economic growth means more goods and services can be produced, and this is either because the resource base has expanded or because there have been technological or human capital improvements that have improved productivity.

Each of these is useful to understand. But the diagram itself is merely a vehicle to help understand the various concepts.

MAKING SENSE OF DIAGRAMS GENERALLY

There will be more diagrams throughout the remainder of this book. For some, they may be a barrier to understanding the points being made, but this need not be the case. They are a means to put a point across that would otherwise take many more words, but with less precision in the meaning. Diagrams really do help and they are not hard to understand.

They are basically 'if–then' statements. They state that if this is the case, then that is the case. With the production possibility curve shown above as an example, it states that *if* this is the level of private sector production *then* this is the maximum level of government goods that can be produced. It then indicates that *if* the desire is to increase the level of public sector production, *then* the level of private sector production must diminish.

This can be stated in words, as it has just been stated. But once you understand how to use diagrams, the rest is easy. And so many seriously important points can be explained that otherwise would have to remain relatively obscure. If you are interested in understanding economic issues, even if you are unsure about the use of diagrams, make the effort. The rewards are worth the minimal time involved in mastering this generally simple technique.

5. Factors of production, finance, innovation and the role of the entrepreneur

It is something of an established tradition in the instruction of economics to discuss early on and briefly the 'factors of production', and then immediately go on to discuss what appear to be more important analytical kinds of issues. Yet it is only here, in a proper discussion of the overall relationship between output and the various inputs that go into the production process, that a true understanding of the underlying dynamics of an economy can be found.

The traditional trio of factors are listed as land, labour and capital. Everything produced needs some combination of the three, and having said so the caravan typically moves on to other things. In many ways this rudimentary discussion is a holdover from early nineteenth century economics where one of the major questions was how income was shared out between workers, capitalists and the owners of the land. Yet in spite of the way such discussions have diminished over time, the roles of the various factors, and how they are brought together, are essential to understanding how an economy works.

And although the factors are traditionally referred to as land, labour and capital we will introduce a fourth, which is often brought into the story but just as often left out. That fourth factor is the role of the entrepreneur, which is actually the utterly indispensable element whose absence leaves the rest completely without direction and purpose. We will even introduce a fifth factor, and then, after that, a sixth, and then, later still, a seventh.

The first two of these factors, land and labour, are generally straightforward and relatively easy to understand. Capital and the role of the entrepreneur, however, are much more complicated both in their meaning and in the roles they play in an economy's success.

LAND

'Land' is a metaphor for all of the natural resources used in the production process. Land thus includes water, as well as any and all other inputs which come as 'gifts' of nature. Refashioning and relocating resources to put them in a form and at a location where they can be used by others is what economic activity almost entirely consists of.

In a farm community, land is just that. It is a piece of ground in a particular place upon which crops are grown or animals raised. Even then, it is seldom, if ever, the case that land can be used without other productive factors preparing the groundwork.

But in using natural resources, almost never are they where you want them in a form in which they can be used. Coal and iron ore, oil and trees, may in some sense have been provided by nature. But in their natural state they are very far from usable for productive purposes; coal is not heat and trees are not timber. They are a potential which can only be fashioned into a final output sought by consumers through being mixed with other productive inputs.

Moreover, farmland requires preparation and fertilizers. Land in its raw state is very seldom available for productive use without some form of preparation.

Even air and water are far from available for anyone to use in any way they please. Although air was once thought of as the one and only example of a free gift of nature, such times are long gone. Air has a scarcity value and its use must in many circumstances be parcelled out amongst those who wish to use it.

Some people, for example, would like to have air to breathe; while others, as part of some industrial purpose, would like to use that same air to dump poisonous gases. How to allocate the uses made even of air is an economic problem of the highest order.

LABOUR

To land must be added labour. Labour represents the human effort in the production process.

Labour, of course, comes in the widest variety of forms. There are vast ranges in age, talent, skills, abilities, experience, knowledge and application. Different people are located in different places, either near to or far from where the particular work that needs doing is located.

There are, moreover, different combinations of such personal characteristics embodied in every single individual, making each either more or less suitable for each and every particular kind of work.

The bringing together of different workers who bring different abilities to a productive process is one of the major tasks of a properly functioning economic system.

CAPITAL

Capital is a more complicated matter. Capital is made up of the inputs into the production process that have themselves been outputs from the production process. They are comprised of that part of value added that is not just used to produce goods and services for consumption, but also used in the production of inputs into the production process and even for the production of other forms of capital. Machines, for example, are used to produce other machines.

The production of capital is a drawing down of the productive capabilities of an economy in the present for the purpose of adding to the economy's productive capabilities at some later stage in the future.

Capital is made up of plant and machinery, shops and office buildings, roads and railways, pens and paper. It includes the stocks kept on hand by manufacturers and retailers.

Capital is any and every form of an economy's already existing stock of productive assets that are used by their owners to earn an income. It is the decision to use an item in some form of commercial activity that turns some tangible good into an item of capital. A car is a car, but what turns it into capital is the decision by its owner to use that car in earning an income.

A car can be used as a taxi, or to transport goods for payment, or in any number of ways that are part of some enterprise's productive efforts. Non-profit organizations and governments also make use of capital, so that, for example, a car may be used by a charity or by the police.

Capital items, to repeat, are items that have themselves been produced which are then, in turn, used in the production process. It is how they are used that matters not what they are. If they are used to produce other goods and services, then they are capital. If they are used by final users in creating the satisfactions that material well-being can provide, then they are not.

Money most emphatically does not count as capital. Since money as notes and coins cannot be used in the production process directly, so far as economics is concerned it does not form any part of an economy's capital base. Money can certainly be exchanged for items of wealth that can be used productively, but money as money is not capital.

Nor does capital include stocks, shares, bonds or any other financial asset. Although often referred to as capital in financial circles, they are only titles to an income stream or to partial ownership of an enterprise. They are not in themselves part of the productive apparatus of an economy. They are therefore not part of an economy's capital base.

Capital is made up of those produced inputs which can be used in creating additional value. Think of capital as technology and machines as the perfect examples of a capital good and you should not get it wrong. But in so doing, bear in mind that much that is part of the capital of a nation is the intangible technological know-how embedded in the physical capital used. An aeroplane is a capital good but the increasing sophistication of its embodied technologies is what causes its increase in productivity.

It might also be noted that *human capital* is now often included as a produced input into the production process and in this way exists separately from the actual labour component. Human capital is thus included as part of an economy's capital stock. The stock of human capital is the result of the efforts made by individuals to increase their own ability to add value during the production process, and not incidentally, to earn a higher income for themselves.

But when all is said and done, capital should be seen as everything that has been developed and produced to be used within the production process.

MILL'S FUNDAMENTAL PROPOSITIONS ON CAPITAL

John Stuart Mill provided four 'fundamental propositions respecting capital' whose validity remains as intact today as when first written in 1848. But for all that, economics has sailed away from these fundamental propositions, much to the cost of our understanding of how economies operate. Without their guidance, it is difficult to understand how an economy works.

The first three of the four are universally accepted by economists even though seldom explicitly taught. The fourth is now explicitly taught as being false, even though it remains perfectly valid. But the loss to our understanding of the disappearance of this fourth proposition has had devastating consequences for economic theory and policy alike.

Industry is Limited by Capital

The first of his fundamental propositions, Mill noted, was so obvious as to be taken for granted but, as he also wrote, 'to see a truth occasionally is one thing, to recognise it habitually, and admit no propositions inconsistent with it, is another'.

This first proposition is that industry is limited by capital. You cannot produce more output than the amount of capital in existence will allow you to.

There is only so much that can be produced during any particular period of time, and that amount is kept within its certain limits by the amount of capital available. But more important than this obvious statement is its corollary. In Mill's very nineteenth-century words, 'every increase of capital gives, or is capable of giving, additional employment to industry; and this without assignable limit'.

To translate: it is not possible to produce so much capital that production would overwhelm the willingness of the community to buy every last bit of the extra output which the additional capital allowed an economy to supply.

Mill wrote in support of the necessity in understanding this doctrine that 'there is not an opinion more general among mankind than this, that the unproductive expenditure of the rich is necessary to the employment of the poor'. Mill believed this opinion to be completely fallacious.

Today that same doctrine would be stated as, 'there is not an opinion more common than this, that the expenditure of governments on just about anything at all is necessary to create employment, especially during recessions'.

The basic form in which economic theory is taught today specifically teaches that if the community increases its level of saving, the level of economic activity will fall along with the level of employment.

There was a time when this modern view of things was seen as utterly false. Today it is seen as the highest truth, a core belief amongst economists. To quote Mill again, whose meaning in spite of his now archaic mid-nineteenth-century language should be crystal clear: 'The limit of wealth is never deficiency of consumers, but of producers and productive power. Every addition to capital gives to labour either additional employment, or additional remuneration; enriches either the country, or the labouring class.'

This cannot be emphasized enough: the limit to wealth creation is *never* the result of a deficiency of consumers, the *only* limits are the limits imposed by the existing availability of producers and productive power.

To produce more does not require additions to consumption, it requires additions to the productiveness of an economy. And these never occur on the demand side of the economy but only on the supply side.

Ignorance of this simple proposition has led to some of the worst mistakes in economic policy ever made.

Capital is the Result of Saving

The second of Mill's fundamental propositions was that if capital is to be produced, saving must take place. Without saving, the stock of capital cannot grow.

Saving is the feedstock of investment. Capital comes into existence only because saving has taken place. To return to Mill, 'all capital, and especially all addition to capital, is the result of saving'.

There are only two possibilities so far as production is concerned. Either what is produced in the present is not intended to add to the economy's productive capabilities, or what is produced is directed towards becoming part of the store of productive assets that can be used in the production process. The first of these possibilities is consumption, and the second is investment. It is from investment that capital is created.

Economists know this, yet the way in which macroeconomics is often taught is to portray saving as a villain, since if you think of the most important driving force in an economy as its level of demand, then saving, because it supposedly reduces demand, leads to a fall in consumption and therefore in the level of activity.

That is the fundamental core proposition embedded in the way macroeconomics is taught today.

In reality, only if not everything produced is directed towards consumption spending but some of our resources are used to improve the productive capabilities of the economy, can growth occur. Investment comes from not using up everything we produce in current consumption. Investment is the result of saving. Only if there are resources available after we have produced for current consumption is there any capacity to use such resources for investment purposes to add to our stock of productive capital. And note most especially that saving is a proportion of the economy's entire resource base and not just the difference between current income and current consumption.

What is Saved is Spent

Mill's third fundamental proposition is to point out that what is described as saving is actually a form of expenditure.

The words Mill uses do, however, require some explanation since they are not the modern way in which these words are used by economists. But to understand what Mill wrote is to move to a deeper understanding of how economies work.

In Mill's words, this third proposition states that capital 'although saved, and the result of saving, it is nevertheless consumed'.

Today the word 'consumption' merely refers to purchases made for personal use by buyers at the end of the production chain. To Mill, to consume meant to put something to use, whether by consumers or by investors. Consumption then meant to use up, as we might still say how a house was 'consumed' by a fire.

So in an economy, if electricity has been consumed, then the electricity has disappeared. It has been used up while being put to use in producing one thing rather than another. If what has been used up is a machine or building, then that machine or building has also been used in one particular way rather than having been used to produce a different and goods and services that might have been produced instead.

But one way or another, the use of our resources during production has deprived society of all the other ways those resources might have been used. Whatever else, those resources did not lie idle.

Mill was perfectly aware of how difficult it was to get this principle understood. He wrote:

> The principle now stated is a strong example of the necessity of attention to the most elementary truths of our subject. It is one of the most elementary of them all. . . Yet no one who has not bestowed some thought on the matter is habitually aware of it. Most are not even willing to admit it when first stated.

Mill goes on to describe how these things are looked at by those who have not considered the issues properly and more deeply. To them, he wrote:

> it is not at all apparent that what is saved is consumed . . . Saving is to them another word for keeping a thing to oneself; while spending appears to them to be distributing it among others. The person who expends his fortune in [personal] consumption, is looked upon as diffusing benefits all around . . . The eye follows what is saved, into an imaginary strong-box, and there loses sight of it; what is spent, it follows into the hands of tradespeople and dependents.

Those who save have limited their current purchases of consumer goods and services to less than what they might have bought and have allowed those unbought resources to be transferred to investors.

The very fact that incomes had been earned means that something had been produced and sold to the market. Saving allows the resources that exist to be used in various forms of productive activity, either by those who own them already or by someone else. It is this saving which enables the economy to grow. Unless there are decisions to transfer resources to those who intend to build productive assets – that is, unless there are decisions to save – the economy cannot and will not grow. This transfer of savings is what the financial system is for. On the surface it is a transfer of money, but what are actually transferred are the productive resources used to build up the capital structure of the economy.

Whether it is personal consumption taking place or investment, resources are being used up in the production process. They have disappeared and been reformed into the products being produced. But in the first case there is nothing to show for it so far as future productivity is concerned; while in the second case, with investment, the economy has been more than compensated for the resources that have been used up.

This is the kind of choice that individuals might face in their own lives. They can choose to take a prolonged international holiday or they can instead decide to build an extension on their home. In both cases the resources of the community have been drawn down, but only in the second is there anything productive to show for it.

It is this choice which every community must face; how much of its resources to use up in day-to-day living and how much to use in adding to its productive capabilities.

To explain what Mill had in mind, look at the production possibility curve in Figure 5.1. On one axis is current consumption (C). On the other axis is investment (I). The point where the production possibility curve meets either axis represents the total productive capability of the economy if either one or the other constituted the total level of production.

If all output is consumed, there is then nothing left over for investment.

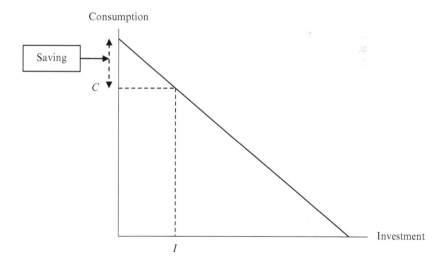

Figure 5.1   Production possibility curve in an economy with only consumption and investment

Only by not consuming all of our incomes – that is, only through saving some of our incomes – are resources made available for investment. That saving is shown on the diagram as the difference between the level of total potential output on consumer goods and the actual level of consumption at C.

The existence of saving allows productive resources to be redirected into investment. Without that saving, no investment could ever take place.

Saving is not an absence of spending. Saving is a decision to transfer to someone else the resources that one might have caused to be absorbed in the production of goods and services for oneself. But whatever those who have received those savings choose to do, saving does not represent an absence of production, a void to be filled. Saving is actual production, just as Mill said.

To believe anything else is as wrong as it is possible to be wrong about economics. Yet it is this very error that modern economic analysis has chosen, as we shall see, to base its understanding of macroeconomic issues on.

The Demand for Commodities is Not Demand for Labour

Mill's fourth proposition was once considered the touchstone of economic thinking, 'the best test of a sound economist' as it was once said. If you could not understand why it is true, you were seen as incapable of understanding how an economy works. This proposition has, however, now grown so far from present usage that it would be a very rare economist who has even heard this statement, let alone accepts what it says. Yet for all that, it remains as valid today as the day it was first penned.

Mill's fourth proposition states that 'demand for commodities is not demand for labour'. Its meaning: when you buy goods and services you are not increasing the number of jobs. This is how it was put by Mill: 'To purchase produce is not to employ labour . . . the demand for labour is constituted by the wages which precede the production, and not by the demand which may exist for the commodities resulting from the production.'

What this means is this. When someone buys goods they are not themselves employing the labour or paying the wages. By the time the good is bought, the work has already been done and workers have already been paid their wages. The employment of labour is an entrepreneurial decision made in advance of production and sale. It is not the consequence of someone having finally bought the product.

In explaining what he meant, this is how it was expressed by Mill: 'Almost all [economists] occasionally express themselves as if a person who buys commodities, the produce of labour, was an employer of labour, and created a demand for it as really, and in the same sense, as if he bought the labour itself directly, by the payment of wages'.

About which view Mill makes this very dark statement: 'It is no wonder that political economy advances slowly, when such a question as this still remains open at its very threshold.'

That this view – that the demand for goods and services is equivalent to the demand for labour – is now accepted across the economics profession with virtually no dissention is a matter of some considerable interest. A very great deal depends on whether Mill was right or wrong.

What, then, did Mill and the classics mean? This is how, in modern language, Mill explained why the contrary is so nonsensical.

If it is the case, he argued, that it all comes to the same thing so far as working people are concerned whether someone entirely consumes their own income – buying cars for themselves and overseas trips, let us say – or instead uses up resources on productive activities or on charitable contributions, then what sense is there in having their money taken from them in tax revenue to fund welfare expenditures?

For, as Mill wrote, 'since my unproductive expenditure would have equally benefited them, while I should have enjoyed it too', why bother removing the purchasing power from their original owners if their spending it themselves on themselves would amount to the same thing?

The conclusion that should never be lost sight of in understanding how economies work is that buying things creates no value. To purchase is not to produce, nor is it to employ. Demand of itself creates no value and cannot put people to work.

To lose track of this fundamental proposition will render useless any and every economic judgement based on the belief in its opposite. Stimulating demand with non-productive forms of spending can only slow an economy. Only productive activity – genuine value-adding activity – only this can create growth. That was Mill's message, a message that has all but disappeared from economics as taught in the modern world.

THE ENTREPRENEUR

The last of the traditional factors of production is the most important one of all, the entrepreneur, the factor which rents, hires and purchases the other three and then directs them towards their productive use.

What makes a market economy work, what makes any modern economy work, is that often ignored fourth factor of production. Economies do not, cannot and will not work in anything other than the most primitive way without free, private, individual decision makers who earn their living based on the success of the businesses they own and run.

It is, of course, possible to have some clunking assemblage of enterprises and business entities run by employees of the state. It is always possible to try to mimic free enterprise and the private sector by surrounding decision makers within a supposedly productive enterprise with a series of incentives.

All this has been tried time and again with tragic results that impoverish any nation that puts such a pseudo-market framework at the centre of its economic structure.

It does not work because as soon as the individuals at the controls of businesses are employees of government, rather than being self-selected individual members of the community who have chosen to run their own particular businesses in their own particular ways, the very process that drives production onwards instantly disappears.

An entrepreneur should be understood as the ultimate decision-making authority in a business enterprise. Entrepreneurs take on the risks that come from being unable to make a business profitable. Someone must be the final decision maker of all of the major decisions in an enterprise. The success or failure of an enterprise is in the hands of the entrepreneur and can be found nowhere else. It is the entrepreneur who experiences a personal loss if the business does not succeed that is the essential ingredient in creating economic growth and prosperity.

ENTREPRENEURIAL EXAMPLES

To understand the role of the entrepreneur as one of the factors of production, think of a symphony orchestra. There, in miniature, we see the factors of production in operation.

There is first the 'land'. The ground on which the concert hall sits has a location and a series of other possible uses, which means that it has value of itself. Labour then consists of the various members of the orchestra, each with their own specialized roles to play and each of whom embodies skills which have taken many years, often many decades, to learn properly.

Capital then comes in the form of the various instruments as well as the music stands and sheet music. These are all produced means of production. Indeed, the concert hall itself is an item of capital, along with all of the seats in the auditorium. Capital consists of all of the previously produced items that are part of the apparatus that enable the concert to go ahead, as well as the human capital embodied in the musicians themselves.

Finally there is the entrepreneur. But just who is the entrepreneur in an orchestra? Most assuredly, whoever else it might be, the entrepreneur is not the orchestra's conductor. The conductor, so far as this example goes, is an employee, often a very highly paid employee but an employee all the same. The entrepreneur was someone else, the person whose role was to ensure that the orchestra was assembled, concerts were arranged, tickets sold and expenses paid.

In any enterprise, such as an orchestra, there is someone who takes the ultimate responsibility for deciding that a concert will take place, ensures that an orchestra, including its conductor, is hired, and then undertakes, or organizes to have undertaken, all of the steps along the way to ensure that a concert finally takes place. In almost every circumstance of this kind, almost no one knows who the entrepreneur behind the scenes has been. But the certainty is that there has been someone, because unless there was, nothing would ever have happened.

Another example is film making. Land in a film is typically called 'the location'. Labour consists of all of the actors and the rest of the production crew. Capital is made up of the various items of equipment that turn the actions of individuals on a set into the finished product that ends up within a cinema. But when it comes to the entrepreneur, the director is only an employee and has not been the person ultimately in charge. A director is hired by someone else but is not typically in charge of the entire film-making process.

In film-making, the entrepreneur is called 'the producer', someone often unknown by name to almost anyone in a movie audience. But behind every film there is someone who has been responsible for bringing together all of the elements that were required to put the film together, from the finance to the actors to the equipment and so on down. Someone is in charge, someone makes those final decisions and ultimately pays the bills. And unless such a person exists, the film will never be made.

RISK VERSUS UNCERTAINTY

The essence of the business world is uncertainty and it is to deal with uncertainty that is the primary task of the entrepreneur. No one can know what is going to happen next, which makes every business decision a risk of one kind or another. Uncertainty is in the nature of the future. Risk is the willingness to make a potentially loss-making decision where nothing about the world as it will become can be known with certainty at the time the decision is made.

About the future, there are only forecasts and conjectures. Business decisions must be made in a world where no one can be sure about what will come next.

It is the role of the entrepreneur, even in the face of such uncertainties, to decide what to produce, how to produce, where to produce and what prices to charge. That in a large enterprise there are managers who make such decisions does not diminish the crucial significance of the entrepreneur. It is the entrepreneur who has that final responsibility, and on that judgement the entire enterprise depends.

It is the entrepreneur who takes on these risks, and risks exist because the future is uncertain. If the future were known in advance with perfect clarity, there would be no risk-taking required in running a business. It is only because outcomes are so unpredictable and the future is so entirely uncertain that entrepreneurial judgement is of such immense value to an economy.

COMPETITION AND THE ENTREPRENEUR

Such willingness to take on this organizational role comes with many motivations, the desire for personal gain being only one. In the commercial world, however, where production for profit predominates, the role of the entrepreneur is guided not only by personal gain, but also by the force of competition whose pervasive presence guarantees that there is very close attention paid to ensuring costs are contained, profits made and that the products sold are as good as can be found at the prices paid.

It may not work out that way, but that is the aim, and those are the pressures that come from the existence of other competing businesses which would like nothing better than to take for themselves the customers of the firms with which they compete.

Business leaders, the entrepreneurs of a free enterprise economy, reach the top by having made decisions along the way that have rewarded their firms with sufficient profitability to ensure that they have paid their way in the world. Anyone may start a business. Anyone may enter a business as an employee and work their way to the top. But whichever may have been the case, success has been registered in the profit and loss statement of the firm. The commercial world is a proving ground for success in business.

And this is true irrespective of the size of the firm. Whether businesses are run by a single person, or are structured as partnerships, or are limited liability companies under the management of boards of directors, it is only because the firm is directed by those whose allegiance is to the success of that particular business that there is any prospect of the firm remaining viable and itself contributing to economic growth.

Loss-making firms also draw down on the resource base of the community, but ultimately, because they are unable to pay their way, must let those resources go to others who will then try to make better use of the capital and labour that the managers of such loss-making firms had been directing.

The market system succeeds by a process in which resources are placed under the direction of those who are able to cover all of their costs through sales revenues received, while it takes the ability to direct resources away from those who cannot. Whether through bad management or bad luck, if a firm cannot pay its way, it will either contract in size or completely disappear.

It is precisely here that the role of the entrepreneur comes into view. The major decisions of an enterprise are determined by its management with the aim of commercial success as the crucial indicator of success. It is entrepreneurs who make the major decisions of deciding what, how and where to produce and sell.

Every major innovation which you might think of as nothing special, just part of the world we live in – whether the telephone, computer or kitchen sink – is the product of entrepreneurial decision making by someone. Goods and services do not end up in our possession through magic, but are the result of business decisions made by individuals trying to earn a living by working out what others would be willing to pay high enough prices for, and in large enough numbers, to cover every single one of the many, many costs of production that have been incurred along the way.

FINANCE

It is possible to think of a fifth factor of production which is in many ways different from the others. Finance is not normally thought of as part of the underlying factors of production since it is not an actual input. But without the ability to pay for the various factors of production put to use before there are any returns on the outlays made, productive activity on the scale to which we have become accustomed could not occur.

So although money or various financial instruments should not be thought of as forms of capital, there are strong reasons to include finance as one of the necessary ingredients in the overall structure of a business enterprise.

A major part of what an entrepreneur does in organizing a business is to secure lines of credit so that in conjunction with normal business cash flows, payments can be made as bills come due. And far from being a minor part of this process, it is often amongst the most important. Without an ability to cover production costs as these come due, a business will fail.

Finance is often ignored because, unlike the other factors, it is more abstract. It is not visible in the way the others are, and there would have been times and places in history when finance played almost no role in productive activity. But these were, almost without exception, more economically primitive communities.

Once commercial activity began to grow, the need for financing activity became immediately evident. Someone or some group was often needed to provide the financial backing to allow purchases to occur before any receipts had flowed into the business. Even where entrepreneurs provide their own finance, this is a separate function, in the same way that working proprietors might provide their own labour even while being the entrepreneur within the businesses they own and manage.

The finance role is a very specialized area of the economy. What finance does is transfer purchasing power from those who wish to save part of what they have earned to those who wish to spend but do not, at the time, have sufficient earnings to cover all of the expenditures they wish to undertake.

And it is of utmost importance here to distinguish between finance, which is almost always provided as some form of credit, and the real savings of the economy, which are in the form of various resources of one kind or another. Finance allows an entrepreneur to buy in inputs before enough revenue to pay for the inputs has been earned.

A business needs actual resources: labour, buildings, machinery, transport and much else. These are the nation's savings that an entrepreneur is seeking to make use of. The money and credit borrowed are merely a means to an end, the end being the ability to purchase these needed inputs before a sufficiently high revenue stream exists to pay for the inputs they are putting to use.

Finance allows buying to take place before revenue is received, but the buying consists of the inputs that are used to produce. Keeping separate the two parallel flows – the flow of money and the flow of inputs – is critical if one is to understand what is taking place.

THE NATURE OF INTEREST

Those who provide finance to others do so to earn interest, which is the name given to the payments made in exchange for the purchasing power that has been made available by others. There is a vast economic literature on the reason that interest is actually paid but here I will only provide the most basic. Interest is the payment made for the use of part of someone else's property – in this case someone else's purchasing power – and can thus be seen as a form of rental. One lends out one's ability to buy at the present time in the same way as one might rent out one's house. At the end of the rental period, the aim is to have the full amount lent out returned, in the same way that one intends to reclaim one's house when the tenant moves out.

It is always easy to find others who wish to borrow. It is far more difficult to find borrowers who will be able to repay the funds they have received.

Business Loans

There are three general classes of recipients of such transferred savings. The first, and economically the most important, are businesses which intend to repay their debts with the receipts from the business enterprises which they manage and often own.

From the lenders' perspective, what they are looking for are enterprises that will be sufficiently profitable that the money they lend will be returned. To assess and make proper judgements on the various applications for the use of funds is one of the most difficult tasks in the business world. That is what banks and other such financial institutions do, and it is from successfully discriminating between *potentially* successful businesses and those which are less likely and even unlikely to succeed that a bank will earn a profit of its own.

But it is only through this process that an economy is able to prosper. It is only by ensuring that funding reaches potentially profitable businesses – that is, funding reaches those who will be able to repay their loans, while funding is steered away from the unprofitable – that an economy grows.

Saving, and a sound financial system that allocates savings to the potentially most productive users of those savings, are amongst the most crucial determinants of whether an economy will itself succeed or instead remain impoverished and unable to genuinely prosper.

It should finally be noted that there are other forms of finance for business besides direct lending, but all of these are forms of saving in which funds are transferred to a business from those who do not wish to spend at the present time. These include the purchase of shares, corporate bonds and other financial instruments that are designed to finance the activities of firms.

Savers in each of these instances are again likely to take whatever steps are needed to ensure that their savings are protected and will even grow over time. There is often more risk, but there are also often greater rewards. But from an economic point of view, the issue is the transfer of purchasing power from those who wish to save in the present to those who wish to spend.

Personal Loans

The second class of borrowers do not intend to use the funds in a money-making operation but intend to finance their loans from other income-earning activities. The most common form of such loans is the housing loan where individuals borrow to buy a house but do not intend to use the house to generate the income that will repay the loan. Instead, the payment of the loan will come from other sources of income, usually from working in some business from which an income is earned.

Again, the financial system is required to ensure that those who receive the savings from others are able to repay the loans they have received. Whether it is to finance a house, a car or an overseas trip, the role of the financial institution is to ensure that the money is likely to be repaid.

Government Borrowing

There is then a third area of borrowed savings, and this is by governments. Some of what governments borrow is used productively, some is used unproductively but to fulfil some social purpose, and some is wasted. But irrespective of how the funds are used, where the government is in charge of the money creation process, the money will almost certainly be repaid to those who lent the funds.

That is why lending to governments is often preferred, but it is also why interest rates paid by governments are usually the lowest on the market. It is because governments can borrow so easily that problems are often created for business. The more funds a government secures, the more a government can spend. The more that a government spends, of course, the less there is for business, and the greater the cost of funds will be.

Governments are also more likely to waste the funds they receive, which means savings are used less productively than they might otherwise have been. In an ideal world, government spending would add enough to the productivity of an economy that tax revenues would rise naturally to allow the debts incurred to be repaid. But even if this does not occur – that is, the economy does not expand as much as would be required to generate the required revenues – tax rates can usually be raised, and as a last resort the government can print more money to repay its debts.

KNOWLEDGE, TECHNOLOGY, KNOW-HOW AND SKILLS

A factor of production is a needed requisite, an essential ingredient if value-adding production is to take place. Walk into any workplace and there you will find land, labour and capital. Looking further, there will be an entrepreneur responsible for the success of the entire operation. And since whatever it is that is being produced has not yet been sold to those who will buy them eventually, somewhere there has had to have been some kind of financing in place so that each of these factors can be paid in advance of the actual sale.

Labour Force Skills

But there is something else needed as well. There are the competencies, the abilities, the skills, the knowledge, the know-how embodied in each employee. There is no such thing as an unskilled employee. Every employee has an expertise in the kinds of work they do, and some of that has been developed through many years of study along with further years of on-the-job experience. New employees on a job are not as productive as they will eventually become; the 'learning curve' is an expression that reflects an actual reality.

The phrase 'human capital' is sometimes applied to this stock of skills possessed by the working population. No matter how advanced the capital stock of a nation is, there must be people who are able to make that technology perform and to make repairs when it breaks down. The fantastically large outlays on education and training that occur in every developed economy are undertaken because the returns are so high in having a skilled and educated workforce.

So it is not just labour as labour that matters, but labour as in a skilled workforce able to take on the productive tasks an economy is in need of having done. The skills, knowledge and practical know-how are a separate factor that could be included as part of labour, since that is where these abilities are embedded. But it is important also to separate these out so that they are recognized as independent as well as essential ingredients of an operating economy, while their improvement is seen as crucial to the improvement of economic well-being in general.

Technology and Innovation

And while skills are the necessary complement of labour, technology and innovation are the complements of capital. Capital is not just some single entity but is made up of the untold millions of individual items that are used in the production process. It is not just the quantum of capital that matters – assuming we could even devise some measure of the amount of capital in existence. What also matters is the ability of the available capital to be used in ways that ultimately satisfy the demands of the population for goods and services.

All other things being equal, the more capital, the stronger the economy. All other things being equal, the more suited to its productive tasks the capital is, the stronger the economy. Investment consists of three elements: increasing the amount of capital available for productive purposes, improving its efficiency, but thirdly, undertaking tasks that in many cases no one had ever imagined could be done.

Technology continues to evolve. There are newer and better ways of doing just about everything. The word 'telephone' has had a meaning going back to the 1870s but in each decade since, what actually constitutes a 'telephone' has vastly changed, as it continues to do right to this minute. The telephone of the 1870s and the telephone of today are only very distantly related and virtually every one of the changes that have occurred have been the result of some action taken by some entrepreneur.

Entrepreneurs run their own businesses but do what they do in their own way. It is not necessary to innovate to run a business, but virtually all innovations are the outcome of entrepreneurial activity undertaken within a business.

Importantly, the notion of innovation goes well beyond making existing products better. It, more importantly, includes the invention not just of whole new ways of doing things that have never been thought of before, but of whole new products or services that were inconceivable not long before. There is no reason that the future will not be just as astonishingly different as the present has been from the past. We have various industry categories: transport, communications, manufacturing, healthcare, for example. But the changes that have occurred in each industry over the past hundred years are a reflection of the astounding changes that have resulted from innovations that have been developed through entrepreneurial activities.

TIME

And moving perhaps one step further into the realm of abstraction, there are some who include time as an actual factor of production. If one bottles wine, the fermentation can require years. The timber industry requires trees to grow for many years before they can be harvested. Indeed, every process takes time.

It is, in fact, a great error to leave time out of economic considerations. No process is instantaneous. All require a period of time to elapse between initial conception and final execution. Coordination takes place in time. Sequences are important. Projects that take longer are, other things being equal, more expensive. Hastening the production process can lower costs and is a consideration when business decisions are made. Economizing with time can assist businesses and therefore an economy. The time taken to get things done is an aspect of the production process that should not be ignored.

FACTORS OF PRODUCTION

Each of the factors of production are necessary components in the growth of industry and the commercial world. They are the components that make up the totality of an enterprise, with the entrepreneur at the very pinnacle of the process.

It is the entrepreneur embedded within the private sector of the economy that coordinates the other factors in a profit-making productive enterprise. The private sector entrepreneur is the keystone of the entire edifice of productive activity. Without the entrepreneur, freely able to operate within an environment which is regulated by those who understand the crucial contributions the entrepreneur provides, an economy cannot be expected to prosper.

The entrepreneur provides direction, focus and innovation, orchestrating the other factors of production into an outcome that will, if all goes well, lead to value creation and a rising standard of living. There is, in fact, no other way that rising living standards can be achieved.

STOCKS AND FLOWS

In understanding how an economy works it is essential to keep one final distinction in mind, the difference between the amount of something already in existence and the most recent increments. This is the difference, in the language of an economist, between stocks and flows.

Thinking in terms of the factors of production, at any moment in time there is an amount of each of those factors available. When constructing the production possibility curve, beneath it is the notion that at some moment in time there are only so many factors available and that is all there is. Those factors can be used in different ways but they set a limit on how much can be produced at any one time. That quantum of existing factors is a *stock*.

The *flow* represents the amounts of newly produced output that is added to what already exists. A flow, as it is sometimes said, is the change in a stock. Again in terms of the production possibility curve, the growth rate is shown by the outwards movement of the curve. And while such curves are typically drawn as if growth is shown by a massive outward shift from period to period, over the course of a year the actual increase would not even be represented by so much as the thickness of the line if the diagram were to be drawn to scale.

If one looks around at an economy, the legacy from the past is the capital on which economic activity is built. The buildings, the roads, the communications networks and all of the other structures in place are the inheritance. This is a stock. What is added every year to what exists – what we describe as the flow – is a minuscule amount in comparison. Much of the flow in each year is merely to replace what has been used up in production during the previous period.

6.   Supply and demand

An economy is a perfect storm of activity buried inside the ongoing activities of a nation. It is not something separate but is entirely all of a piece with the whole life of a community. There is hardly a thing any of us do that does not involve some kind of economic activity, even if not by ourselves, then by someone else.

Even our recreational activities are part of the market. It is hard to think, even amongst our leisure activities, of what could be done without there being someone else whose job it is to make sure it happens. Not the movies, not a sporting event, not a trip to the beach, just about nothing at all can be done without there having been some kind of commercial transaction somewhere.

Our lives are surrounded by the products of the market, which means they are surrounded by the almost entirely invisible forces of supply and demand.

THE MARKET

But what is this entity called 'the market'? It is an abstraction that draws upon the village marketplace for its imagery, once an actual location where those with produce would find buyers for what they had to sell. Such purchase and sale was a personal one-to-one transaction as goods were exchanged for money and money was exchanged for goods.

The market price, then as now, is the number of units of money that need to be exchanged for the produce bought. The value of the money is thus understood in relation to what it can buy. Other than in periods of hyperinflation both buyers and sellers have a reasonably good idea of the price of goods in relation to the units of currency needed to make the purchase. When in another country, using a foreign currency, it invariably takes time to understand the exchange value of the currency being used, which is why everyone when in foreign countries automatically converts the local price into the currency they are familiar with.

The market price is the number of money units required to purchase a specified quantum of some good (or service). And while this is as obvious and familiar as the morning sun, almost no one ever thinks twice about the way in which each price is determined or how the products became available for purchase. Yet at something as basic as a farmers' market, there will be a range of fruits and vegetables up for sale – tomatoes, potatoes, cabbages and beans – each product having a price of its own. Yet for each of these, and for the millions of other items put on sale across the world, there is at any moment in time a *price* that is asked and a *quantity* available for sale. For each individual product – for each of those millions of products – there is an individual market in which the number of units sold and the price of the product has been determined in some way. And even though two products might sit next to each other on some shelf, their product histories in reaching that point are almost invariably completely different.

In thinking about how modern economies work, they must be seen as the summation of the millions of separate individual markets for each of the millions of separate individual products. Every entrepreneur almost certainly produces more than just one of these products, but whatever item is produced has a market of its own in which other producers usually compete to make the sale.

There is a market for clothes, and a market beneath that for shirts, and below that there is a market for work shirts and then underneath that there is a market for shirts to wear to an office. No centralized bureaucracy could possibly sort this out, which is why these things are left to the market, that is, to individual entrepreneurs who try to anticipate what buyers would like to buy and who would be willing to pay prices that would, in aggregate, cover all of the production costs incurred. Production decisions are then based on these entrepreneurial assessments. Which brings us to supply and demand.

PRODUCTION AND SALE

The most fundamental of all diagrams in economics relates the supply curve to the demand curve. The supply curve incorporates what sellers are expected to do in response to the economic environment in which they operate. The demand curve does the same for buyers. It outlines how those who buy are expected to behave, given the circumstances in which they find themselves. And the circumstances they typically find themselves in are to be surrounded by a vast multitude of products that have been put up for sale that they must choose amongst, always bearing in mind the amount of money they have to spend.

But understand this. No one has ever actually seen supply and demand curves outside of an economics text. No business has ever used supply and demand curves to decide what prices to charge. They are like the fundamental particles of physics. In physics, we posit the existence of various sub-atomic particles with certain properties to account for the structure and behaviour of the visible world. In economics, sense is made of the behaviour of people in buying and selling through conjecturing the existence of these two forces, forces which cause goods and services first to exist, and then to end up in the hands of particular individuals and not of others.

Start with supply. A supply curve is intended to show how sellers of a product will behave if prices are changed. A demand curve is designed to show how buyers of some product will behave when prices are changed. The central question being asked is how many units of whatever happens to be available for sale will be bought by buyers and sold by sellers at various possible prices.

And beneath it all is the ancient *ceteris paribus* proviso. All other things must be equal if the simple relationship between price and production is to hold good.

The theory underlying supply and demand is designed to explain how the particular price and the particular volume of sales are eventually arrived at through the competitive forces of the market.

The very existence of goods or services to buy is the result of a decision by someone or some group to produce and put such goods and services up for sale. The market is another name for human will as applied to the production process.

In a market economy, it is the individual members of the community who set businesses up and make their decision to sell. It is thus very important logically and in actual fact to recognize that the words 'supply' and 'demand' do not just represent two separate words, but are in the natural order in which events occur. There is first supply, and only then can there be demand for what has been supplied.

In almost every textbook presentation the ordering is to teach first about demand and then about supply. This reverses the logic of what really happens in causing goods and services ultimately to find their way into the world before being put on their way to the individual buyers.

THE MARKET

The market is neither a place nor a moment in time. It is entirely notional, abstract, a way of understanding the everyday routine of purchase and sale. A market is a conceptual frame of reference in which transactions are seen to take place in isolation from everything else that is going on. A transaction occurs when a good or a service is exchanged either for money paid immediately or, if not paid immediately, for a promise to pay at some time in the future.

To this transaction is brought either an existing good or service or a promise to provide some good or service at a predetermined moment in the future.

Producers, to be in a position to supply, must have created in the past a production chain that has led them to the particular moment in which the transaction has taken place.

Buyers similarly must have put themselves in a position to buy whatever they are buying, either by immediately paying the price or else by being in a position to convince the seller that they will be able to complete their side of the exchange when the payment they have agreed to make comes due.

It is in thinking about market activity that supply and demand become relevant. It is in this context that the process by which total strangers are able to exchange one set of goods for another through the use of money takes place.

Understanding the dynamics of supply and demand is crucial for understanding how an economy operates.

SUPPLY

Start with supply. In fact, the only place to start is with supply, since it is only with the decisions made to supply that anything can ever be bought. There is no demand without supply. And in starting with supply, we are starting with the entrepreneur.

For something to come to market, someone must make a production decision, and in most instances put a price on the goods and services that have been put up for sale. There is an actual human will that exists behind the actual actions taken. And it is in recognizing this that an understanding of the information available to the seller needs to be appreciated first.

What every seller is thinking about is how the needs of other people can be fulfilled. For final consumers, it is to provide utility. For other businesses, it is to supply a needed input. But one way or another, it is to put up for sale some good or service that can be sold to buyers, certainly at a profit, but more importantly because these are the items buyers want to have.

The structure of supply and demand curves, the centrepiece of this analysis, shows the price of the product on the vertical axis and the number of units that will be sold at different prices during some period of time on the horizontal axis.

Price

Quantity

Figure 6.1   The certain information available to a firm introducing a new product or service

In thinking about supply, the business has to think through, at its most primitive, how many units will be demanded at different possible prices. The relevant information available to the business in introducing a new product for sale is shown in Figure 6.1.

For a new product or service, what is shown is what is known with certainty. That is, nothing is known with certainty. The level of sales at each price is a guess, even if an educated guess based on intensive market research and review. The kinds of certainty a business would like to have simply cannot exist.

A business in setting up is taking a step into the unknown. The business failure rate for new start-ups is high, and the survival rate for firms making it past even the second year is depressingly low. Every business, of course, sells more than a single product.

With supply and demand, however, the market for single products taken one at a time is examined. For a firm putting that product up for sale, there is simply no reliable information that can let a business know ahead of time how well that product will sell. There is no scientific way for the firm to determine the price to put on the item. What finally takes place is often no more than a matter of judgement and experience.

Free market economics

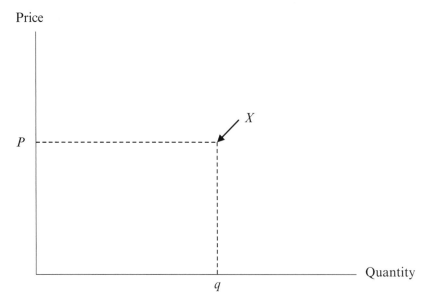

Price

P

X

q

Quantity

Figure 6.2   Information available to a single business about the price and volume of a good or service it is already selling

PRICE AND VOLUME OF AN INDIVIDUAL PRODUCT

But let us get to the next step and think about a product that has already been put on the market. In this case, something is known, and what is known is shown in Figure 6.2. The small '*q*' is used because this is a single firm. The volume of sales across the entire market is designated by the capital '*Q*' in the figures that follow.

What does a business know about any of the products it has put up for sale? It knows the price and generally has a pretty fair idea about its own volume of sales in each period of time. It therefore knows *P* and it generally knows *q*, but so far as this diagram is concerned, not necessarily all that much more.

And here it might be emphasized that the point in question may or may not be on the firm's supply curve since it may have been willing to supply more had there been the demand. The point may also be on the demand curve, since that is the number of units being bought at that price. It is, however, possible that more could have been sold at the price had more been put up for sale, so that the actual level of demand at that price may be greater than shown by the actual level of sales.

Of course, aside from the information shown on this graph, what this business almost always also knows is what competitors with the same sorts of goods or services are selling, and the prices at which they are being sold. There is for most goods in most places an active market where there are substitutes for everything any individual firm puts up for sale.

The marketplace is typically a crowded square. There are often many other sellers of identical, similar or closely related goods and services. Even distantly related goods and services can affect each other, such as the way that the demand for restaurant meals might be affected by the relative attractiveness of other forms of evening entertainment (as in, 'Shall we go out to dinner or to a film instead?').

EFFECT OF AN INCREASE IN PRICE

But knowing the level of sales at a particular price is a very limited piece of knowledge. Start with the question of what would have happened if the price had been higher or lower, even assuming that all of the other underlying *ceteris paribus* conditions remained the same (which they never are for very long).

What would have been the effect of raising the price? Any business thinking about a higher price immediately considers the effects on two groups: its customers and its competitors.

Raise the price, and every business will assume that the level of sales will fall. Higher prices reduce the number of units customers will buy, and that would be the case even if all of the competing firms raised their own prices at the same time by the same amount.

But then, suppose the other competing firms in the industry chose not to raise their prices. The effect on the level of sales would almost certainly be even greater. The loss of customers to other producers would be larger, often much larger, than if all firms raised their prices at one and the same time.

So there the business is at point X in Figure 6.2, and is thinking of the consequences of a price rise. What does not exist for this business is a nicely presented, already worked-out demand curve that sets out what would happen to the level of sales if the price happened to be higher. All that exists are different possible reactions from customers and competitors, all of which will affect the level of sales either hardly at all or to a very great extent, but which can only be guessed at. All this is conjecture. Nothing is known for sure.

This is the reality of business decision making at its most basic level. The product has already been developed. It is on the market and is selling

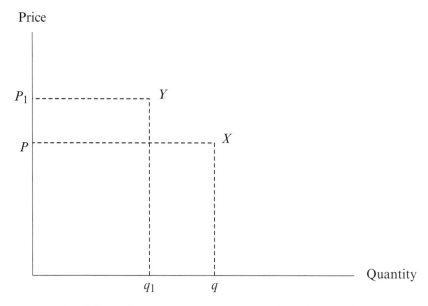

Figure 6.3   Effect of a price increase on the number of units sold

q units at price P in each period of time. The business has views about its customers, it has views about the products sold by its competitors. It also knows its level of sales and is very conscious of how rapidly this product is selling relative to the past. It knows its costs and presumably has a reasonable idea about the costs facing other firms in the industry. It knows what is happening to the prices of similar products elsewhere. There are many, many such facts which are known. What is not known is what will happen to the level of sales if the price is increased.

Suppose the price is raised from P to P_1. The effect on the number of units sold is a fall in sales from q to q_1 (Figure 6.3). Thus, in a sense *but not actually*, we have traced out part of the demand curve for this one particular business selling this one particular product which would be found in drawing a line from X to Y.

It is not necessarily a true demand curve since between two time periods it is not necessarily the case that the underlying *ceteris paribus* conditions had remained the same. A true demand curve shows all the prices and quantities during a particular period of time when every one of the *ceteris paribus* conditions are assumed to be constant. In this example, however, when changing the price we have moved to a different time period since two prices for the same product cannot be charged in the same place at the same moment in time.

All kinds of other things might have changed, including the prices charged by competitors. But nevertheless, in some simple way, the increase in price and subsequent fall-off in sales may have given this business some idea of the shape of its demand curve.

THE FIRM'S SUPPLY CURVE

Now it might be noted that for the firm no 'supply curve' independent of the demand curve has been traced out. At each price there is a maximum amount that would be put up for sale in each period of time which in some sense might be known to the firm.

This is a notional supply curve that exists in a somewhat more concrete way than the presumed demand curve. Individual firms do have some notion of how many units of a product would be supplied to the market at different prices.

There is a level of sales and the firm is scaled to meet that level of sales. With the capital and labour available, there is an absolute maximum that could be produced, but no one really thinks about it except during those rare occasions when sales come up against capacity constraints.

Nevertheless, there is a notional amount that is the maximum and this maximum would tend to increase as the price increased. The fact that with the higher price, fewer units would be sold, tells nothing about the productive potential of the firm. At the higher price, if more could be sold than the original number of units, q, more would be produced even if there were additional costs involved.

At price P in Figure 6.4, the most that might be produced is q but at the higher price P_2 the number of units of output that would be produced per unit of time would rise to q_2. In this way, by connecting X and Z a rudimentary supply curve for the firm can be traced out.

It slopes up and indicates that the higher the price, the more that this producer would be willing to produce. Or at least, that is what those who run this business believe, since all of the businesses in the industry have not tried to increase their production levels together at the same time. If they did, all may find shortages of labour and raw materials that they had thought would be available, which turns out not to be the case.

Nevertheless, there is a notional supply curve for each firm that is, at its most concrete, the tacit belief by each producer of what would be produced were the price to rise by different amounts. And there are even some firms which are not even producing this product which would enter the market if the price rose high enough.

The supply and demand curves for individual firms are in a sense the

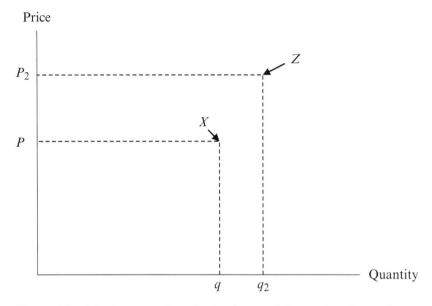

*Figure 6.4   Maximum number of units that would be produced at each
             price in each time period*

individual components of the supply and demand curves for the market
as a whole. If they were all added together, they would provide the totals
for all buyers and all sellers, actual and potential, assuming no unexpected
constraints suddenly show up because everyone was trying to produce
more.

And as much as the supply and demand curves for individual firms are
merely a conceptual notion with no possibility of calculation, the data for
the market as a whole are even more phantasmagorical. They have no
existence other than as a conceptual tool for understanding how markets
work. We will come to that in the section after next, on 'Market Supply'.

COMPETITION

The term we use for what happens in markets is 'competition'. As the
name suggests, competition presents what is taking place as a form of
contest which, as normally conceived, suggests that someone must win and
therefore someone else must lose.

So it is important to think very carefully about just who is engaged
in whatever this contest is, and who really are the winners at the end of

whatever competition is going on. How does one tell at the end of the contest who has actually won?

To the extent that it is a competition, the winner is the business that is able to provide buyers with whatever it is that those buyers prefer from amongst all of the alternatives presented. The contest is between sellers. The winner is determined according to which of those sellers buyers prefer to buy their goods and services from.

Thus, the judges in this competition are the buying public. The laurel wreath is given in the form of sales and profitability. And the result is a structure of production made up of just those businesses which have been able to satisfy buyers more completely than any of the other businesses who had offered their goods and services up for sale.

Of course, at any one time, there is usually more than one supplier of any particular product. But there are also usually many more who had tried to supply that product but had been forced to leave the market because they did not provide whatever it was that buyers were looking for.

This jostling amongst sellers to make the sale is the essence of the market system, and it is this that continues to ensure – so long as markets are free, open and contestable – that the products on offer continuously improve in quality while falling in price.

In understanding what takes place, it is the supply side where all of the true action happens. It is on the supply side that decisions on what to produce, how to produce, where to produce and what prices to charge are made. Demanders really do no more than choose amongst the different possibilities that have been put before them.

It is true that there is also competition amongst buyers for the supplies of the goods and services made available. But it is the producers who make all of the decisions of consequence, right up to the moment when buyers decide to purchase one set of products rather than another. Until that moment, everything that has taken place has been under the direction of a string of entrepreneurs, from the producer of the first of the inputs to the final decision to put some item or service up for sale in some retail establishment.

Until some good or service has been sold to its final purchaser, every step along the way has been the outcome of a series of decisions made by the owners and managers of various firms, from the producers of the most minimal inputs to the eventual retail shop where it is ultimately bought.

It is this that is embodied in the market supply curve. It is the summation of all of the previous decisions to transform various inputs into final output put up for sale.

Price

Quantity

Figure 6.5   Market supply and demand space before the decisions are made to supply some product

MARKET SUPPLY

And again, with the market supply curve the first place to start is with the blank market supply and demand open space (Figure 6.5). It is on this empty field that actual decisions will be imprinted by entrepreneurial decision.

Name the product: it is not available for sale until someone has decided to produce it.

Having decided to produce, with only some very odd exceptions, the price found in the market is the result of business decisions.

And finally, however many units there might be available for sale, those units are available only because entrepreneurs have made the decision to bring those to market, either from new production or from out of some inventory that has itself been the result of earlier decisions to produce.

In thinking about the market situation, beneath it are the various considerations made by each of the potential sellers. All have applied their judgement in one way or another in deciding how many units to put up for sale. And the kinds of supply-side considerations that are of most concern to such entrepreneurs in making such decisions include:

- the cost of inputs including the cost of labour;
- the capital stock available;
- the kinds of technologies available;
- the skills available within the workforce;
- expectations about the future;
- government taxes and regulations.

And then in thinking about who will buy, there are still many considerations that go through the mind of the seller:

- how many can be sold;
- what the competition will charge;
- what innovations might affect my sales.

Each of these is based on the expectations held within the firm. There are no concrete facts that it can depend on to tell it how many units it will be able to sell. Production decisions depend on the business judgement exercised within the firm.

Having factored in all of these matters, a decision will be made on how many units to produce and what price to charge. These factors are the *ceteris paribus* conditions. The price and quantity decision that is finally made is based on some assessment made of all of these. And when each of these changes, the prices charged and/or the number of units produced at each price might also be changed in response.

'SUPPLY' MEANS THE WHOLE CURVE

But the notion of supply in economics is more than just about the decisions that each of these entrepreneurs has made about what quantities to sell and at what price. It also goes further, much further, and asks how many units would be put up for sale if the price were higher or lower.

Supply is *all* of the different volumes that would be sold at *all* of the different prices that might realistically be charged where all of the underlying factors remain unchanged. Supply is not an amount. Supply is a relationship between price and quantity (Figure 6.6).

Supply to an economist is that whole line. It is a schedule showing how many units would be supplied to the market at each price.

A supply curve should be seen as an 'if–then' statement. It states that *if* the *expected* price is at some particular level shown on the horizontal axis, *then* the number of units that will be supplied to the market will be some number shown on the horizontal axis. If the price is P then the number of

Price

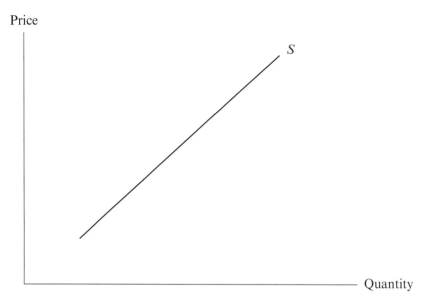

Figure 6.6   Supply

units that will be supplied to the market will be Q for all possible levels of P. Each point on the supply curve shows a particular relationship between the price and the number of units supplied.

SUPPLY AS A BARRIER

Crucial to understanding the notion of supply is that the curve, which is so clearly drawn in the text, is unknown to anyone actually participating in a market. The supply curve should be thought of more along the lines of an invisible force field that constrains and limits both what producers can do and what buyers can buy.

If we are thinking about some particular price, the supply curve shows that there is some maximum amount of that product that sellers will put up for sale at the price. Where exactly that is, no one can ever know. But what is known is that there is some upper limit on the amount that producers would produce at that price or at each possible price.

There are many market constraints, from limited amounts of capital and labour, other products that can be produced instead, through to bottlenecks in trying to raise production levels. The result is that at each price there is a maximum that will be put on the market.

Raising the price may help to relieve some of the pressures on suppliers but might not increase the amounts available in the short run. The supply curve in that short run might be completely vertical and unresponsive to the pressures of demand. But in the longer term, as producers are able to respond to the pressures of demand, more can be produced. And as will be discussed in the next chapter, the effect may lead to an increase in price but may also lead to prices falling.

The supply curve also provides a constraint of a different kind. It sets the lowest possible price for any particular amount supplied. If buyers in total would like Q units of some product, then given existing economic conditions, the lowest possible price that will bring that number of units to market is P.

Once again, no one knows what this price is. There are risks and uncertainties in every market, there is only a certain proportion of the productive agents of the economy that can be applied to the production of this particular product and lowering the price below P will only mean there is insufficient return to those who produce the good or service.

The market process is one of trial and error but also innovation. Since neither supply nor demand are known quantities, but a reflection of the constantly shifting forces of the market, businesses and their customers must constantly adapt to circumstances as they change.

But with innovation, the particular product may be improved or its production costs brought down, so that where supply is and, more uncertain still, where it will be in the future, are deep unknowns. The market is a region of discovery where the new is continuously replacing the existing. Thinking of supply in terms of supply curves is the traditional approach but must always be tempered with the recognition that in many important ways it provides a false picture of what is really going on.

SUPPLY VERSUS QUANTITY SUPPLIED

People often do talk about supply as if it is a specific amount and it is therefore important to make sure that when someone is talking about 'supply', one is aware of which meaning they have in mind.

Compare these two statements:

1. if the price goes up supply goes up (and who would deny this is so?)
2. if supply goes up the price goes down (and similarly, who would deny this?)

This becomes the following conclusion if the two statements are run together:

3. *if the price goes up* [supply goes up; if supply goes up] *the price goes down.*

That is, if the price goes up the price goes down. A higher price is the cause of a lower price. Obvious nonsense, but it comes from using the word 'supply' in its two different meanings.

In (1), this is using the word 'supply' to mean a movement along the supply curve when the price happens to rise. In (2), this is using the word 'supply' to mean a shift of the entire supply curve when one of the underlying factors has changed.

It is therefore essential to always make sure which meaning of supply is intended. You can usually tell from the context of what is being said, but the words here are slippery and can lead you into trouble.

And the same cautionary note is applicable to demand when we come to it. The words 'supply' and 'demand' have two separate meanings, one meaning the whole curve and the other a point on the curve. Knowing which one is being discussed is important. Not being aware of this distinction will lead to endless confusion.

The supply curve is in a particular position, *all other things being equal.* But these other things change, as they always do. And when they change, the supply curve changes along with them.

MOVEMENTS OF THE SUPPLY CURVE

When any of the underlying *ceteris paribus* conditions change – in fact, when anything changes that affect the willingness of businesses to put a good or service onto the market, *other than the price of the product itself* – the entire curve will shift.

If the change makes entrepreneurs willing to produce greater amounts at each price, we say supply has gone up, which is represented by the supply curve shifting to the right. In Figure 6.7, it moves from S to S_1. So if costs go down, technology improves or business taxes fall, then the response of businesses would be to increase the amounts they would be willing to provide to the market *at each price*.

If, on the other hand, whatever has changed has made businesses willing to provide only a reduced amount at each price, then we say that supply has fallen, and this is represented by a shift of the supply curve to the left, in this case from S to S_2. This might occur because of an increase

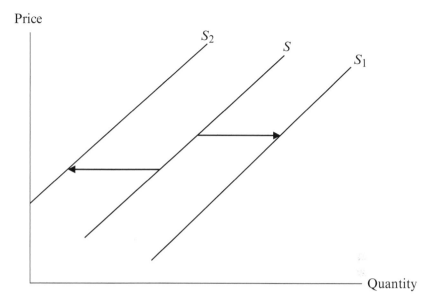

Figure 6.7   Changes in supply

in business costs, higher wages let us say, or expectations of a slowdown in the economy. Whatever makes businesses less willing to go to the expense of producing for the market will cause the supply curve to move to the left.

The movement of the supply curve is merely the application of common sense to economic events. And never forget that beneath the curve are entrepreneurs making business decisions about what they should do.

MARKET DEMAND

Then we come to demand. Demand represents the actions taken by the buyers of all of the products that entrepreneurs have put up for sale. And this is not just the final goods found in shops, but includes everything that is sold by one business to another. Iron ore is never bought by consumers, but there is a very large demand for iron ore all the same, by businesses that make steel, for instance.

Those who buy are almost invariably choosing amongst products that have already been produced and in any event are known to exist, and can be brought to market. For demanders, supply and demand is not an empty space. There are, instead, all kinds of goods and services that have already been made available and in virtually every case already have a price attached.

Demand curves, like supply curves, are a relationship between a range of realistic prices and the number of units that would be bought at each of those prices. Demand is not an amount. But again, beneath the position of the demand curve there are a host of *ceteris paribus* assumptions about all of the other factors that are assumed to remain constant while the price and quantities vary. These factors include:

- incomes;
- tastes;
- the prices of alternatives (substitutes);
- the prices of goods or services used in conjunction with the product (usually referred to as 'complementary' goods or services);
- government decisions, regulations and taxation;
- expectations about future prices or future availability.

Demand is influenced by anything and everything that makes a product either more or less desirable to buyers.

The demand curve is a relationship between the price and the number of units of a product that will be bought during any period of time, all other things being equal. A market demand curve invariably has the downward slope found in Figure 6.8.

Demand is *all* of the different volumes that would be bought at *all* of the different prices that might realistically be charged where all of the underlying factors remain unchanged. Demand is not an amount, it is a relationship between price and quantity.

Demand, like supply, to an economist is that whole line. It is a schedule showing how many units would be demanded at each price.

A demand curve should also be seen as an 'if–then' statement. It states that *if* the price is at some particular level shown on the horizontal axis, *then* the number of units that will be bought will be some number shown on the horizontal axis. If the price is some particular P then the number of units demanded will be some particular Q.

DEMAND AS A BARRIER

Like with supply, crucial to understanding the notion of demand is that the curve, which is so clearly drawn in the text, is unknown to anyone actually participating in a market. The demand curve should also be thought of as an invisible force field that both constrains and limits what buyers

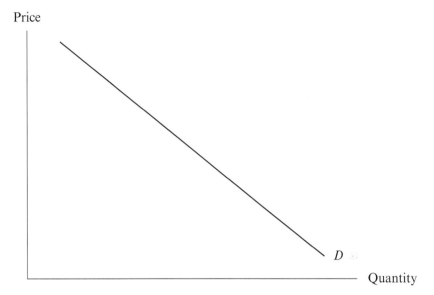

Price

D

Quantity

Figure 6.8   Demand

in aggregate will buy, but also puts a constraint on sellers in regard to the prices they can charge.

If we are thinking about some particular price, the demand curve shows that there is some maximum amount of that product that buyers would be willing to buy during some period of time. Where exactly that is, no one can ever know. But what is known is that there is some upper limit on the amount that buyers will buy at that price or at each possible price.

There are many market constraints, from the amount of income individuals have, the other products they might buy instead, to the actions of competitors who supply the same kind of product. The result is that at each price there is a maximum number of units that buyers will be willing and able to buy, but no one knows or can know how many units that is.

The demand curve also provides a constraint of a different kind. It sets the highest possible price any particular quantity of some product could be sold at. If sellers would like to sell Q units of some product, then given existing market conditions, the highest possible price that will enable that number of units to be sold is P. Once again, as with supply, no one knows what this price is.

The market process on the demand side is one in which individuals are in constant search of the array of products that their incomes, actual and expected, will allow them to buy that will lead to the highest level of utility being reached. Since neither supply nor demand are known quantities but a reflection of the invisible yet constantly shifting forces of the market, buyers are constantly adapting to the circumstances created by suppliers.

The market is a region of discovery where the new is continuously replacing the existing, so that buyers must keep an eye out for what would suit them best. Thinking of demand in terms of demand curves is the traditional approach but must always be tempered with the recognition that in many important ways it provides a false picture of what is really going on.

DEMAND VERSUS QUANTITY DEMANDED

Demand, like supply, is often discussed as if it is a specific amount rather than a relationship. And as with supply, it is important to be able to make the distinction between statements such as:

1. 'the price went up so demand went down'.

and statements such as:

2. 'demand went down so the price went down'.

Here, too, you can run the two statements together and end up with a complete contradiction:

3. 'the price went up [so demand went down' – 'demand went down] so the price went down.'

That is, the price went up so the price went down. The reason the price went down was supposedly because the price had first gone up. Once again, the problem is that the word 'demand' has been used in two different ways. In this example, (1) means a movement along the demand curve induced by a rise in price. In (2) it is a movement of the entire demand curve which has led to a fall in price.

With the first meaning, it is often recommended that the movement along the curve should be called a movement in 'quantity demanded'. Yet even economists will regularly speak of demand and mean either shifts of or movements along the curve. It is necessary to be able to recognize which meaning is intended, because you cannot count on anyone else maintaining the distinction consistently.

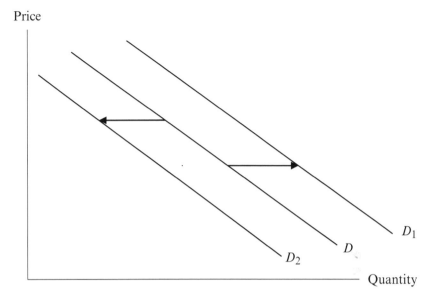

Price

Quantity

Figure 6.9   Changes in demand

MOVEMENT OF THE DEMAND CURVE

A shift in demand, as in a shift of the entire curve, will occur when any one of the underlying factors change. Then things have not remained equal. The underlying demand conditions have changed and this is represented by a movement of the entire curve (Figure 6.9).

The movement of the curve from D to D_1 represents an increase in demand. At each price, the number of units of the product that will be bought has increased. Some change, such as an increase in incomes or a rise in the price of other similar goods, means that more of this product is desired. The entire curve therefore shifts to the right.

A fall in demand is represented by the shift of the curve from D to D_2. With this reduction in demand, there is a fall-off in the number of units that will be bought at each price. Some underlying factor, such as the product going out of fashion or no longer being needed as an input into some other production process, has reduced the number of units that others want to buy at each price.

When any of the underlying *ceteris paribus* conditions change, in fact when anything changes that affects the willingness of buyers to buy a good or service, *other than the price of the product itself*, the entire curve will shift.

And just as it was with supply, the movement of the demand curve is merely the application of common sense to economic events.

THE SANDWICH SHOP

Figure 6.10 shows the situation facing the entrepreneur of a sandwich shop at the start of the day. The entrepreneur may have been in business for 20 years, at the same location for the whole time, have made good profits every year, and yet even then there is no certainty how many sandwiches will be sold on any given day.

The $6 price chosen is based on past experience and the prices charged by competitors. But at 6 am the question remains as to how many sandwiches should be made, since once the shop is opened it is too busy to make more. If not enough are made, sales are lost. If too many are made, then there is waste and loss.

By 6 pm, at the end of the day, the entrepreneur will know how many were sold. But before the shop has opened, it can only be an estimate. The demand curve that we might draw in class, and describe as the constraint on the shop owner, is in reality invisible and never known. Everything done is projected forward.

The sandwich shop is a representative example of every firm in every

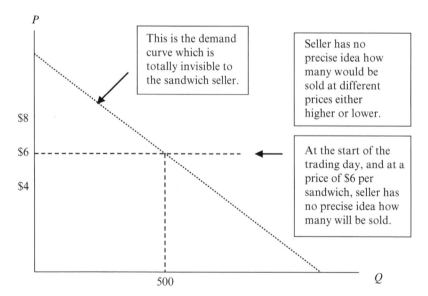

Figure 6.10   Sandwich shop

market at all times. No one in any business ever knows how many units at each particular price can and will be sold of any product they produce. No demand curve can be drawn that can fill in these unknown details. The information needed is literally unavailable and could never be made available. We discuss supply and demand as if they are concrete entities but they are the very reverse. They are abstractions providing a false picture of what is in fact the actual situation, the deep uncertainty every business must have in making decisions on what to produce, with that decision often wrong, and sometimes so badly wrong that the business must actually fail.

The reality of business decision making must therefore never be allowed to fall away in trying to understand the operation of the market. The successful are working out ahead of time what others would like to buy, and then supplying the market with the goods and services that are eventually bought. The unsuccessful do exactly the same, supplying the market with what they believe buyers will buy, but this time with goods and services that do not match buyer demands.

Over time, it is only the successful that remain and they will only remain if they continue to be successful. That success depends on their being able to anticipate what others would like to buy. This is the reality of the market upon which our communal prosperity depends.

EQUILIBRIUM

The supply and demand curves together provide the equilibrium position which allows for the *simultaneous* determination of the number of units of the product that will be sold in each time period and the price at which those units will be sold.

Bringing the supply and demand curve together on the same diagram show the mutual determination of the two outcomes at one and the same time (Figure 6.11).

The point where the supply curve S and the demand curve D cross is the equilibrium position. It is at this price that the number of units that buyers are willing to buy and sellers are willing to sell are the same. At no other price is this the case.

If nothing else changed, the market for this single product would come to a rest. Nothing else would happen, other than that for time period after time period the same amount Q would be produced and all of it would be sold at the equilibrium price P. This is precisely what would never happen in the real world, but it is an important place to start if one is to make sense of economic events.

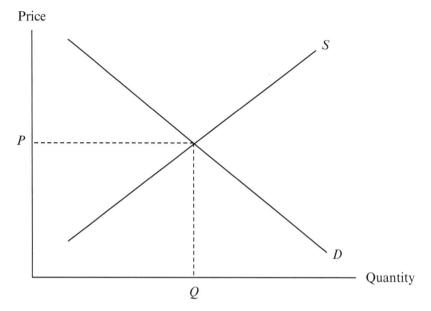

Figure 6.11   Market equilibrium

7. Supply and demand: beyond equilibrium

The entire notion of equilibrium is something like a diversion to take your eye away from what is really important in markets, and that is change and how people deal with such change.

Figure 7.1 shows the equilibrium position for a single product out of the millions being put up for sale. At price P there will be Q units of the product bought and sold in each time period. And this would go on literally forever unless something changed. But since something can always be counted on to change, it does not go on forever.

Importantly, change can only come from a change in one or more of the underlying factors that cause a shift in the position of one of the curves.

Start with something simple: an increase in the incomes received by buyers of this good. If it is a *normal* good, higher incomes will lead buyers

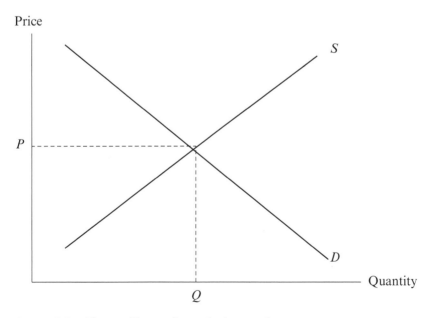

Figure 7.1   The equilibrium from which everything starts

to buy more. (If it is what is known as an *inferior* good, an increase in income will actually lead to a fall in the demand for the product as buyers switch to the more expensive, higher-quality products.)

Here the assumption is that higher incomes have led to an increase in demand. The question is, how would anyone in business know, firstly, that there has been an increase in the incomes of the industry's customers and then, secondly, that this increase in income has been followed by a desire to buy more of the industry's output? The one action that no one in business can take is to look at what is happening to the demand curve, either for the business or for the industry. There is no demand curve. There is no one to alert a firm. There are only the clues to a changed situation that the market provides.

In Figure 7.2, the supply and demand curves were drawn to meet at an equilibrium point *E*. The only actual point on either curve that was known to anyone was where price *P* and quantity *Q* met. Even then, the only part that anyone may really have known, so far as the industry was concerned, was the price. The total volume of sales across the industry may not have been known to anyone and will probably never be known.

If we are talking about the market for black umbrellas, let us say, there

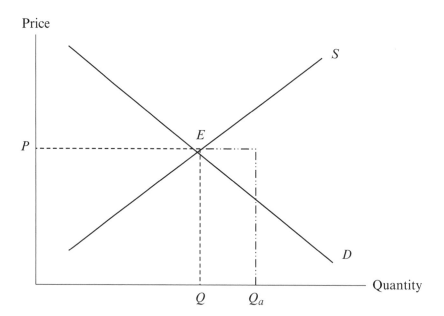

Figure 7.2   An increase in quantity demanded

would never be a mechanism for knowing the total level of sales, and as far as the market is concerned, no one would ever likely care. But the picture in Figure 7.2 could occur for any good or service you might care to name.

HOW A BUSINESS KNOWS THERE HAS BEEN AN INCREASE IN DEMAND

There is that original equilibrium point E. And something has happened so that rather than selling Q units of output, the same amount that had been produced, the market is now trying to buy Q_a units at the existing price. In that first instance, only the volume of sales has changed and it is setting up quite a disturbance within the industry.

Businesses selling this product are finding they are selling more units than their past experience would have led them to expect. This may or may not have created a commercial opportunity. There may or may not be an obvious reason for this change. There may or may not be an obvious response to the different level of sales.

What has happened, though, is this. More are being sold at the existing price than on previous occasions and either their stock levels are running out (for a good) or the sales staff is far busier than in the past (for a service). The questions then are, first, to decide whether the change is permanent or just a statistical fluke, and then, if it does seem to be permanent, what action to take.

Because on top of all of the other considerations that go into making a decision, there is the front-row question of what the other firms in the industry are going to do.

But the one certain fact is that more is being bought than is being produced. There is therefore pressure on businesses all around the industry to increase production levels and possibly raise the price. And if this shortage persists, then the response may well be to increase production levels and push prices up.

This will be the attitude of many in the industry and eventually, given the unknown supply and demand situation, through a process of trial and error the price will lift, and the quantity demanded will cut back to some extent but not to the full extent of the previous increase in sales. Eventually a new equilibrium is established at a higher price and a higher volume in which the level of sales is matched by the level of demand. That is what is shown in Figure 7.3, except that the unknown demand and supply curves are drawn in. D has moved to D_2.

Note very carefully that the supply curve has not moved. There is, of

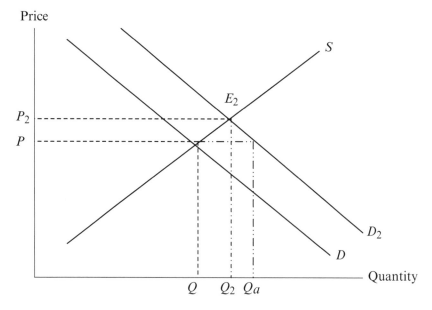

Figure 7.3   Market adjustment with supply and demand

course, a supply response but it is shown by the movement along the curve, not by a shift of the curve. More is being supplied, but only because the price that can be charged is higher.

The supply curve, being an absolute barrier, shows the maximum that will be provided at each price. If more units are sought than in the past, the price must be higher than in the past unless supply conditions have changed.

Ultimately, the price goes from P to P_2 while the level of sales increases from Q to Q_2. But it has been a process of market adjustment that required a series of entrepreneurial decisions at every stage along the way. An increase in the volume of sales did not just happen. Someone had to decide to produce more and raise the price.

EFFECT ON BUYERS

As we do economic analysis, we state that demand has shifted. This is a short-form statement about there being new facts on the ground that those who run businesses must take into account. To leave out the need for business decisions to be made by actual human beings, who raise the level of production, and who put up the price, leaves out the actual dynamic processes involved.

It also leaves out the decisions that face the buyers of the product. For them, there was a product they bought whose price has suddenly increased. In most circumstances, each customer had bought only a tiny fraction of the total volume of sales. And for no particular reason that they can see, the price has risen and they have to make a decision on what to do.

Relative to the original equilibrium, they are in aggregate buying more. Relative to the intermediate position, when demand had risen but price had not, now that the price has gone up from P to P_2, fewer units are being demanded, with the number of units bought falling back from Q_a to Q_2. But here too there are real live people making decisions on how many units to buy, with all of these decisions being finally registered as the total number of units demanded that is also, when everything has worked itself through, the same as the total number of units supplied.

But as for the curves themselves, they will never be seen. It is only a diagrammatic way to explain the changes in behaviour that are taking place across the entire market for this product which have led to an increase in price and an increase in the level of production and sale.

CHANGE IN SUPPLY

Suppose instead we think about some change that affects the willingness to supply at each and every price. The initial market equilibrium is shown in Figure 7.4, but again no one knows where these curves are.

So far as these diagrams are concerned, a business knows only its own price and sales volume. It would also know what price it would need to receive to be willing to put various amounts onto the market, but as far as the market itself is concerned, it would often know very little.

Originally the willingness to supply is shown by the firm's supply curve S. This represents the costs of selling around the existing level of production. This is the kind of information that a firm might have readily available. Higher prices would lead to more production and lower prices to less.

But basically, unless an expansion was in the works, the effect on the level of production of a large change in the price, either up or down, would not be part of the calculation.

But into this setting, suppose there is an increase in costs. This moves the notional supply curve for the individual firm in Figure 7.5 from S_1 up to S_2. At the level of production, the price would have to rise to P_2 to cover the entire increase in costs for that level of production. And that is what you would expect to happen if there were no effect on the level of demand.

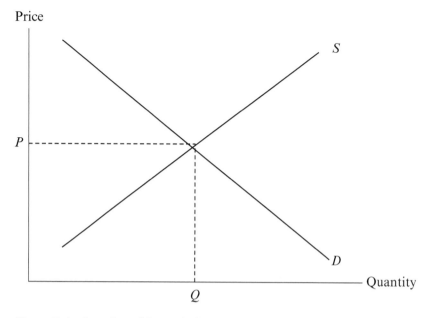

Figure 7.4   Initial equilibrium before an increase in supply has occurred

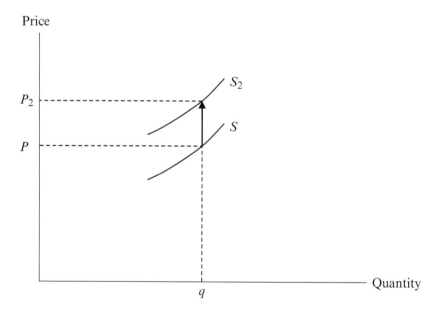

Figure 7.5   What a firm might know

The higher price, however, leads to a lower level of sales. Behind the scenes is the unknown and invisible demand curve which, if the information could be known, would instantly tell sellers what the new price ought to be if only such a demand curve existed. In reality, there is a process of adjustment that businesses must go through in finding their way to the new equilibrium.

The oft-stated lament from businesses, that they could not pass on their entire increase in costs, is a tacit recognition that they are facing a downward sloping demand curve. They do not know its shape although they have some sense of it from past experience. But what they do know is that in raising the prices they charge, the consequence is a loss of sales. An entrepreneur does not need to have seen a demand curve to have had this experience in business.

INDUSTRY SUPPLY

Translate these shifts across to the industry supply and demand curves. For convenience, we keep the same supply curve shape that was drawn for the individual firm. Nothing about the underlying analysis has to change.

Both the shape and position of the demand and supply curves are unknown and unknowable. Costs have gone up but have almost certainly affected each firm in a different way. But as shown in Figure 7.6, the

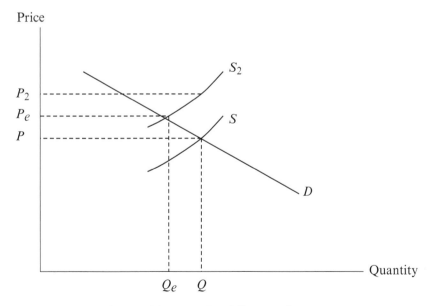

Figure 7.6   Market equilibrium with a fall in supply

higher price has a powerful effect on the level of sales across the industry. Prices do not rise to the full extent of the increase in costs. Perhaps with lower volumes, input costs are lower or overtime is no longer needed, perhaps even allowing costs to fall. Some high-cost producers may drop out of the market.

HORIZONTAL AND DOWNWARD-SLOPING SUPPLY

But it is just as possible that the supply curve may be horizontal over the relevant range, or, with economies of scale, perhaps even downward sloping. Both of these are genuine market possibilities.

With a horizontal supply curve over the relevant range, changes in demand lead to changes in production levels but not to changes in prices (Figure 7.7). Businesses may even be absorbing higher costs. The supply curve merely traces the response of suppliers to higher or lower levels of demand.

Market demand curves are invariably downward-sloping which is why the relevant principle is called the *law* of demand. Supply curves can go in any direction, particular over what might be described as 'the relevant

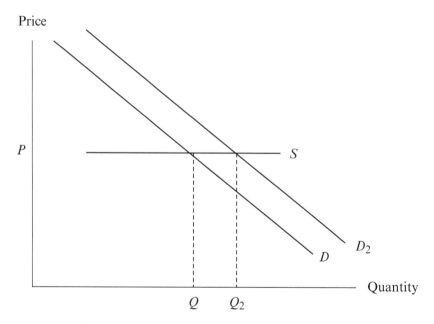

Figure 7.7   Effect on price and volume with horizontal demand

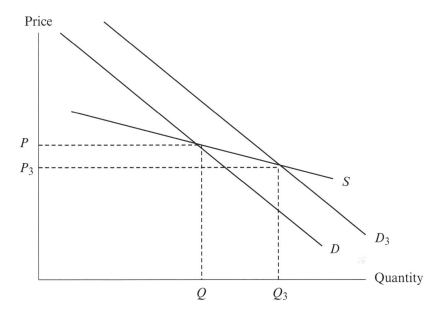

Figure 7.8 Economies of scale and increased demand

range', which is the output level in proximity to the current level of production.

Horizontal supply curves show that over a broad range of output, given the existing workforce, technical know-how, input costs and any of the other *ceteris paribus* supply conditions, it is quite possible to maintain the same price irrespective of the particular level of output.

There is also no particular reason that the supply curve might not be downward-sloping in some industries, particularly when the longer run is taken into account (Figure 7.8). In industries where there are large economies of scale that can be captured, so that as output goes up average production costs go down, it is possible that higher volumes will bring prices down.

In this case, an increase in demand will lead to a lower price for the product. From cars to cameras to calculators to computers, an increased volume of sales has brought prices down by spreading overheads over a larger number of units sold.

Moreover, the shape of these curves is to some extent determined by the time period we are looking at. In the short term, extending no farther than the immediate future, the supply curve would in most cases be almost vertical since for most products there is only so much and no more.

As the time frame is extended, the supply curve may begin to bend forward until in the longest of runs, the supply curve may actually be downward-sloping as the most efficient approaches to production are introduced.

In trying to think past these very abstract supply and demand curves, it is imperative to remember that at every stage there are individuals reacting to the economic circumstances they must themselves personally face. These curves provide a short-form means to summarize everything that is happening in a generally simple way across a large number of individuals.

But beneath it all, it should not be forgotten that there are individuals on both the supply and demand sides who are making decisions to produce and buy.

The answers these diagrams provide ought to be powerful reminders of the ways in which markets operate. Where both entrepreneurs and their customers are permitted to act in ways that provide themselves with the greatest good – the highest utility for consumers, the highest profits for producers – this will lead to a continuous improvements in living standards and increased satisfaction with life, to the extent that satisfactions come from an increased command over goods and services.

INNOVATION

But the role of innovation must be introduced into the notions of supply and demand. Innovation is typically thought of as some technological improvement that lowers the cost of production for some particular good or service. The result is a shift to the right of the supply, which means that at each price more can be produced. Or it may be thought of as showing that for each level of output, the minimum price has become lower than it was.

This is, of course, a correct understanding, but in the greater scheme of understanding how an economy works it is almost trivial. Yes, of course, there are innovations that bring down unit costs, increase supply and lower price. But these are not the innovations that usually matter.

Innovation in an economy is the introduction of either an entirely new product that had never existed before, or a major improvement in one that has already existed. Think of the telephone, car and aeroplane and their development from the end of the nineteenth century, right up to the present. Drawing supply and demand curves for each of these at ten-year intervals is to consider products that are so different compared with what had existed before that almost no genuine comparison is possible.

The innovations in each industry have been so immense that to describe a change in market conditions as a movement of either the supply curve or the demand curve immediately shows how inadequate such a representation would be.

Market conditions are overwhelmed by new products, new ideas and new production technologies. The flat two-dimensional supply and demand apparatus provides only a dim appreciation of what actually takes place in entrepreneurially driven markets.

Such markets are totally reformed, if not year by year, then certainly decade by decade. Products are introduced with a fantastic regularity, and not just products that are better versions of what had been previously done by other, older technologies. These are products that do things that were inconceivable not all that long before.

The actual reality behind supply and demand is made up of entrepreneurially driven change in virtually every product, with consumers adjusting to the ever-expanding array of goods and services being offered by business. What is more, these goods and services are forever changing in price, based on the pressure of demand and the unit costs of production. It is innovation that leads to change, not just efficiency improvements that allow the same products to be sold at a lower price.

SUPPLY AND DEMAND IS TOO NARROW IF ONE IS TO SEE EVERYTHING TOGETHER

And while it is demand that largely determines the price in the short run, since in the short run the number of units available for sale is more or less fixed, over the longer term almost the only thing that matters, for goods that can be produced at will, is their cost of production.

Reducing market activity to supply and demand curves leaves out the important parts in far too many ways. It leaves out the innovation that makes the market for many of the products bought in one year a matter of history a year or two later.

It leaves out the crucial importance of factor markets which determine the lowest possible price any particular volume can be sold at, and this includes the factor markets for those factors themselves.

It leaves out that most of the innovations in an economy are not about the products that are bought but are related to the technology and inputs used in production (such as the way plastic has replaced steel).

It leaves out that the entire economy is one large recursive mechanism where outputs from one industry are inputs not just into other industries, but often into that industry itself (think about electricity as one obvious example, where electricity is used in the production of electricity).

It pushes into the background the role of relative prices, since supply and demand are about only a single product. Changes in the relative prices of each and every good or service affect the willingness and ability of the economy to produce each of the products put on the market.

It leaves out the structure of production. That is, it leaves out the entire network of millions of goods and services that are inputs into the millions of goods and services being produced. Changes in the supply or demand conditions for any one of these inputs will change the supply and demand conditions for other products, as prices and the availability of different inputs affect the markets across a broad array of industries.

As long as these considerations are kept in mind in looking at supply and demand, no harm is done. But it should never be forgotten that supply and demand is only one part of a more complete story that needs to be understood. Each pair of supply and demand curves relates only to a single product amongst the millions produced. That is the way in which markets are normally explained, but it is not anything like the whole story nor is it everything you need to know. You must go beyond the purchase and sale of individual products if you are to see how an economy unfolds in real time.

USING SUPPLY AND DEMAND

The key to the use of supply and demand is to recognize that they are a relationship between price and quantity, *all other things being equal.* Moreover, so far as economic theory is concerned, *a market price does not change unless there is a change in the conditions affecting either demand or supply or both together.* If market price or market volume have changed, one or the other of those two underlying forces must have changed first.

That is, either the supply curve has moved, or the demand curve has moved, or both have moved.

Unless there has been some government decree, within economics there is no other valid explanation for a change in prices charged or in the volume of output produced in any market other than a shift in supply or demand or in both at the same time.

Therefore, if there has been a change in a market price or in the level of sales, an explanation must be given in terms of a movement in one or the other of the supply curve or demand curve. If a price has gone up, then either the demand curve has shifted to the right (that is, demand has increased) or the supply curve has shifted to the left (that is, supply has gone down).

Similarly, if a price has gone down, either the demand curve has shifted to the left (that is, demand has fallen) or the supply curve has shifted to the right (that is, supply has gone up). When prices change, this is where one needs to look.

And in regard to volumes, if the level of sales has gone up, either the supply curve or the demand curve have shifted to the right (that is, supply or demand have increased); while if sales levels have gone down, either the supply curve or the demand curve has shifted to the left (that is, supply or demand have fallen).

It is perfectly pointless to have gone to the trouble of learning about supply and demand without understanding that it is precisely when P or Q have altered that supply and demand curves are needed if one is to understand why.

THINKING THROUGH PRICE MOVEMENTS

The price of electricity has gone up, let us say. Why might this be? That is where the *ceteris paribus* issues come in to play. On the supply side, we might think that any of the following could have been important:

- the cost of inputs including the cost of labour might have increased in price;
- the capital stock available has diminished because there has not been sufficient maintenance of electricity generating capacity;
- there are expectations that demand is going to increase and more capital will be needed;
- taxes on the industry have gone up.

If, instead, one thinks about the various factors that might have affected the willingness to purchase electricity, then going through the list of demand-side *ceteris paribus* conditions we might think that one or more of these were part of the explanation for the higher price of electricity:

- incomes have risen and more energy is demanded;
- the population has gone up;
- there has been an increase in the use of products that use electricity;
- the prices of other sources of energy have risen.

These are just examples. For most price movements there are usually readily understood reasons for prices to have moved. But whatever they are, they should be thought of in relation to shifts in supply and demand.

PRICES AND INFLATION

During an inflationary period, it is almost always the case that wages and other labour costs are rising much faster than technological change can produce productivity increases. The supply curves of many products are therefore moving to the left. At the same time, because incomes in nominal terms are rapidly rising, which is the same thing as higher labour costs but from a wage earner's perspective, the demand curves for many products are moving to the right.

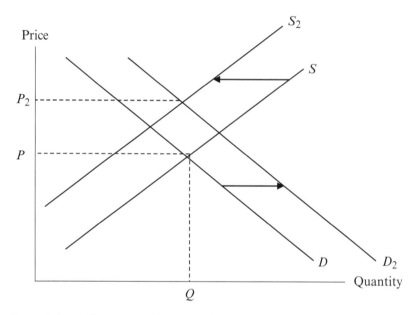

Figure 7.9   Inflationary effects on individual prices

As Figure 7.9 shows, the effect on the level of prices is certain to be positive, but the effect on the level of sales could be anywhere, either rising or falling depending on whether the supply curve or the demand curve shifts to a greater extent.

It is also useful to be aware that in an inflationary period, the prices of different products are rising at different rates. Some prices may even be falling. Thus, while inflation may mean that the 'average' price level has risen, individual prices for individual products will experience different rates of change depending on the effect on the underlying shifts in the supply and demand curves for the products.

USING COMMON SENSE

It is usually a matter of common sense to understand the effect that some underlying factor will have on the willingness of producers to supply, or the willingness of buyers to buy. The formal use of supply and demand clouds some people's minds so that what they once understood intuitively, they lose their grip on by seeing it in this way.

Just understand this:

- if producers have become more willing to produce, then the supply curve will move to the right – they will supply more at every price;
- if, on the other hand, producers have become less willing to produce, then the supply curve will move to the left – they will supply less at every price;
- then, amongst buyers of a product, if demanders have become more willing to buy, then the demand curve will move to the right – they will buy more at every price;
- and finally, if demanders have become less willing to buy, then the demand curve will move to the left – they will buy less at every price.

Understanding this will take you a long way towards thinking like an economist. Not understanding this means you never will.

PRICE CEILINGS

Governments frequently attempt to influence the prices of various goods and services by imposing prices on the market. It happens less than it once did, partly because the level of economic knowledge has improved somewhat. But the attempts by governments to gain popular approval by in some instances holding prices down, and in other instances holding prices up, is often irresistible. It is always, however, a bad decision economically, no matter how it might be received politically.

A price ceiling is a maximum price imposed by governments below the equilibrium point. The prices of particular goods or services are seen by decision makers as a political problem, and rather than subsidizing the sale of such goods or services (which would move the supply curve to the right at every price) they merely either impose a maximum price on the market or restrict the rate at which such prices may legally increase in the future.

A very popular use of the price ceiling was once to control rents, which is still done in some places. Rapidly rising rents are very unpopular and

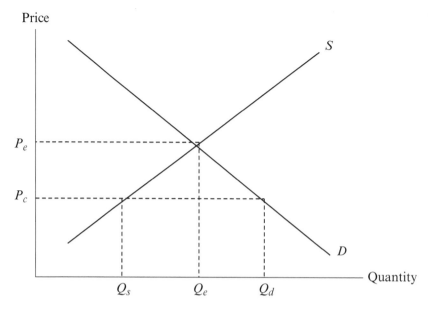

Figure 7.10   Price ceiling

governments have on occasion tried to do something about the increased price of rental accommodation by imposing rent controls. The inevitable result is harm to many of those the decision was intended to help.

This is shown in Figure 7.10. And as in the use of all other diagrams, here too the aim is to explain the principle, not some exact situation.

If the market were allowed to find its own equilibrium, the rental price would be P_e. However, the government, for reasons of its own, decides that the market level of rent is too high, so it imposes a maximum rental. Here the ceiling is shown to be at price P_c.

Is this good for renters? And if so, which renters?

According to the diagram, three things are sure to happen: (1) after the price ceiling is imposed, rents are lower than they otherwise would have been; (2) with lower rents, more people try to rent, with the level of demand for rental accommodation moving up from Q_e to Q_d; (3) with lower rents, meanwhile, fewer landlords are willing to take on the expense and hassle of renting, and the quantity of rental accommodation supplied falls from Q_e to Q_s.

In these circumstances, the rents may be lower to those who can actually find a place to rent, but there are not enough places to rent relative to the number of people trying to find a place to live. Even some of these who had been renting before no longer have a place, since the number of rented places falls as dwellings that had previously been rented out are removed from the rental market. What is worse, there are even more people looking to rent than before rents were lowered. Accommodation looks more affordable, if only they could find someone to rent them a place.

The original equilibrium price did two things. It encouraged producers to build and maintain rental accommodation, and it encouraged those with places to rent out to put them on the market. It pulled up the quantity supplied.

But at the same time it made renters economize. They would rent smaller units or share with others to help pay the rent. They might stay at home with their parents. Since there is only so much rental space in any urban setting, leaving it to the market allows rents to adjust until the number looking for a place to rent and the number of places being rented out are the same. And if there is a shortage and rents are moving up, it also encourages the construction of new places in which to live. If the aim is to have more places for more people, rent control is the exact wrong way to go about getting it.

The basic moral is this. Keeping the price of anything below its equilibrium price will create shortages. More units will be demanded than supplied. The evidence from history is overwhelming. Although supply and demand curves are totally invisible, the world operates in just the way we would expect if these curves could actually be seen.

PRICE FLOORS

The opposite of a price ceiling is a price floor. A floor price is the lowest price allowed by law, or the price at which the government will buy everything not bought by the market.

Figure 7.11 shows a price floor. Examples are the minimum wage, where it is illegal to pay a wage lower than that stated in law, or agricultural price supports, where the government promises to buy up any production not sold on the market at the government-established price.

The equilibrium is P_e but the floor price imposed is at P_f. Let us say that this is the market for butter and the government wishes to assist farmers. They therefore promise to maintain the price of butter by paying the higher price, P_f.

The result is an excess supply of butter, what became known as the 'butter mountain' in Europe where this was tried. Farmers, responding to the price, produce a quantity of butter equal to Q_s. Buyers, however, do not buy all the butter produced at a floor price above the equilibrium price, buying only Q_d.

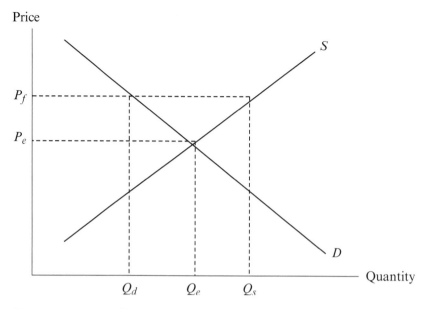

Figure 7.11   Price floor

Here again there are three certain results: (1) after the price floor is imposed, prices are higher; (2) with higher prices, there is less of the good or service bought in the market than had been bought before; (3) with higher prices, however, more is produced even though less is being bought in the market.

Price support programmes in agriculture have ended up exactly as the theory of supply and demand have said they would. There have been literally mountains of unsaleable butter produced. The same has happened in grains and milk. Pushing the price above equilibrium causes more of the product to be produced than the market is prepared to buy at that price.

This is how markets can be expected to work. In a well-ordered economy, with prices allowed to adjust as circumstances dictate, output adjusts itself to the willingness to produce on the one side, and to the willingness of buyers to buy on the other.

This is because behind these adjustments are the individual buyers who are shifting between the various goods and services being put on the market on one side of the ledger, and the different amounts of every good and service being put up for sale.

Implementing a minimum wage is less messy since those workers priced out of the market are indistinguishable from the rest of the unemployed who are without work, although for other reasons. But for all that, some people are not working because the wage rate has been kept too high.

ELASTICITY

Amongst economists, there are actual specific terms that are used to describe the tilt of supply and demand curves. Rather than describing these curves as 'horizontal' or 'vertical', the words used are 'elastic' and 'inelastic'.

The economic point about elasticity is to gauge the *responsiveness* of changes in one economic variable to changes in another.

Demand, for example, is said to be elastic if there is a large change in the quantity demanded following a relatively small change in price.

A typical economics text will spend quite some considerable time on explaining how such elasticities are measured, which of course can only be done if there is an actual supply or demand curve which can be drawn.

You cannot calculate the tilt of a line without being able to see the line. Since the line can never be seen, such calculations are almost entirely beside the point. Other books will teach you how to calculate elasticity. You will not find that here.

DEMAND ELASTICITY AND TOTAL REVENUE

But elasticity is a useful concept since it is a reminder that different businesses and industries face a different demand response to changes in prices. And elasticity has an important conceptual point related to changes in the total revenue earned as the price is changed.

The definition of elasticity of demand shows the significance:

$$\varepsilon = \frac{Percentage\ change\ in\ quantity\ demanded}{Percentage\ change\ in\ price}$$

Suppose that a price went up 10 per cent, which led to a 20 per cent fall in the number of units bought. That is, at whatever was the price, the response to a 10 per cent increase in the price was a 20 per cent fall in the volume of sales.

In terms of the elasticity calculation, the percentage change in quantity, being 20 per cent, is divided by the percentage change in price, which was 10 per cent, which comes to 2.[1]

So what? So this.

Suppose the price had originally been $20 per unit and the number of units sold was 1000. Total revenue is therefore $20 per unit × 1000 units = $20 000.

But then the price went up by 10 per cent which meant the price rose to $22. However, the number of units sold fell by 20 per cent, that is by 20 per cent of 1000 which is 200. Thus, there were 800 units sold at the higher price. The total revenue is now $22 per unit × 800 units = $17 600.

The price went up and total revenue went down. This might seem obvious, but that is not necessarily how it goes.

Try this instead. The price goes up by 20 per cent but this time the level of sales falls only 10 per cent. In elasticity terms, the percentage change in quantity is 10 per cent while the percentage change in price is 20 per cent. Elasticity is now 10 per cent divided by 20 per cent which comes to 0.5.

So to put in a set of numbers: suppose again that the price had originally been $20 per unit and the number of units sold was 1000. Total revenue is $20 per unit × 1000 units = $20 000.

This time, however, the price goes up by 20 per cent which means the price rises to $24. Meanwhile, the number of units sold falls by only 10 per cent, that is, by 10 per cent of 1000 which is 100 units. Thus, there were 900 units still being sold at the higher price. The total revenue is now $24 per unit × 900 units = $21 600.

This time the price went up and so too did total revenue.

ELASTIC AND INELASTIC

In the first instance, when the price went up the quantity demanded was generally responsive to the change in price, with the definition of 'generally responsive' being that the percentage change in quantity was greater than the percentage change in price. The elasticity measure was thus calculated to be greater than 1.

Where quantity demand is generally responsive to change in price, demand is said to be *elastic*.

Meanwhile, in the second instance, when the price went up the quantity demanded was generally unresponsive to the change in price, with the definition of 'unresponsive' being that the percentage change in quantity was smaller than the percentage change in price. The elasticity measure was thus calculated to be less than 1. And where quantity demand is generally unresponsive to change in price, demand is said to be inelastic.

Where the effect on the number of units demanded is greater in percentage terms than the effect on the price, demand is said to be elastic and total revenue will move in the opposite direction to the movement in price.

On the other hand, where the effect on the number of units demanded is less in percentage terms than the effect on the price, demand is said to be inelastic and total revenue will move in the same direction as the movement in price.

And what is interesting is that the very same demand curve will typically shift from being elastic at higher prices to becoming inelastic at lower prices. That means that as the price comes down, at first total revenue will go up and then, having reached a maximum, total revenue will come down.

ELASTICITY USUALLY CHANGES ALONG A DEMAND CURVE

The numerical example shows a fall in price in the first column of Table 7.1, and a corresponding increase in the quantity that would be purchased at each of those prices. As the price falls from $14 to $7, total revenue rises from $0 to $49. This is because the percentage change in quantity is greater than the percentage change in price. We are in the elastic part of the demand curve.

However, from a price of $7 per unit down to a price of $0, as the price falls so too does total revenue, until when the price goes to zero, total revenue again goes to zero. This is because the percentage change in the fall in output is greater than the percentage change in the fall in price. Here we are in the inelastic portion of the demand curve.

Table 7.1   Price–quantity demand relationship

Price	Quantity	Total revenue	
14	0	0	elastic
13	1	13	elastic
12	2	24	elastic
11	3	33	elastic
10	4	40	elastic
9	5	45	elastic
8	6	48	elastic
7	7	49	unit elastic
6	8	48	inelastic
5	9	45	inelastic
4	10	40	inelastic
3	11	33	inelastic
2	12	24	inelastic
1	13	13	inelastic
0	14	0	inelastic

Now it should not be forgotten that this process works in reverse. In the inelastic range, a rise in price will lead to a rise in revenue. However, from the moment that the demand curve moves from the inelastic portion to the elastic section, the rise in price is associated with a fall in revenue. This is shown in the diagrams in Figure 7.12.

As price goes down, total revenue rises until there is a point at which

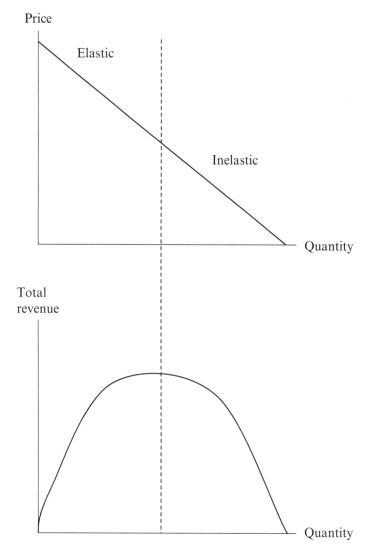

Figure 7.12   Effect of elasticity of demand on total revenue

revenue reaches its maximum level. From then on, as price descends, total revenue descends as well.

But what should not be thought is that the point of maximum revenue is the point at which business decisions will drive output levels. Missing still is the level of cost at each level of output.

The point of maximum profit is the point at which the total level of revenues exceeds the total level of costs to the greatest extent. This is the level of output that firms are directing their activities towards. Which brings us to marginal analysis, discussed in the chapter that follows.

NOTE

1. Arithmetically it should be −2 since the fall in demand was −20 per cent, but I leave out the minus sign for convenience.

8. Marginal analysis

Marginal analysis, the very core of economic thinking, is based on an understanding that every decision takes place in the present. The past was once the present, when all of the decisions were made that affect the world as it is today. Today's decisions will affect the future, cannot alter the past, and in reality cannot alter the present either.

What is more, decisions are made without certain knowledge about what will happen in the period ahead. There is always a degree of uncertainty about every decision, and the farther into the future one must be forced to look, the more uncertain that future becomes.

In regard to an economic decision to invest, there is normally reasonable clarity looking forward a month or two. Looking forward a year, issues become more opaque and are even more difficult if one projects forward two years or five. Looking ahead ten years or 20, there is no mechanism to determine how the world will look then, and therefore to determine how sensible today's decision will turn out to be.

Yet decisions do have to be made with these kinds of time frames in mind. Twenty-year-olds make such decisions all the time by choosing which areas they will study. Those decisions made at 20 will often affect the entire direction of their lives as they choose to take on skills in one particular area rather than another.

Businesses, in choosing the shape to give to their capital, are making decisions that may require decades for the full realization of the initial outlay. Planting forests, to take a simple and obvious example, requires outlays to be made in the present without any chance of repayment for years on end. How do such decisions end up being made?

The framework in which decisions are presumed to be made is referred to as marginal analysis. Decisions are, it is said, made at the margin.

DECISIONS AT THE MARGIN

And here the word 'margin' is used to mean 'at the edge'. And the edge at which marginal decisions are made is at the very end of all past history until that moment, that moment being the always-with-us present.

Economic decisions can only affect the future since the past is gone and the present is now. Marginal analysis is based on what can still be changed going forward. The past sets the circumstances in which a decision is made, but only what can be made different is ever included as part of marginal analysis.

The past does, of course, affect the present. It is the feedstock that created the circumstances we are now in. There are past decisions that will continue to affect conditions in the present and on into the future. You can never escape the past.

A factory has been built. A factory has burned down. Debts have been taken on. Particular skills have been acquired. Unexpected events have occurred. Each of these remain crucial aspects of the present that absolutely must be taken on board when a decision is being made. Past decisions often reduce our options going forward, just as they also create opportunities as well. The decisions of the past are the baggage we carry into the present.

But when making a decision, this carryover from the past may narrow our options – may raise by an immense amount the costs which must be borne into the future – but this carryover is nonetheless not the subject of the decision itself. Decisions are about what can be changed. Bad decisions in the past may mean that the optimal decision in the present is to declare bankruptcy and close the business. It is the fact that the past is unchangeable that can often make it so unendurable. But whatever has happened in the past, it is the past. It is a *fixed cost* whose effects endure into the present. These circumstances must be taken into account but are not themselves part of any decision that is made.

Time moves in one direction only. Decisions are about the future. Sunk costs are sunk. The only question is: given where someone is, what can be done that will add more to the benefits received in going forward relative to the costs that will be incurred in trying to obtain those benefits?

This is the weighing up that is the basis for decision making in an economy. It can be rules of thumb and back-of-the-envelope estimates of the relative costs and benefits all the way to the most sophisticated decision making techniques that management science has so far developed. The greater the potential costs involved, the more detailed will tend to be the assessment process.

But whatever the means used to make the assessment, it comes down to this: to a weighing up of all of the potential costs against all of the potential benefits brought back to the present. That is, brought back to the moment that the decision is made.

COSTS AND BENEFITS

Every time a cost is taken on, it is taken on with some projected benefit in mind that exceeds the costs being borne. No one will make decisions that are expected to make them worse off (unless becoming worse off is seen to provide some kind of net benefit).

People may be wrong about outcomes. That happens all the time. But at the moment of decision, so far as economics is concerned, the expectation is that the outcome will be a net positive. The return will be greater than the costs.

That is what is meant by rationality in economics. The decision maker alone decides what the benefits to be had are. More money, prestige, fame or whatever; benefits can be both tangible and intangible. But before the decision is made to achieve some end, the *expected* costs are compared with the *expected* benefits to determine whether the game is worth the candle, that is, whether the return is sufficiently large to repay all of the costs and effort involved.

If the expected benefits are greater than the expected costs, then the first threshold is passed in deciding to go forward. If the expected benefits do not exceed the expected costs, then the project is rejected.

But that is only the first threshold. In many instances, there is more than one possible project with a positive net return. In this case, the project with the largest excess of benefits over costs, as estimated by the decision maker, is chosen.

OPPORTUNITY COST

This is what is meant by opportunity cost. There are almost always alternative possibilities that have to be ranked. In choosing one project from amongst all of the alternatives available, the choice is the one with the greatest excess of benefits over costs.

In a sense this is a roundabout way of saying the obvious. It is a set of circumstances that also faces governments in deciding what they should do. With governments, however, it is usually political considerations that matter most and the financial that come later.

But in the world of business, when the private decision maker, the entrepreneur, is considering all of the alternatives, there is the best alternative and then there is the second best from amongst the full range of possibilities. The opportunity cost is defined as the best foregone alternative. It is this that is considered the cost of going forward with the alternative that is actually chosen.

Suppose there are three projects, the first with a return of $100 million, the second with a return of $70 million and the last with a return of $40 million. The cost of taking up the $100 million project is the lost opportunity to undertake a project that was potentially worth $70 million. That was the project's opportunity cost.

TIME AND ECONOMIC RETURN

But there is yet another complexity that needs to be negotiated, at least conceptually. That is the time frame in which the forecast returns are expected to accrue.

Using the tree plantation as an example, if it take 25 years for the trees to reach maturity and become commercial, the cost of planting the trees now must be set against an expected return that can occur no sooner than a quarter of a century later.

Meanwhile, there may be another project that might require the same initial outlay in the present that will achieve a smaller return but sooner.

These are the everyday kinds of calculations that everyone in business must regularly make. These are the kinds of decisions that must be made in every economy by someone. Balancing distant gains against an earlier return, where the distant gain is expected to be larger, but because it is farther into the future, is potentially less certain and less attractive.

The choice of $100 million in one year or $200 million in seven years is a commercial decision that require some delicate weighing up. The cost of finance, an assessment of the risks involved, time preference and a host of other considerations will be stirred into the decision making brew. This is the kind of entrepreneurial decision that must, however, be made all the time, for which no hard and fast rules can be made.

There are techniques that have been developed to deal with such problems at the managerial level. '*Present* value' calculations try to estimate the costs of a project against its expected revenues where these costs and revenues are of different amounts and will occur at different dates in the future. These calculations are an attempt to bring back to the present moment, that is, to the only moment that ever actually exists, an estimate of how much will be earned (or lost) if the project actually went ahead.

All such techniques are merely means to deal with these uncertainties, but can never eliminate them. Such uncertainty is intrinsic because the future is unknowable.

But everyone makes these kinds of decisions routinely. Minimizing costs relative to benefits is a constant process that becomes second nature.

Look at the following example. In Figure 8.1, there are four different

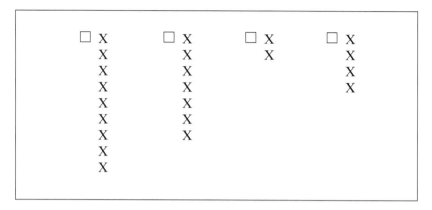

Figure 8.1　Why are a different number of people in the different
supermarket queues?

supermarket checkout queues and each is of a different length. Yet no one looking at these queues of different length would have any doubt as to why that is.

It is because each individual person coming to check out at the supermarket would look at the amount of groceries in each of the shopping carts in the different queues and make an assessment of which one would take the least amount of time to get to the front. People make mistakes about which queue will take the shortest time, but this they will only know when time has passed and the different queues have moved forward at different rates.

This is a minimalist example of what happens at every stage in the business world, and indeed, amongst both producers and buyers. We make decisions all the time that are intended to reduce costs to ourselves (in this example, the cost being the time required to get through the checkout). Whether things turn out as planned is often quite another story.

MAXIMIZING PROFITS

In looking at businesses and what they do, the most basic of the economic assumptions is that firms attempt to maximize profits.

We say this either because the assumption is made that this is in the nature of the kinds of people who run businesses, or because the nature of competition is such that if a firm does not try to get as much profit as its circumstances will allow, competitive forces will threaten it with extinction. Profit maximization in this second case is a form of self-preservation.

Again, profit maximization is a notional concept. There are so many considerations, both short run and long run, that go into thinking through the course of action to take, that all that can be said is that businesses try to work their way through the minefield of all of the different issues, both large and small, that must be dealt with in order to make as much money as possible.

But the time frame in which this money is being made is impossible to specify. If we again think of that forest plantation, how can any calculation be made about the profit to be earned, when it will be earned and the uncertainties along the way? To use as a catch-all notion that those making the decision are trying to make the most money possible given the possibilities available to them, balancing all considerations including the need to take a more long-term perspective, we are very seldom likely to go wrong in trying to make sense of the economic world we find ourselves in.

It need hardly be pointed out that sometimes profits in the short term will be sacrificed for profits in the long term. It would be normal business practice to accept lower profits in the present to increase profitability over the longer haul.

A retailer, for example, might implement a no-questions-asked returns policy on items sold. And certainly, for any item returned there is a loss, but if the difference can be made up through an increased sales volume then profits are potentially higher because of the practice. This is how businesses can be expected to operate.

They will choose actions which they believe will lead to the largest difference in revenues relative to costs over the relevant time period. The time period they have in mind will, of course, be decided by the business itself.

TRADITIONAL MARGINAL ANALYSIS

It is not so much that traditional marginal analysis is wrong as that it is so pointless that is its problem. This and the next section of the chapter outline this traditional approach, but you are being warned as well. Thinking about marginal analysis in this traditional way will make it harder to understand how an economy works, and will take you further from seeing how a market economy works as well.

Economists use the concept of marginality at every stage. It is a forward-looking concept. In the traditional analysis, it in effect asks this question: taking all that exists already as a given, what will be the effect on one economic variable if there is a change (usually described as a 'one-unit change') in some other economic variable?

Marginal cost, for example, asked what would be the effect on production costs of a change in the level of production. *Marginal revenue* asked the same question about the effect on sales revenue of an increase in quantity demanded.

There is then marginal utility. We cannot even measure total utility, so there is nothing in actual fact that is being measured when marginal utility is discussed. But the notional concept is what is the *increase* in total utility that follows from a one-unit increase in the possession of some good or service. That is, how much does utility rise for some individual through the purchase of one more shirt to go with all of the other shirts already owned?

Marginal product asks about the effect on the level of production that occurs through the addition of one more unit of some input while holding all other inputs constant. Here again, as an example, it is supposed to show the effect on total output that would occur if one additional worker were added to all of the other workers already employed. This would be the marginal product of the last worker. If you do not know which one was the 'last worker', that is not the point. And if you think that each worker is different and has different capabilities, again that is not the point.

The concept is notional and tries to focus attention on the decision maker in each case. With utility, the focus is on the buyers of final goods and services. With marginal product, the focus is on producers who must decide whether to add more employees to the payroll.

And almost invariably, the marginal measure is used in comparison with something else as part of a decision-making process.

For a consumer deciding whether to buy one thing rather than another, the question is which will provide a higher level of marginal utility, that is, a greater improvement in personal welfare as decided by themselves.

Looking at the marginal productivity of labour, the same kind of question underlies the concept. The comparison is typically made with the wage that has to be paid for the additional employee added on. If the expected money value of the addition to output is greater than the money cost of employing one new person, then the person is employed. If the expected value is less than the wage, the person will not be employed.

In general, though, the use of marginal analysis is based on understanding the process that anyone making a decision must go through as they, embedded in the present as they must necessarily be, compare future states of the world with one decision having been made rather than another (with the decision to do nothing at all always a realistic option).

Marginal analysis concerns itself with making a decision in the present while trying to make judgements about the future consequences of that decision. It is what people generally do. It is how most people normally behave when faced with uncertainty. They weigh up the options and choose one course of action in preference to all of the others. That things seldom come out as planned is just the way of the world.

MARGINAL REVENUE AND MARGINAL COST

This section of the chapter is also presented because it represents the traditional approach, not because it will enable you to better understand how an economy works. Learning marginal analysis in this way may even delay your ability to make sense of the way in which an economy works. You are therefore being warned. For a more detailed understanding of these issues, see the Appendix to this chapter.

The notions that lie beneath the decision making process as understood by economic theory are bundled under the names 'marginal revenue' (MR) and 'marginal cost' (MC) and are applied to the price determination of a single product. When MR and MC are equal for any particular product, the greatest level of profit is made in selling that one product. It is therefore said that 'profit maximization' occurs when $MR = MC$. There is then quite an elaborate discussion on these concepts, both with figures and with charts (and in more mathematical treatments using calculus) to show that this is so.

Reduced to its essentials, the argument is basically this. A business will continue to increase its production of some particular good or service so long as every time it produces one additional unit of output it can add more to its revenues than it does to its costs.

The trick is in understanding that a business faces a demand curve that slopes down. Therefore, to sell another unit of production, it has to lower the price for all of the units that it is already selling.

To sell more it must lower the price per unit. So even on the revenue side there is a potential trade-off. A business can increase its level of sales, but it must lower the price of the product to do so.

As we saw, along a straight-line demand curve, as prices fall total revenue first goes up and then after some point begins to go down. Meanwhile, the more is produced, the higher is the level of costs.

For a while, as the price is lowered and more units are sold, revenues rise faster than costs. But at some level of production and sales, there is a crossover where costs begin to rise faster than revenue. It is at this crossover point where MC equals MR that profits reach their maximum level. It is at this level of output that the firm will produce, and the price it will charge will be the price associated with this level of output.

PROBLEMS WITH TRADITIONAL MARGINAL ANALYSIS

The problem with this analysis is that it assumes too much knowledge on the part of those who own and manage firms. It firstly assumes that they know the shape of the demand curve they face. It assumes that they can tell what would happen to their own revenues if they adjusted the price. It assumes that costs are generally static and can be foretold for each level of production.

What is also left out is time. There is no sense in this analysis of the considerations that any business gives to the trade-offs that it might accept in the present to increase its profitability over the longer term.

It makes it seem that business decision making is a mechanical exercise in looking at marginal revenue on the one side and marginal costs on the other, and then setting a price while producing the relevant volume.

It almost completely assumes away the fact that virtually every product sold is a 'joint product' with other goods or services produced and sold by the same firm at the same time. It ignores cross-subsidization of every good or service sold, as costs are spread over many different products.

In going about things in this way what is really important about marginal analysis is buried. Because what is really important is that decision making in a firm takes place within an environment surrounded by radical uncertainties. Those who make the decision cannot know at the time those decisions are made whether the outcomes will in reality add to profitability or lower it. This no one in business can ever know before the fact.

But what may be the largest problem with the marginalist approach to business decisions is that it has traditionally focused on the effect of a small increase in the sale of a *single unit* of some product. It therefore takes the entire notion to the point of utter vacuity. Production of one more unit of anything, unless we are discussing house construction or some such, are not decisions but matters of routine. They just happen.

But if marginal analysis is seen as it ought to be seen, as a step into the dark of the future where *conjectures* about what will happen to revenues are balanced against *conjectures* about what will happen to costs, then it brings home just how difficult it is to find that point of maximum profit. Indeed, it underscores just how hard it can be to earn any profits at all.

MARGINAL ANALYSIS IS ABOUT DECISION MAKING AND NOT SINGLE PRODUCTS

And there is this. Marginal analysis is about making a decision. Marginal analysis is useful in understanding the nature of entrepreneurial decision making. It helps to explain the process that people in business (in fact, people generally) go through in reaching decisions.

They weigh things up. They look at the pros and cons. They look at different time perspectives. They wrestle with a host of unknowns and recognize the existence of unknown unknowns.

Marginal analysis is about actively deciding what to do in a situation of uncertainty. It is *not* one unit of this or that being discussed. It is about the effect on revenues and costs of moving in one direction rather than in some other. It takes the entire situation into account, not some infinitesimal increase or decrease in the production of some individual product.

Traditional marginal analysis studiously ignores what is actually interesting about marginal analysis.

APPLYING MARGINAL ANALYSIS TO THE THEORY OF THE FIRM

To look just a bit further at what is wrong with the traditional theory, let us examine what is described in many texts as the 'theory of the firm'. The business firm in economic theory is a very abstract entity. It is a series of costs related to a series of potential revenue streams in which the level of production for a single product is determined in isolation from every other product a firm might in fact be producing. The standard microeconomic theory of the firm corresponds with no actual existing firm found in the real world.

The concentration in the theory of the firm is on the product and not on the business itself. It is supply and demand writ large. But if one is to understand what firms do, it needs to be seen that they do not concentrate on any particular good or service, but once in existence do whatever they believe will earn them a profit.

Could one seriously imagine a department store using a form of analysis that focused on the price and quantity relationship for single products? Could one think of the supply and demand for shirts when the variety of actual shirts in the market must mean that at any one time hundreds of different products could be described as a shirt?

The point of marginal revenue and marginal cost analysis is essentially sound but it takes much too narrow a compass in how it looks at things. Firms do act so that they will maximize profits. But they do so not by selling one product but by selling many, and not by staying with whatever original line of production they were originally in but through a willingness to seek opportunities wherever they may open.

They also try to maximize those profits, not in some kind of immediate term, but are always thinking strategically as best they can where there is a trade-off between earning as much money as possible in as short a period of time, or taking a more longer-term perspective by earning less in the present than might have been possible so that more might be earned over the longer term. Considerations of time are a very large part of how business people think. None of this is shown in the traditional analysis.

ALL DECISIONS ARE MADE IN THE PRESENT

Here, instead, is what you need to understand in applying marginal analysis.

All decisions are made in the present. Whenever any decision has been made, it was at that moment, the present, which then instantaneously became the past. And what may be the best way to understand a 'decision' is to recognize that some action was taken. Something was done. A contract was signed. A purchase was made. A cheque was issued. A building was demolished. A person was hired.

Or perhaps the contract was not signed, the cheque not issued, the building not demolished or the person not hired. But whichever way it went, time moved on and a new set of circumstances presented themselves in which the past was whatever it was and the future still remained unknown.

Generalizing beyond a single product to the way business people think about everything is essential if marginal analysis is to be understood properly. Broadening $MR = MC$ into a theory of decision making in general is what is required. This is in fact a major aspect of economic technique. What is called cost–benefit analysis (CBA) is a short-form name for the application of MR and MC to a vast range of questions, and not all of them economic.

At the core of CBA is the need to bring into the present moment an estimate of the value of the flow of future benefits (usually quantified as the receipt of sums of money at different dates in the future) that would be expected to follow this decision, which are compared with the value of the costs that are expected to be incurred (also usually quantified in money terms). A project gets past at least the first threshold if the expected flow of revenue, as quantified in the present, exceeds the expected flow of costs, also quantified in the present.

This kind of technique is applied to all manner of project from the smallest to the most immense, projects which can often take many years before they reach a stage where they are even breaking even. The assumptions made are guaranteed to go wrong and projects often miscarry for any number of reasons. But the technique itself is an attempt to think through questions about whether some project is even worth consideration.

And when cost–benefit analysis is finally boiled down to its essence, the technique itself turns out to be a question of the expected additions to revenue of taking some decision (that is, the marginal revenue) balanced against the expected additions to costs (the marginal costs), as they are each perceived at some particular moment in time.

SUMMARIZING MARGINAL ANALYSIS

A proper understanding of marginal analysis comes down to this. A decision is to be made, and in the economics of the firm, it is a commercial decision. Some entrepreneur must decide what to do.

The decision, like all decisions, is to be made in the present. The consequences of that decision will unfold in the unknowable future.

In this circumstance, marginal revenue means the entire additional flow of benefits that are expected to accrue from making this decision. Since the flow of benefits will take place at different dates in the future, some means of bringing the value of such benefits back to the present needs to be made.

But the essence of the decision-making process is to have some means – whether rule-of-thumb or highly sophisticated mathematical technique – available to make these revenue projections and return those projections to a figure that relates to the present moment.

There are then the marginal costs. Marginal costs are the additions to costs that the decision will entail. To achieve the benefits – the revenues that will be earned – various costs must be borne, and in most economic decisions a large proportion of the costs, which may be spread over a considerable time, come before the revenues.

Some means must be found to estimate what those costs will be and then bring those costs back to some form of money valuation that can be compared with the expected present value of the revenue stream.

That there are far more complications in such an analysis, such as just ensuring that every cost can be financed along the way as the project goes ahead, is understood. But when all is said and done, a project will be undertaken when the *expected addition* to revenue is greater than the *expected addition* to costs. That is, when marginal revenue is estimated to be greater than the marginal cost.

To think in this way is to think like an economist.

GRAPHICAL REPRESENTATION OF MARGINAL REVENUE AND MARGINAL COST

The core notion, if you are to understand decision making in an economic setting, is to recognize that every decision to do something will entail

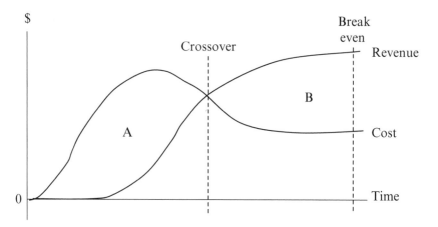

Figure 8.2   Marginal revenue and marginal cost where expected revenues
*   exceed expected costs*

costs. Since the aim in commencing commercial activity is to generate a
profitable outcome, for that to happen the amount of money brought
in must exceed the amount of money paid out. Not instantaneously, of
course, but over time.

Because what is especially important to understand is that, almost
invariably, the costs will need to be met before any money at all is earned,
and for a period of time costs will be in excess of revenues.

And the final element to understand is that at the time the decision is
made, every part of the project is merely a set of expectations with varying
degrees of certainty about what the eventual outcome might actually be.

The marginal revenue is the *addition* to revenue that this new venture is
expected to earn. The marginal cost is the *addition* to costs that will have
to be paid out in running this venture. And the likelihood of such additions to revenues and costs is judged not after the results are in, but at the
moment when its future prospects are being considered before anything
concrete is known.

Figure 8.2 provides the proper means to understand the nature of marginal revenue and marginal cost. The horizontal axis shows the time frame
over which the costs and revenues are being calculated, starting from the
present moment, which is the moment the decision is being made, which
for every decision is the immediate present.

The vertical axis shows the expected amount of money to be received
or spent during different periods of time. At the moment the decision is
made, all past costs are past. The only issue is what is expected to occur in
the future, which is why both the revenue and cost lines start at the origin

at the far left of the figure. There may well have been an immense series of payments that led up to that moment, but all that is past. Now we are looking forward and considering what will happen from this point on.

The Revenue Curve shows a stylized estimate of the revenue that is expected to be earned during each time period as a result of this decision.[1] Since in each time period there is an amount of revenue being earned, the total revenue earned is shown by the area under the Revenue Curve. As with virtually all projects, no revenue is earned until some stage in the future, which is why the curve runs along the horizontal axis for a period of time.

The marginal revenue is thus the cumulative additional revenue over some time frame in the future expected at the moment the decision is being made as the result of this decision having been made.

Unlike revenue, costs begin to accumulate almost immediately, as shown by the costs line. This too is a stylized representation since costs will typically be intermittent – in some periods higher and in some lower. The cost curve, however, shows a smoothly continuous increase in costs starting from the vertical axis, rising for a period of time as the initial start-up costs are met, and then coming down to settle in at some level, which are essentially the running costs of the venture. The area under the costs curve represents the total expected costs of the project.

Thus the marginal costs are the total addition to costs that are expected to occur also from the perspective of present moment, the moment the decision was made.

These are merely expectations but the aim is eventually to reach a position where the addition to revenue exceeds the addition to costs. Importantly, it should be understood that this position does *not* occur where the two lines cross.

In any successful project, at some stage the two lines must cross to allow revenue to become greater than costs. At that moment, the project has begun to pay its own way, meeting all of its expenses out of revenue. But it has not yet repaid all of the costs that had allowed the project to get under way.

The funding for the project has come out of the accumulated savings of the community. Whether it was the raw materials used in construction, the capital equipment that has been put to use or the wages paid to employees, all of that can only have come out of accumulated savings. And do note that these are not savings in the form of money and credit but savings in the form of actual products and services.

The venture will only have finally covered its cost when the area B, which is the revenue over costs past that breakeven point, is finally equal to area A, which are the costs in excess of revenue that will have been borne before the project began to earn a positive return.

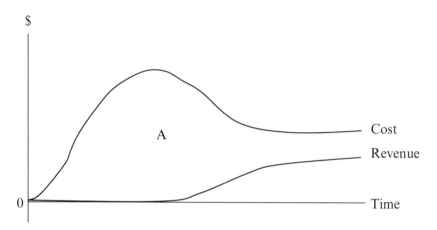

*Figure 8.3   Marginal revenue and marginal cost where expected costs
            exceed expected revenue*

At that moment, but not before, the expected revenue is exactly equal to
the expected costs. Only thereafter will the project show a positive return.

But what cannot be emphasized enough is this. The revenue and cost
line are projections. They are estimates of what might happen. And in any
conjectures such as this, there are almost always alternative possibilities
that fail to show a profitable outcome.

It is just as possible that in looking into the future, there are also
loss-making outcomes that are thought of as realistic possibilities, one of
which is shown as an example in Figure 8.3. Here the costs are the same
but the revenue projections never rise above the costs. This is a project for
which the expected addition to costs, the marginal cost, is greater than the
expected addition to revenue, the marginal revenue. This is a venture that
would never be undertaken since marginal costs are well above marginal
revenue.

The message of the figure is broader than just economic decision making.
It shows how actual decisions in every part of life are determined, from
personal decisions through political calculation and onto every important
commercial consideration. Every decision is based on some weighting of
the *expected* benefits against *expected* costs looking from the present and
into that unknowable future. As solid as the lines may appear on the page,
they are curves of conjecture, mere thoughts in someone's head about how
things might turn out if some particular action were actually taken.

Finally, even if there is a positive expectation, there is no certainty an
actual decision to go ahead will be made. There may be a range of projects that are being considered with further judgements required to pick

and choose amongst them. The risks may just be too great relative to the expected return.

The best alternative use of these resources is the opportunity cost – what is not undertaken so that this project can be. But merely because marginal revenues are greater than marginal cost is not enough to ensure a project will be undertaken.

INNOVATION, ENTREPRENEURS AND MARGINAL ANALYSIS

The traditional form of marginal analysis is seriously deficient in one additional way as well. What it does is look at a product already being sold and incorporates all of the forces that determine the price charged and volume produced. It therefore excludes what may be the single most important factor in determining our economic welfare, which is the introduction of new products and new production technologies.

The notions that lie behind marginal cost and marginal revenue are related to existing products. The concepts introduced in this chapter are about making the world new over again, with entrepreneurs driving change. $MR = MC$ is a world without the entrepreneur. Products are produced, priced and sold without so much of a mention of the role of the entrepreneur. Everything is determined by the existing forces. The outcome happens almost by itself. These are the forces of demand, these of supply, and there is the price.

The reality is that producing and selling are processes that require a great deal of prior thought. Decisions are made at every step of the way. Products do not appear by themselves. They are brought to the market by the deliberate actions of their producers. And all along the way, as each of the necessary decisions between conception and production has been taken, there are the true forces of marginal analysis.

At each stage, in other words, there are decisions being made where the effect on future revenues is compared with the effect on future costs. Marginal analysis is thus not a one-off matter where the product has finally been brought to market, and these are the costs at different levels of production and these are the revenues. It is instead a process that never ever stops.

And the most important way in which this process is ongoing is the way in which new products are continually replacing older products, just as new services are replacing other, older services. Entrepreneurs and innovation are the core elements in the processes of a market economy.

Marginal analysis is so incorrigibly static that rather than helping to explain what is going on, in many ways it inhibits the ability to understand the underlying dynamic. Nothing in a market is finished. Nothing is ever settled. Everything is provisional and temporary. There is literally nothing that might not be replaced.

Thinking about $MR = MC$ may cause you to miss everything that really does matter since it will divert attention from the entrepreneur. Marginal analysis is about plotting the future before that future arrives. And when it does arrive, plotting a new future to come after that.

If you are going to understand how an economy works, you have to see that the commercial world is determined by entrepreneurs who act within the law to produce new products. And at each step of the way, they are thinking about what would be the best thing to do. That is the reality of the economy that you must understand if you are going to make any sense of the economic world in which you live.

INDUSTRY STRUCTURE

There are many different ways to characterize firms, from the number of employees or the level of sales through to the kind of industry they are in and the type of products produced. The economy adapts itself to the production techniques of the time as shaped by, amongst many other things, entrepreneurial initiative, the capital stock in existence, the availability of savings, the characteristics of the workforce, the existing technological knowledge, and the regulatory and tax structures that governments have put in place, not to mention, of course, the kinds of goods and services such firms think they can sell at a profit.

In a market economy, no one deliberately chooses in advance how the commercial world will evolve, but at any moment in time it is possible to gather statistics to identify what actually happens to exist, or if not exactly that, what existed in some relatively recent period in the past. The structure is what it is, but not because it was planned in that particular way.

Amongst the various industry characteristics that some have deemed of significance is the question of industry concentration. The issue in regard to concentration is how many firms are found in an industry and how large each firm is relative to the size of the industry as a whole.

How to decide what actually constitutes an industry is itself never so obvious (for example, is the 'industry' shirt manufacturing, menswear, clothing in general or even something else?). There are also issues of geographical distribution. When we speak of concentration, how large an area should be included. Almost nothing is highly concentrated if looked at on a global scale. Narrowing the area over which one is looking increases the proportion of sales any one firm is likely to have made.

So even to determine just how few or how many firms are in an industry is never clear cut.

Nevertheless, economists have provided a kind of division between different industry structures based around the idea that a greater number of firms in an industry is better than fewer. The divisions are generally something like this:

- *monopoly*: where there is only a single seller of a product;
- *oligopoly*: where there are a few sellers of a product which may or may not be differentiated, that is, which may either be identical to the products sold by all other competitors (think iron ore production) or may instead be highly individualized (such as with car manufacturing);
- *monopolistically competitive*: where there are many relatively small sellers of a generally differentiated product (such as restaurants);
- *highly competitive*: where sellers are very small relative to the size of the market and where each seller sells what is for all practical purposes a product indistinguishable from the products sold by competitors (such as with milk producers). No firm in a highly competitive industry has any control of the price it charges. They are 'price takers' where the price is determined in the market and not by the individual firm.

Each industry structure is to an important extent driven by the nature of the products sold. The largest determinant of structure is the efficient size of an individual firm. In some industries, the most efficient size is very large relative to the market, so that only one or a few firms may be in operation. In other industries, such as with barber shops and bakeries, an efficiently sized operation may be quite small in comparison with the size of the market as a whole.

The tendency for some to worry over industries where a few large firms dominate seems excessive. There are genuinely anti-competitive practices but they are not particularly associated with the size of firm. These practices are attempts to get around market competition, often based on private side agreements reached with other firms which are supposed to be in competition with each other.

Such side agreements are designed to reduce the amount of competition by reducing the uncertainties faced by each of the businesses in the market. Most such agreements work against the interests of the buying public, and are almost invariably made illegal.

But a similar kind of process occurs where businesses argue that the forces of competition are so stacked against the efficient operation of individual firms that the government must come in and prevent certain normally fair practices by other firms. A firm lowering its price because it can employ economies of scale, and in that way lowering average costs and therefore average prices charged, is not an unfair practice, even though some small businesses try to have such price reductions declared illegal.

But determining whether falling prices are due to lower average costs, or are the result of a large firm going out of its way to drive smaller competitors from the market by keeping prices low until the smaller businesses leave the industry, is central to knowing what a regulator might do. How to differentiate between the two is often difficult to determine in practice.

But this everyone should understand. Market competition is often hard and the risks can be very high. Running a business is not for the faint-hearted.

NOTE

1. This is equivalent to a discounted cash flow since all revenues and costs are referenced to the present moment.

APPENDIX: THE TRADITIONAL THEORY OF PROFIT MAXIMIZATION

Profits are Maximized where $MR = MC$

This appendix should be seen as a 'no-go area' for all but the most intrepid. If you want to see how economists traditionally look at things, you can find out below. But in looking at this material, beware of getting caught up in the numbers. It is the concepts that matter if you are to understand how economics is taught.

The theory of profit maximization in economics states that in a business profits will reach their highest level where marginal revenue equals marginal costs: $MR = MC$. To understand what the words mean is to understand that this is so.

But the analysis is based on the production and sale of a single item. It says almost nothing at all about how production and sale occur in the real world, where everything is sold accompanied by the sale of many other products which are often close substitutes. In the traditional microeconomic presentation, we see only how the price and volume for a single product are determined. Only in the most abstract way does it discuss what a business firm in general might do.

Marginal revenue in this traditional analysis is defined as the change in revenue from producing one extra unit of output. You are selling, let us say, Q units of output at a price P. Total revenue is P times Q. To sell one more unit, given the barrier created by the demand curve, the price must fall. The new price is then Pn and there are now $Q + 1$ units being sold. The revenue is now Pn times $Q + 1$.

The price is lower, which drags total revenue down. But the number of units sold is higher, which drags total revenue up. What happens to total revenue depends on which of the two effects – the price effect or the revenue effect – is greater.

Based on the data from a normal demand curve, total revenues will first rise and then fall. As the price falls from the point where the demand curve hits the price axis, since this is the elastic portion of the demand, curve total revenue at first continues to rise.

This is shown in Table 8A.1. As the price falls from $14, where zero units are sold and therefore no revenue is earned, total revenue keeps rising until the price falls to $7, where 105 000 units are sold.

As the price descends below $7 more units are being sold, but as this is the inelastic part of the demand curve, total revenue begins to fall. Eventually, the price reaches zero, where the good is free. Total revenue here is also zero.

Table 8A.1 Revenue

Price $	Quantity 000s	Total revenue 000s	Marginal revenue 000s
14	0	0	
13	15	195	195
12	30	360	165
11	45	495	135
10	60	600	105
9	75	675	75
8	90	720	45
7	105	735	15
6	120	720	−15
5	135	675	−45
4	150	600	−75
3	165	495	−105
2	180	360	−135
1	195	195	−165
0	210	0	−195

Marginal revenue is the *addition* to revenue that comes from selling one extra unit of output. Forget for the time being that no business knows what its demand curve looks like and therefore there is no certainty about what will happen to total revenue if the price were to be brought down. Here we pretend that we can see the demand curve and that we can calculate what happens when the price falls again.

The highest level of revenue this firm can earn comes at a price of $7. There it is capable of taking in receipts of $735000 per time period. But whether this is the price to charge depends on what the business's motivation is. If the aim is to earn as much revenue as possible, then that will be the price.

But if the aim is to make the highest level of profits possible, then it is necessary to introduce production costs. Production costs are shown in the hypothetical example in Table 8A.2. Shown are the various forms of costs at each level of production, from zero units all the way up to 210000.

And whatever else might happen in the long run, over the short and medium term to produce more means that costs are higher. You have your fixed costs and they cannot be varied (which is why they are called 'fixed'). Therefore, when the quantity being produced is zero, total costs are equal to fixed costs which is $100000.

Only in the long run are there no fixed costs, which is the definition of the long run. In the long run, everything can be changed and therefore in the long run no costs are fixed.

Table 8A.2   Production costs

Quantity 000s	Total fixed costs 000s	Total variable costs 000s	Total costs 000s	Average total costs 000s	Marginal costs 000s
0	100	0	100		
15	100	30	130	8.7	30
30	100	75	175	5.8	45
45	100	130	230	5.1	55
60	100	195	295	4.9	65
75	100	270	370	4.9	75
90	100	370	470	5.2	100
105	100	480	580	5.5	110
120	100	600	700	5.8	120
135	100	740	840	6.2	140
150	100	915	1015	6.8	175
165	100	1135	1235	7.5	220
180	100	1395	1495	8.3	260
195	100	1715	1815	9.3	320
210	100	2090	2190	10.4	375

However, once output begins to rise, costs keep rising as output keeps rising. When there are no items being produced, total costs are $100 000 and when 15 000 items are being produced, variable costs rise by $30 000 (as shown in column 3).

The next column shows total production costs for each level of production. It is calculated as the sum of fixed costs plus variable costs. When no units are being produced, the total is $100 000. When 15 000 units are being produced, total costs are then estimated at $130 000.

Average total costs are shown in the next column. They are calculated by dividing total costs by the number of units produced. When this business is producing 15 000 units, the average cost of production is $8700.

The final column shows what is the most important of these calculations. Shown here is the *addition* to costs of producing extra units of output, the *marginal* cost.

There is found the addition to total costs of producing 15 000 additional units of output. To go from zero units to 15 000 units adds $30 000 to the total. To go from 15 000 units to 30 000 adds $45 000 to the total, and so on down the column.

Here it might be noted that it is normal to discuss marginal costs and marginal revenue in relation to the addition of a single extra unit of output. This is so trivial as an example of how businesses work, or how anyone normally looks at things, that it is dispensed with here. Therefore, to add a (very limited) sense of realism to the argument, the gradients have been reckoned in the thousands rather than in terms of a single extra unit of output.

Profit Maximization

From the above, we have, according to economic theory, all the information needed to calculate how many units a business should sell of this product and at what price it should be sold if profits are to reach a maximum in this short-run situation, which is, by assumption, what a business is aiming to do.

The point here is metaphorical but explains the way economists think about how economies work. Businesses are in business to make money. And the point at which a firm makes the greatest amount of profit is where marginal revenue is equal to marginal cost ($MR = MC$).

Having said that, however, the danger is that you might get so entangled in the arithmetic and lose the economics. Even as you are looking at the numbers, try to think instead about the underlying logic and not the numbers.

If one is in a situation in which doing something would add more to revenues than to costs, then economists assume that this action will be taken. Thus, if someone can get $1000 by spending $1, it is assumed that the $1 cost will be absorbed and the $1000 will be earned for a net profit of $999. In this case, MR is $1000 and MC is $1 so that one would happily make the decision to go ahead with whatever project would produce this return.

A more realistic example is shown in the example that makes up the rest of the appendix.

Reading across Table 8A.3 from a price of $14 down to a price of $9, it can be seen that total revenue rises and total costs rise and total profits rise. As the price moves down, marginal revenue keeps falling from but at each point remains higher than marginal cost until the price reaches $9.

The extra revenue earned by selling additional units of output remains higher than the extra costs taken on until the price is $9, when marginal revenue and marginal cost are both equal to $75000. Here the level of profit reaches its highest at $305000.

Unfortunately, this is not exactly the case. In fact, as you will see, as far as this table is concerned, profits reach the same maximum at a price of $10 where the business is also earning profits of $305000 per time period.

What is in fact the actual situation is that profits reach their maximum level at a price somewhere between $9 and $10. Therefore, the entire

Table 8A.3   Profits are at a maximum where MR = MC

Price $	Quantity 000s	Total revenue 000s	Total costs 000s	Marginal revenue 000s	Marginal costs 000s	Profit/loss 000s
14	0	0	100			−100
				195	30	
13	15	195	130			65
				165	45	
12	30	360	175			185
				135	55	
11	45	495	230			265
				105	65	
10	60	600	295			305
				75	75	
9	75	675	370			305
				45	100	
8	90	720	470			250
				15	110	
7	105	735	580			155
				−15	120	
6	120	720	700			20
				−45	140	
5	135	675	840			−165
				−75	175	
4	150	600	1015			−415
				−105	220	
3	165	495	1235			−740
				−135	260	
2	180	360	1495			−1135
				−165	320	
1	195	195	1815			−1620
				−195	375	
0	210	0	2190			−2190

exercise will be done again, this time with the pricing points in 10 cent intervals between $9 and $10. In this way we can see exactly where profits reach their highest point, and that it occurs where marginal costs are equal to marginal revenues.

This is shown in Table 8A.4. We have the prices between $10 and $9 where the number of units sold per time period rises from 60 000 at the higher price to 75 000 at the lower price. At the same time, total costs rise as production levels rise, from $295 000 to $370 000. Revenues at the same

Table 8A.4   How profits are maximized

Price $	Quantity 000s	Total revenue 000s	Total costs 000s	Marginal revenue 000s	Marginal costs 000s	Profit/loss 000s
10.00	60	600	295			305.00
				7.10	6.60	
9.90	61	607	302			305.47
				7.20	6.80	
9.80	63	614	308			305.88
				7.30	6.90	
9.70	64	622	315			306.21
				7.40	7.10	
9.60	66	629	322			306.48
				7.50	7.30	
9.50	67	636	330			306.68
				7.50	7.40	
9.40	69	644	337			306.80
				7.60	7.60	
9.30	70	652	345			306.84
				7.70	7.80	
9.20	72	659	352			306.81
				7.80	7.90	
9.10	73	667	360			306.68
				7.90	8.10	
9.00	75	675	370			306.48

time rise from $600 000 to $675 000. All this information is found in the previous tables. What is added are the increments in between.

Also added are the increments for marginal costs, which are scaled down because we are adding much less to costs each time since we are not adding as much to production each time. Similarly with marginal revenue. The numbers are lower because the increments are lower.

What we see, however, are the point of maximum profit. It comes at a price somewhere around $9.30 per unit when around 70 000 units are being sold. There marginal costs and marginal revenues are both equal to $7600. Profits reach a maximum at something like $306 840 in each period of time.

The economist's point is that businesses will keep adjusting what they do so that the level of profitability will rise as high as can be estimated, given how little is known about what conditions are really going to be like when production finally takes place. If some change can be made which is expected to add more to revenues than to costs, then that decision is made.

Incrementally, businesses will continue to take those steps that will cause them to reach a maximum level of profits.

But it is not the arithmetic that matters but the process. It is a step-by-step process in which decisions are made whose aim is to create a business structure that will make more money than any other structure the business might have chosen. That there are other motivations is understood, but you really cannot go too wrong assuming that businesses act in ways that will make them additional profit.

Where people often do go wrong is in thinking that businesses acting in this way are somehow acting against community interests, which is not the case. But it is sentiment and prejudice that often cloud the minds of those who are trying to understand how things work. Profitability is the engine of economic growth, and we are all materially far better off because of the way businesses go about their business.

But there are other aspects of the table which should be noted. Firstly, the level of profit made at the profit-maximizing price is hardly different from the profits that are to be made at other price-quantity pairings nearby. This kind of exactness is never to be expected from business. There are so many considerations when a business is trying to decide what to do, that profit maximization in this crude proximate kind of way is never going to be attempted, let alone achieved. And if it were achieved, who would know, because how could they tell?

Secondly, we are here discussing a single product. This is not a depiction of how businesses behave in general but is presented to provide a supposed understanding of how a firm decides the price and volume of production for a single item that it is putting up for sale. It is almost not worth pointing out how utterly unrealistic it is to think of business decisions in individual product lines being made in this way.

Finally – and this cannot be emphasized enough – none of the demand-side information can be known other than as conjectures about what might happen around the existing price. The information shown in the standard diagrams is unknown in virtually every instance. There is therefore no way whatsoever to derive the marginal revenue figures, even assuming that any firm would ever bother even if it were possible.

The cost data are knowable for a single firm and there are specialists who can estimate the total potential costs at different levels of production, and therefore can estimate the marginal cost.

But this approach is provided not because this is how businesses actually work things out in setting price, but to explain how an outcome will arise given that there is a level of demand at each price, that there are costs of production, and that businesses are typically trying to make money in a very competitive world in which others will take their customers if they can. The forces of the market will push firms in these directions without their necessarily knowing the data beneath.

Marginal analysis provides guidance on how businesses, guided by beliefs about the level of demand for their own products, their production costs and the effect of different pricing strategies of their competitions and customers, will behave. What it definitely does not say is that the decisions will be the right decisions. Business make wrong decisions all the time.

But if they are private decisions, in which individuals are putting up their own money, the certainty is that those who make the decisions will do everything they can think of to ensure that the decisions are the right ones. That is, they will do whatever they can to ensure that the decisions will lead to the greatest excess of benefits over costs, however those decision makers might wish to make the calculation.

Graphical Presentation

This discussion would not be complete without including something about the figures that are associated with marginal revenue, marginal costs and profit maximization. They are far from intuitive and difficult to understand, but every economist at some stage must make the journey.

Let us take, first of all, average and marginal revenue (Figure 8A.1). Average revenue is the demand curve. If each good sells for a particular price, which is what every point on the demand curve specifically states, then the price is also the average amount received per unit of output sold.

Marginal revenue is derived from the average revenue curve and shows the change in total revenue for each additional unit of output sold. And the specific and crucial point to remember here is that if one is already on the demand curve, then to sell additional units the price must be lowered, not just for the last unit sold, but for all of the others put up for sale.

Where the *MR* curve cuts the horizontal axis is the dividing point between elastic demand to the left and inelastic to the right. Therefore total revenue rises from the point where the demand curve touches the vertical axis and nothing is produced, right up to the point where $MR = 0$ as the *MR* line crosses the quantity axis. It will be clear why if you understand the nature of these two curves.

Figure 8A.2 shows average costs (*AC*) and marginal costs (*MC*). The *MC* curve cuts the *AC* curve at its lowest point. If you understand what each of these curves is intended to explain, you will also immediately understand why this is so.

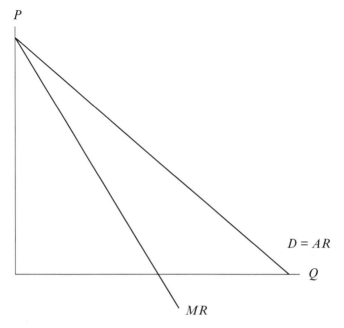

Figure 8A.1   Average and marginal revenue

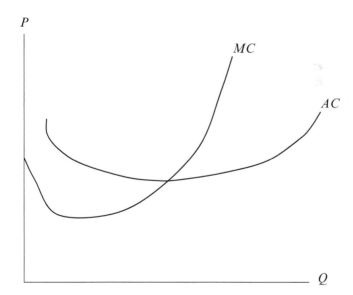

Figure 8A.2   Average and marginal costs

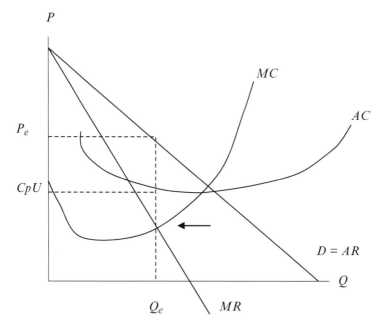

Figure 8A.3   Profit maximization where MC = MR

Maximizing Profits Shown Diagrammatically

Each set of curves in the two figures taken on their own are readily under-standable. They are just the two sets of data transcribed onto a chart. Where there is often confusion is when the two sets of lines are brought together onto a single graph so that one is overlaid on top of the other. Yet if we are to use a diagrammatic approach to understanding how profits are maximized, this is what needs to be done. This is shown in Figure 8A.3.

There is an arrow on the figure to point out where *MC* is equal to *MR*. That directly tells you the number of units of production, simply by looking to the horizontal axis. But for the price it is necessary to look at the maximum price that number of units of output can be sold for. This means running upwards to the demand curve for that level of production.

In this case, we have an equilibrium quantity of Q_e and an equilibrium price of P_e. This is the point at which profits are at their highest.

The figure for cost per unit of production (marked CpU) shows what the *average* cost for each unit of production would be at the profit-maximizing level of production. The price shows the average revenue. The difference between the average revenue and the average cost will be the average level of profit for each unit of output. Multiplying profit per unit by the number of units sold gives the figure for total profit.

What this analysis is supposed to explain is how a price is determined for an individual product, but the fact is that no one could seriously believe that it does. In some vague way, it might tell you something about a business that sold only a single product, such as an electricity company. But even there things are far more complicated, since to provide electricity at different times of day or on weekends comes with different production costs and a different level of demand. This would provide no real explanation of how a business behaves.

The analysis is for the most part a study in mathematical logic without really being a study in economics. It diverts attention from what is really useful, which is how businesses reach decisions in the face of uncertainty. Instead, it acts as if everything that needs to be known is knowable and actually known, and that products are priced one by one using marginal analysis.

Certainly there are some things that can be picked up mechanically using marginal cost and marginal revenue. The following are some of the more direct lessons that are explained:

- profitability is a process in which changes are made to prices charged and volumes sold and these changes are dependent on management expectations of what will happen to costs and revenues;
- there is a point of maximum profit for every product based not just on the revenues it generates but on keeping its cost of production under control;
- firms cannot charge just any old price but are usually well constrained by the market;
- businesses are forever trying to adjust what they do so that profits are as high as possible;
- average costs may fall for a while as production levels increase, but in most firms in the short run especially, average costs start rapidly rising as capacity constraints take effect.

These are certainly worth knowing but are hardly earth-shattering. This analysis, with $MC = MR$, is found in textbooks around the world. To become an economist requires someone to learn what is not so, to enable them to eventually learn for themselves, if they are lucky, how business decisions really are made in the real world.

9. Measuring the economy

Beyond individual markets is the economy as a whole. This is the entire network of purchase and sale of all goods and services, plus all of the actions taken by governments in raising revenue and spending their receipts, plus all of the actions of financial markets in taking in savings and allocating funds, plus all of the transactions, both physical and financial, that take place between one country and another.

And in trying to understand the processes involved, the aim of theory is to guide policy so that economies are able to achieve rapid rates of growth, low rates of unemployment, low rates of inflation as well as exchange rate and balance of payments stability.

The branch of economics that deals with these questions is referred to as macroeconomics. It is the area that tends to be of most interest to the community generally since such macroeconomic issues appear to affect them most directly while the operation of markets seems more distant and abstract.

Yet it is markets that matter most for prosperity, and even beyond that, it is only in understanding the interaction of entrepreneurs, financial institutions, businesses and consumers that the greater macroeconomic questions can be understood and answered.

MEASURES

To coincide with the four major macroeconomic issues of economic growth, unemployment, inflation and balance of payments stability there are four major measures of economic activity that are essential in understanding the direction in which an economy is travelling. These are:

- Gross Domestic Product (GDP);
- the unemployment rate;
- the Consumer Price Index (CPI);
- the balance of payments.

There are many other economic statistics produced by governments around the world (and there are still others produced by the private sector), but these are the four that are most frequently discussed. They are the ones that are looked at most closely and it is these that provide the most important guide to policy.

At the end of the day, the question really is: what purpose are the figures to serve? Each set of data requires a statistical agency to put in place a methodological framework for collecting the underlying figures. The questions the final statistics are asked to answer determine which numbers are collected and how they are put together. That is, the process begins with what you would like to know, and works backwards to try to establish what you can actually find out.

Most statistical collections are expensive. Therefore a good deal of thought is given to the uses that are to be made of the statistics once they have been collected. Statistics are not naturally occurring numbers that merely require a count, such as with a census. They are highly complex artefacts that occur only at the end of a very long process of thought and methodological refinement.

Every major statistic has gone through a period of evolution to reach its present stage, and it may be stated with certainty that as time goes by, every statistical series will continue to be improved.

THE NATIONAL ACCOUNTS

The 'National Accounts' is the name given to the most comprehensive measure of overall economic activity. They are a drawing together of amongst the most important economy-wide data on production within an economy.

The data answer questions such as: how large is the economy overall, how much is being produced, how fast is it growing, which areas of the economy are expanding or contracting and how rapidly is change taking place? Such statistics are particularly useful in making comparisons with the past, with the economy's official growth rate estimated from these data.

The data are also designed to indicate the economy's ability to increase the level of employment. The National Accounts were first conceived during the Great Depression, in the 1930s, when no such measure of the economy as a whole existed. The aim was to devise a measure based on the commonsense belief that an increased level of production would lead to an increased level of employment.

This, it may be noted, is the reverse of John Stuart Mill's fourth proposition on capital, that demand for commodities is not demand for labour. But the belief is now well established within economic theory that increased aggregate demand for goods and services is directly correlated with an increase in the number of jobs available. Raising the rate of economic growth is now seen as amongst the most important means by which to increase employment.

But in thinking about the National Accounts, it is crucial to understand that most of what differentiates the living standards in one community in comparison with another are not shown by the published data. To know that one economy had a growth rate of 10 per cent and another's growth rate was 3 per cent does not necessarily tell you all that much about either economy's standard of living, rate of unemployment or future prospects. These are tricky figures that have to be understood to be interpreted properly.

STOCKS AND FLOWS

The National Accounts show the level of current production. Production is a flow concept. It measures what has been made newly available for use. When it is said that the economy has grown by 5 per cent over the year, the comparison being made is between how much was newly produced this year in comparison with how much was newly produced the year before. It is a comparison of the size of the increments.

But what separates countries between rich and poor is not so much the *flow* of newly produced goods and services but rather the *stock* of capital and other productive assets that the economy already possesses that allow that flow of output to be produced.

To understand the difference, think of a production possibility curve. The distance of the curve from the origin – that is, the amount of output of all kinds that can be produced – is determined in part by the capital, which embodies a particular array of productive technologies and capabilities; in part by the available labour, which is not just a total for the number of workers but embodies all of the knowledge, skills, abilities and personal qualities they possess; in part by the decisions of the economy's entrepreneurs, who have brought all of the factors of production together in the individual enterprises they direct; and finally, by the decisions made by the government in relation to the manner in which the economy was regulated and the wisdom of its spending and taxing decisions.

But crucially, it is the stock of available inputs that is the prime constraint on any economy. And from this stock of particular assets flows the output which we either consume during the year – that is, that we collectively use up entirely – or add to the stock of assets available for future production.

In understanding this, it is also important to appreciate how small the additions are each year. In terms of the production possibility curve, the distance from the origin can be thought of as the flow of output emerging from the stock of productive assets, while the thickness of the curve may be thought of as representing the actual scale of the additional increment made to productivity through the improvements made to the asset base in any year. The offices we work in, the houses we live in, the roads we drive on – most have been there far longer than a year. The accumulated stock of productive factors is what makes the crucial difference in a community's standard of living which will grow only slowly from year to year.

Think of a typical city and its multitude of houses. That is the stock of housing. Each year there is an addition of a number of new houses which are added to the rest. That is the flow. It is the stock of housing that determines whether there are enough places to live. It is the flow of new houses that adds incrementally towards the future, but in any one year hardly makes a dent in the total number of homes available.

In thinking about the National Accounts, the figures are designed as flow variables. They measure the additions to our totals. The figures are estimates of the increase. The underlying stock of productive assets is what makes the flow as large as it is. But what is not measured is the stock of productive assets that are the actual supporting superstructure for the economy taken as a whole. Yet it is this that determines our standard of living and, following Mill, even determines the level of employment a community can sustain at the given level of wages.

GROSS DOMESTIC PRODUCT (GDP)

Within the national accounts, the most commonly used measure of the overall strength of the economy is the data on Gross Domestic Product or GDP.[1] It is an attempt to answer the question of how much is being produced during some period of time, and more importantly, it is used as a measure to show how much more (or less) has been produced during some period in comparison with some earlier period.

On its own the figure is almost meaningless and is almost never presented without placing it in the context of other data at the same time. For GDP itself, the most useful comparative measure is GDP per capita. How much output has there been relative to the number of men, women and children living in the country? Even then the figure is not all that useful since much of what has been produced is not for personal consumption, but at least it is something. The GDP figure on its own says close to nothing and is almost without interpretive value.

The figures are also used to make comparisons of one country with another, either in terms of output levels, or in relation to their relative rates of growth. The problems with such measures are notorious, starting with finding a single currency to measure local GDP in two economies, and then working out from there.

But with all its deficiencies, the rate of growth in this statistic is the most common way in which GDP figures are used in examining an economy. The conceptual aim is to calculate the amount that has been newly produced and compare this increment with the increments made in earlier years. The problem is deciding what to include in the composition of a country's output, and then in finding some way to summarize all of the information contained within a meaningful set of numbers.

A country in one year might produce one set of goods, and then a decade later a quite different set of goods. Comparing the value of the earlier set with the later set requires a large number of issues to be thought carefully about.

Of course, the time frames involved are usually much shorter than a decade. In relation to GDP, the usual periods are between financial years or between quarters, such quarters being the three months ending 31 March, 30 June, 30 September and 31 December. It might thus be said that the growth in the June quarter relative to the March quarter was such-and-such per cent.

But what was growing? The aim is to have some measure of production: how much was produced in one time period, relative to another time period, or in one place relative to some other place.

But in trying to make such estimates, here are a few of the problems:

- There is an enormous variety in the kinds of goods and services that are produced, literally tens of millions of items from paper clips to aircraft; how can they all be added up together?
- Some of what is produced is sold on the market for money while some – such as what is produced in the home or much of what is produced by governments – is not
- Since the only common denominator amongst most of the goods and services produced is the price that has been placed on them by their sellers, where comparisons across time are sought it is necessary to find some means to isolate the change in the level of prices from changes in the level of production. If GDP has doubled, was it because output doubled, or prices doubled, or some combination of the two?
- The range of goods and services produced changes year by year so that in comparing two time periods, especially distant time periods, one is almost literally comparing apples with oranges.

- The range of goods and services produced is different in different places, so it is hard to make comparisons with the production taking place in two different locations.
- Most of what is produced is used as inputs into the production of something else, so the danger of double counting in adding it all up is large.
- Some of what is produced is used as final goods and services which disappear almost immediately after being produced (a restaurant meal, let us say), while some, even if produced as final goods, remain in existence and are used for years on end (such as a kitchen stove).
- There are different levels of production in different time periods with, for example, a fall in output often occurring during the summer months and a large increase in the production of retail items in the period before Christmas.
- Some of what is produced are capital goods used in the production process which last beyond the current time period. How should the stock of accumulated assets be incorporated into current production data?

Each of these questions has been the subject of international debate since the 1930s. It became crystal clear during the Great Depression that some kind of measure of economic output was needed, and it is still needed. How production is measured is a continuously evolving process.

The approaches used by national accounting statisticians have now become so complex that it would be impossible to explain how what is done is actually done. But the following provides some idea of the methodologies now used to provide some sense of how these figures are produced and, more importantly, how they can be interpreted.

Variety of Goods and Services

It is quite clear that an inventory of all of the goods and services produced during some period of time would not provide the kind of information that anyone could possibly use. What is sought is a number which summarizes the whole of the amount produced.

The first approximation of the answer was to find the total sale price of all of the goods and services sold during the relevant time period. For goods sold in the market, each item had a sale price. Adding up all of the prices paid for all of the goods and services sold provides a total aggregate cost of the goods and services that had been bought.

If one adds up everything bought, in that total must also be included the various goods and services that were put up for sale and sold by governments. These might include public utilities such as electricity and telecommunications, public transport and public housing. If government goods or services are sold on the market, they are included as part of purchases and sales and dealt with in the same way as the output of private sector firms.

Government-Produced Goods and Services

Many government-produced goods, however, are not sold on the market and have no prices attached. Governments provide schools, roads, hospitals and the like, often with no direct payments by any of the users. There is also the vast apparatus of the public service for which no market payments are ever made.

These are forms of production that obviously cannot be left out and yet there is no associated market price for any of them. The answer, therefore, has been simply to include public sector activity 'at cost'.

What does it mean to include these expenditures 'at cost'? It is to incorporate the entire non-marketed segment of public expenditure into the National Accounts by using the amount that the government has paid as a proxy for value added. If the government paid an annual salary to someone of $75 000, irrespective of what that person did, it would be recorded as $75 000 worth of value. The expenditure would just go in as it is.

Government investment would be included in the same way, with its full production costs being recorded. The outlays would be recorded as its addition to value.

In that way, while the wages of teachers in the private sector would only be incorporated as part of the income received from private school fees, the cost of employing teachers in public schools would have their wages included directly without the intermediation of anyone actually paying for the service other than through taxation.

As a result, even government activities that have created no value added, or have created less value than the government outlay, appear in the National Accounts as having contributed to GDP to the full extent of the government expenditure. This is an area that can and does lead to overestimates of an economy's real level of production.

The famous example of a stimulus programme that consists of one group of people digging holes and a different set of people filling in these same holes again is recorded as economic activity, enters straight into GDP but obviously creates no additional economic value.

Home-Produced Goods and Services

But it is not just government-produced goods that fail to go through the market and whose value adding is therefore difficult to estimate. There are also home-produced goods and services. A meal eaten in a restaurant is a marketed activity. An identical meal prepared and eaten at home is not. There is therefore no actual market transaction to provide a valuation. It is the same thing with home-made wines or home-made anything. There is no market transaction, although there clearly has been value-adding activity. Since value-adding production has obviously taken place, what should be done so far as the national accounts are concerned, especially since such activities are so immensely difficult to measure?

The answer has been to ignore for national accounting purposes the value produced by home production. If an activity is undertaken by private persons in the home but there is no sale transaction, then it is left out of the national accounts. This may cause some underestimate of the total level of production, but so long as there is not much variation between time periods in the amount of home production, the growth rate between periods, the actual figure that is usually being looked for, will not be much affected.

But while there may be a small effect, that is not the same as no effect. Comparisons between distant time periods or different countries are affected.

GDP is by no means an accurate measure of the elusive estimate of total production that is the underlying aim, since with government activities much is included that does not represent actual value created, while with home-produced goods much is left out that does. It may not matter if the aim is to measure employment-creating activity, which is the assumption of a Keynesian model, but it does seriously underestimate per capita production.

Range of Products

One further complication in making comparisons of the level of production between two time periods is the certainty that there will be changes in the composition of goods and services offered up for sale. Between two quarters the differences are minimal, and even over the period of a year the changes are unlikely to be significant.

But as time goes by, the larger the differences become. New products are introduced while older products disappear. Innovation and product development continue at every moment. The wider apart two time periods are, the more diverse the products on sale are certain to be.

There are also shifts in the level of demand for some goods relative to others, so that even if there were exactly the same products put up for sale, they would be found in different proportions. Demand for some products increases while the demand for others falls away, if for no other reason than that relative prices change. This ebb and flow is ongoing.

Beyond even the goods that have come and gone are the improvements in goods and services which now take place routinely. What might have been classified as a 'stove' in 1950 is a far different device from a 'stove' today. The national accounts must be able not just to record expenditure, but to incorporate quality improvements as well.

Differences in the Range of Products between Geographical Regions

Production statistics are used to make comparisons between regions as well as time periods. And here again it is typical for different regions to produce a different range of products. In fact, it would be unusual to the point of impossibility for two geographical areas to be producing or even purchasing exactly the same goods and services.

Different parts of the world, even different parts of the same country, will have different demands made on their productive apparatus. Even the weather will affect the kinds of housing constructed and clothing worn.

Amongst the most important reasons for the production of different goods and services in different regions is the existence of trade. Some parts of the world specialize in particular kinds of products and exchange those for the products of other regions. This is almost as true within individual nations as it is internationally. Specialization and trade are certain to cause production to be different in one region in comparison with another.

Double Counting

Most of the outputs in an economy are inputs into something else, as some product that is either almost immediately transformed through production, such as cloth in the making of a shirt, or used as a necessary component in value-adding production, such as the fuels in a transport network. These disappear into the productive process and no longer exist as they once did.

Thus, where cloth is used in producing an item of clothing, it would be double counting to include the production of the cloth separately from the production of the shirt. The economy did not produce two separate items, a piece of cloth and then a shirt. It produced, first, a piece of cloth and that piece of cloth was transformed into a shirt.

Ensuring that production of the cloth and then production of the shirt are not separately added into the production total is absolutely necessary to prevent a vast overestimate of the amount of actual production which did take place.

Consumption Goods versus Capital Goods

There are then the capital goods which are produced so that they can be used to produce something else. There are machines which are used to produce other machines, such as the capital equipment that is used to build industrial sewing machines. There are then machines which are used as part of the production process, such as these sewing machines which are used to produce clothing.

The production of such capital equipment presents a much larger problem than the production of the various forms of inputs that are totally used up during a period of time. The labour time, electricity and cloth used up are gone, but not so the capital equipment. Capital equipment will under normal circumstances survive the period of production and often continue to contribute for years on end.

And, of course, a sewing machine can be bought by a business and can be bought by a final user for the home. The same item, depending on the use to be made of it, can be either a final good or an input into the production process. These two entirely different purposes for an identical item need to be distinguished when calculating the level of production.

Depreciation

The use of Gross Domestic Product is a reflection of the fact that the national accounting data are not adjusted for depreciation. That is, they are not adjusted for the effects on the future productiveness of capital equipment that is eaten away during the production process.

The wear and tear on capital equipment is part of the cost of production. Each day that an item of capital is used brings it a day closer to the moment when it loses all effective economic value. The amount worn away by use is the depreciation. That GDP is a gross estimate means that no adjustment is made for this loss in economic value.

Depreciation is the opposite of investment. It is the value lost in the use of capital equipment. The national accounts ignores this lost value. The only aspect of capital equipment that is recorded is its first sale to its first owner. After that, since it is no longer part of the production process, its existence forms no part in the recording of GDP.

That these are gross estimates is a serious shortcoming in the measure of output. As discussed under stocks and flows, the productiveness of an economy is dependent on the already existing stock of capital and only very slightly on the new increments added in any year. Part of the annual investment is replacement for what has been used up, so that the gross investment data published do not fully reflect the net addition to the capital stock. Even a positive investment figure may cover an actual reduction in the stock of productive capital in an economy if the additions do not fully compensate for the productive losses which are not recorded.

Seasonality

When dealing with quarterly data, movements between periods will be affected by the normal levels of production that can be expected at different times of the year.

The most obvious shifts in the level of activity related to the calendar are the large increases in production and retail sales which typically occur in the lead-up to Christmas. It can be expected that December quarter production levels will typically be far greater than the level of production in the March quarter.

If growth statistics do not take this into account, there will at certain times in each year be an apparent drop in output that is fully predictable, has no economic meaning, but which will affect perceptions about the actual underlying rate of economic growth, unless adjustments are made to the statistical series. These will be followed by upturns that are equally meaningless in economic terms.

These factors are described as seasonality, and statistical series which are adjusted for these factors are referred to as the 'seasonally adjusted' data. Most economic series are produced in both the non-seasonally adjusted and seasonally adjusted forms, but no discussion of statistics ever deals with the non-seasonally adjusted series where seasonally adjusted data are available. The non-seasonally adjusted data are almost always used only as a staging post on the way to calculating the seasonally adjusted and trend figures.

Trend

Even within the seasonally adjusted data there are large and frequent movements that cause the data to move upwards and downwards. These are due to irregular and usually unpredictable changes that are unrelated to the seasons. But whatever might be their cause, this can have a significant effect on the data.

There are therefore shifts in statistical data that again can cloud the ability to see into the data and understand their longer-term underlying direction. Therefore, there has been the introduction of trend data in some series.

What the trend data do is to remove the effects of these irregular events so that the statistical series is 'smoothed'. The irregular upwards and downwards jags in the numbers are taken out, and what is left is a series that is intended to show the actual underlying movement in the direction of some economic variable.

Measuring GDP

So to summarize, in measuring production, what is needed is a means to do all of the following:

- find some kind of summary statistic representing all of the immense number of goods and services produced during a period of time;
- find some means to deal with goods and services provided outside the market, which are usually either those goods and services produced by governments for which direct payments are not made, or those goods produced by individuals for themselves where no payments are made;
- find some means of incorporating changes in the composition of the goods and services produced between time periods or between different geographical regions;
- bring together both goods that have been sold on the market and those that have not;
- recognize that some goods and services are used as inputs into the production of other goods and services, while some are produced for final consumers or as capital investment;
- for quarterly data, incorporate into the data the 'seasonally' different levels of production that can be expected to take place at different times of the year;
- and also for the quarterly data, adjust for the irregular events that can distort the pattern of production and disguise the actual direction of an economic statistic.

Clearly, the only common factor that can be used in recording the vast range of goods and services produced in an economy during a period of time is to put some kind of monetary value onto the level of output. Only by providing a valuation can everything be reduced to some measure that is, for most of the goods and services produced, easily found.

GDP is therefore measured as a money value. A figure for output is provided that, at its crudest level, represents the total amount of money that would be required to purchase everything that has been produced and included as part of this measure.

But not everything produced is included. The most important exclusions are goods and services produced by individuals for themselves, and which have not been part of a market transaction. A bed made at home is not a market activity and is therefore excluded; a bed made in a hotel by someone else and for payment is included. They are both productive activities, but one is left out and the other is kept in.

Adding Together Private and Public Sector Activity

Of goods produced outside the home, there are firstly those goods and services which have been produced and put up for sale. These are virtually all private sector forms of production as well as some produced by the public sector (such as public transport).

Private sector activity comes with a ready-made price and transaction cost. These can be directly recorded.

A large proportion of public sector activity, however, occurs outside the market (such as public service activities and state-run schools) and therefore does not have a sale price. Since there is no price attached, as has already been noted, the convention has become to include public sector activity 'at cost'. That is, whatever the level of public sector outlay, this is included as the value added of these forms of activity.

Thus, at the very core of the national accounts is a methodology that equates the results of market-directed private sector activity which can only survive where a profit has been earned, with public sector activity which requires no test other than that the government has chosen to fund whatever the expenditure happens to be.

It need hardly be pointed out that governments are not profit-oriented entities but choose to fund activities for a wide variety of reasons, the creation of net value not necessarily being the most important.

Exports and Imports

It is also important that goods sold to overseas residents (exports) and bought from overseas residents (imports) are properly accounted for.

Imports are made up of goods and services which are bought within the domestic economy but were not produced within the domestic economy. Exports are goods produced within the domestic economy but not bought within the domestic economy.

Therefore, if we are interested in the level of production in an economy, we have to net out the level of imports. At the same time, we have to include within our production totals our exports, the amount of output produced domestically but not purchased domestically. There is therefore a need to add in exports (usually designated by the letter X) and take away the amount of imports (usually designated by M). Therefore, within the national accounting identities, there is often the expression '$X - M$' which means exports minus imports.

CALCULATING GDP

There are three methods used to calculate GDP which in theory are identical, but because of computational problems as well as some conceptual questions never come out exactly the same. The most often discussed methodology is what is known as the 'expenditure' method. The other two are referred to as the 'value added' and 'income' approaches to measuring national output.

Expenditure Method

The most well-known approach used to calculate GDP, the method most commonly found in public discussion, is what is known as the expenditure method. It attempts to calculate how much it would have cost to buy everything that was produced. But even though it is the most frequently discussed methodology, because its framework has been adopted into macroeconomic theory, it is in its own way the most confusing to understand properly.

In understanding this approach, it is important to recognize that only final goods and services are counted. Since produced inputs are embedded into the production of other outputs, there would be a massive level of double counting if these inputs were not factored out of the estimates.

The methodology employed is to add together the expenditure on all final goods and services bought. A final good is classified either as a good or service sold to its final consumer, or as a form of capital (that is, machinery, plant and equipment) expected to last for an extended period of time and not be immediately used up during production.

In addition, capital is an item of production that has been added to the inventory of a business even if the intention is eventually to sell whatever it is to its final consumer.

The production of capital goods and inventories is classified as investment, with investment listed as a separate category of final good.

A shirt bought by its final consumer is classified as a consumption item. The cloth that goes into making a shirt, however, is classified as a purchased input. It is left out as an independent item of production since it was not purchased by the final user but embodied in the production of the shirt which was bought by a final user. The purchase of a sewing machine by the business, even though also used in the production process, is included independently as a form of final good and recorded as investment.

There are thus two categories of final good whose demands begin in the private sectors, consumption goods (C) and investment (I) goods. These are typically identified in economic discussions by the following arithmetical expression, in which Y is used to designate GDP:

$$Y \equiv C + I$$

That is, total output consists of the total dollar value of final goods and services bought by consumers and business investors.

There are then goods and services bought by governments. These include expenditure on the public service and other forms of public outlays not sold on the market (such as, roads and schools). The letter used in economic discussions to refer to public sector expenditures of this kind is G. The formula can now be written:

$$Y \equiv C + I + G$$

There are then exports, the goods and services purchased by overseas residents. The letter used to designate exports amongst economists is X. The formula for total purchases is now:

$$Y \equiv C + I + G + X$$

This is the total of everything bought from domestic sellers *but it is not the total level of production.* Some of what was sold within the domestic economy was imported from other countries. Imports are designated by the letter M.

We thus have everything bought: $C + I + G + X$.

We have everything imported: M.

If, from the total of everything bought, those parts which were imported are removed, what is left must be what was produced. The expenditure measure of production of GDP is therefore:

$$Y \equiv C + I + G + X - M$$

This is the central identity of the expenditure approach to measuring GDP. The formula will turn up again when looking at macroeconomic theory but rather than it being an identity (note the identity sign ≡), it will then be shown as an equation, where it will be written:

$$Y = C + I + G + X - M$$

There is a very large difference between these two expressions, to which we now turn.

UNDERSTANDING THIS IDENTITY

In using the identity to determine the level of production, it is imperative to understand that what we are dealing with is a *definition*. There is nothing about this formula that indicates that the left-hand side of the expression is the direct result of activities on the right side. Y is of necessity equal to $C + I + G + X - M$ because that is how Y is defined.

The identity sign (≡) is used below to show that in this expression we are dealing with an accounting definition. It is simply true because that is how things have been defined:

$$Y \equiv C + I + G + X - M \tag{1}$$

But when used as part of macroeconomic theory, the expression is typically written in the following way using an equals sign:

$$Y = C + I + G + (X - M) \tag{2}$$

If you are to understand the calculation of GDP using the expenditure approach to the national accounts, this is how the expression should be written using the identity sign, which was shown in (1) above, and with a different set of brackets:

$$Y \equiv (C + I + G + X) - M$$

In this way, the meaning ought to be immediately clear.

$(C + I + G + X)$ is the total amount bought within the economy.

M is what has been imported.

Since there are only two possible places where what has been bought can be produced – that is, either in one's own country or in some other country – if from what has been bought is subtracted what has been imported, what must of necessity remain is what had been produced in one's own country. Thus: Y represents domestic production.

GDP is thus estimated by subtracting imports from total domestic spending. If something was not produced somewhere else, then it must have been produced here.

INTERPRETING GDP

So note this. If the level of imports, M, increased and nothing else changed, the level of production represented by Y would fall. But it should be obvious that an increase in imports does not, of itself, cause a fall in domestic production.

In the same way, GDP does not go up because consumer demand (C) or investment (I) has gone up. It is output that has gone up, and the statistician then makes a decision under which category to record the increased production.

It is an error that many make, and few can resist, to believe that production (Y) changes because of changes in any of the elements on the right-hand side. In an accounting expression the two sides must balance. There is no causation; no change on the left side was 'caused' by what had occurred on the right side of the identity sign.

Whether a change in C, I, G, X or M leads to a change in Y is a matter for determination by economic theory. What is found here is strictly measurement.

Value-Added Method

The aim of the national accounts in estimating the level and growth of production is to measure the level of value-adding production. Here what is done is to add together all of the value added at each stage of the production process. If one thinks only of the private sector, and if an economy were made up only of private sector firms, this would be conceptually the most straightforward.

For each firm there are the total input costs and there is the total revenue. The difference between revenues received and all of the costs incurred is the value added created by the firm. Adding up all of the value added created by every producer in an economy provides a measure of total value added.

However, because much production takes place in the public sector, it is impossible to employ such a straightforward methodology. Instead, government spending is included as if all such public outlays are of themselves value adding and growth producing in the same way as private sector value-adding activity.

Income Method

The final method for calculating the level of production is what is known as the income method. It is, in a sense, a reworking of the value-added methodology. Using value added to measure output, the net receipts are the measure. Using the income method, the distribution of those receipts to their different recipients is recorded.

Businesses receive payments when they sell their productions. These payments are then divided amongst a series of groups and individuals. Some go to wage earners. Some go to those who have rented their premises to businesses. Some go to those who earn profits. And some are taken by government in the form of indirect taxation.

Thus, in the income method, all payments received are broken up into the different ways in which business income can be distributed. A business receives various amounts of payments from its customers and these payments become the various forms of income received by those with a claim to share in the amounts outlaid. These are:

- the wages, salaries and other forms of compensation received by employees;
- the profits earned by entrepreneurs;
- the rental incomes of property owners;
- the indirect taxes received by governments.

Adding up these payments must give the same total as the amount originally spent, and also equal the total value added of the economy. This is the third measure of GDP.

ACCOUNTING FOR MOVEMENTS IN THE PRICE LEVEL

The total level of GDP when first calculated is recorded as a sum of money spent at the time of purchase. Whichever approach is used, the figures are recorded at the time the transaction was made and therefore each is recorded at the price level when the transaction occurred. This is described as GDP in *nominal terms* or at *current prices*.

But there is little interest on most occasions in the total money value of production. What in fact is of interest is the growth in production that has taken place between two periods of time: how much more output has there been in the second period relative to the first.

But the total level of GDP as measured in *current* prices of the time can increase because either more output has been produced or the prices charged have gone up. That is, in the first period there is the volume of output (Q_1) which was sold at first-period prices (P_1). That is, GDP in period 1 is the total amount produced multiplied by the prices at which this production was sold:

$$GDP_1 = P_1 * Q_1 \text{ (or more precisely, } GDP_1 = \Sigma P_1 Q_1\text{).}^2$$

And in the second period there is the volume of output (Q_2) which was sold at second-period prices (P_2):

$$GDP_2 = P_2 * Q_2 \text{ (or again, to be more precise, } GDP_2 = \Sigma P_2 Q_2\text{)}$$

The interest is in the increase in the volume of output from Q_1 to Q_2. How is this increase to be measured? How can the effect of increasing prices be removed from the totals?

The answer, which is fantastically more complex to do than to state, is to calculate GDP in every period at the prices charged during some arbitrarily chosen base period. This is described as the level of *real* GDP. Thus:

$$Real\ GDP_2 = P_1 * Q_2$$

The real level of GDP in the second period is calculated as the second period's output at first-period prices. So when the real growth rate is calculated, prices cancel out.

Numerical Calculation

The real data are usually only calculated for the individual components of the expenditure series. It is a very complex process but all a user needs to know is that adjustments have been made for the individual components of the calculation, for *C*, *I*, *G*, *X* and *M* as well as each of the individual sub-components beneath these.

But while the necessary price indexes can only be calculated for the expenditure series and its components, the real figures are provided for each of the GDP estimates, although even here the necessary price indexes are usually calculated from the expenditure series.

The figures are published as an amount denominated in the local currency. It will thus be said that GDP was so many millions for the year, and in the most recent quarter the seasonally adjusted level of GDP was also so many millions, which is usually a figure around one-quarter the size of the annual total.

GROWTH RATES

In virtually all cases, the interest in the figure produced is not in the level of output but in its rate of growth. There is seldom an interest in the GDP figure itself, and even GDP per capita is seldom quoted. The usual interest is in comparing GDP during some period of time with the same statistic during a different period of time.

Suppose, for example, in the previous year the real annual level of GDP was $480 000 million and in this year the figure rose to $501 600 million, again estimated in real terms.

To calculate the annual growth rate, the procedure would be the normal means of calculating a percentage change:

$$Annual\ Real\ Growth\ in\ GDP = \frac{501\,600m - 480\,000m}{480\,000m} \times 100$$

$$= \frac{21\,600m}{480\,000m} \times 100$$

$$= 4.5\%$$

Thus, the real level of GDP has been estimated to have grown by 4.5 per cent over the previous year.

The growth rate between any two periods can be found in this way, and it can be calculated for any of the series produced in the national accounting statistics.

Usually, of course, the calculation does not work out to some exact whole percentage movement, so that the growth rate must be rounded. The convention is that for almost all economic statistics, only a single decimal point is shown for growth rates.

CONSUMER PRICE INDEX

Measurements of price movements in general have a wide variety of uses and are essential to the monitoring of the state of the economy.

At the very minimum, measures of price movements are needed as a measure of inflation, the rate at which prices are growing.

But possibly even more important is the use of a price index to convert economic indicators, which are shown in terms of current or nominal prices, into real measures of activity.

Nominal wages, for example, is the average wage rate calculated in the price level of the time. But if the interest is in comparing the purchasing power of wages at different times, since the price level will have changed between the two periods, they must be converted, using some indicator of price movement, into a measure of the real wage.

Price measures are almost invariably calculated as an index, which means that these figures are pure numbers. That is, they have no units associated with them. GDP measures, for example, are typically calculated in terms of the local currency, while a price index will have no units of any kind.

Price indexes being just a number, their sole purpose is to examine the rate of increase in whatever is being measured. Sideways comparisons with other measures, such as the level of prices in different places, cannot be calculated using price indexes. Only the rate of increase in prices in a single place between two time periods can be measured.

An economy produces many forms of price index. Anything that has a price, such as manufactured goods, airline services or imports, can have a price index calculated. However, the most frequently discussed price index is for consumer prices.

The Consumer Price Index (CPI) is calculated in virtually every country, and all are based on the same international standard although with much local variation. It is a system that has continued to evolve, as has every other statistic, but the basic outline for calculation is generally clear, at least in concept. Creating the index and keeping its estimate relevant is, however, difficult.

The Basket of Goods and Services

To create a price index of any kind, it is necessary to know which prices are to be included in the index. Food, but which foods? Clothes, but which clothes? And so with every kind of good or service put up for sale. Which among all of the consumer goods and services sold are to be included in the index?

But not only do you need to know which items to price, you also need to have some idea of how many units of each item to include. A price index has to match the average expenditure patterns of the population who are paying the prices. It is not enough to know that they buy bread but how much bread? It is useful to know that people go to the doctor, but how often?

The aim in constructing an index is to mirror the 'average' expenditure of whichever group the prices relate to. If it is manufactured goods, then you have to know not just what was bought but also how many units were bought of each item.

With the purchases of consumers, it is not enough to know that a typical household has bought bread, furniture and overseas trips, but also how much is spent on each of these during the measurement period.

Therefore, what is whimsically called a 'basket of goods and services' is put together, which is in reality a list of the average number of units of each individual good or service bought by the target population during some specified period of time, such as a quarter or across a full year.

The first step in making price estimates is usually to conduct some kind of household expenditure survey to find out what people buy and in what quantities. For some items, like loaves of bread and cartons of milk, more than a single item is bought in each time period. But others, such as home computers, cars and fridges, are bought only every so often, so that only a fraction of a unit would be bought during the relevant period.

The list would be different in different countries, even in different locations within a single country. A different mix of products can be expected to be purchased in different places, because of different income levels, relative costs, cultural traditions or any number of other factors that would lead to a preference for one set of goods and services rather than another.

The list of items in the basket of goods – and there are typically hundreds of items included in the CPI of most major economies – is then priced. Employees of the statistical agency go to places where these items are sold, find the prices, which are then recorded. If a product is on special offer and the price is lower than usual, the actual sale price, not its normal price, is included.

The total cost of the basket of goods becomes the basis for the Consumer Price Index.

How the Index is Constructed

When all of the items are priced, the cost of purchasing this set of goods is calculated. The total is the basis for the index but is not the index itself.

Suppose in the base year – that is, the year from which all movements are calculated – the total cost of the basket of goods was $850. Because it is the base year, the index is arbitrarily given the value of 100.0. Although there are exceptions, the base year is almost invariably given this value.

But the arbitrary attribution of the index at 100.0 is irrelevant to the purpose that these indexes are for: it is the growth in the level of the index that is important.

In the base year the cost of the basket of goods and services is $850 and the index is equal to 100.0. In the second year, the cost of buying exactly the same basket of goods and services may have risen to $880. This is an increase, after rounding, of 3.5 per cent.

The index number is then raised by 3.5 per cent, in this case from 100.0 to 103.5. The statistical agency then publishes the 103.5 index as the CPI.

One can then calculate the growth in the level of prices by calculating the percentage change in prices in the normal way, using the indexes in the two years. What is therefore published is not the money cost of the bundle of goods and services but the movement in the index which reflects the underlying movement in the cost of the basket of goods and services. Therefore, in this instance what is published is a new index, which is 3.5 per cent higher than the previous index, which is 103.5.

Then with the index figure of 103.5 the increase in the price level relative to the previous period can be calculated as a normal percentage change.

$$\text{Movement in CPI} = \frac{103.5 - 100.0}{100.0} \times 100$$

$$= \frac{3.5}{100.0} \times 100$$

$$= 3.5\%$$

Suppose that in the next year, the total cost of the bundle of goods and services rises to $916. This is an increase over the previous year's cost of $880 of 4.1 per cent. But again, the cost of the basket of goods and services is not published, only the index number, which is made 4.1 per cent higher than the previous year's index of 103.5. The index thus becomes 107.7 which is 4.1 per cent higher than 103.5.

To calculate the movement in the price level, again a percentage change between the two indexes is calculated in the normal way.

$$Movement\ in\ CPI\ (2nd\ period) = \frac{107.7 - 103.5}{103.5} \times 100$$

$$= \frac{4.2}{103.5} \times 100$$

$$= 4.1\%$$

It would then be said that consumer prices had risen by 4.1 per cent.

The movement in the price level can then be calculated between any two time periods. Suppose the interest was in the growth in prices over the two-year period. This would be done by calculating the percentage change in the index over that two-year period, when it rose from 100.0 to 107.7. The calculation, as before, would be:

$$Movement\ in\ CPI\ (2nd\ period) = \frac{107.7 - 100.0}{100.0} \times 100$$

$$= \frac{7.7}{100.0} \times 100$$

$$= 7.7\%$$

That is, the growth in prices across the two years would have been 7.7 per cent.[3]

Real Movements in Economic Indicators

Price indexes are also of immense value in calculating the 'real' movements in economic indicators which are given in current prices. Take, for example, the data on wages which show the following changes:

Year 1 $50 000
Year 2 $52 000
Year 3 $53 500

If, during this period of time, the price level has also risen, the question then is whether the purchasing power of the money wage has increased. The way to do this is to use movements in a price index to estimate the real growth in wages.

Using the CPI calculated in the previous section, the means to estimate the growth in the real wage is firstly to calculate the real wage in each year:

$$Real\ Wage = \frac{Nominal\ Wage}{Index} \times 100$$

Therefore, to calculate the real wage in each of these three years:

$$Real\ Wage\ Year\ 1 = \frac{\$50\,000}{100.0} \times 100 = \$50\,000$$

$$Real\ Wage\ Year\ 2 = \frac{\$52\,000}{103.5} \times 100 = \$50\,240$$

$$Real\ Wage\ Year\ 3 = \frac{\$53\,500}{107.7} \times 100 = \$49\,675$$

Thus, in Year 2 the real wage was higher than in the first year, while in Year 3 it fell not just below its real level in the previous year but below the real level even in the first year.

This technique can be used to bring any series affected by changes in the price level to a set of base-year prices so that changes in the real level of an economic indicator can be monitored.

EMPLOYMENT AND UNEMPLOYMENT

The third measure of economic activity is in many ways the most important. Certainly in political terms it is the most important, since allowing the number of unemployed to rise significantly will create problems for any government that is at all responsive to community concerns.

In purely economic terms, unemployment is a measure of wasted opportunities for an economy. Those who are unemployed could have contributed to the productive potential of the economy. Their being unemployed has deprived the community of the goods and services that could have been produced had they found productive work. And for the unemployed themselves, their workplace skills can atrophy so that the longer they are out of work, the less employable they become. And for that same reason, the longer an individual is out of work, the more difficult it becomes to find an employer.

But there is also the human dimension which is even more important, since it is largely through paid work that individuals earn the incomes that allow them to buy the goods and services they need and want. There are potentially even deeper psychological and emotional effects of unemployment that can make being without work a personally devastating experience.

Keeping unemployment as low as possible is therefore one of the crucial tasks that a government is responsible for.

The Unemployment Rate

The unemployment rate is the most important measure of unemployment. And here the underlying definitions are in some ways quite straightforward, but because of the difficulty in measuring each of the core concepts this is nonetheless more complex than would at first appear.

To calculate the unemployment rate you first need to know the number of persons who are unemployed. You then need to know the total number of persons who are already working so that you can have an estimate of the total number of persons in the labour force, since not everyone without a job wants one.

The unemployment rate is then calculated as the number of persons unemployed as a proportion of the labour force. And who is considered to be a member of the labour force? Everyone who is already working plus everyone who is not working but is *officially* classified as unemployed.

At its most simple, the number of unemployed is a ratio of those who would like to have paid work as a proportion of the labour force. And who is considered to be a part of the labour force? Everyone who is already working, plus everyone not working but who wants to have a job. That is:

Labour Force = Number of Employed Persons + Number of Unemployed Persons

Or to rearrange this expression, we can see that the number of unemployed persons is represented by the following:

Number of Unemployed Persons = Labour Force – Number of Employed Persons

And to calculate the unemployment rate the following calculation is used:

$$Unemployment\ Rate = \frac{Number\ of\ Unemployed\ Persons}{Labour\ Force} \times 100$$

These are the concepts. How are the individual elements measured?

Labour Force Survey

In every country there is an official unemployment rate. Where does it come from? How is it possible to know how many people in an economy are working, not working, want to work or are available to take a job?

The aim is to turn these concepts into a statistical measure. Because even if one has a precise idea of what ought to be measured, operationally it is less clear-cut since each term in the calculation must have something that can actually be measured.

Moreover, it is necessary to have a means to put numbers to the items that are to be included. To say that the unemployment rate is a ratio of the number of unemployed relative to the labour force still requires someone to know how many there are in each category.

The means of calculation is therefore preceded by a statistical survey of a sample of households, in which individuals are asked whether they are employed or unemployed. Thus, not all households are in the survey, only a very small proportion of the total population is at any time included. But it is from this labour force sample survey that the data are taken.

The way this is done is as follows. Someone from the national statistical agency makes contact with those households that have been selected to be in the survey. A series of questions are prepared which are asked of individuals living in the selected households. It is the answers to these questions that determine the number of those who are recorded as employed, those who are determined to be unemployed and those who are considered to be outside the labour force.

The Employed

The first issue is to separate the employed from those who are either unemployed or outside the labour force. It is also necessary to make a distinction between those who have chosen not to work and those who are deemed too young to work.

The first threshold question asks who is over the official working age, because only those over that age can be considered part of the labour force. The minimum age for inclusion is different in different countries. No international standard exists.

The second set of questions then relates to whether the person had paid work during the survey week. Each statistical agency chooses its time period that the data are restricted to.

Who, then, is counted as employed? Which comes down to the question: how long does one have to have worked for payment during the survey period to be considered employed? So far as the official statistics are concerned – which is the international standard – someone need only have had one hour of paid work in the previous week to be considered to have been employed.

For many of those unused to such statistical definitions, it often appears ridiculous that the division between employed and not employed is a paltry single hour of paid work. The statistic is not, however, intended to differentiate between those who had a full satisfying week of work that will provide an adequate income, but merely to register those who had worked at all.

Certainly, as a measure of what we would like to really know, there is something lacking. But as a statistical measure of employment, it is seen to be preferable to pick up virtually everyone who was paid for their efforts during the sample week than to leave such individuals out.

The issue is thus not whether they would have preferred to have worked longer than they did, particularly since most of those who had worked only one hour in a week probably would have preferred more hours of paid work. But here the issue is whether they have been paid for any work at all, and one hour is the length of time required for statistical inclusion into the paid workforce.

Then, if an individual has not worked, there are questions to determine whether someone was away from their paid employment because they were on holiday or sick leave. If they normally worked but were ill or on vacation, they are included in the total of those employed.

The Unemployed

To be unemployed is, so far as the statistics are concerned, not as simple as it sounds. It is not enough to have been without work and have wished to work. There are a series of criteria that must be met that determine whether one is to be officially included as unemployed. An individual:

- must want paid work;
- must be old enough to be included in the labour force statistic;
- must not have worked for a single hour during the sample week;

- must have actively taken steps to find work (for example, applied for a job, looked at newspaper adverts, and so on);
- must be capable of commencing work in the period immediately ahead (for example, not finishing a course, no child-minding problems, and so on).

If the person wants to work, is over the minimum age, did not work in the previous week, actively took steps to find a job and was able to start paid employment, then that person would be officially counted as unemployed. Otherwise, they are classified as not part of the labour force. They are considered neither employed nor unemployed.

From these survey results, the statistical agency then publishes a number showing the official level of unemployment, employment and the total labour force.

Seasonally Adjusted Data

Even these raw numbers are not sufficient, since the figures are often not of much use on their own.

Because there are periods when employment is typically high, say in the period leading up to Christmas, and other periods when employment is typically low, such as during the summer months, an adjustment to the data is required. If there were not some adjustment made for these seasonal differences then the numbers would not be of much use in monitoring month-to-month movements.

There is therefore a calculation done to 'seasonally adjust' the employment data in the same way that is done with the National Accounts, and indeed with virtually every other series produced by national statistical agencies.

With the employment and unemployment data, the raw data are virtually never quoted. The figures most often quoted are those which have been seasonally adjusted. (There are also in many economies 'trend' data, which are adjusted for both seasonal influences and the irregular occurrences that affect employment levels.)

Calculating the Unemployment Rate

Suppose the figures in Table 9.1 are collected by the national statistical agency on employment and unemployment.

In the first period there were 10 000 persons employed and 500 who were unemployed. The 'labour force' was the total of the employed and unemployed, which is 10 500 persons.

Table 9.1 *Sample data on the employed, unemployed, labour force and the unemployment rate*

Period	Employed	Unemployed	Labour force	Unemployment rate
1	10 000	500	10 500	4.8
2	11 000	600	11 600	5.2
3	12 000	700	12 700	5.5
4	13 000	800	13 800	5.8
5	14 000	850	14 850	5.7
6	15 000	880	15 880	5.5

The unemployment rate is found as a simple percentage of the number of unemployed relative to the total labour force:

$$Unemployment\ Rate = \frac{Number\ of\ Unemployed\ Persons}{Labour\ Force} \times 100$$

$$= \frac{500}{10\,500} \times 100$$

$$= 4.8\%$$

In the table, it will be seen that the unemployment rate continues to rise from 4.8 per cent in Period 1 until it reaches 5.8 per cent in Period 4. It then falls to 5.7 per cent in Period 5 and 5.5 per cent in Period 6.

But what is worth noting is that the number of unemployed persons keeps rising. The higher the number of persons in the labour force, the larger the number of unemployed people it takes to raise the rate of unemployment.

Discouraged Workers and Underemployment

It might have been noticed that to be unemployed it is necessary to be actively looking for work. Some people, however, are unemployed, would like to work, but have given up trying to find a job after making the effort but not being taken on.

There is a specific category for such people and it is within a classification called 'discouraged workers'. Such potential workers are not included in the labour force data and are therefore not included in the unemployment data. The unemployment data, therefore, to the extent that discouraged workers are an important group, underestimate the actual dimensions of the unemployment problem.

There are also many who work part-time but would prefer to work full-time, but cannot get a full-time job. The economy is therefore deprived of the additional hours of work they would prefer to contribute, while they earn less income than is optimal from their perspective.

Together with discouraged workers, such underemployment is also a measure of the underperformance of the labour market in generating jobs for all who want them.

BALANCE OF PAYMENTS

Balance of payments statistics are the numbers that are of least interest to the general public. And in many ways, this is a reflection of the difficulty in making clear-cut judgements about the figures and what they show.

What the balance of payments data provide are, firstly, a recording of the purchase and sale of goods and services between the home country and the rest of the world. These data are then combined with a series of measures of the flow of monetary payments that always allow the total to balance. The balance of payments data are literally a series of accounting records.

Since the sales of goods and services to foreign countries (exports) will never precisely equal the purchases of goods and services from foreign countries (imports), which is what is what is calculated in the *current account*, the *capital account* records the balancing flow of payments and debts incurred that have permitted the flow of exports and imports to take place.

There can, for example, be a deficit on the current account if imports are greater than exports. Deficits have a negative connotation, but the reality is that there is nothing intrinsically wrong with such deficits. It is the way economies work, and that there is a balancing item on the capital account is merely how the two sides of the accounts are made to be equal.

Some idea of the economy itself and its strengths and weaknesses is needed to make sense of the balance of payments statistics on their own.

These are accounts as devised by accountants. Therefore here, and only here in this chapter, the word 'capital' refers to money, finance and credit. Everywhere else, capital means goods and services used in production.

In the days of fixed exchange rates, which meant that the value of a currency in relation to other currencies was specified by every country and never varied other than during a crisis, the balance of payments data held a deadly fascination for governments. If imports began to grow much more rapidly than exports, leading to larger and larger deficits on the current account as time went by, the probability would grow that the country could no longer finance its imports through its exports and raising capital. There could then be weeks of political instability until either the currency was devalued (lowered in price relative to other currencies) or the crisis dissipated as evidence grew that no actual problem existed.

In the present, however, with most exchange rates now *floating*, so that the value of the currency moves upwards and downwards depending on trade and financial conditions, such periodic episodes have almost completely disappeared. The balance of payments has therefore become of little interest outside professional circles, and even then there is no consensus on when a problem can even be said to exist.

Exchange Rates

There is still, of course, widespread interest in the exchange rate, which can and does have profound effects on an economy. Exchange rates in the world of floating currencies are determined in the market, with the supply and demand for a particular currency the subject of the desire of others to own that currency, for trade purposes, finance, travel needs or speculation.

The supply and demand curve shown in Figure 9.1 is for some currency. Its value is determined by the supply and demand for the currency in terms of other currencies.

And as always, it is the *ceteris paribus* conditions that matter most. Whatever causes an increased need or willingness to hold a currency will move the demand to the right, and if there is less need or willingness to hold that currency, then the demand moves to the left.

Since with each exchange rate the price is in terms of the value of every other currency being bought and sold, the underlying complexities are many and varied. But in the market for currencies, expectations play a very large role, with anything expected to cause an increased willingness to hold a currency immediately reflected in a shift to the right of the demand curve, which causes an immediate rise in the value of a currency. Similarly, a fall in the expected value of a currency will cause the value of the currency to immediately fall, since there will be an immediate fall in the demand for the currency. Central banks in every country, however, typically act to stabilize the value of their currencies through buying and selling foreign exchange.

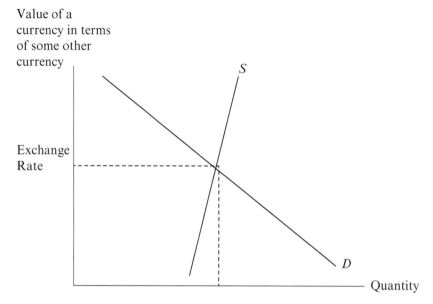

Figure 9.1   Determination of an exchange rate in the market

NOTES

1. Sometimes the most important measure within an economy is the data on Gross National Product (GNP) rather than Gross Domestic Product. The difference for most economies is trivial. It hinges on whether the output was produced within the country (GDP) or was produced by the citizens of a country with some of that production having taken place in foreign lands (GNP).
2. Σ means 'the sum of', here being the total of all transactions that took place.
3. It might be noted that the growth rate is higher than if the 3.5 per cent were added to the 4.1 per cent. This is not rounding error but is due to the effect of compounding. Adding growth rates to get the arithmetical total is inaccurate, and the larger the growth rates involved, the larger the error would be.

APPENDIX: AVERAGE ANNUAL RATES OF GROWTH

One of the most useful techniques for examining data is the appropriate statistical technique for finding the average of a series of growth rates. If one is interested in the average annual growth in some series over the last decade, for example, because of the effects of compounding, merely to divide by ten is inaccurate, and the larger the growth rate, the more inaccurate the measure will be.

Suppose that over that decade the growth was 50 per cent. Dividing by 10 will suggest that the average growth per year had been 5 per cent when in reality it had been 4.1 per cent (after rounding to a single decimal point).

The proper methodology is as follows.

1. Calculate the number of periods (n) between two figures.
2. Divide the later figure by the earlier figure.
3. Using a calculator take the nth root of the answer in (2).
4. Subtract 1 from the answer in (3).
5. Multiply the answer in (4) by 100.

Thus, if between 1969 and 1985, some index had risen from 120.0 to 198.0, the means to calculate the average annual growth rate would be, following the above methodology:

1. The number of periods is found by subtraction: 1985–1969 = 16.
2. Dividing 198.0 by 120.0 leaves a figure of 1.65 (which by subtracting 1 from this result shows that the growth across the period was 65.0 per cent).
3. The 16th root of 1.65 is then shown to be 1.03179. On some calculators this is worked out by the expression '1.65^(1 ÷ 16)'.
4. Subtracting 1 from 1.03179 gives 0.03179.
5. Multiplying 0.03179 by 100 and rounding to one decimal place shows that the average growth rate per time period was 3.2 per cent.

This technique can be used for any kind of statistical series, whether calculated as an index, such as with the CPI, or as a whole numbers, as with the data on GDP.

10. An interlude on the history of economics

In moving from the microeconomic side to macroeconomics, it is a strategic moment in which to have a look at the way in which economic theory developed. An appreciation of how economic theory became what it is, and the steps it took along the way to become what it has now become, will make textbook and mainstream theory easier to follow. Rather than just looking at the theory as if it had been handed down to us as a finished product on tablets, it is useful instead to recognize that it was actual human beings, living in societies in many ways similar to our own although in many other ways different, who carved out of the solid rock of an underlying reality the way we make sense of the world at the present time.

It is also important, as a matter of general cultural awareness, to know the great economists of the past who have had an influence on the way in which we think about economic matters. For good or ill, these people have influenced our lives more than any other group in the social sciences, because it is based on their theories that our economic structures are now organized. This is true irrespective of the kind of economic system one happens to live within.

There is one other reason to read what they wrote: they have an awful lot to teach us about how economies work.

ORIGINS

People have always fed, clothed and housed themselves, but for most of past history what was done was seen as just how it was done. Alternative ways of going about organizing economic structures and institutions was not on anyone's agenda. The traditional way of managing production was generally considered the only way. Whatever evolution did take place, was slow. Any improvements were generally imperceptible to those living at the time. Most of any writing on economics was undertaken as a form of ethical discussion in relation to what was fair and just. What virtually no one discussed until the eighteenth century was how to make economies more prosperous or how to raise the living standards of a community.

What changed all of this came from a number of directions. The industrial revolution was in its infancy but was effecting real improvements in production levels. Rather than all economic and political issues remaining local, the nation state had begun to emerge as the political organizing principle, at least for those nations bordering the North Atlantic. And political theory had begun to point towards individual rights and freedoms as an ethical principle. In England, in particular, the rise of Parliament in relation to the monarchy opened up possibilities that had not existed before.

It was in this environment that the first major writings on economics, then referred to as 'political economy', began to emerge. And while there were many writers at the time, one name emerged which has towered above all others as the first great economist. It was Adam Smith and his *Inquiry into the Nature and Causes of the Wealth of Nations* that changed the entire way economic issues have been conceived ever since. The book was published in 1776 and became an immediate sensation. It has never been out of print.

ADAM SMITH AND CLASSICAL ECONOMICS

The aim of this first great work of economics was to demonstrate the power of individuals acting in their own interests as the potential driving force of economic activity. Rather than needing governments to direct economic activity from above, and making every economic decision a matter for review by government, what Smith argued was that economies were social institutions that could be left to run themselves.

Invisible Hand

At its centre is the argument that individuals, if left to act in their own best interests, would create a world of wealth more efficiently and with more certainty than any other possible way of arranging a nation's economic affairs. The following passage may be the most famous, most quoted passage in the whole of economic theory. It may also have been the single most influential:

> [A merchant] generally, indeed, neither intends to promote the public interest, nor knows how much he is promoting it . . . He intends only his own security; and by directing that industry in such a manner as its produce may be of the greatest value, he intends only his own gain, and he is in this, as in many other cases, led by an *invisible hand* to promote an end which was no part of his

intention. Nor is it always the worse for the society that it was not part of it. By pursuing his own interest he frequently promotes that of the society more effectually than when he really intends to promote it. (Smith [1776] 1976: Book IV, Chapter II, emphasis added)

The 'invisible hand' of Adam Smith was a metaphor for the market. In this passage, Smith made a number of points:

- people who run businesses do not do so because they have some larger social purpose in mind;
- business people do what they do as a way to earn an income;
- but in going about earning their incomes, they actually do a great deal of social good even though it was not their specific intention to do so;
- business people are only trying to create as much value as they can, because whatever value they create they can exchange for other things and in this way earn a living;
- but, unbeknownst to these business people, in acting in their own best interests, by creating value, they are led by that 'invisible hand' to act in ways that often turn out to be very good for society as a whole;
- indeed, had these business people actually decided to do things with the intention of benefiting society, it is uncertain whether they could have done so as effectively as they have by just building their own businesses and running their own firms.

The clear message was that no one had to run the market or the economy in general. The spontaneous actions of individuals seeking to do what is best for themselves would provide the direction and impulse for economic activity. And leaving such matters to the market would create a greater improvement in economic output and human welfare than any other possible set of arrangements. This is how Smith put this argument:

As every individual endeavors as much as he can both to employ his capital in the support of domestic industry, and so to direct that industry that its produce may be of the greatest value; every individual necessarily labors to render the annual revenue of the society as great as he can. (Book IV, Chapter II)

That is, individuals have only so many resources, skills, and so much capital at their disposal. Since individuals are each trying to create the greatest amount of value they possibly can in order to earn their own incomes, when what each individual is doing is seen in relation to society as a whole, the entire economy must at the same time be creating as much value in total as that society is capable of.

Self-Interest and Economic Outcomes

Smith pointed out the motivations behind the production of goods and services by individual businesses. This, too, was a famous and very influential passage from the *Wealth of Nations*:

> It is not from the benevolence of the butcher the brewer, or the baker that we expect our dinner, but from their regard to their own interest. We address ourselves, not to their humanity, but to their self-love, and never talk to them of our own necessities, but of their advantages. (Book I, Chapter II)

In an economy where complete strangers produce for each other, there is nothing to offer someone else to produce for oneself other than what can be given in exchange. We do not go to those who sell to us and tell them how much we need their products. We instead offer something of value to them (usually money) in exchange for what we want.

This is certainly the world in which we live, and it was the world in which Smith lived. Past the village and the world of tradition – outside a world where economies are directed by a central government – economic activity was a process in which both parties saw themselves as gaining through exchange. There was, of course, the entire society of morals, laws and regulations that surrounded the operation of the market whose existence was assumed. But this common-sense statement made an immense impact because things had never before been said just like that. It made the world of commerce and industry appear for the first time as a benevolent activity which would result in greater prosperity for an increasing number of people, which is exactly how it has turned out.

Attitude to Merchants

Not that it should be thought that Smith had a benign view of the merchant class. In one of the more famous passages from the *Wealth of Nations* he discusses the actual motivations that lie behind the ways in which business people act: 'People of the same trade seldom meet together, even for merriment and diversion, but the conversation ends in a conspiracy against the public, or in some contrivance to raise prices' (Book I, Chapter X).

It has been pointed out that Smith, amongst the first true defenders of the market, at no point in the *Wealth of Nations* makes any statement that could be interpreted as partial to merchants and business people as a class. He is highly cynical about their acquisitiveness. But he nevertheless sees these characteristics as being beneficial to society as a whole. Their focused pursuit of gain will ensure they are focused on the management of the businesses they run.

Attitude to Governments

Nor should it be thought that Smith had a kindlier view of governments, which he in fact thought of as even more wasteful, destructive and pernicious than businesses. And in this quote, where Smith talks about employing 'their capitals' he is referring to how private individuals manage their own wealth. This is a statement that has lost none of its relevance since the day it was first penned:

> The statesman who should attempt to direct private people in what manner they ought to employ their capitals would . . . assume an authority which could safely be trusted, not only to no single person, but to no council or senate whatever, and which would nowhere be so dangerous as in the hands of a man who had folly and presumption enough to fancy himself fit to exercise it. (Book IV, Chapter II)

Smith in this passage emphasized the dangers of placing too much economic power into the hands of a government, and especially into the hands of individual political leaders who believe they are capable of directing economic activity. He makes no bones about it. Such concentrations of power are a danger, not just to our economic welfare, but also to our personal freedoms.

Smith also wrote of the dangers of government spending with the kind of insight that the years since have done nothing to diminish the relevance of. The propensity of governments to profligate waste was recognized by Smith in ways that every generation has had to learn over again for itself:

> It is the highest impertinence and presumption, therefore, in kings and ministers, to pretend to watch over the œconomy of private people . . . They [governments] are themselves always, and without any exception, the greatest spendthrifts in the society. Let them look well after their own expence, and they may safely trust private people with theirs. If their own extravagance does not ruin the state, that of their subjects never will. (Book II, Chapter III)

The consequence of the *Wealth of Nations* was to move the economy of England, and thereafter the economies of an increasing proportion of the world, in the direction of market forces. The effect of a greater reliance on markets in every economy where they have been introduced has been unmistakeable and positive. The growth in productivity and economic well-being have been direct results of the introduction of private direction for economic activity.

In looking at Smith, it should be noted that most of what he had described was what would now be called a 'macroeconomic' view of the world. He did not particularly discuss individual markets. He talked literally about the wealth of entire nations; how increased levels of wealth for a country and improved standards of living for the individual inhabitants could be effected. The microeconomic side of Smith's approach was in the concept that leaving economic decision making to individual decision makers would set in motion processes that would lead to a vast improvement in value added per person employed.

The Importance of Saving

Amongst the most important messages provided by Smith was his insight into the crucial role of saving. It was saving that allowed investment to occur; saving, being a decision to postpone current consumption and allow the resources that would otherwise have been used up in producing consumer goods to be used by others to invest, is thus the only mechanism through which economic growth can occur. For a society, saving means increasing expenditure on capital assets such as machinery and buildings. The more that is invested in capital, the faster an economy will grow:

> Wherever capital predominates, industry prevails . . . Every increase or diminution of capital, therefore, naturally tends to increase or diminish the real quantity of industry, the number of productive hands, and consequently the exchangeable value of the annual produce of the land and labour of the country, the real wealth and revenue of all its inhabitants. (Book II, Chapter III)

The basis for investment is saving, which Smith calls 'parsimony'. Saving allows a community's resources to be employed productively, that is, to be used in ways which increase the productive capacity of the economy in general:

> Whatever a person saves from his revenue he adds to his capital, and either employs it himself in maintaining an additional number of productive hands, or enables some other person to do so, by lending it to him for an interest, that is, for a share of the profits. As the capital of an individual can be increased only by what he saves from his annual revenue or his annual gains, so the capital of a society, which is the same with that of all the individuals who compose it, can be increased only in the same manner. (Book II, Chapter III)

Without saving there can be no investment and therefore no economic growth. Saving is the most crucial aspect of economic activity. It is the absolutely necessary ingredient for increasing prosperity:

> Parsimony, and not industry, is the immediate cause of the increase of capital. Industry, indeed, provides the subject which parsimony accumulates. But whatever industry might acquire, if parsimony did not save and store up, the capital would never be the greater. (Book II, Chapter III: 359)

The stock of productive assets available within an economy are the result of past saving, and without that saving they would not exist. This is a conclusion that has remained one of the major insights into the operation of an economy. It is saving that finances investment. It is a conclusion that tends not to be taught, because saving, rather than being an essential for prosperity, is now often portrayed as the villain because saving in excess is now seen (wrongly) as the most important cause of recessions and unemployment.

It is saving that is the absolute necessity as a foundation for economic growth. The modern attitude to saving as the cause of recession is a dangerously misleading view of the true importance of saving in creating growth and prosperity.

Specialization and the Division of Labour

Smith's major microeconomic insight was what he described as specialization and the division of labour. At the workplace, more output per person could be achieved by breaking an entire production process into smaller tasks in which individual workers could excel at the specific parts of the process they had been assigned: 'As it is the power of exchanging that gives occasion to the division of labour, so the extent of this division must always be limited by the extent of that power, or, in other words, by the extent of the market' (Book I, Chapter III).

The division of labour is limited by the extent of the market. This was, in its way, a comment on the advantages of international trade. The greater the size of the market, the more an economy could benefit from the productivity growth that would accompany division of labour at the enterprise and industry level. Small markets are less efficient. Being able to produce and trade would improve the amounts of output available for sale.

Free Trade

On free trade itself, Smith wrote in its defence in ways that have appealed to economists ever since. It is difficult to get around the logic of what he wrote, and the growth in world trade and prosperity since his time has confirmed what was then more intuition and logic than an empirical reality upon the evidence of which he could count. He starts with the observation that if an object is cheaper to buy than to make, then it should be bought and not made. From this he points out that what is true for an individual is true for an entire nation:

> It is the maxim of every prudent master of a family, never to attempt to make at home what it will cost him more to make than to buy . . . What is prudence in the conduct of every private family, can scarce be folly in that of a great kingdom. If a foreign country can supply us with a commodity cheaper than we ourselves can make it, better buy it of them with some part of the produce of our own industry, employed in a way in which we have some advantage. (Book IV, Chapter II)

This, along with much else in Smith, has become part of the central message of economic theory. There has been much elaboration along the way, and much has been qualified in comparison with Smith's views in 1776, but the *Wealth of Nations* remains a repository of economic ideas that provide a very good first approximation of the ideas that may be found in economic texts to this day.

DAVID RICARDO

It was not to be for another 41 years that a book as influential in its own time as the *Wealth of Nations* would be published. This was David Ricardo's *Principles of Political Economy and Taxation*, published in 1817.

What made this book so entirely different and yet revolutionary in its own way was that it was an economics treatise that was modern in its approach. Smith had been expansive and literary. Ricardo was narrowly economic and deeply analytical. His *Principles* began with a series of propositions about how economies worked, and from these axioms he deduced the conclusions that would be translated directly into policy.

And while most of what is found in Ricardo is largely of historical interest, there are, however, a number of aspects of what he wrote that have had a major impact on economic theory up until this day. The first was the core issue of his writings which concerned itself with the distribution of income. Income was distributed with wages going to labourers, rents to property owners and the residual ending up with the owners of business in the form of profits.

Ricardo's discussion of profits, and especially their existence as a residual, was later taken up by Marx who used the same concepts to show, at least according to himself, that profits were nothing other than a surplus skimmed from the productivity of the workers. The workers produced while the profit owners earned large incomes although contributing nothing. Marx therefore argued that it was perfectly sensible to do away with those who took the profits, since payments for their nil contribution to production had no justification. These views, it need hardly be pointed out, are now seen as absolutely erroneous, with the irreplaceable role of the entrepreneur firmly recognized.

Comparative Advantage

There was then Ricardo's theory of comparative advantage, which remains an integral part of economic discussion to this day. In explaining not just why trade occurred but why it could be of advantageous to both parties (something not easily seen, as discussions of trade-related issues down to the present continually show), Ricardo developed a deeper understanding of the role of specialization and trade.

The central idea of comparative advantage is that it is not whether one country is *absolutely* more productive than another that allows trade to occur. What matters is whether one country is *relatively* better at producing something. And note: there are two relativities involved, the first being the relative cost of products within each economy, which is then compared with the second of these relativities, the relative cost of production in both countries taken together.

Take a simple example:

- Suppose in Country A, in *one* hour it can produce either one car or 1000 shirts.
- And suppose in Country B, in *two* hours it can produce either one car or 500 shirts.
- Country B is therefore not as good at producing either cars or shirts, since in one hour it can only produce half a car and 250 shirts.
- But note this. In Country A the cost of one car is 1000 shirts, since every time a car is produced 1000 shirts could have been produced instead. Meanwhile, using the same reasoning, in Country B the cost of one car is only 500 shirts. (That is, in A the *opportunity cost* of one car is 1000 shirts and in B the *opportunity cost* of one car is 500 shirts.)
- So although Country A is *absolutely* better at producing *both* products, it is *relatively* better at producing shirts. Country B is however, not as good at producing either good, but is relatively better at producing cars.

- According to the theory of comparative advantage, Country A should produce only shirts, which it is relatively better at producing. It should sell shirts to Country B and use the money received to buy cars. Meanwhile, Country B should produce only cars and sell these to Country A, and use the money it received to buy shirts.
- The result is that both countries are better off, since both will have more of both products because each is concentrating on what it does comparatively better than the other.
- A, since it is buying cars from an economy where the price is 500 shirts, is better off if it gives anything less than the 1000 shirts it used to pay for each car. Meanwhile B is better off if each time it sells a car to A it receives more than the 500 shirts in return that it used to receive for each car produced.

The 'law of comparative advantage' remains an important element in the explanation of why trade takes place. It shows that countries trade with each other because it makes them better off. If trade did not make a country better off, you may be sure that trade would disappear.

JEAN-BAPTISTE SAY

Given his subsequent importance, the French economist Jean-Baptiste Say must be brought into the story. Say was for the most part a popularizer of the arguments that had been presented by Adam Smith. His *Treatise on Political Economy* was published in 1803 to acquaint the French public with Smith's ideas. But it was not merely a restatement of Smith: Say had a number of innovations of his own.

The first of these was the introduction of a fourth factor of production beyond land, labour and capital. This was the additional input that was brought to the production process by the *entrepreneur*. Say explicitly recognized the crucial importance of the entrepreneur as the initiator and organizer of the production process. It was, as he wrote, through the entrepreneur that value-adding activity was able to take place.

For reasons unknown, independent discussion of the role of the entrepreneur remains relatively uncommon even to this day. Yet without the entrepreneur to identify value-adding possibilities, introduce innovation and then superintend the process all along the way, value-adding production would remain far less common and prosperity would possibly have remained as elusive as it had been in all of the centuries prior to the arrival of the industrial revolution.

Say's Law

But Say's other innovation was the popularization of an economic principle which would be given the name Say's Law, but not until more than a century had gone by since its first discussion by Say in his *Treatise*.

Although there were a number of strands to the surrounding principle, in brief it may be stated as: demand for goods and services is created by value-adding production and by nothing else. For goods to be bought not only must goods be produced, but precisely those goods that others would be willing to buy must be the ones that need to be produced.

From this principle, there arose three broad conclusions that were accepted by the mainstream of the economics profession through until 1936. These are the conclusions based on an understanding of Say's Law:

1. 'Goods buy goods': to buy, one first had to produce goods of one's own, *sell these goods for money* and then use the money received to buy the goods produced by others; thus it is the production of one's own goods that leads to the ability to purchase someone else's, even though money is used as the medium of exchange
2. 'Demand is constituted by supply': in an exchange economy one cannot buy unless they have first supplied, since unless someone supplies they have no money with which to demand
3. 'There is no such thing as a general glut': it is impossible for an economy to produce so much output that there would not be enough buyers for what had been produced, *so long as what has been produced is what people want to buy*; therefore demand deficiency across an entire economy can never be a realistic explanation for recession.

It was the reversal of this last principle in particular, following the publication in 1936 of *The General Theory of Employment, Interest and Money* by the economist John Maynard Keynes – the most influential text on economics written during the whole of the twentieth century – that led to what became known as the 'Keynesian Revolution'. There is more about this below and in the chapter to come.

THOMAS ROBERT MALTHUS

Thomas Robert Malthus wrote one of the most sensational and influential books of all time. In 1798, he published his *On Population* which argued that food production increased only 'arithmetically' while population grew 'geometrically'.

He believed that natural rates of human reproduction if unrestrained, would lead to geometric increases in population. The population would grow in a geometrical progression in a ratio of 2, 4, 8, 16, 32, 64. At the same time, however, food production would increase only in arithmetic progression: 2, 4, 6, 8, 10.

The consequence of these differential rates of growth was that population growth could be expected to outrun food production. Therefore, the availability of food for most people could be expected to be no better than just enough to prevent starvation; while for some, starvation was inevitable.

Population, Malthus argued, would expand right up to the limits set by food production. Moreover, even when productivity grew and economies were able to produce more food, the only result was that population numbers would rise and keep rising until there was again only just enough food to go round.

The sole way out of this dilemma, Malthus argued, was through checks to population growth. 'Moral restraint' would be exercised, so that numbers would be kept down because marriage was delayed and the number of children diminished. And then there were the positive restraints, which would be imposed on populations by external factors, which he named as war, starvation, disease and plague.

Malthusian population theory was embedded into what was described during classical times as the 'iron law of wages'. The purchasing power of wages could never for long rise above the level that would just keep most members of the working class alive. This theory found its way into classical economic theories, including those of Ricardo and Marx. Wages would always descend to subsistence levels, which was why the principle was called an iron law.

There is also an interesting sidelight to Malthus's population theory. Both Darwin and Wallace, the two originators of the theory of evolution by natural selection, reached their conclusions after reading *On Population*. Since population would outrun the available food supplies, there would be a life-and-death struggle amongst all organisms for food to eat. Since only the fittest amongst living organisms would be expected to survive, only those best suited to producing children within existing conditions would win out over the rest, who would perish. The fittest would leave the most descendants, and so it would be the characteristics of those who survived that would predominate in the generations that followed.

UNDERSTANDING SAY'S LAW: MALTHUS AND THE 'GENERAL GLUT'

It was because of his already established fame as the author of *On Population* that when he came to write his own *Principles of Political Economy*, which was published in 1820, his book immediately attracted attention. It commenced a debate that involved every major economist of the time and led within half a dozen years to the publication of a large number of books and pamphlets designed to refute the arguments Malthus had made.

What was at the core of this debate was Malthus's argument that the depressions which had followed the ending of the Napoleonic Wars in 1815 had been caused by a deficiency of demand. Too much was being saved and not enough was being spent to employ the entire working population of England. The result was a 'general glut', or overproduction: too much output relative to the willingness of those with incomes to buy.

Leading the opposition to Malthus's view was Ricardo. In one of the odder aspects in the history of economics, Ricardo and Malthus were the best of friends and frequent visitors to each other's homes. But on general gluts as well as much else, they were in complete disagreement. Their differences were carried on not only in public but also in an ongoing correspondence which was conducted for many years on many topics. And amongst the issues that they corresponded on was the question of overproduction. It was this correspondence that a century later would lead to a revolution in economic thought and the development of macroeconomic theory to demonstrate the possibility of demand deficiency.

JOHN STUART MILL

It was also in this debate that the contours of the classical theory of recession were developed. Indeed, the controversy continued for a generation and was only ended with the publication of John Stuart Mill's *Principles of Political Economy* in 1848. And the overwhelming view of the entire mainstream of the economics profession was that Say's Law was valid, so that demand deficiency, or overproduction as it was more generally called at the time, was never seen as an actual cause of recession.

While there were many theories to account for recessions, and many more would be developed as time wore on, it was accepted with virtual unanimity that recessions were not caused by glutting of markets – that is, by a failure to sell what had been produced – but that the glutting of markets was, whenever it occurred, due to some other set of circumstances.

Mill in his *Principles* spoke for the entire classical school, and his conclusion would be accepted right through to 1936 when Keynes published his *General Theory*. In concluding his argument, Mill wrote:

> I know not of any economical facts . . . which can have given occasion to the opinion that a general over-production of commodities ever presented itself in actual experience. I am convinced that there is no fact in commercial affairs which, in order to its explanation, stands in need of that chimerical supposition. (Mill [1871] 1921: 562)

Nor was this seen as a mere sidelight to other more consequential issues. There are two entirely different sets of assumptions and conclusions that one might reach, depending on whether or not one accepts the existence of demand deficiency as a realistic possibility. Because if one believes that demand deficiency is a realistic possibility, then not only is it necessary to devise policies to ensure that goods are produced and distributed, but it is also necessary to devise policies to make sure that everything produced gets bought. This is Mill again making this argument:

> The point is fundamental; any difference of opinion on it involves radically different conceptions of Political Economy, especially in its practical aspect. On the one view, we have only to consider how a sufficient production may be combined with the best possible distribution; but, on the other, there is a third thing to be considered – how a market can be created for produce. (Ibid.: 562)

To Mill and the classical school, to believe that demand deficiency was even possible so completely confused anyone trying to understand how an economy works that ultimately they would never get past the most basic aspects in trying to think through the mechanics of economic activity. As Mill wrote:

> A theory so essentially self-contradictory cannot intrude itself without carrying confusion into the very heart of the subject, and making it impossible even to conceive with any distinctness many of the more complicated economical workings of society. (Ibid.: 562)

This is the judgement that classical economists made of the economic theories of Malthus. As we shall see, it was these same Malthusian views that would a century later be introduced into mainstream theory by Keynes, who would be convinced that Malthus had been right all along. It was his own interpretation of Malthus's letters to Ricardo, which he read at the depths of the Great Depression in October 1932, that would lead Keynes to this complete reversal of what had been the hardest and fastest of classical conclusions.

THE LABOUR THEORY OF VALUE

From the earliest days of economics, the question of what created 'value' in the goods and services bought and sold was ongoing. With the influence of the *Wealth of Nations* came the acceptance of the notion that the value of a good or service was in some way related to the amount of labour that was embodied in each item of production. Thus, Smith wrote:

> Labour was the first price, the original purchase-money that was paid for all things. It was not by gold or by silver, but by labour, that all the wealth of the world was originally purchased; and its value, to those who possess it, and who want to exchange it for some new productions, is precisely equal to the quantity of labour which it can enable them to purchase or command. (Smith, [1776] 1976: Book I, Chapter 5)

And then as the conclusion of an extended argument: 'Labour, therefore, it appears evidently, is the only universal, as well as the only accurate measure of value, or the only standard by which we can compare the values of different commodities at all times and at all places.'

Money, Smith argues, is the medium through which goods and services are exchanged, but relative monetary values represent the relative amount of labour found in the various products. It has been argued that in Smith's time, before the growth of the huge enterprises that we now associate with the nineteenth century, that labour may have been a reasonable proxy for the exchange value of goods and services. Be that as it may, it was at some level that labour was seen to embody the goods and services produced with their relative worth. It was this conclusion that was referred to as the 'labour theory of value' (LTV).

Ricardo took up the LTV, although he was somewhat troubled by the obvious inconsistencies that had arisen by the start of the nineteenth century. But he nevertheless endorsed some version of the LTV in his 1817 *Principles* (Ricardo, [1817] 1951: 73). There he wrote: 'The value of a commodity, or the quantity of any other commodity for which it will exchange, depends on the relative quantity of labour which is necessary for its production, and not as the greater or less compensation which is paid for that labour.'

MARX AND THE LABOUR THEORY OF VALUE

But it was the extension of these concepts to the notion of the division of output amongst the three classes that would become the basis for socialist and Marxist agitation. There are capitalists, land owners and workers who earn profits, rents and wages. But the only source of value, according to Ricardo, was labour. Ricardo wrote: 'It is not by the absolute quantity of produce obtained by either class, that we can correctly judge of the rate of profit, rent, and wages, but by the quantity of labour required to obtain that produce'.

It was from this that the socialist and then later the Marxist theory of the exploitation of the worker took much of its drive. If all value came from labour, that is from the efforts made by workers, then the profits earned by the capitalists in running their businesses are unjustifiable incomes taken from the workers who had created all of the value but did not receive all of the return. This became, in Marx's hands, the theory of surplus value. It is, in essence, a theory in which the entrepreneur creates no value and can therefore be discarded.

Marx's two main works were, firstly, the *Communist Manifesto*, which was published in 1848, and then secondly, his *Capital*, the first volume of which was published in 1867. *Capital* was his major work of economics in which the issue of capitalist exploitation of the worker was laid out in what would eventually become three massive volumes of near-unreadable prose. The following is part of Marx's discussion of the theory of surplus value which is presented only as an example of the way in which the book was written. It is to be looked at only for its interest as a specimen of Marx's style of writing – do not attempt to make sense of what it says:

> We have seen that the labourer, during one portion of the labour-process, pro-duces only the value of his labour-power . . . The portion of his day's labour devoted to this purpose, will be greater or less, in proportion to the value of the necessaries that he daily requires on an average, or, equivalently, in proportion to the labour-time required on an average to produce them. During the second period of the labour-process, that in which his labour is no longer necessary labour, the workman, it is true, labours, expends labour-power; but his labour, being no longer necessary labour, he creates no value for himself. He creates surplus-value which, for the capitalist, has all the charms of a creation out of nothing. This portion of the working-day, for a definite period of time, I name surplus labour-time, and to the labour expended during that time, I give the name of surplus-labour. (Marx, [1867] 1918)

In the history of world politics, Marx's writings have been as influential as anything ever written. They created what became revolutionary move-ments in one country after another, and Marx's writings remain influential still, both in practical politics and amongst social theories in every area aside from economics.

In terms of economics, however, so far as the mainstream economic theories found in market economies are concerned, Marx has had, and continues to have, almost no influence. Marx is seen as part of the classical tradition of Smith and Ricardo and is not associated with the development in economic theories that have occurred since then. The labour theory of value, which is embedded in Marx, was discarded during the next major development in economics, and as a result there has been little penetration of Marxist thinking into economic theory in general nor into the market-oriented economies of the West.

THE BREAKDOWN OF THE CLASSICAL SCHOOL

As the industrial revolution gained momentum, the economics of the classical school were no longer seen as capable of providing a sufficient basis either for understanding economic issues or in providing practical policy advice. At the centre of this break was the theory of value that had been at the core of classical economics.

The labour theory of value simply could no longer even pretend to give an account of the relative prices of the goods and services sold on the market. The growth and prevalence of massive industrial businesses, whose most obvious characteristic were the immense amounts of physical capital that were built into the costs of production, rendered impossible any theory based on the assumption that relative values were based on relative labour content. Something did not cost twice as much as something else because there was twice as much labour content. Some other explanation for the relative value of products was clearly needed.

The development of massive industrial structures also destroyed the basis for *laissez-faire*, that is, the notion that one could safely leave economic activity to the market without detailed government involvement and regulation. When Smith and Ricardo wrote, industrial enterprises were small and generally non-intrusive. By the middle of the nineteenth century, the complex industrial societies which had arisen demanded the imposition of social controls to limit their impact. These issues have been very well described in the following passage:

> The 'market' model of Civil Society may be applicable to the very special conditions prevailing in eighteenth-century Britain, in the course of the first emergence of industrial society. Those conditions included the existence of, above all, a fairly feeble technology, one just about capable of improving significantly on traditional methods of production, and making sustained innovation appear attractive, but not capable of very much more. A feeble technology of such a kind can be given its head and it will not disrupt either the social order or the environment, or at any rate not too much. Compare this with the technology available at present: any unrestricted use of it would – and quite possibly

will – lead to a total disruption of the environment and the social order. The indirect consequences of modern technology are terrifying. Moreover, technical innovation is often on a very large scale and irreversible. In brief, both its scale and its consequences are such that they cannot but concern society as a whole. (Gellner, 1994: 89)

Economic theory needed a means to think clearly about these questions, but without also abandoning the desirability of organizing economic activity around the actions of the entrepreneur. The growth of output per person and the astonishing increases in per capita incomes demonstrated the powerful forces that had been put into play by the capitalist modes of production. What was needed was a theoretical structure that would preserve the role of the entrepreneur while providing governments with a technical apparatus that would guide the structuring of a sound regulatory environment.

Also, under the pressure of socialist agitation, and especially because of the labour theory of value, immense political pressures had developed over the distribution of incomes. If all value came from labour, what justification could there be for earning profits? For the mass of workers, although their real standard of living was rising, there was a desire for an even larger slice of the income available. Economics therefore needed to provide a theory which, firstly, explained the role of the entrepreneur, and which showed that entrepreneurial incomes were not exploitation but a return for value-adding input. But economic theory also needed an explanation for the relative wages of workers, of why some were higher than others.

Beyond this were the many conflicts of interest that became more and more evident as industrial society became entrenched. In feudal aristocratic societies, most people had their place in society set at birth. But by the time of the industrial revolution, this aristocratic division of political power had almost completely broken down. How to resolve differences between individuals and groups over economic questions became a more and more important question.

Externalities

Many questions then surrounded the problems that would eventually be described as '*externalities*'. In an industrial society, where the indirect consequences of modern technologies are potentially devastating, a means was required to assess more comprehensively not just the costs and benefits of buyers and sellers, but also the effects on those who are not even involved in the transactions. An economy not only produces goods, it also produces various bads as part of that same process. A seller of a good or service whose production pollutes air and water, but at no cost to themselves, is creating damage for those who are harmed by the production process but receive no direct benefits.

The buyers of these goods and services are made better off by the product, but the costs they are made to bear are only the direct costs of production: the resources, labour and capital used up. They are not asked to compensate those who have been harmed by the increased pollution as well as other forms of harm. There is thus a third party to the industrial process, those who are damaged by production but who are not considered during the normal operation of market processes since they are neither buyers of the product nor suppliers. Even those buyers of the product may be harmed by the industrial processes that have produced the goods they buy.

It thus became apparent that such externalities had to be taken into consideration by economists and embodied in economic theory. Without recognition of the harmful effects of economic activity on third parties, economic activity would not accurately reflect the desires of the community for various goods and services, nor would prices properly reflect the actual social costs of production.

MARGINAL REVOLUTION

It is frequently argued that what set this reconstruction of economic theory in motion was a passage found in the *Wealth of Nations*. Smith had written in 1776 about what has since been described as the diamond–water paradox:

> The word VALUE, it is to be observed, has two different meanings, and sometimes expresses the utility of some particular object, and sometimes the power of purchasing other goods which the possession of that object conveys. The one may be called 'value in use;' the other, 'value in exchange.' The things which have the greatest value in use have frequently little or no value in exchange; and on the contrary, those which have the greatest value in exchange have frequently little or no value in use. Nothing is more useful than water: but it will purchase scarce anything; scarce anything can be handed in exchange for it. A diamond, on the contrary, has scarce any value in use; but a very great quantity of other goods may frequently be had in exchange of it. (Smith, [1776] 1976: Book I, Chapter IV)

This was a return to the question of the sources of value. From where did value come? Why were diamonds expensive but almost useless, while water cost nothing but was necessary for life?

The answer was supplied during the first years of the 1870s with the almost simultaneous publication of three different works in three different languages, each of which supplied more or less the same answer. In England and in English, the answer was supplied by William Stanley Jevons in his *Theory of Political Economy*. In German, Carl Menger paved the way, and in French, Léon Walras was the economist who began this revolutionary shift. All modern economics has descended through the concepts that were first put forward then by these three. Here I will concentrate on the approach taken by Jevons.

For Jevons, the value of a product was determined by how much one already had in relation to how many additional units one wished to have. Sale price was therefore determined by the price that could be charged for the *final* unit sold. Moreover, it was the personal estimation of the buyer that determined value, not some external source such as labour. It was utility, and in particular the additional utility that was given by that final additional unit bought – that is, its *marginal utility* – that determined a product's value. With diamonds, because they are so scarce, only those uses for which people would be willing to pay high prices can be satisfied. With water, on the other hand, because of its abundance in normal times, its use in keeping us alive is satisfied by the first amounts we use, but by the end, the value we receive in each time period from additional units of water is so low that there is hardly any amount of money we are willing to pay for that last unit of water we use, the marginal unit. Pricing was therefore done 'at the margin'.

If, as Jevons wrote, value 'depends entirely upon utility', then all value is determined on the demand side of the economy. The classical economists had been production-oriented in their thinking about how economies evolved. By placing value onto the demand side, a very different perspective developed.

Marginal analysis then became the core of economic theory and was applied in more and more situations. In dealing with incomes, it was argued that each person receives as their income the value of their marginal product. That is, they receive the value of their own contribution to the production process. Therefore, because wage earners are not the sole producers of output, their return is only equal to the value of what they contributed. Similarly, those who run business firms, the entrepreneurs, also receive the value of their own contribution to total output.

This was the answer to Marx's labour theory of value. Distribution of incomes was related to contribution to production. Labour received a fair return for its efforts, which was related to the value of the output it had been responsible for creating. The goods produced have value only because those who buy them are willing to repay the costs of production. Wages, through supply and demand, would adjust to ensure that the return was equitable at least as far as the level of national productivity was concerned. Similarly, the owners of capital would receive their own return, which was justified by their having caused capital to come into existence, and in the specific forms that would create the greatest amount of value. Those who built and owned the capital would receive their own fair return which was again related to the value of the final product on the market.

But the most important consequence of the 'marginal revolution' was that the focus was concentrated more and more onto individual decision making rather than the theory of national wealth and prosperity. Much of what mattered in relation to the traditions, customs, historic circumstances, moral views, social outlook and institutional structures was disregarded. These were momentous changes that haunt economic theory to this day. Although not described using the more modern term, microeconomics, the consequence of the marginal revolution was the development of an approach to economic theory that concentrated on the individual. And at the core of the individual approach were the theories that related to marginal revenue and marginal cost.

THE THEORY OF THE BUSINESS CYCLE

Yet the classical approach to economic issues did not completely disappear but was melded into what became known as the theory of the business cycle. For all of the increased focus on individual decision making, the theory of the business cycle, the rudiments of which can be traced back to the eighteenth century, was continuously developed to build greater understanding of the causes of economic fluctuations and variations in the level of employment. In many ways, the cycle was seen as representing the not insubstantial cost of the tremendous net good achieved by market forces. A typical example put the argument this way:

> Believing as I do, in Competition, although fully aware, from personal experience, of its frequent hardship to the individual, I cannot see anything but a vast balance of good in a system which throws the weight of the competitive struggle on capital and organising brains – that is, on the factors most able to bear it – while it does so much for the consumer and the worker classes. (Smart, 1906: vii–viii)

The business cycle attempted to explain what was straightforwardly obvious. Economies were cyclical in their level of activity. There were periods of prosperity, rapid growth and high employment which were followed by periods of recession, often deep recession, where economies slowed and employment fell. The pain that arose during the downturn in the cycle was offset by the good that came during periods of innovation and strong rates of growth.

A theory of the cycle had, however, developed with the intention of first explaining the causes of recessions, and then with the growth of knowledge of the underlying dynamic, thereafter devising a programme to limit the depth and duration of the downward phase.

In Adam Smith's work there is already recognition that there are variations between periods in the level of activity and employment, and this was before there had been anything like the full development of an industrial civilization in which a general downturn in activity would become a regular feature of economies. It was only during the first half of the nineteenth century that it became evident that economies were subject to regularly recurring downwards and upwards periods of recession and prosperity.

The theories of recession which economists had developed were based on acceptance that the different phases of the cycle were interrelated. The downturn would contain the seeds of the future upturn, just as periods of prosperity would lay the groundwork for the subsequent recession. The one aspect all agreed on was that, following Say's Law, whatever might be the cause of recession and unemployment, it would not be demand deficiency. Economies would never enter recession due to a lack of demand.

SAY'S LAW IN THE 1920S

Because these economic principles are associated with an economist whose books were written during the early years of the nineteenth century, there is a tendency to consider that these views were already musty and ancient when Keynes came to write his own economic analysis. In actual fact, the principles which underlay Say's Law remained an intrinsic part of economics throughout the nineteenth century and well into the twentieth.

The very phrase, 'Say's Law', is itself twentieth-century in origin and was introduced to help explain the then universal belief amongst economists that demand played no role in creating growth and employment. It was in a textbook first written for his own students by the economist Fred Taylor and then published as a text in the 1920s that the term first entered into general economic discourse (Taylor, 1925). There he discussed the universally accepted principles associated with aggregate demand during the 1920s which he explained was a fallacious form of economic thought. In discussing these issues, Taylor wrote:

> Among the fallacious notions in popular thinking that have gained very wide currency are to be found a number which grew out of misconceptions as to the real source of the *general or total demand for goods*, and as to the methods by which that demand is increased or diminished. Several types of these fallacious notions may be cited. Thus, **governmental improvements of all kinds, including even those of questionable value, are often supported by business men and others on the ground that such improvements increase the total demand for goods**. (Taylor, 1925: 196, emphasis in bold added)

Taylor traced the refutation of this argument back to the early classical writers, and to J.-B. Say in particular. He therefore explicitly states that this is why he has given the proper principle showing the identity of aggregate supply and aggregate demand the name 'Say's Law'. The first sentence of the passage, given that this is the precise reverse of modern economic theory, is especially ironic since Taylor emphasizes that at the time of writing the notions behind these principles were perfectly obvious to everyone:

> The points just brought out with respect to the relation between demand and the output of goods are so evident that some will consider it scarcely legitimate to give them the dignity derived from formal statement. On the other hand, the continued prevalence throughout the larger part of the community of the fallacious notions which these considerations are designed to correct seems to furnish ample ground for any procedure which gives these points adequate emphasis. I shall therefore put the proposition we have discussed in the form of a principle. This principle, I have taken the liberty to designate Say's Law; because, though recognized by many earlier writers, it was particularly well brought out in the presentation of Say. (Taylor, 1925: 201)

And what is this principle?

> *Principle* – Say's Law. The Ultimate Identity of Demand and Product.
> In the last analysis, the demand for goods produced for the market consists of goods produced for the market, i.e., the same goods are at once the demand for goods and the supply of goods; so that; if we can assume that producers have directed production in true accord with one another's wants, total demand must in the long run coincide with the total product or output of goods produced for the market. (Taylor, 1925: 201–2)

Taylor makes the qualification, 'if we can assume that producers have directed production in true accord with one another's wants', that is, if we can assume that producers have made no errors in what they choose to produce but have correctly anticipated what others will demand, then total demand must coincide with total production. They are then exactly the same. In aggregate, the demand for goods and services is funded by the supply of goods and services. That is all that can exchange because that is all there is.

Recessions are caused by a failure of producers to anticipate correctly what others will demand. The theory of the cycle, among the many and varied forms in which explanations for recessions were found, was based on explaining why businesses in general might fail to anticipate what consumers would demand.

KEYNESIAN REVOLUTION

The essence of the next major revolution in economics was the overturning of Say's Law by the English economist John Maynard Keynes (rhymes with 'brains', as he used to say). What made Keynes's arguments so formidable was that, like Malthus, at the time he was writing he was the single most famous economist in the world.

Malthus's fame had come from his writing *On Population*. Keynes had become equally famous for having written *The Economic Consequences of the Peace* at the end of World War I (Keynes, 1920). The book argued that Germany would be driven into national bankruptcy by the victors' demand that it pay reparations to the French for the damage the German army had caused while camped on French soil and occupying the northern half of France from 1914 to 1918. *The Economic Consequences of the Peace* was a worldwide best seller that made Keynes famous overnight. He remained the world's most famous and influential economist in 1936 when he published a book that would change the way in which recessions are understood and policies would thereafter be designed.

The Keynesian Revolution overturned the principles that underlay the actual set of beliefs that had been held by classical economists on the causes of the business cycle and the means for dealing with such downturns, by substituting Keynes's own straw man version of Say's Law. It is these conclusions which are now embedded in macroeconomic theory and therefore also in macroeconomic policy, right up to the present time.

HARLAN MCCRACKEN AND SUPPLY CREATES ITS OWN DEMAND

It is from Fred Taylor that the term 'Say's Law' has come. But it was from the work of another American economist, Harlan Linneus McCracken, that the standard definition of Say's Law has come. In a book cited by Keynes in an early draft of his *General Theory* and titled *Value Theory and Business Cycles* (McCracken, 1933), is found the following passage:

> The Automatic Production–Consumption Economists who insisted that
> *supply created its own demand*, that goods exchanged against goods and that
> a money economy was only refined and convenient indirect barter missed the
> significance of a money economy entirely. (McCracken, 1933: 159, emphasis
> added)

The actual interpretation of Say's Law found in the passage is incor-
rect, but it was this error that was nevertheless taken up by Keynes.
McCracken's error was to argue that Say's Law assumed a barter
economy in which the existence of money played no part in the unfolding
of economic events. It is an error that no economist at all familiar with the
ways an economy unfolds would ever have been likely to make, and was
an error no classical economist had ever made.

But apart from reinforcing in Keynes's mind various ideas about
the economic beliefs of classical economists, it is also in this passage
that Keynes found his own definition of Say's Law. In McCracken's
words, it was 'supply created its own demand'. These words were
slightly altered by Keynes to become 'supply creates its own demand'.
But the meaning Keynes employed is identical to McCracken's: goods
exchange against goods, and a money economy is only a refined and
convenient form of indirect barter. The existence of money makes no
significant difference to an economy other than to make exchange far
more convenient.

This is in complete contrast to the classical view. Going back to J.-B.
Say himself, in his own discussion of the principle which bears his name,
he had emphasized that to buy one first had to produce goods of one's
own, sell those goods for money and then use the money received to buy
the goods produced by others. It was clear to Say, just as it had been
clear to the entire classical school, not only that money was intrinsically
involved in economic transactions, but also that monetary dislocations
could destabilize an economy to its very foundations.[1]

Keynes misinterpreted the classical theory of the cycle by stating that it
had denied any role to money in causing economic dislocation, and then
corrected it by inventing a theory of his own to show that monetary disturbance does cause such dislocation. But in this sleight-of-hand Keynes was
able to introduce his refutation of Say's Law. As a result, and to this day,
the main economic argument used to explain recession and large-scale
unemployment is a deficiency of aggregate demand, the very proposition
that Say's Law had originally been designed to refute.

NOTE

1. Book II, Chapter 2 of Adam Smith's *Wealth of Nations* deals as far back as 1776 with money and monetary issues. His discussion of the failures of a succession of Scottish banks just prior to the publication of the book (Smith [1776] 1976: 327–328) and the Mississippi Bubble induced in France by his fellow Scot, John Law, also just a few years before (ibid.: 337–338), should dispel any notion that economists during classical times held such benign views of the impact of money on an economy.

11. The Keynesian Revolution and Say's Law

The Keynesian Revolution, and therefore the origins of virtually all macroeconomic theory today, can only be understood in relation to Keynes's coming across Malthus's economic writings in 1932. In particular, it was his reading of the Malthus side of the Malthus–Ricardo correspondence, which had been unearthed in 1930 by his close associate Piero Sraffa, that turned Keynes's mind to the possibility of demand deficiency as a cause of recession. Until that time, economists had been near unanimous in arguing that insufficient demand as a cause of recession was fallacious, and until reading the Malthus–Ricardo correspondence, this possibility had never crossed Keynes's mind.

There has been universal recognition amongst historians of thought that something did happen in late 1932 to turn Keynes in a new direction. Yet not one of the works devoted either to understanding the nature of the Keynesian Revolution, or to examining the road between the *Treatise on Money* published in 1930 and the *General Theory* published in 1936, has suggested that the reason for this change in focus occurred specifically because Keynes was at that time updating his essay on Malthus for inclusion in a collection of his biographical writings. Indeed, there is no reason given of any kind for why at that particular moment Keynes came to the conclusion that demand deficiency was the missing link in the theory of the cycle.

Yet it is as close to a certainty as one can have in such reconstructions that Keynes would never have written the *General Theory* as he did, focusing on demand deficiency as the cause of recession and unemployment, had he not become deeply interested at the end of 1932 in Malthus's economic writings. It was Malthus, of course, who had been the leading advocate in the nineteenth century of demand deficiency as a cause of recession, and of increased levels of unproductive spending as the cure. Reading Malthus's letters to Ricardo, and then the text of Chapter VII of Malthus's *Principles*, both of which Keynes did at the end of 1932, ought to be recognized as the single most important reason why Keynes was to write what he wrote in the way that he did.

Recognizing that this was the inspiration should make it easier to understand what the intent of the *General Theory* was and to understand the nature of the change in economic theory that occurs as a result. In the *General Theory*, Keynes is very clear about what he has learned from reading Malthus:

> The idea that we can safely neglect the aggregate demand function is funda-
> mental to the Ricardian economics, which underlie what we have been taught
> for more than a century. Malthus, indeed, had vehemently opposed Ricardo's
> doctrine *that it was impossible for effective demand to be deficient*; but vainly.
> For, since Malthus was unable to explain clearly (apart from an appeal to the
> facts of common observation) *how and why effective demand could be deficient*
> or excessive, he failed to furnish an alternative construction; and Ricardo con-
> quered England as completely as the Holy Inquisition conquered Spain. Not
> only was his theory accepted by the city, by statesmen and by the academic
> world. But controversy ceased; the other point of view completely disappeared;
> it ceased to be discussed. *The great puzzle of Effective Demand* with which
> Malthus had wrestled vanished from the economic literature. (Keynes, [1936]
> 1987: 32, emphasis added)

It was the 'great puzzle of Effective Demand' that Malthus had been wres-
tling with which had disappeared, and it was this that Keynes was intent
on restoring to economic theory.

Nor was Keynes wrong on the implications of Say's Law to his con-
temporaries. It is precisely this issue that is the dividing line between
pre-Keynesian economics and the economics that has dominated macroeconomic theory ever since. Mainstream economists before 1936 had
actively denied any role for aggregate demand in understanding the
business cycle. Although there had been some previous attempts to
overturn Say's Law, demand deficiency as an explanation for recession
was until then almost entirely the province of cranks. The two most
important diagrammatic innovations of the 1930s were the 'IS-LM'
curves published by Sir John Hicks in 1937, and the 'Keynesian-cross'
diagram, first drawn by Paul Samuelson in 1939. Both were developed
in response to Keynes's *General Theory*, both explain the role of demand
deficiency in causing recessions and both may be found in economics
texts to this day.

The problem of recession as conceived in the *General Theory* was that an
economy, once it has passed a certain level of production, will run out of
demands for the goods and services it produces. This is not excess supply
for individual goods and services, the 'particular glut' whose existence
no one had ever denied, but an actual excess supply of all goods taken
together, that is, a 'general glut'. Keynes made the possibility of demand
failure the very focus of his argument at the end of the introductory
chapters of the *General Theory*:

The celebrated *optimism* of traditional economic theory, which has led to economists being looked upon as Candides, who, having left this world for the cultivation of their gardens, teach that all is for the best in the best of all possible worlds provided we will let well alone, is also to be traced, I think, to their having neglected to take account of **the drag on prosperity which can be exercised by an insufficiency of effective demand**. (Keynes, [1936] 1987: 33, emphasis in bold added)

The possibility of a failure of effective demand is the very point behind the macroeconomic theory taught to students to this day. It is taught to undergraduate economists worldwide, and is embedded almost universally in economic policies designed to pull economies out of recession. And while other possible explanations for recession are now usually discussed as well, demand failure remains the single most important concept most economists are taught in relation to the causes of recession and involuntary unemployment. It is the argument that recessions can best be understood as occurring because of a fall in aggregate demand that continues to mark economic theory, along with the implication that stimulating demand through deficit spending is a valid and useful approach to take in dealing with recessions when and where they occur.

Aggregate demand is intrinsic to the modern understanding of the level of economic activity. The implication is that it is the level of aggregate demand that is responsible for the level of output, the rate of economic growth and the number of persons employed. An insufficient level of aggregate demand is held generally responsible for high levels of unemployment and it is almost universally accepted that deficit-financed public spending can permanently raise the level of output and thereby lower the rate of unemployment. There is an aggregate supply curve associated with aggregate demand, but its principal role is the determination of the rate of inflation. Production levels are not determined by supply capabilities but by the willingness of individuals to buy what has been produced with the incomes they have received.

Indeed, the issue went farther than this. Keynes argued (wrongly) that if Say's Law were valid, continuing and persistent unemployment simply could not occur and this was unrecognized by classical economists, whom he was about to correct. As he wrote:

Say's law, that the aggregate demand price of output as a whole is equal to its aggregate supply price for all volumes of output, *is equivalent to the proposition that there is no obstacle to full employment*. If, however, this is not the true law relating the aggregate demand and supply functions, there is a vitally important chapter of economic theory which remains to be written and without which all discussions concerning the volume of aggregate employment are futile. (Keynes [1936] 1987: 26, emphasis added)

For the vast majority of the economics profession even now, this is the way in which Say's Law and its implications are understood.

UNDERSTANDING SAY'S LAW: MALTHUS AND THE 'GENERAL GLUT' DEBATE

What is relevant about Say's Law cannot be contained within a single statement. Say's Law, if it is to be understood in full, must be understood as a series of related propositions which when taken together constitute the basic ingredients of the classical theory of the cycle. The most extraordinary of the many ironies that have surrounded this issue since Keynes first pronounced on it in 1936 is that Say's Law was the foundation stone within classical theory for understanding why a cycle exists at all. Keynes's argument was that belief in Say's Law meant that classical economists assumed there was never at any stage an obstacle to full employment. The reality is that Say's Law was an integral part of the explanation as to why in fact unemployment actually occurred.

Keynes, in attacking 'Say's Law' in 1936, was not attacking some one-sentence statement of principle. In attacking Say's Law, he was attacking the entire classical theory of the cycle. Unless this is understood, it is impossible to understand in full exactly what Keynes was able to do. The propositions associated with Say's Law need to be seen as the constituent elements of the classical theory of the cycle, and to understand why this was so, it is necessary to enter into some of the early history of economic theory itself.

What became the classical theory of the cycle was formed during what is now known as the 'General Glut' debate that lasted from the publication of Malthus's *Principles of Political Economy* in 1820 through until John Stuart Mill published his own *Principles of Political Economy* in 1848. What in particular distinguished Malthus's arguments from virtually all other writings on economic issues at the time was his belief that the recessions experienced by England at the end of the Napoleonic Wars in 1815 had been caused by oversaving and demand deficiency. And so a debate was commenced across the whole of the economics community of the time, with a raft of books on economic theory published over whether there could be an excess supply of all goods and services taken together.

Importantly, it was not a debate over whether recessions and large-scale unemployment were possible. On this there was obviously unanimity. The only question was whether recessions, when they occurred, were the result of too much saving and too little effective demand. That this could never be a realistic explanation was ultimately accepted by the whole of the mainstream of the economics community.

Moreover, during classical times there was no economic principle known as 'Say's Law'. As discussed in the previous chapter, the term would not be coined until the twentieth century, nor enter economic discourse until the 1920s. There was Jean-Baptiste Say's *théorie des débouchés*, known in English as the 'law of markets', which stated that demand was constituted by supply. It was the law of markets that was employed as part of the response to Malthus's views, but as only one strand in a far more complex series of counter-arguments. It was a crucially important part of the argument, but it was only one of the arguments in a longer chain of reasoning. It was the entire set of counter-arguments that when taken together became the related propositions that formed the classical theory of the cycle. Leaving Say's Law in Keynes's vague and imprecise form of words – 'supply creates its own demand' – not only reverses the point that classical economists had tried to make, that demand in real terms can only be derived through the production of value adding goods and services, but ignores every other related aspect that was central to an understanding of the classical theory of the cycle.

By discrediting the crucially central idea that demand is formed on the supply side of the economy, the related propositions that had emerged from the debate over Malthus lost their coherence. The publication of the *General Theory* caused the entire classical perspective on the business cycle to disappear. The propositions presented below are therefore intended to reassemble the arguments that were at the core of pre-Keynesian business cycle theory and need to be seen as the full meaning of Say's Law as it emerged during the General Glut debate. They are also put in a form so that the entire argument can be seen not just as a full and complete response to Keynes and the arguments of the *General Theory*, but also as a reply to modern macroeconomics to the extent that it continues to rely on demand deficiency to explain why recessions occur.

THE RELATED PROPOSITIONS OF SAY'S LAW

What follows are the related propositions which make up Say's Law. These were integral components of classical thought and must be appreciated to follow the classical theory of the cycle. Prior to the publication of *The General Theory*, these propositions were accepted by the entire mainstream of the profession.

Proposition 1: Recessions are never due to demand deficiency.

This is the starting point for any understanding of the pre-Keynesian theory of recession and Say's Law. Four examples of how this statement was an integral part of economic theory across the entire classical period, written by three of the greatest economists who have ever lived, will help to put the law of markets into its proper context.

First, Adam Smith. He specifically denies that there is any danger from oversaving and that a community has anything to fear from the saving of its more provident members. It was this argument that Keynes specifically set out to deny:

> What is annually saved is as regularly consumed as what is annually spent, and nearly in the same time too; but it is consumed by a different set of people. That portion of his revenue which a rich man annually spends, is in most cases consumed by idle guests, and menial servants, who leave nothing behind them in return for their consumption. That portion which he annually saves, as for the sake of the profit it is immediately employed as a capital, is consumed in the same manner, and nearly in the same time too, but by a different set of people, by labourers, manufacturers, and artificers, who reproduce with a profit the value of their annual consumption. His revenue we shall suppose, is paid him in money. Had he spent the whole, the food, clothing, and lodging, which the whole could have purchased, would have been distributed among the former set of people. By saving a part of it, as that part is for the sake of profit immediately employed as capital either by himself or by some other person, the food, clothing and lodging, which may be purchased with it, are necessarily reserved for the latter. The consumption is the same, but the consumers are different. (Smith, [1776] 1976: Book II, Chapter III)

A second example is Alfred Marshall writing in a publication co-authored with his wife, Mary Paley Marshall, in 1879. Here it is made abundantly clear that deficient aggregate demand is not the proper explanation for depression:

> After every crisis, in every period of commercial depression, it is said that supply is in excess of demand. Of course there may easily be an excessive supply of some particular commodities; so much cloth and furniture and cutlery may have been made that they cannot be sold at a remunerative price. But something more than this is meant. For after a crisis the warehouses are overstocked with goods in almost every important trade; scarcely any trade can continue undiminished production so as to afford a good rate of profits to capital and a good rate of wages to labour. And it is thought that this state of things is one of general over-production. We shall however find that it really is nothing but a state of commercial disorganisation. (Marshall and Marshall, [1879] 1881: 154)

And lest it be thought that this is the early Alfred Marshall which was later subsumed by a different point of view, in a section introduced into the fifth edition of the *Principles* in 1907 he emphatically made the point again. Note that problems on the demand side are seen only to exacerbate a problem that has been due to other causes: 'It is true that in times of depression the disorganization of consumption is a contributory cause to the continuance of the disorganization of credit and of production. But a remedy is not to be got by a study of consumption, as has been alleged by some hasty writers' (see Marshall, [1920] 1961: 711n).

Finally, Friedrich Hayek. His 1931 article, 'The "paradox" of saving', is a full-scale discussion, more than 40 pages in length, on the arguments of two economists who had argued during the 1920s and 1930s that oversaving was the cause of recessions. Hayek's opening paragraph is not only an attack on the belief that excess saving is a cause of recession, but he also specifically refers to the *théorie des débouchés* as providing the appropriate position. It is nothing other than a straightforward statement of the classical position. Hayek wrote:

> The assertion that saving renders the purchasing power of the consumer insufficient to take up the volume of current production although made more often by members of the lay public than by professional economists, is almost as old as the science of political economy itself. The question of the utility of 'unproductive' expenditure was first raised by the Mercantilists, who were thinking chiefly of luxury expenditure. The idea recurs in those writings of Lauderdale and Malthus *which gave rise to the celebrated Théorie des Débouchés of James Mill and J.B. Say*, and in spite of many attempts to refute it, permeates the main doctrines of socialist economics . . . But while in this way the idea has found a greater popularity in quasi-scientific and propagandist literature than perhaps any other economic doctrine hitherto, fortunately it has not succeeded as yet in depriving saving of its general respectability. (Hayek, 1931: 125)

It is highly noteworthy that it was only five years later that the *General Theory* would in fact do what Hayek had feared, and 'deprive saving of its general respectability'.

Proposition 2: Demand is created by supply and by nothing else.

This proposition is a restatement of Jean-Baptiste Say's original *théorie des débouchés*, wrongly characterized by Keynes as 'supply creates its own demand'. Moreover, the statement that demand is created by supply may be the most important concept in coming to grips with the classical theory of the cycle, but because it is so foreign to modern macroeconomic thought, it may also be the most difficult. Yet it was fully accepted by pre-Keynesian economists.

Here is James Mill, in the first presentation during the early years of the nineteenth century of what would become the classical theory of cycle, explaining the significance of this principle. He could not be more emphatic, nor does he leave any doubt about just how crucial he believes this principle to be:

> No proposition however in political economy seems to be more certain than this which I am going to announce, how paradoxical soever it may at first sight appear; and if it is true, none undoubtedly can be deemed of more importance. The production of commodities creates, and is the one universal cause which creates a market for the commodities produced. (Mill, [1808] 1966: 135)

Moving forward a century, the same concept is found in the following passage from one of the most widely used economic texts ever published, in which this principle is stated in very clear terms:

> It is only because our exchanges are made through money that we have any difficulty in perceiving that an increase in supply is (not 'causes') an increase in demand . . . An increase in the supply of cloth is an increase in the demand for other things; and *vice versa*, an increase in the supply of anything else may constitute a demand for cloth. What is divided among the members of society is the goods and services produced to satisfy its wants; and the same goods and services are both Supply and Demand. (Clay, [1916] 1924: 242)

The notion of aggregate demand separate from aggregate supply was foreign to pre-Keynesian economic thought. Aggregate demand grows at the same rate and by the same amount as aggregate supply, and will not grow unless supply has grown. It is not, however, just any production that will lead to an increase in aggregate demand. What creates demand is the production of forms of output for which enough buyers can be found whose payments cover in aggregate the entire costs of production. Only if the goods and services produced can be sold for more than was paid for the inputs that went into their production can it be said with certainty that value has been added during the production process. Conversely, if the goods and services produced do not create more value than is used up in the production process, there can be no increase in aggregate demand because there has been no increase in aggregate supply in any relevant sense.

Proposition 3: The process involved in purchase and sale is the conversion of one's own goods or services into money and then the reconversion of the money one has received back into other goods and services. There is no implication of a barter economy. Money is intrinsic to the processes involved.

At the very core of the classical propositions surrounding Say's Law is an appreciation that money is infused with value only by being received in exchange for value adding production. The process is one that may be characterized in the formula $C - M - C'$ where the set of goods or services in one's own possession (C) are converted into a different set of goods or services (C') by the sale of what one owns for money (M), and then the reconversion of the money received into what one wishes to buy. Keynes had accused classical economists of confusing a barter economy with the operation of a money economy, but from the first statements on Say's Law by Say himself, that had never been the case. Here is J.-B. Say, in the fourth edition of his *Treatise*, trying to explain the obvious.

> Should a tradesman say, 'I do not want other products for my woollens, I want money,' there could be little difficulty in convincing him that his custom-ers could not pay him in money, without having first procured it by the sale of some other commodities of their own . . . You say, you only want money; I say, you want other commodities, and not money. . . To say that sales are dull, owing to the scarcity of money, is to mistake the means for the cause; an error that proceeds from the circumstance, that almost all produce is in the first instance exchanged for money, before it is ultimately converted into other produce. (Say, [1803] 1821)

But more importantly, the process lay in ensuring that those who pro-duced actually did create value. Demand was only constituted by the value added that arose from the sale of goods or services to others. If output could not be sold at prices which repaid the costs of production, then no value added had occurred. That this frequently did take place provided the core insight into the classical theory of the cycle. That demand was built on productive activities was also pointed out by the economist Ludwig von Mises who was explicitly following Say in making this point: 'Commodities, says Say, are ultimately paid for not by money, but by other commodities. Money is merely the commonly used medium of exchange; it plays only an intermediary role. What the seller wants ultimately to receive in exchange for the commodities sold is other commodities' (Mises, [1950] 1980).

To understand demand being constituted by supply, it is necessary to recognize that in a properly functioning economy, purchases are effected by the revenue from the previous sale of goods and services, or with money borrowed from others who have earned incomes by producing. For those who earned their incomes from the sale of goods and services, the process is direct. The creation of value and the sale of what had been produced provided the income for the purchase of other goods and services. For businesses investing borrowed funds, the purchases are effected through the transfer of funds through a saving–investment process. For govern-ments, purchases are effected through revenues raised through taxation of the incomes of those who had sold goods or services to the market.

Proposition 4: Recessions are common and result in high levels of involuntary unemployment.

It really ought to be unnecessary to point out that this proposition ought to be completely non-controversial. It really ought to have been inconceivable to have suggested, as Keynes did in 1936, that economists until then had had no explicit theory of involuntary unemployment and recession. Yet one of the consequences of the publication of the *General Theory* was the belief that classical economists had no theories to account for recessions and involuntary unemployment. It is therefore necessary to make the explicit statement that classical economists did indeed have such theories of recession and that they most assuredly did understand that involuntary unemployment was a frequent feature of economic life. The theory of the business cycle had been developing for over a century by that stage, so that for Keynes to have stated of his fellow economists that they had no theory of involuntary unemployment was absurd.

A compendium of all of the theories of the cycle is found in a League of Nations publication by Gottfried Haberler, titled *Prosperity and Depression*, whose first edition was published in 1937, the year following the publication of the *General Theory*. The first words of the Preface ought to make it absolutely plain that recession and unemployment were amongst the most important questions under examination by the economics community of the world during the 1930s, and had been for generations:

> This book has its origin in a resolution adopted by the Assembly of the League of Nations in September 1930 by which it was decided that an attempt should be made to co-ordinate the analytical work then being done on the problem of the recurrence of periods of economic depression.
>
> The literature concerning economic depressions and what is currently and somewhat loosely described as the trade cycle is abundant ... It is apparent from the persistence with which depressions occur, from the gravity of their economic and social effects, and from the growing consciousness of that gravity, that – however abundant the literature on the subject, however elaborate and specious the theories – our knowledge of the causes of depressions has not yet reached a stage at which measures can be designed to avert them.

That what ought to have been seen as absurdly improbable was nevertheless accepted from the moment it was first published is an issue that demands the attention of historians of ideas. Here it should merely be noted that Keynes's statement, that economists before him had no theories to explain recessions and unemployment, is false, as a moment's reflection ought to have led anyone to recognize at the time, just as it ought to be recognized today.

Proposition 5:   Recessions are due to structural problems of one kind or another. In particular, recessions occur where the structure of supply does not match the structure of demand.

For anyone basing their understanding of these issues on Keynes's writings, it is something of a surprise to discover that the law of markets was at the very centre of the classical theory of the recession and, in fact, provided the foundation for the theory of the cycle as understood by classical economists. Because demand was constituted by supply, cyclical activity was understood to be the result of individuals and businesses producing what could not be sold at prices which covered costs. Why this might happen was the underlying issue, but that it frequently did happen, of this no one had the slightest doubt. The more than 100-year classical literature on the nature and causes of the business cycle, written before the *General Theory* was published, is a testament to the recognition that pre-Keynesian economists gave to unemployment and recession.

Torrens, writing in 1821 in a direct response to the arguments presented by Malthus, makes the point as explicitly as it is possible to make it. The classical theory of the cycle was built on these very concepts. Demand is constituted by supply but only so long as supply consists of what those with incomes to spend want to buy. Keeping demand and supply properly proportioned was the imperative, but once that had been achieved all went well. It was when the proportions were not maintained that recessions would occur. Torrens in making this point firstly notes that there is no possibility that supply will ever outrun demand if producers make the right production decisions:

> So long as the proportion is preserved, every article which the industrious classes have the will and power to produce, will find a ready and profitable vend. No conceivable increase of production can lead to an overstocking of the market . . . *Increased production will create a proportionally increased demand.* (Torrens, [1821] 1965, emphasis added)

What is particularly notable is that Torrens uses almost the very words Keynes would use to summarize Say's Law: 'Increased production will create a proportionately increased demand' is the lineal ancestor of 'supply creates its own demand'. Torrens is invoking Say's law of markets to show that demand deficiency is never a problem. But he does not conclude from this that economies cannot therefore go into recession or that there are no obstacles to full employment. He instead uses this very principle to explain why recessions occur. Following on from the above passage, Torrens immediately sets out the consequences, should something happen to disturb the balance between the structure of production and the structure of demand: 'This happy and prosperous state of things is immediately interrupted when the proportions in which commodities are produced are such as to disturb the equality between effectual demand and supply . . . Then gluts and regorgements are experienced' (ibid.).

Even in 1821 Torrens was not the first to make this point, but he made it very well. A lack of proportion between supply and demand in aggregate is the cause of a descent into recession. The problems of recession are due to structural problems in an economy, not because of a failure of demand. And it required an understanding of the law of markets to understand that recessions occur when what has been produced does not coincide with what those with incomes want to buy.

In these passages, Torrens captured the theory that became during the following century the common ground amongst the economics community in discussing the business cycle. Recessions and depressions were due to structural problems. Haberler, in his *Prosperity and Depression*, provided a synopsis of the theory of the cycle as it had been understood until then. In summarizing the views of the economic profession of his time, he wrote: 'An expansion or contraction may be interrupted on the one hand by an accident . . . or it may on the other hand itself give rise to maladjustments in the economic system . . . Most cycle theorists have tried to prove that the second type of restraining force is all-important' (Haberler, 1937).

This is Torrens once again. It is this maladjustment in the structure of production, where demand and supply are out of proportion with each other, that was the fundamental explanation for recession. Demand deficiency played no part in the process within orthodox theory.[1]

Where demand was crucial was in relation to the structure of demand relative to supply, that is, in situations where what buyers would have been willing to pay the full costs of production for did not match what suppliers had actually put on the market. Starting from the proposition that demand is constituted by properly proportioned supply, recessions are caused by events that mislead producers into producing goods and services that cannot be sold at cost-covering prices.

Proposition 6: Overproduction of individual goods and services occurs continuously within economies and can lead to a general downturn in an economy.

Walter Bagehot, the editor of *The Economist* during the middle years of the nineteenth century, wrote one of the most influential works on the operation of the money market. As part of this work, he included a chapter on the nature of the business cycle, in which he described the evolution of a general downturn built out of a downturn in one part of the economy. Given Keynes's accusation that classical economists had ignored monetary factors and their effects on economic activity, it should not go unnoticed that the following is from Bagehot's *Lombard Street*, which had as its subtitle, *A Description of the Money Market*. What Bagehot wrote was this:

> No single large industry can be depressed without injury to other industries; still less can any great group of industries. Each industry when prosperous buys and consumes the produce probably of most (certainly of very many) other industries, and if industry A fail [*sic*] and is in difficulty, industries B, and C, and D, which used to sell to it, will not be able to sell that which they had produced in reliance on A's demand, and in future they will stand idle till industry A recovers, because in default of A there will be no one to buy the commodities which they create. (Bagehot, [1873] 1919: 121–2)

The essence of this process is the creation of an economic downturn built upon the systematic failure of producers to sell what they have produced in their own markets. It accepts that when the recovery comes there may be different firms and industries in different proportions. But the conception that lies behind it is that the pieces in the economy must interlock as firms provide a market for each other with the entire structure ultimately aimed at producing goods and services for final home consumption.

Proposition 7: Monetary factors, most notably structural imbalances in the market for credit, can also be and often are an important cause of recession. Even where monetary instability has not been the originating cause of recession, monetary factors will often deepen a recession brought on for other reasons.

It is because Keynes argued that classical economists thought only in terms of real variables that such an obvious statement even needs to be made. It was, in fact, the specific conclusion reached by Becker and Baumol, writing as long ago as 1952, that ought to have put this issue to rest for all time, and also have raised some questions about the foundations of the Keynesian economic theory that had been built on the rejection of so flimsy a straw man. Becker and Baumol could not have been more explicit in dealing with this caricature of classical theory which they labelled 'Say's Identity'. In discussing what they term 'the clearest statement on the point' – in a famous essay published by John Stuart Mill in 1844 – they wrote: 'It is all there and explicitly . . . In reading [Mill's essay] one is led to wonder why so much of the subsequent literature (this paper included) had to be written at all' (Becker and Baumol, 1952).

Monetary factors can and do cause recession. It is stating only what ought to be obvious, that classical economists were fully aware that monetary factors were often part of the process even when not the initiating factor in causing recessions to occur.

The approach to economic policy becomes very different if one begins from a classical perspective rather than from one that commences with demand deficiency. These different perspectives are part of the matrix of ideas that were part of the structure of understanding that existed under a theory of the cycle built on classical foundations.

Proposition 8:   Because recessions are not due to a failure of demand, practical solutions to recession do not encompass large increases in the level of public spending.

The policy consequences of Keynesian theory have over the years provided ample evidence that on this matter classical economists were correct. There has been no instance of a peacetime increase in public spending during recession that has led to recovery. Reductions in taxation have a different effect on economic outcomes, and can be consistent with classical principles in generating economic growth. Increases in public spending, however, are not. John Stuart Mill's statement is about as clear-cut as one could find: 'The utility of a large government expenditure, for the purpose of encouraging industry, is no longer maintained . . . It is no longer supposed that you benefit the producer by taking his money, provided you give it to him again in exchange for his goods' (Mill, [1874] 1974).

Since the publication of the *General Theory*, all this has changed round again. The utility of large government expenditure, for the purpose of encouraging industry, is precisely what is maintained by standard macroeconomic theory today.

UNDERSTANDING THE CLASSICAL THEORY OF THE CYCLE

It was Keynes himself who made it clear that the economics of the *General Theory* was to be seen as a refutation of Say's Law. Recessions, he wrote, were caused by a deficiency of aggregate demand. This was contrary to mainstream classical thought. Classical economists argued that economies are not driven by demand but by value-adding production, which is what they referred to as 'supply'. They were virtually unanimous in arguing that raising demand without an increase in the level of value-adding output cannot be an answer to recession and unemployment.

This was summarized by classical economists in various ways: demand is constituted by supply, there is no such thing as a general glut, overproduction is an impossibility. However, the most remarkable short statement, not just on the nature of aggregate demand but also on the related issue of how recessions occur, can be found in David Ricardo's reply to Malthus in a personal letter written on 9 October 1820. Ricardo was writing a few months after Malthus's *Principles* had been published and was trying to explain why Malthus's explanation for recession, a deficiency of demand, was wrong. Ricardo therefore wrote: 'Men err in their productions, there is no deficiency of demand' (Ricardo, 1951–73, Vol. VIII).

This is, to begin with, a statement on the causes of recession: 'men err in their productions', that is, there is some kind of market disequilibrium which has occurred across the economy. The wrong goods and services – that is, goods and services that cannot find a buyer – had for some reason been produced. And beyond that, it is a statement of what does not cause recessions: 'there is no deficiency of demand'. Whatever might have caused the recession, it is not due to a lack of demand. What is found in Ricardo's short statement is in summary form the classical theory of recession with its explicit rejection of demand factors as their cause.

Within Ricardo's short and to-the-point statement there is no ambiguity of meaning, none of the uncertainty that currently exists over what 'supply creates its own demand' does or does not mean. Ricardo's brief statement of the classical principle means that when recessions occur, they cannot be understood as a consequence of too little demand but should be understood as some sort of derangement within the market process.

Macroeconomics replaced the classical theory of the cycle in the 1930s and has been Keynesian ever since. No metaphorical statement on the death of Keynes or of Keynesian economics can be true so long as aggregate demand maintains its presence at the core of macroeconomic theory and policy. Because of the near universal acceptance of Keynesian theory within the mainstream, economists have repeatedly formulated policies around the need to stimulate demand during periods of high unemployment. The pervasive presence of the theory of aggregate demand has caused a blackout curtain to fall across the whole of macroeconomic theory, making it all but impossible to understand the underlying workings of an economy or to provide useful advice when recessions occur, as they inevitably must.

NOTE

1. There was, however, an under-consumptionist literature which argued that too little demand from consumers was the systematic cause of economic recession.

12. The basic Keynesian macroeconomic model

The basic macroeconomic model taught across the world is a direct descendant of the economic theory proposed by Keynes in his *General Theory* published in 1936. Therefore, since a complete understanding of economics must include a discussion of modern macroeconomic theory, in this chapter and the next, modern macroeconomic theory is explained in just the way it might be explained by someone who thought the theory was valid. In this case it must be understood that the reason it is being explained is because it is the basis for the standard macroeconomic model used by economists across the world, not because it is seen as a valid theory of economic behaviour.

So you are hereby warned. So far as this text is concerned, the model discussed in this chapter does not properly reflect reality. It does not explain how an economy functions. Attempting to create economic growth during recessions by raising the level of aggregate demand, so far as this text is concerned, is doomed to failure. Raising the level of aggregate demand does not create the conditions for higher growth and employment. Such actions will not lead to recovery. Attempting to stimulate an economy by increasing aggregate demand will, instead, cause an economy to stagnate and the labour market to falter.

The final chapters of the book will outline the classical theory of the business cycle. These chapters will explain how an economy knits together, why it can on occasion enter into recession and what steps can be usefully taken to restore full employment when recessions occur. In the meantime, this chapter and the chapter that follows will discuss the basics of modern macroeconomic theory and its associated theory of recession, based as it is on the original Keynesian model first published in 1936.

THE ORIGINAL KEYNESIAN MODEL

What is found in virtually all macroeconomic texts at the present time are models that are descendants of the model first discussed by Keynes in his

General Theory and subsequently developed since that time. This is how the original Keynesian explanation for recession worked:

- As income rises, the level of consumption rises, but not at the same rate.
- Therefore, the higher the level of income, the greater will be the level of saving, not just in absolute terms but as a proportion of income.
- If the level of output is going to soak up all of the additional savings being generated, investment must also rise at the same rate as savings are rising, which means that investment must rise proportionately more rapidly than incomes.
- Business confidence, called 'animal spirits' by Keynes, is essential if businesses are to invest.
- More technically, for the economy to grow fast enough to employ all those who seek employment the rate of interest must fall enough to encourage businesses to spend a sufficient amount on investment goods to soak up all of the savings generated. Because of what is termed a 'liquidity trap', interest rates do not fall sufficiently, which means not all savings generated at a full employment level of output will be used.
- Therefore, the level of savings will be greater than investment at the level of Gross Domestic Product (GDP) required to create full employment or to put this in a different way, there will be a deficiency of aggregate demand.
- Therefore, the economy will reach an equilibrium level of GDP even though there are high levels of unemployment.
- The problem is too much saving relative to the willingness of businesses to invest.
- Therefore, the only adequate solution is for governments to increase their own level of spending to soak up the savings that private sector firms have refused to borrow and invest.

Keynes described such recessionary conditions as the 'fate of Midas'; that is, a community can become so rich that it ends up being poor. As he wrote in his *General Theory* to explain the cause of the Great Depression:

> Of two equal communities, having the same technique but different stocks of capital, the community with the smaller stock of capital may be able for the time being to enjoy a higher standard of life than the community with the larger stock; though when the poorer community has caught up the rich – as, presumably, it eventually will – then both alike will suffer the fate of Midas. (Keynes, [1936] 1987: 219)

Why should a poorer community with less capital enjoy a higher standard of living than a richer one with more capital? Because a rich community will save so much that mass unemployment is the result.

And was this some prospect far down the track when the world had become far richer than it was then? Why no, not at all. It was the very condition of the UK and the US right then, in the period immediately after the end of World War I. Again, this is Keynes in 1936 writing in his *General Theory*:

> The post-war experiences of Great Britain and the United States are, indeed, actual examples of how an accumulation of wealth . . . can interfere, in conditions mainly of *laissez-faire*, with a reasonable level of employment and with the standard of life which the technical conditions of production are capable of furnishing. (Keynes, [1936] 1987: 219)

These countries have become so wealthy that they have become poor. This is the Keynesian message, and the fault lies in the saving that takes place in richer communities.

MAKING SENSE OF THE KEYNESIAN MODEL

Central to macroeconomics is the study of what causes the level of output to deviate from its highest potential level. It therefore attempts to explain why unemployment exists and almost as an afterthought, it attempts to explain changes in the rate of inflation. Finally, macroeconomics makes a stab at explaining economic growth.

Following Keynes, the single most important element in macroeconomic analysis is *aggregate demand*. In macroeconomics, the driving force behind the level of activity, and therefore the rate of unemployment, is the level of demand in an economy for everything that the economy produces.

Whatever might be the productive potential of an economy, it is the total amount that buyers wish to buy that will determine how close to full employment an economy is.

These buyers are typically divided into a series of classes, the same as those used to calculate the level of GDP using the expenditure approach:

- *C*: consumption – purchases of goods and services, the end products of the production process, by consumers;
- *I*: investment – purchases by private sector firms of assets to be used in the production process by businesses;

- *G*: government spending – purchases made either as forms of public consumption (as for example the public service) or as public investment (such as roads and schools) by governments;
- *X*: exports – purchases of domestic output made by buyers living in other countries.

This is domestic demand, the total of everything bought in an economy during some period of time. But what is bought includes not just those goods and services produced within the economy but also includes goods and services imported from overseas.

Therefore, just as with the national accounts, to calculate the level of production, from the total level of domestic demand the level of imports must be taken away:

- *M*: imports – local purchases of goods and services produced in other countries.

The total level of domestically produced goods and services is therefore represented by the following equation. The letter *Y* stands for GDP or production or national income or output, all of which are seen as equivalent so far as their impact on aggregate economic activity is concerned:

$$Y = C + I + G + X - M$$

That is, total *production* (*Y*) is equal to everything bought inside the domestic economy ($C + I + G + X$) minus everything imported from other countries ($-M$). Net exports (*NX*) are defined as exports minus imports ($X - M$). The equation therefore becomes:

$$Y = C + I + G + NX$$

It is this concept, and this equation, that is at the core of modern macroeconomic theory. The level of production (*Y*) is dependent on the aggregate level of demand. The higher are the various components of demand, the higher is the level of production, with this conclusion: the higher the level of production, the higher will be the level of employment (all other things being, of course, equal).

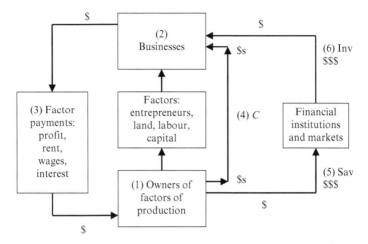

Figure 12.1   Circular flow of income: the basic Keynesian model

CIRCULAR FLOW

The busy little diagram in Figure 12.1 provides an approach to under-standing the direction of expenditure in a very simplified model. It is not perfect as a model, but it moves you closer to what needs to be understood. The numbers in the text below refer to the numbers in the boxes of the figure.

(1) Start with the 'owners' of the factors of production. These are the individuals who supply the market with the various inputs needed to produce. There is an arrow that points north, which shows that there is a real movement of such inputs from their owners to those who put these factors to use.

(2) These factors of production – land, labour, capital and the activities of entrepreneurs – are used by businesses as part of the production process. The first three factors – land, labour and capital – exist in an extraordinarily large number of forms and are shaped into various types of output under the direction and control of entrepreneurs who own and run business firms. These businesses produce goods and services, some of which are in fact themselves used as factors of pro-duction by other firms or by governments. But so far as this highly aggregated model is concerned, most of what is produced are con-sumption goods that are bought by consumers in the current period.

(3) Now we must follow the money. In return for the use of the various factors, payments are made to their owners. These payments come

in various forms, for example, profits, rent, wages and interest. They are a money return to their owners for the inputs they provide. The money in this way comes into the hands of the owners of the factors of production; that is, the factors having originated in Box (1) means that the money payments return to Box (1).

(4)   Those who have received this money for their productive efforts must do something with the money they now have. Some of the money received is spent on consumption goods and goes straight back into the revenue stream of businesses.

(5)   Some of the money received, however, is saved and goes to financial institutions of one sort or another.[1] These can be banks, finance houses or whatever. But wherever these funds go, they are presumed not to go straight back into the revenue stream of business. They must first flow through a financial institution where the saving occurs.

(6)   If the economy is to retain its current level of output and employment, the money placed in financial institutions must be borrowed by others and used for investment purposes. The level of investment spending leaving such financial institutions must be at least as large as the savings that have come in. Otherwise, the level of business receipts – made up of spending on consumer goods and capital investment – will be smaller than the level of incomes paid out at (3).

The circular flow diagram represents what Keynes was getting at when he wrote the *General Theory*, as simple as the diagram may appear to be.

SAVING IN KEYNESIAN AND CLASSICAL MODELS

The circular flow diagram also presents a simplified means of comparing the Keynesian and the classical models. The Keynesian version is that there are serious impediments caused by the different saving and investment decisions that prevent the circle from being closed. In the classical model, this is never the problem when recessions occur.

The obstacle for Keynes occurs in that box marked 'Financial institutions & markets'. It is into these that savings are directed. The question for Keynes was whether the level of investment spending going out would be equal to the level of savings going in.

Keynes made the point that those who invest and those who save are different people who make decisions for entirely different reasons. There is therefore no reason to believe that the amount of money saved at a full employment level of output would be anywhere near the amount of money investors intended to invest.

Indeed, as far as Keynes was concerned, the likelihood was that the level of saving on the one hand and the intention to invest on the other would diverge at the full employment level of output, with the level of saving often far exceeding the level of investment with nothing to close the gap.

In the classical model, however, saving was not the proportion of current income not spent on consumer goods. Saving was instead the proportion of the entire economy's stock of existing resources used to produce additional capital. Interest rate adjustments would ensure that no savings would end up uninvested.

Two differences need to be emphasized. The first is that to Keynes, only current incomes were saved. To classical economists almost all of the savings in existence during some period of time consisted of the massive stock of the economy's resource based used for producing capital.

The second is that savings were not conceived as so many units of money but were seen as actual productive assets. Interest rate and relative price adjustments ensured that the level of saving and the level of investment were equal.

It was Keynes's argument that the rate of interest would not fall to its equilibrium level but would remain above its equilibrating level. There would therefore be an excess supply of money saving at the full employment level of output, and too little demand in aggregate relative to aggregate supply.

The result was that the economy would contract, and as the economy contracted, the level of money saving would fall. The economy would eventually contract until the level of saving in terms of money fell enough so that the amount of money saved was equal to the amount of money spent on investment.

In the classical model there would therefore be no unemployment *due to demand deficiency* while in the Keynesian model there often was. In the classical model there were, as discussed in Chapter 14, a large number of reasons that an economy might go into recession, but demand deficiency was never one of them. In the Keynesian model, all other reasons for recession were ignored, with only demand deficiency identified as the explanation.

LEAKAGES AND INJECTIONS

The basic Keynesian model is, however, only the start. To the circular flow diagram in Figure 12.1 is now added the government sector which involves taxes (T), which leads to a reduction in the level of expenditure across the economy, and government spending (G), which leads to an increase.

With the introduction of the government, incomes received by the owners of the factors of production are either spent on consumption goods (*C*), which adds to aggregate demand, or instead of being spent, incomes are either saved (*S*) or paid to governments as taxes (*T*). Both saving and taxes lower the level of aggregate demand. These subtractions from the spending stream are given the name *leakages* or *withdrawals*, indicating that they represent a diversion of purchasing power away from buying.

For businesses, their revenues can now come not just as spending by consumers on consumer goods and services (*C*), but also as spending by businesses on investment goods (*I*) and as some form of spending by governments on the goods and services sought by the public sector (*G*). These additions to the spending flow are referred to as *injections*.

The equilibrium level of aggregate demand, made up of *C* + *I* + *G*, is equal to the uses made of the incomes received, which is made up of *C* + *S* + *T*. In equilibrium, where the level of injections equals the level of leakages, consumption (*C*) drops out on both sides and we are left with an equilibrium where the level of injections made up of investment (*I*) and government spending (*G*) is equal to the level of leakages made up of saving (*S*) and taxation (*T*).

This is shown in the expanded circular flow diagram in Figure 12.2 which has income earners either consuming (*C*), saving (*S*) or paying taxes (*T*). Businesses also receive payments, in the form of consumer demand (*C*), business investment (*I*) or government spending (*G*). In equilibrium then:

$$C + I + G = C + S + T$$

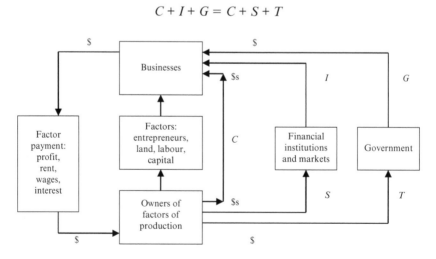

Figure 12.2   Circular flow with government

Or when C is dropped from both sides, this is the equilibrium found in the domestic economy before foreign trade is introduced:

$$I + G = S + T$$

In the Keynesian framework, however, leakages at the full employment level of output can frequently be expected to exceed injections. An important part of the response when such demand deficiency occurs is to increase the level of public spending to make up the difference.

Thus, although leakages might be greater than injections, this could be counterbalanced if the level of injections could be increased through higher levels of government spending. This shift could be further supplemented by a fall in leakages through lower levels of taxation. The aim in putting this model together was not just to demonstrate the cause of recession but to indicate the proper policy response by governments when recessions occurred.

BRINGING IN THE FOREIGN SECTOR

The final addition required to complete the model is the introduction of the international sector. Not all of the income earned necessarily flows back into domestic firms. Some is spent on goods and services produced in other countries. Such imports (M) are another form of leakage, as the expenditure of domestically earned incomes disappears from the domestic spending stream.

Thus the incomes received can then end up being used to buy consumer goods and services (C), or they can be saved (S), or they can be paid in taxes (T) or they can be used to buy imports (M). Only the first of these, C, ends up being spent on buying goods or services produced in the domestic economy. The others are leakages from domestic demand. And in aggregate, these elements can be listed as consumption (C), saving (S), taxes paid (T) and imports (M), $C + S + T + M$. That is, consumer demand plus three different forms of leakages.

At the same time, some of the demand for domestic production comes from the international sector. These are a nation's exports (X) which are another form of injection. They add to domestic aggregate demand which now totals consumption (C) plus investment (I) plus government spending (G) plus exports (X). That is, $C + I + G + X$.

Total spending in equilibrium, $C + I + G + X$, is equal to total leakages from the spending stream, made up of $C + S + T + M$. That is, there is consumer demand plus three forms of injections which in equilibrium is equal to the level of consumer demand plus three forms of leakage:

$$C + I + G + X = C + S + T + M$$

If one again drops C from both sides, it can be seen that the equilibrium condition is where:

$$I + G + X = S + T + M$$

On the expenditure side of this equation, $I + G + X$ is the sum total of possible injections. On the other side of this equation are shown the categories taken from the spending stream, $S + T + M$, the leakages. In equilibrium, injections must equal leakages and the entire economy will adjust its level of output to ensure that this equality is maintained.

THE COMPLETE CIRCULAR FLOW DIAGRAM

All of the other diagrams to this point were mere building blocks so that the full and complete circular flow diagram could be understood. This is the diagram that summarizes the nature of aggregate demand.

There are the various leakages on the lower half, made up of savings (S), taxation (T) and imports (M). Businesses pay out incomes. Those who earn those incomes either consume, or else they save, pay their taxes or purchase imports. These leakages are a deduction from the potential spending stream.

Businesses also receive receipts from four sources. These are firstly from consumer demand (C), or they come in the form of various injections, business investment (I), public spending (G) or export income (X). The various injections are seen on the upper half of Figure 12.3.

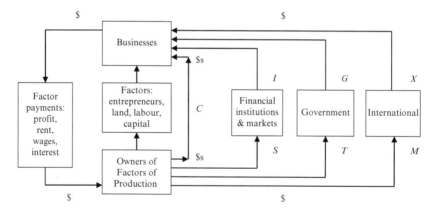

Figure 12.3   Circular flow with international sector

Equilibrium occurs where the level of leakages is exactly equal to the level of injections. If leakages are greater than injections, then money expenditure is draining out of the circular flow, with the most important consequence being that businesses find they are receiving less in earnings than they paid out in costs. The economy will therefore contract as businesses cut back on production and therefore on employment.

The policy answers suggested by this model are again to increase injections through higher levels of government spending (*G*) or via lowering the level of leakages through lowering the level of taxation. Such a response to recession has ever since its introduction been called a 'Keynesian' policy, and the various forms of demand-side attempts to increase the economy's rate of growth have been called a 'Keynesian' stimulus, of course named after John Maynard Keynes who did so much to bring this form of analysis into economic theory.

INVENTORY ADJUSTMENTS

There is one final matter to understand in the Keynesian model, and that is what happens when the two sides of the leakages–injections equation are not equal. Well, in fact, strangely enough they are always equal. But what allows that to happen is that the level of investment is divided into *intended* investment and *unintended* investment.

If part of the production during some period of time remains unsold, then these goods remain as part of inventories. Since they are part of the inventories of businesses that were not intended to remain, they are classified as *unintended inventory accumulation*, which is classified as a form of investment spending even though businesses had not intended to invest as much in inventories as they eventually did

If, on the other hand, the level of expenditure is higher than the level that had been expected, then inventories of goods disappear more rapidly than had been intended, and the fall-off in the level of inventories held is described as *unintended inventory decumulation*.

Equilibrium only occurs when the level of investment at the end of a period is equal to the investment that had been intended when the period began. In each time period, the level of injections will equal the level of leakages. Where the disequilibrium shows up is in the actual level of sales relative to the level of sales that had been expected before the period began.

If sales are higher than had been expected, business inventories fall relative to expectations, leading to more production and investment. If sales are lower than had been expected, then inventories end up higher than had been expected and businesses reduce production.

But it is the level of demand that makes all the difference. It is aggregate demand that drives a Keynesian model either upwards or downwards.

THE BASIC KEYNESIAN EQUATION

The graphical version of the Keynesian model will be built in the same way as the circular flow diagram, adding in additional sectors until the full model is on display. It should also be noted that there will be three different versions of the Keynesian model discussed, each one of which has been part of the traditional approach. These are:

- 'leakages' and 'injections';
- the 'Keynesian-cross' 45-degree diagram; and finally,
- what is known as aggregate demand and aggregate supply.

We start with the traditional way in which Keynesian economics has been taught. There are many other presentations that have been developed but this is the one that gets closest to Keynes's original concept.

And here we begin with a cut-down version of an economy where there are only consumers and investors, C and I. At this stage there is no government sector. Aggregate demand for GDP (Y) is thus the total demand for consumption goods by consumers plus the total demand for investment goods by business. Thus:

$$Y = C + I$$

It was then noted that GDP, that is, total national income, can either be consumed (C) or saved (S). So we have another basic equation:

$$Y = C + S$$

Therefore, in equilibrium:

$$I = S$$

That is, the economy comes to its resting point when the level of business investment is equal to the level of personal saving. What is important about this model is that the labour market has no influence on the level of economic activity. Saving and investment come to an equilibrium and the unemployment rate is whatever it happens to be.

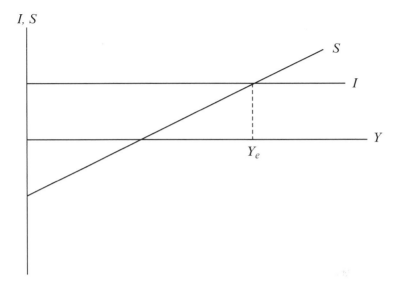

Figure 12.4   Equilibrium where saving and investment are equal

The Basic Leakages–Injections Framework

The basic diagram, showing the equilibrium between investment and saving, begins with the assumption that the level of investment is constant at all levels of income while the level of saving rises with the level of income. These are shown in Figure 12.4.

The level of national income is shown on the horizontal axis and the levels of saving and investment are shown on the vertical axis. The diagram is to be read from the bottom up. You should begin from the horizontal axis and look at each level of national income, Y.

The investment line I states that *if* the level of income is at some level, *then* the level of investment will be whatever it happens to be which can be read from the vertical axis.

In just the same way, the saving line S states that *if* the level of income is at some level, *then* the level of saving will be whatever it happens to be, which can also be read from the vertical axis.

Since by assumption the level of investment is decided independently of the level of saving, and is determined at the start of the period before anything has occurred, the investment is seen as unchanged by whatever actual level of GDP happens to eventuate.

Meanwhile, the diagram shows that saving increases as income increases. The higher the level of national income, the higher the level of savings.

The equilibrium level of output occurs where investment and saving are equal, in this case at *Ye*.

If *Y* is below *Ye*, so that investment is greater than saving, then the level of spending is greater than the level of output being produced. The economy will therefore expand until the level of investment and saving are equal. That is, *Y* will rise until it reaches *Ye*.

If, on the other hand, saving is greater than investment, so that less is bought than has been produced, some businesses begin to reduce production and employment. The economy will therefore contract until it reaches *Ye*. Once at *Ye*, nothing shifts.

The Keynesian Cross

The same sort of equilibrium can be shown from the expenditure side, although it is slightly more complicated to understand.

The basis of the diagram – known as the Keynesian Cross diagram – is the 45-degree line which comes halfway between the vertical and horizontal axis (Figure 12.5). What is notable about the 45-degree line is that everywhere along the 45-degree line everything on the vertical axis is equal to whatever is on the horizontal axis. If one takes any point on the 45-degree line, then if the amount shown on the horizontal axis is $10 million, then the same $10 million is found on the vertical axis.

If, however, the economy is at a point below the 45-degree line, the level of aggregate demand is less than the level of production.

The 45-degree line is used to explain the role of expenditure in an economy. On the horizontal axis in the second diagram below (Figure 12.6) is the level of output. On the vertical axis is the level of aggregate demand, made up, in this simple example, by consumption and investment, *C* and *I*.

There is first the level of consumption at all levels of GDP. It is read vertically and in the form of a typical 'if–then' statement. Any point on the C-curve, the consumption line, states that *if* the level of output is at some particular level, *then* the level of consumption will be whatever is shown on the vertical axis.

The same is shown by the investment curve. It states that *if* the level of GDP is at some particular level, *then* the level of output is at the amount shown on the vertical axis.

The figure for aggregate demand in this model is shown by the *C* + *I* line. It is found by vertically summing the level of consumption and investment at each level of output.

The *C* + *I* line shows that *if* the level of output is at some level, *then* the total level of aggregate demand will be whatever is shown on the vertical axis. And while the level of investment is the same at all levels of

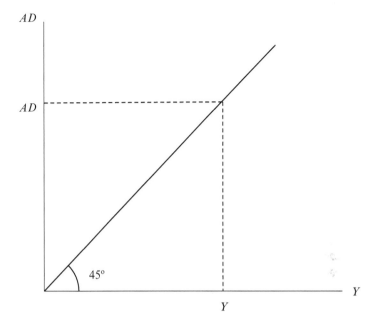

Figure 12.5   The 45-degree line

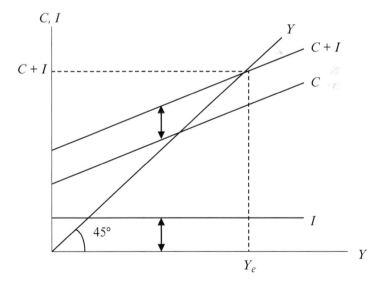

Figure 12.6   Equilibrium where consumption and investment equal production

production, because consumption rises as income rises, so too does the *C* + *I* line. Aggregate demand goes up as the level of national income goes up.

Everywhere along the 45-degree line the level of aggregate demand, shown on the vertical axis, is equal to the level of output, shown on the horizontal axis. It can be useful to think of this 45-degree line as the level of GDP (*Y*) since the core issue will be the vertical distance between the level of demand at full employment and the level of production required to achieve that level of employment.

Since equilibrium occurs where aggregate demand is equal to the level of production, equilibrium therefore occurs somewhere on the 45-degree line.

Neither the *C* nor the *I* line ever appear again and are rarely needed for the rest of the analysis. They are there to show what are the ingredients of the *C* + *I* line discussed next. Indeed, until we get to the final total level of aggregate demand, *C* + *I* + *G* + (*X* − *M*), we will not have reached the full specifications for the economy as a whole. Until then, the additional bits added on should be seen as staging posts on the way to the final theory.

C + I

The question then is, what happens if *C* + *I* does not equal *Y*? If the actual level of *Y* is greater than the equilibrium level, *Ye* – that is, if the actual level of GDP is greater than *Ye* – the level of production is therefore greater than the level of aggregate demand. Buyers across the economy are buying less than has been produced. Inventories are therefore increasing faster than intended and businesses will therefore reduce production. The economy will slow. GDP will fall and move towards the equilibrium level of output.

If, on the other hand, the actual level of production is less than the equilibrium level – in this case the actual level of GDP is less than *Ye* – more is being bought across the economy than businesses are producing. Inventories will be falling. The economy will therefore expand as entrepreneurs try to meet the increase in sales. The economy will grow until production and demand are the same, that is, until *C* + *I* is equal to *Y*.

Production Function

And while the level of employment is not shown on the diagram, it is the very purpose of this analysis. The assumption that lies behind both of these diagrams and all Keynesian models is that the higher the level of demand, the higher will be the level of production and therefore the higher will be employment.

A 'Keynesian' policy, therefore, is to increase the level of production by

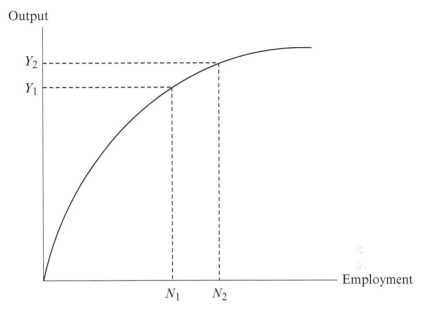

Figure 12.7   Production function

increasing the level of demand. The assumption behind a Keynesian model is that as the level of spending goes up, the level of production goes up, and therefore so, too, does the number of jobs.

Figure 12.7 shows what is known as the *production function*. It may seem an odd term, although there are reasons for it. But what is important is what it shows, which is the relationship between the level of output and the level of employment.

As the level of GDP increases, more employees are required. Thus at an income level Y_1 there is employment level N_1. As the level of production rises, here to Y_2, the level of employment required also rises, in this case to N_2. More production requires more people to have jobs.

The question, though, remains whether Keynesian-type spending on goods and services whose costs are greater than the value being created has a positive effect on employment, especially in the longer run.

Bringing $C + I$ and $I = S$ Together

The two graphical forms of equilibrium determination are shown together in Figure 12.8.

The equilibrium in the top diagram occurs where $Y = C + I$. In the

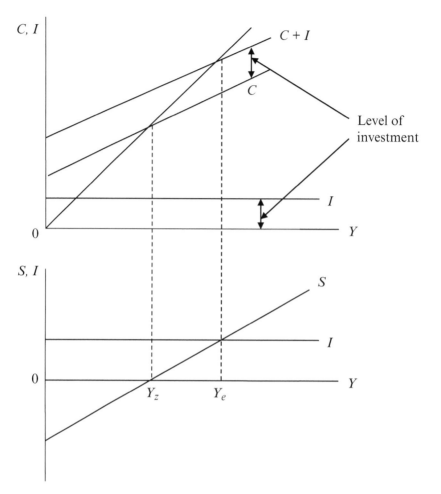

Figure 12.8   Equilibrium income expenditure and saving analysis

bottom diagram, equilibrium occurs where $S = I$. The two diagrams show exactly the same set of relationships, but in a different way.

In the upper half of the diagram, equilibrium occurs where the $C + I$ line meets the 45-degree line. Here the level of total demand represented by consumption and investment on the vertical axis is exactly equal to the level of production on the horizontal axis. This occurs at a production level of Ye. Everything produced finds a market.

The equilibrium in the investment–saving approach occurs where $I = S$. This takes place at the same level of output, Ye. It is towards this level of production, and its associated level of employment, that the economy will move. It might also be noted that where the consumption line crosses the 45-degree line, the level of saving is exactly zero.

It should thus be seen that the information shown on both halves of the diagram is based on the same sets of underlying economic conditions. In the top half, equilibrium occurs where $Y = C + I$, and in the bottom half it occurs where investment equals the level of saving generated at that level of national income, that is, where $I = S$.

INTERLUDE ON SAVING IN MODERN ECONOMIC ANALYSIS

The potential villain of the piece in Keynesian economic theory is saving. Excess saving causes an economy to stagnate. Classical economists had argued that saving is what drives an economy forward. Since it is saving that finances investment and therefore growth and innovation, an economy could not, according to classical economists, have too much saving. The greater the level of saving, all other things being equal, the faster the economy would expand.

In contrast, in modern macroeconomic theory, where demand rather than value-adding production is seen as the single most important impetus for economic activity, saving, rather than being the feedstock for capital investment, is instead a withdrawal from the spending stream. By lowering the level of spending, increased saving lowers growth rather than increasing it.

A prime example of this way of thinking is outlined in the following passage:

> The classical economists argued that saving was a national virtue. More saving would lead via lower interest rates to more investment and faster growth. Keynes was at pains to show the opposite. Saving, far from being a national virtue, could be a national vice . . .
> As people save more, they will spend less. Firms will thus produce less. There will thus be a multiplied *fall* in income . . .
> But this is not all. Far from the extra saving encouraging more investment, the lower consumption will *discourage* firms from investing. If investment falls, the aggregate expenditure line will shift downwards. There will then be a further multiplied fall in national income . . .
> [This phenomenon] had been recognised before Keynes . . . But despite these early recognitions of the dangers of underconsumption, the belief that saving would increase the prosperity of the nation was central to classical economic thought. (Sloman and Norris, 2002: 417)

Much of the policy development that has occurred since Keynesian economics became the basis for macroeconomics has centred around the need to maintain the level of aggregate demand in an economy to ensure that all savings are soaked up. Saving in a Keynesian model remains a problem.

BRINGING IN GOVERNMENT

In a closed economy with only the private sector, equilibrium occurs where $C + I$ equals Y. Domestic private demand is all there is. But in every economy there is more than just the private sector. There is always a government undertaking various activities. The government, and its expenditure, must therefore also be brought into the story.

Using only the 45-degree analysis to begin with, the government can be brought in by adding a constant amount of spending to the level of spending shown by $C + I$. If government purchases of goods and services (designated by G) are added in, then the total level of spending becomes $C + I + G$.

In Figure 12.9 we now find that the level of aggregate demand is made up of the total expenditure by consumers, private investors and the government. G is a catch-all for everything that government buys. So far as public spending goes, whether government spends on its own consumption items (salaries paid to public servants, for example) or whether it

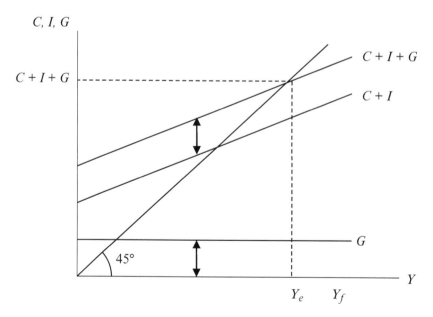

Figure 12.9   Consumption, investment and government spending

represents forms of government investment (such as expenditure on roads or public housing), it all comes to the same thing.

The level of aggregate demand with government spending introduced is made up of $C + I + G$, while the equilibrium level of output is at Ye. Here total demand is equal to the total level of production. Everything produced finds a buyer.

But note that even here there is no necessity that the equilibrium level of production will employ everyone who wants a job. Y_f is the full employment level of production which is a level of GDP higher than the equilibrium level found at Y_e. Y_f represents the level of production that would require the efforts of the entire workforce to produce. Unless the economy is at that level of output, unemployment continues to exist.

EXPORTS AND IMPORTS

$C + I + G$ only represent the domestic economy. What must still be included is the international sector. Part of the demand for the output produced by domestic producers is made up of the exports sold in other countries. Part of what is bought in the domestic economy are forms of output produced in other countries. The level of aggregate demand for the productions of domestic producers must therefore take into account foreign trade, the expenditure from foreign buyers adjusted for the goods and services produced in other countries that is bought domestically.

Adding in expenditure on exports by foreign buyers, which increases demand for domestic production, and taking away the value of imports from foreign producers, which diverts demand away from domestically produced goods and services, provides the final components of aggregate demand.

These net exports (NX in Figure 12.10) are made up of exports minus imports ($X - M$). The equilibrium in an open economy occurs where the total level of production is made up of the total of everything that was bought from within the economy, including the goods and services bought by buyers in other countries, $C + I + G + X$, from which is substracted the total level of imports. As discussed in Chapter 9, if one subtracts the level of imports from the total of what was bought, the remainder must be what was produced in the domestic economy.

In equilibrium the level of aggregate demand $C + I + G + (X - M)$ is exactly equal to the level of production, Ye. It is here, in a Keynesian model, that the entire economy comes to rest.

Again, if the actual level of production is higher than Ye, the level of aggregate demand is less than the level of output so that the economy

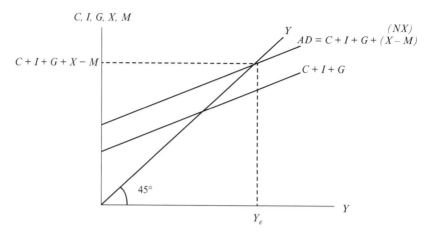

Figure 12.10   Introduction of foreign trade

contracts. If, on the other hand, the actual level of production is less than
Ye, then more is being bought than the economy is producing, with the
result that the economy expands.

It is demand, and demand alone, in this model that determines the
level of economic activity. And once equilibrium is established, unless
something causes the level of demand to shift, the economy will stay
exactly where it is irrespective of how many people happen to be
unemployed.

INJECTIONS AND LEAKAGES

The saving and investment model was also expanded to take into account
all of the various forms of spending, such as investment, as well as all of the
various forms of withdrawals from the spending stream, such as saving.

Just as with the circular flow diagram, to investment (I) on the expenditure side was added government spending (G) and exports (X). All of
these were seen to add to aggregate demand, and the higher they were, the
higher the level of economic activity would be.

These were the *injections*, and they were, in total, $I + G + X$.

On the other side of the ledger as shown by the circular flow diagram,
as a subtraction from the spending stream to go along with saving (S)
were taxation (T) and imports (M). The higher any of these might be, the
lower the level of aggregate demand and therefore the lower the level that
economic activity might be.

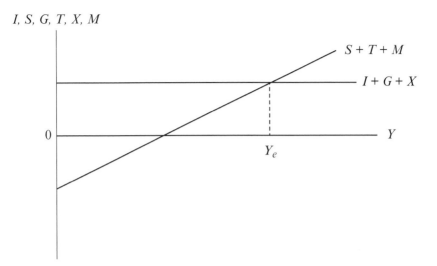

Figure 12.11 Leakages and injections

These subtractions from the spending stream were the *leakages* or *with-drawals* and they were totalled as $S + T + M$.

As shown in Figure 12.11, $I + G + X = S + T + M$ is where equilibrium occurs. All of the expenditure going into the economy is balanced by all of the leakages. Consumption (C), as was shown in the circular flow diagram, is netted out as consumption spending goes straight to business, without any intermediary as is the case with the other forms of spending.

Again saving is a problem. Saving too much slows an economy. Higher saving will, all other things being equal, raise the $S + T + M$ line and therefore lower the level of equilibrium output. You might therefore think that taxation would also be seen as a problem, but since taxes are used to finance government spending there is no necessary problem involved. But if looked at independently on its own, an increase in the level of taxation will add to leakages and slow the economy

Finally, net exports are seen as a potential stimulus to activity. We have, in a sense, conceptually returned to the world before Adam Smith, because here it is exports which are good for an economy, while imports are bad.

From this simplified model can be seen the public policy advice that is given to governments during recessions: increase spending and lower taxes. Higher spending pushes the $I + G + X$ upwards with Y rising as a result. Lower taxes causes the $S + T + M$ line to move down, again raising the level of output.

KEYNESIAN POLICY

Keynes's aim, an aim which remains intact in most macroeconomic models today, was to show how government spending could lift an economy and push it into higher levels of national output, and therefore into higher levels of employment. It was this that has since been named a 'Keynesian' policy.

In the standard Keynesian model in which we have left out the international sector since it makes no difference to these policy considerations, we start with the $C + I + G$ line. If aggregate demand cuts the 45-degree line at a level of economic activity below the full employment level, the economy will remain just there until something happens to change it. Because the economy is in equilibrium, something outside the system must change for this to change.

The Keynesian notion is that governments and governments alone can rescue the economy from its recessionary level of activity. By increasing government spending (G), the total level of aggregate demand will increase. With higher aggregate demand, economic output will increase and therefore the number of persons employed will increase and unemployment fall.

Figure 12.12 shows two aggregate demand curves. The first, showing

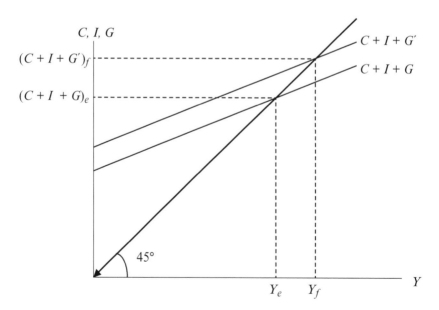

Figure 12.12   Creating full employment through higher public spending

total aggregate demand of $C + I + G$, reaches an equilibrium at *Ye* which is below the full employment level of output, Y_f. The Keynesian answer is to increase the level of aggregate demand through higher levels of public spending.

The level of public spending rises from G to G'. As a result, the level of aggregate demand rises from $C + I + G$ to $C + I + G'$.

The level of national output therefore rises from Y_e to Y_f and the level of employment moves to the full employment level of production.

Since Y_f is the full employment level of output, the actions of the government have brought the economy into full employment which would not have occurred had the government not acted as it did.

DEALING WITH RECESSION

Government spending, of course, exists in every economy and always has, so that $C + I + G$ can represent an economy in full employment or in recession.

Suppose an economy that had been at a full employment level of output goes into recession because for whatever reason, the level of investment falls so that the level of output is below the full employment level of output.

This is shown in Figure 12.13. The level of investment has fallen from *I*

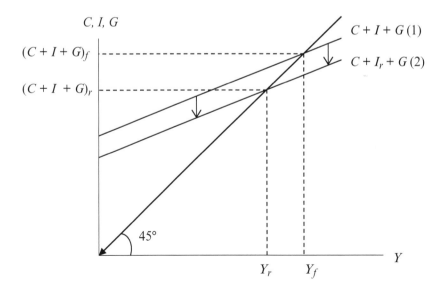

Figure 12.13   A fall in aggregate demand leads to recession

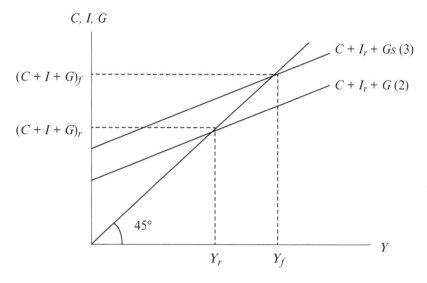

Figure 12.14   Government spending to restore aggregate demand

to I_r. The level of aggregate demand has therefore fallen from $C + I + G$, marked with a (1), to $C + I_r + G$, marked with a (2). The subscript f indicates the full employment level of output while the subscript r indicates that the economy is in recession.

With the fall in aggregate demand, the level of GDP has fallen from Y_f to Y_r. And with nothing to effect change, there output will remain unless something is done to raise the level of aggregate demand.

Figure 12.14 starts where Figure 12.13 ended. The economy is in recession at Y_r with the level of aggregate demand at $C + I_r + G$, again marked with a (2). How can the economy be brought out of recession?

The Keynesian answer is for government spending (G) to rise to take up the fall in aggregate demand. G rises to Gs (s for stimulus) which is comprised of the previous level of government spending plus the additional expenditure on the stimulus.

The level of aggregate demand therefore rises to $C + I_r + Gs$, marked with a (3). To the extent that spending itself is the driver of economic activity, the level of aggregate demand has returned to the full employment level with GDP now at Y_f.

But not all is as it was. Compared with the previous $C + I + G$, there is now less private investment since I_r is lower than the previous I, and there is more government spending, which has gone up from G to Gs. Since public spending is less productive than private spending – and given the haste with which many stimulus programmes are usually introduced may well be completely unproductive, with their costs higher than their economic return – the economy is not as productive as it had previously been, even if employment does return to its previous level which no actual Keynesian stimulus has ever achieved.

THE MULTIPLIER

There is one last piece of Keynesian theory that needs to be included, and that is the theory of the multiplier. The theory states that an initial increase in public spending, say $100 million, will lead to an eventual increase in the level of output of some multiple of that initial spending.

If the multiplier is 2, then $100 million in initial spending will lead to an increase of $200 million in total output. If the multiplier is 4, then an initial increase of whatever amount will lead to spending rising four times as much.

The reasoning is that each person receiving the first round of expenditure will spend some of their increased incomes and save the rest. Their expenditure become second-round effects: the persons who receive the initial spending will spend some of it in turn while also saving the rest. Ultimately, an increase in public spending spreads farther and wider and the benefits of increased activity are amplified.

This story is told in virtually all macroeconomic texts and has been almost since 1936, along with methods of calculation that provide a precise estimate of what the numerical value of the multiplier might be. But as these multiplier effects have never been observed in practice, the concept is not of much use other than to understand what Keynesian economists are saying about the effects of an increase in public spending – even unproductive spending – on the level of GDP in general.

SOME FINAL THOUGHTS ON PUBLIC SPENDING

Amongst the major deficiencies of the Keynesian model is its assumption that all expenditure, no matter who is doing the spending or what the spending is on, in terms of economic activity comes to the same thing. This is obviously untrue, which often translates into policy decisions in which productive private sector spending is replaced by far less productive, and often unproductive, public sector spending. They are not equivalent.

Firstly, public spending directs the economy into a completely different direction than private sector expenditures. This point does not just relate to final goods and services but to the entire structure of production that provide inputs into such public sector projects. An entire network of interrelated businesses are supported through the subsidized projects. Call it charity and welfare if you must; just do not confuse it with an increase in value-adding production or see such spending as a contribution to economic growth.

Secondly, the things that governments produce are not typically sold on the market so that there are no additional consumer goods available to buy with the incomes earned by producing what the government has decided to subsidize. The effect on purchasing power is dubious at best.

Thirdly, because the different direction such additional public spending flows into sets up an entirely different structure of production for the economy as a whole, existing economic relationships are disrupted when there are already major disruptions taking place because the economy has entered recession.

Fourthly, it is a further reminder that when the economy begins to recover, there will need to be a further contrary set of disruptions as resources are redirected to the economic structure supported by private sector activity. One has to assume that most of these emergency forms of public spending, brought on to limit the impact of recession, will be reversed.

Rather than this being a simple shift from one set of final demands to another, it will require a restructuring of all of the industries involved in producing whatever the additional public sector spending had been devoted to producing. Not only will businesses producing the additional public goods experience a fall in demand, but so too will producers of every one of the inputs. They will also be affected with disruptions to demand for their products.

NOTE

1. To be strictly accurate, according to Keynes it was also possible to 'hoard' money, meaning that individuals would keep their purchasing power literally in the form of cash. With interest rates low, there would be a 'liquidity preference' where individuals kept cash on hand because they feared a capital loss on their savings if their money was tied up in the bond market as interest rates rose. The money thus held was an even more relentless reason to explain why money earned in production would not re-enter the spending stream. (See *The General Theory*, Keynes, [1936] 1987: 166–70, if you think no one would be so absurd as to suggest any such thing.)

13. Aggregate demand and aggregate supply

This chapter is about the application of Keynesian theory to dealing with both unemployment and inflation. And again it comes with a warning that this is being taught not because the theory is seen to be valid, but because it is how macroeconomics is taught across the world. Following policies based on this model will deepen recessions rather than promote recovery. But as this is the standard model now taught everywhere, here it is so that you can know what others believe, and understand the policies they introduce.

This chapter also contains quite a few diagrams. None of them are difficult but all are necessary to get a sense of the policies that are used to keep unemployment and inflation down to 'acceptable' levels.

But the central point of this Keynesian analysis is this: an economy has only so much capacity and if you try to push an economy beyond its productive capabilities, it will 'overheat'. This overheating will create an inflationary environment which comes with a series of very harmful economic consequences of their own.

On the other hand, if there is not enough demand, then the economy will slow and unemployment will rise. So policy makers, even while they are worried about the inflationary effects of too much demand must also be worried about the employment effects of too little.

HISTORICAL INTERLUDE

The 45-degree line model with its 'Keynesian cross diagram' was the core of macroeconomic teaching from the 1940s through to the early 1970s. It was near enough all aggregate demand and not much else. But as there were no major recessions during the period, although a few minor downturns did occur, the model continued to be taught in this way because events in the real world had not yet shown it to be dangerously incomplete.

It was in the late 1960s and early 1970s that the first major post-World War II economic downturn took place, and the causes were very far from anything related to the demand side of the economy. If anything, it demonstrated that a demand-side understanding of economic events provided no insight into many of the most important problems an economy might face.

The Vietnam War had pushed public spending in the United States upwards since the cost of the war had to be added to the normal activities of government. In the United States, as well as in similar economies, there was also a push for much greater spending on social welfare programmes.

Yet rather than these economies flowering under the increase in demand, they began to wilt. What made matters worse was the continuing upwards pressure on the price level as inflation began to accelerate across the world. But what caused inflationary pressures to rocket were the almost simultaneous 'oil shock' and wage explosions of the early 1970s.

The oil shock, as it was called, quadrupled the price of a barrel of oil virtually overnight. It caused a massive and almost immediate rise in prices of products produced from crude oil as well as energy, transport and related costs. It slowed economic activity while at the same time pushing inflation well up.

Coincident with, but also in many ways caused by the rise in oil prices, were the worldwide wage explosions which affected one economy after another. Annual wage increases well beyond 10 per cent became common. Again this led to a slowdown in economic activity and an even larger rise in the price level.

It therefore became immediately evident that the simple Keynesian-cross 45-degree line diagram could not explain what was taking place. The Keynesian-cross was therefore replaced with another model almost completely patterned after the supply and demand curves found in micro-economics. These were the *aggregate* supply (*AS*) and *aggregate* demand (*AD*) curves which are now staples within macroeconomic theory.

What *AS–AD* brought to attention was firstly the fact that the supply side of the economy had something to do with the level of activity. The second aspect it focused attention on were the forces causing inflation. Keynesian-cross diagrams had no price-level dimension while *AS–AD* curves did.

Eventually, even the *AS–AD* apparatus was modified to return economic theory towards classical pre-Keynesian thought by the introduction of the long-run aggregate supply curve (LRAS). It was an attempt to show that in the long run, fluctuations in aggregate demand have no effect on the level of economic activity; almost, in its own way, a reintroduction of Say's Law. But that was in the long run. In anything shorter, aggregate demand was still seen to have large effects, which is why from a Keynesian perspective an economist's work is never done.

AGGREGATE DEMAND AND AGGREGATE SUPPLY

Most important in understanding the short-run version of *AS–AD* is that there are no changes in the underlying conditions of aggregate demand or supply. The aggregate demand and aggregate supply curves are schedules of different possible combinations of the price level and aggregate output over a period of time, say a month or a quarter. Nothing much changes in the underlying structure of an economy in a month or during most quarters.

The most important assumption is this: the level of nominal (money) wages is kept constant. Although along both the *AD* and *AS* curves the price level is rising, nominal wages do not change. Therefore, higher prices have a negative effect on aggregate demand, while those same higher prices have a positive effect on aggregate supply.

Or to put it another way, as the price level goes up, buyers, whose incomes by assumption do not change, become less able to buy as much as they did before; while sellers, whose labour costs also by assumption do not change, become more willing to produce.

If, for example, wages are some fixed amount, say $6000 a month, and the price level (represented here by the Consumer Price Index, CPI) is at 100.0, then the real wage is $6000. If, however, the wage is $6000 and the price level has risen to let us say 120.0, then the real wage will have fallen, in this case to $5000 a month. The higher the price level, the lower will be aggregate demand. This relationship is found in Figure 13.1.

The aggregate demand curve shows different combinations of the price *level* and the level of aggregate demand. At higher prices less is demanded while at lower prices more is demanded.

The diagram is again in the form of an 'if–then' statement. It states that *if* prices were at some level, say P_1, *then* the level of aggregate demand would be Y_1. If, however, the level of prices were lower at P_2, then the same nominal incomes in combination with a lower price level would mean that real incomes were higher, since with the same nominal income you can buy more if prices are lower. Aggregate demand in real terms will therefore be higher, in this case at Y_2.

It is a similar idea for aggregate supply. Shown in Figure 13.2 is the *short-run* aggregate supply curve (*SRAS*). This shows how much output producers would be willing to put up for sale at different prices. Since business costs remain constant along this curve, the higher are the prices they receive while their costs have remained the same, the more that sellers would be willing to produce and sell.

Here, too, is an if–then relationship that is read from the price-level axis. Since we are dealing with the short run, everything is assumed constant, and especially the cost of labour.

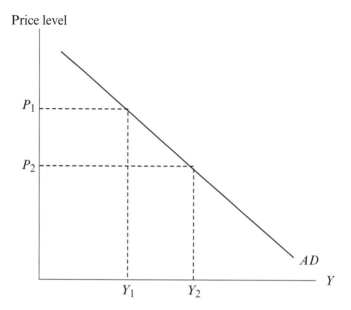

Figure 13.1   Aggregate demand

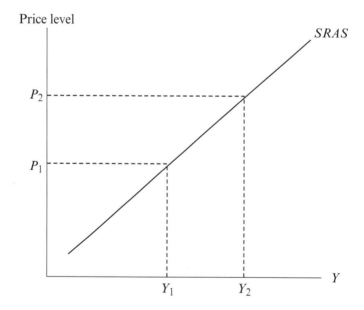

Figure 13.2   Aggregate supply

The higher the price level, that is the more that can be received for each unit of output, the more businesses will be willing to produce. Since labour costs in particular are assumed not to change during the period, if prices are higher more will be produced.

Thus, *if* the price level is at P_1, *then* businesses in aggregate would be willing to produce a level of output represented by Y_1. *If,* however, prices were higher at P_2, with all production costs constant, businesses would be willing to produce an even greater amount of output, here represented by Y_2.

Hence the upwards slope of the short run aggregate supply curve. With higher prices come higher profits and therefore higher levels of production.

EQUILIBRIUM

Equilibrium, as with the microeconomic supply and demand, occurs where aggregate demand equals aggregate supply. This is shown in Figure 13.3.

Where the two curves meet is found a simultaneous determination of the price level for the entire economy and the level of production. Output is at Y_e and the price level is P_e.

There is again nothing in this equilibrium position that would ensure that the economy is at full employment. It is a Keynesian model. Therefore

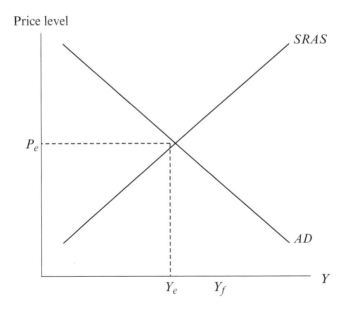

Figure 13.3   Macroeconomic equilibrium

the equilibrium in the aggregate demand and supply for goods and services places a limit on the overall level of production from the demand side. The full employment level of production may be at Y_f, at a higher level of production than Y_e.

Behind the *AD* curve are all of the usual elements of aggregate demand: *C*, *I*, *G*, *X* and *M*. Whatever pushes the components of aggregate demand upwards will push the *AD* curve to the right. If these underlying factors reduce the collective willingness to buy, then *AD* moves to the left.

So far as the *SRAS* curve is concerned, its position is dependent on production costs. Anything that reduces production costs per unit of output will move the curve to the right. Anything that raises production costs per unit of output will move the curve to the left.

Although the curve is short-run, and most of the underlying elements are supposedly frozen, if wage or other production costs move up or down, there is a shift in the curve. Higher costs move the curve to the left, reducing the level of production at each price level. Lower costs move the curve to the right.

But note this. In the short run, there is almost nothing that policy makers can do that would cause the *SRAS* curve to move to the right. Moving the *SRAS* curve to the right requires long, patient efforts to raise the productiveness of the economy. Technological change, improving skill levels, innovation are the kinds of changes that will lead to the slow drift of the *SRAS* curve to the right.

But there are many changes that can move the *SRAS* curve to the left, and these are generally changes that raise the costs of production. Thinking back to the 1970s, the combination of the rise in the cost of oil and coincident wage explosion would have moved the *SRAS* curve very firmly to the left. The result would have been the rise in the price level and a large fall in output. With the large fall in output would have come the fall in employment.

TYPES OF UNEMPLOYMENT AND THE NATURAL RATE

Modern macroeconomic policy cannot, however, be understood without first understanding the modern classification of unemployment. There are, broadly speaking, three types. Although each has the same immediate consequence – someone is without a job – they are very different for policy purposes.

Frictional Unemployment

There is, firstly, *frictional unemployment*. Frictional unemployment is the naturally occurring unemployment that cannot be escaped in even the best-managed economies. It is the unemployment that exists because economies are dynamic. Some businesses are shutting down while others are opening up. Jobs are being lost in one enterprise while other jobs become available somewhere else.

People therefore lose their jobs as the economy adjusts, and until they find their next job, they are unemployed. Some people just quit their jobs and look for another. Others are new entrants to the labour force who are unemployed while they look for their first jobs.

This kind of unemployment is actually healthy. Workers look for the jobs in which they can make their highest valued contribution to output as reflected in the wages they receive. This can take time, so even their period of unemployment can be seen as productive.

Structural Unemployment

The second form of unemployment is what is referred to as *structural unemployment*. This is a very difficult form of unemployment to overcome. It comes about because not only do people lose their jobs, but the very skills they have are no longer sought by the labour market.

Logging as an industry slows, and people whose jobs it has been to fell trees lose their jobs. Their sole commercial skills, however, may only be related to their forestry work. They are unemployed and willing to work but no jobs available in the economy match the kinds of things they can do.

New technologies have typically created structural unemployment. With the coming of desktop computers, the role of typists has completely disappeared. Few jobs are any longer secure from the forces of innovation and technological change.

Cyclical Unemployment

The final category of unemployment is described as *cyclical unemployment*. This is the kind of unemployment associated with downturns in the economy. The most notable characteristic of an economy in recession is the large and often rapid rise in unemployment.

Related as such unemployment is to the business cycle, it would be expected to go down as soon as economic recovery began. When the economy has returned to its full employment level, all cyclical forms of unemployment will have disappeared.

This is, in fact, the very definition of *full employment*. There will always be frictional and structural unemployment in even the best of economies, but cyclical occurs only when the economy is performing below its potential.

POTENTIAL GDP AND THE NATURAL RATE OF UNEMPLOYMENT

The level of economic growth, when resources are being used efficiently and labour is fully employed, is described as *potential* Gross Domestic Product (GDP). The unemployment rate when GDP has reached its potential is described as the *natural rate of unemployment*.

The natural rate of unemployment is the rate of unemployment when cyclical unemployment is zero. And what is that particular rate? It is different in every economy and is only determined by those responsible for economic management.

If the actual unemployment rate is below the natural rate, inflation would be expected to go up. If instead the actual unemployment rate is greater than the natural rate, the inflation rate would be expected to fall. It is this relationship, as discussed below, that is at the centre of the modern theory of inflation control.

INFLATION AND ITS PROBLEMS

Unemployment is not, of course, the only problem an economy must deal with. Inflation also creates massive problems on its own, and must therefore also be avoided. The dilemma here is that many of the actions that lower unemployment also tend to raise inflation, while many of the actions taken to lower inflation raise unemployment.

Inflation is a continuous ongoing reduction in the exchange value of money. When inflation occurs, the purchasing power of a unit of currency continues to fall, so that as time passes, each unit of currency buys less than it did in the time period before. It is an insidious process that creates many problems in the management of an economy.

The most obvious manifestation is a rising price level. Inflation comes in many forms, from the creeping 2–3 per cent growth in prices that most economies now tolerate as an acceptable price to pay for lower rates of unemployment, to the many thousands of per cent annual growth rates that are found during hyperinflations.

But because inflation has so many who gain from its existence, especially governments, and because the cures are almost always extremely painful, once inflation sets in it is difficult to root out.

THE PROBLEMS CAUSED BY INFLATION

The problems caused by inflation, however, need to be understood:

1. Money no longer maintains its secure role as a store of value. The purchasing power of a unit of currency continues to fall, so that other means of holding wealth are sought. Since all other forms of wealth holding are more costly and less fluid, the effect of inflation is to make it more difficult to conduct one's daily life.
2. Personal savings are eroded and can be entirely lost. Money kept as cash loses value. But even money kept in interest-bearing deposits may be subject to loss if interest rates do not rise as rapidly as the price level.
3. This problem is worsened to the extent that interest earnings are taxed. Even if money is earning a nominal return as rapid as the growth in the inflation rate, once taxes are paid, the real value of the sum of money saved will diminish. Unless interest covers not only the inflation rate but also the tax rate on savings, the purchasing power of savings will fall.
4. Forward planning within business becomes more difficult. A large part of the planning process involves estimates of future costs and revenues. In an inflationary environment such projections become much more uncertain.
5. Businesses become much more tentative in terms of investment. The more clouded future state of the economy adds to entrepreneurial risk and reduces confidence. Businesses seek a higher than normal return on their investments before they become willing to commit their funds.
6. Wage increases accelerate and industrial disputation is certain to increase. Workers act to protect their earnings by pressing for higher incomes as prices rise. Various techniques, such as cost of living adjustments, are included in contracts entrenching the inflationary process. Industrial disputes increase as wage earners intensify their attempts to maintain their real incomes.
7. Lenders are robbed, while borrowers receive an unearned return. Those who lend money out on the expectation that the payment of interest, and eventually the repayment of the principal, will provide a positive return find out, instead, that the money returned

to them is lower in real value than the money originally lent out.

8. In contrast, debtors receive a windfall return which allows them to pay their contracted debts in a debased currency.

9. Interest rates rise to quite high levels as an inflation premium is added to the other factors that will induce lenders to lend. High interest rates become a major deterrent to investment.

10. Additional unemployment is created as the economy fails to adjust fully to the movement in relative prices. The lower level of real investment, and the slower growth in sales as prices rise and businesses find it more difficult to cover costs, lessens the willingness of firms to employ.

11. Inflation does not affect all prices to the same extent, nor does its effect descend on all members of a community at the same time. Those selling products whose prices rise last, or in occupations where incomes are the last to increase, find they are losing out to those whose product prices or nominal incomes rise sooner than theirs. Others are able to buy before prices adjust to their new higher level.

Governments, in particular, are able to profit from inflation since taxes rise with the price level, and most importantly, because of progressive taxes, government revenues rise more rapidly than the economy. The effect is to increase public spending as a proportion of total economic output. The losses to government revenues as inflation subsides can also create disincentives for governments to implement policies that bring inflation to an end.

SUMMING UP ON INFLATION

Inflation lowers living standards, reduces growth and adds to uncertainty. It makes individuals waste time and effort on finding means to protect themselves from inflation rather than adding to the aggregate production of value-adding goods and services. They try to hedge against inflation rather than contributing to the sum total of products available on the market.

Yet once the process begins, it becomes a political nightmare to bring such inflations to an end. No one wants to become the first to choose not to demand an inflationary increase in payments that compensates them for the rise in the price level. Whether it is income earners thinking about the wages they receive, or business owners and the prices they charge, or government concerned with taxes and other imposts they impose, by being the first to restrict their income for the national good, they have chosen to reduce their own command over goods and services while allowing others to move ahead.

So rather than anyone being willing to step back, each group, and most individuals within each group, continue to work in their own interests, seeking higher nominal returns for the goods and services they provide. It is a problem which is almost impossible to end without a major economic downturn and a huge dislocation in activity.

NATURAL RATE OF UNEMPLOYMENT AND LONG-RUN AGGREGATE SUPPLY

This brings us back to the natural rate of unemployment, which has a very important additional characteristic. The natural rate of unemployment is the rate of unemployment at which the rate of inflation will remain unchanged. It is not where the inflation rate is zero, but where the inflation rate stays at whatever rate it already is.

According to the theory, if the actual unemployment rate falls below the natural rate, the rate of inflation will begin to rise. If, for example, the natural unemployment rate is 6 per cent and the actual unemployment rate is lower at 5 per cent, the assumption is that inflationary pressures will increase and the price level will rise.

If, however, the actual unemployment rate is above the natural rate, the inflation rate will diminish. Therefore, if the natural rate is 6 per cent but the actual rate of unemployment is 7 per cent, the rate of inflation will begin to fall.

Only where the actual rate of unemployment coincides with the esti-mated natural rate will the inflation rate stabilize. If inflation is at 3 per cent per annum, then it will stay at 3 per cent per annum. If it is at 5 per cent, then it stays at 5 per cent. Therefore, if the aim is to lower the rate of inflation, the only way this can be done, according to the theory, is to raise the actual level of unemployment above the natural rate and maintain that higher rate of unemployment until the inflation rate falls to the inflation rate desired. At that point, the unemployment rate can be lowered to its natural rate and kept there.

It is the manipulation of the actual rate of unemployment relative to the estimated natural rate which is at the centre of anti-inflationary policy. Or to put this in a more straightforward way, inflation is brought down by deliberately, and as a matter of policy, pushing the rate of unemployment up.

INFLATIONARY POLICY AND THE SRAS

In understanding this policy, it must first be seen that a rise in inflation will set off a series of responses throughout the economy by which various groups will attempt to defend their real levels of income. Since inflation lowers the purchasing power of incomes earned, an acceleration of inflation will create increased pressures for higher money incomes and especially for higher wage rates, because of the higher prices that have to be paid for goods and services.

Higher incomes will push the *SRAS* curve to the left, which means the level of GDP will fall. Thus, the economy cannot for very long break past the barrier imposed by the natural rate of unemployment. There is an upwards limit imposed on the economy by technology, existing capital and labour force numbers and skills. Any attempt to move the economy to a higher level of activity will create bottlenecks, labour shortages and inflationary pressures that will by themselves cause the economy to slow. The effect is to create higher inflation but no sustainable addition to output.

In Figure 13.4, there has been an increase in aggregate demand, with the AD curve moving from AD_1 to AD_2. It might have been caused by an increase in consumer confidence or in investment expectations or public spending. But whatever may have been the reason, the equilibrium level

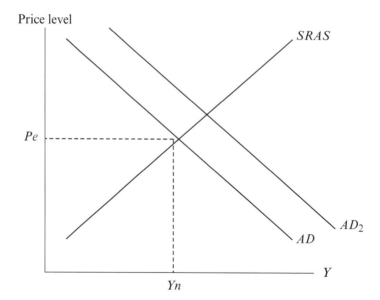

Figure 13.4   Macroeconomic equilibrium

of output has moved beyond its natural rate, indicated by *Yn*, and is attempting to produce more output than is sustainable given the economy's resource base.

But whatever may have been the cause, it is the consequences that matter. There are many things that might push aggregate demand outwards, but if the economy is already at its natural rate of unemployment, the concerns about an acceleration of inflation begin to mount in the minds of those responsible for managing the economy.

In Figure 13.4, the new equilibrium occurs at a level of GDP higher than *Yn*, where *Yn* is the full employment level of output, being the level of output at which the unemployment rate is at its natural rate. Because the economy is trying to produce beyond its potential – it is outside of its production possibility curve – there are shortages of all kinds of inputs, and particularly of labour. Prices begin to rise, and it is at this point that wage earners become concerned about their loss of purchasing power.

The result is a far more intense effort by working people to increase their wages to compensate for their loss of purchasing power. And it is through circumstances such as these that an inflationary spiral begins to gather momentum.

LONG-RUN AGGREGATE SUPPLY (LRAS)

The increase in aggregate demand beyond the economy's potential level of GDP, which occurs where the unemployment rate is below its natural rate, sets off a sequence of events:

- Aggregate demand having gone up for whatever reason, the *AD* curve moves to the right.
- This sets off inflationary pressures since demand pressures begin to exceed the ability of the economy to produce. Of particular importance is the effect on wage rates which begin to increase, which in turn pushes the *SRAS* curve to the left.
- The increases in money wages received also leads to an increase in the demand for goods and services, which pushes the *AD* curve even further to the right.
- The higher inflation that then occurs leads to further strikes and wage increases as wage earners attempt to maintain the purchasing power of their incomes
- The continuous shifting of *SRAS* to the left as costs increase, and the almost simultaneous shift of the *AD* curve to the right as more money is being earned and spent, traces out a series of points.

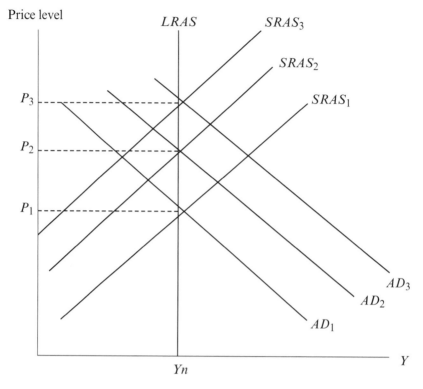

Figure 13.5   Tracing out long-run aggregate supply

- The points traced out become what is known as the long-run aggregate supply curve (*LRAS*).

As shown in Figure 13.5, the long-run aggregate supply curve is in practice the equivalent of the production possibility curve. It is the maximum an economy can produce without creating unsustainable inflationary pressures. If demand is greater than potential supply, whatever may happen in the short run, ultimately forces are set to work that bring the level of production back down to *Yn*.

Yn is the level of output that represents the economy's potential level of GDP. It is the level of output in which cyclical unemployment just reaches zero. There is still frictional and structural unemployment but the unemployment rate is at its irreducible minimum rate given all of the circumstances that exist in that economy at that time.

GETTING INFLATION DOWN

In fact, once inflationary pressures intrude, the level of output may fall below *Yn* for an extended period, which is how the inflation rate is brought down. If inflation only increased prices but had no effect on output, there would be little need for concern about prices. That, however, is not how things work.

To get inflation down requires a prolonged period of high unemployment to beat inflationary expectations out of the system. Only when inflationary expectations have been contained, so that wage earners settle for moderate increases in incomes, will the inflation rate begin to subside and return to an acceptable level.

It is the role of policy makers to do their utmost to convince those who set prices and pay wages that inflation has finally disappeared. Only then will wage increases be set at rates that keep inflation rates within some kind of either notional or explicit target range.

Thus, as shown in Figure 13.6, an anti-inflationary policy will need to pull the *AD* curve so far to the left that the equilibrium occurs at Y_2, which occurs below *Yn*. Below *Yn*, the actual rate of unemployment is above its natural rate and the economy is growing below its potential growth rate.

Such reductions in aggregate demand could occur through cuts to

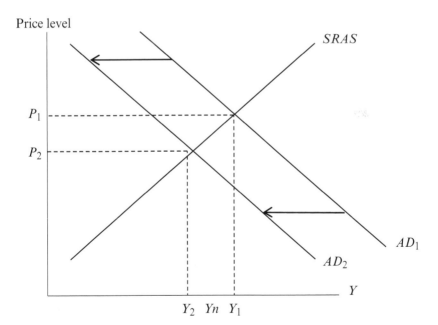

Figure 13.6   An anti-inflationary policy on aggregate demand

government spending but almost never do. The technique used is to raise interest rates to reduce private sector expenditure, especially private sector investment.

Keeping the level of economic activity below the economy's potential at *Yn* will eventually squeeze inflation out of the economy. At that point the economy can once again be allowed to grow at its potential where the unemployment rate is at its natural rate. It is a long process, and in the meantime the economy must experience higher rates of unemployment and lower levels of production than it is capable of. It is immensely costly, but then so too is inflation. Curing inflation never comes cheap.

PHILLIPS CURVE

The last piece in the conceptual matrix within the modern macroeconomic framework is the Phillips curve. According to the Phillips curve relationship, the lower the level of unemployment, the higher the rate of inflation would become. As aggregate demand increases, the greater the pressure on resources and especially on labour costs. Therefore, inflationary pressures rise with higher employment which itself is derived from increasingly rapid economic growth.

Similarly, as growth slows there is less pressure on resources, fewer wage demands and a lower rate of inflation. This relationship is shown in Figure 13.7 and is called a Phillips curve, named after the economist Bill Phillips.

Phillips curve analysis remains at the heart of the inflationary control policies of central banks.

As Figure 13.7 shows, there is a choice, a trade-off, between higher inflation but with lower unemployment on the one hand, and lower inflation but with higher unemployment on the other. (Δ is the Greek letter delta and is used to indicate a change in some variable, thus ΔP is the change in prices, the inflation rate.)

The theory suggests that the lower the unemployment rate, the greater are the inflationary pressures. Lower unemployment creates pressure for wage increases and price movements in general. Higher unemployment reduces the pressure on wages and prices.

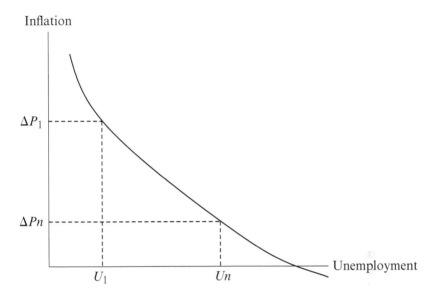

Figure 13.7   Phillips curve

ANTI-INFLATION POLICY

Anti-inflationary policy has therefore been designed to limit the growth in prices through adjustments to the rate of unemployment.

In every economy those in charge of economic management estimate the natural rate of unemployment. This is the rate of unemployment at which the 'optimum' rate of inflation will occur.

Interest rate adjustments are then used to either lower or increase the unemployment rate as needs be. If the actual unemployment is lower than the natural rate – that is, if the economy is seen to be overheating – then interest rates are raised. If, on the other hand, the actual unemployment rate is higher than the natural rate, then interest rates are lowered to cause the economy to accelerate and unemployment to come down.

And what is this 'optimum' rate of inflation? It is the rate of inflation that those in charge of managing an economy are prepared to live with over the longer term.

In the Phillips curve diagram in Figure 13.7, the natural rate of unemployment is shown at Un. At this rate of unemployment, the inflation rate will be at ΔPn, which is low enough to satisfy those who manage the economy.

If unemployment falls below this rate, say to U_1, the inflation rate rises to ΔP_1, well above the optimal rate. Those who manage the economy then take steps to raise the unemployment rate, which essentially consists of raising unemployment. According to the Phillips curve, the higher unemployment rate will lead to a lower rate of inflation. As crude as this mechanism is, this is the way in which inflation is kept low.

The natural rate of unemployment will, however, rise and fall over time depending on various factors that affect how prone an economy is to inflation. If, for example, unions become less militant, the Phillips curve will move inwards towards the origin. The unemployment rate associated with the optimal inflation rate will therefore fall.

This is shown in Figure 13.8. The outermost Phillips curve indicates that the desired inflation rate, ΔPn, to begin with requires an unemployment rate of Un. But if unions become less militant, and the economy is less strike-prone, or indeed if there is structural change of any kind that reduces pressures on the price level, the Phillips curve moves inwards towards the origin.

With the Phillips curve having shifted to the left, it is now possible to achieve the same desired inflation rate, but with a lower rate of

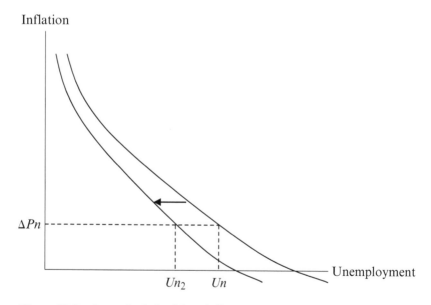

Figure 13.8   Inwards shift of the Phillips curve

unemployment at Un_2. Unfortunately, such changes take time and require institutional changes often of the most profound kind.

LONG-RUN NON-INFLATIONARY GROWTH

Over time, as technology improves, the quantum of capital is increased and labour force skills improve, the *LRAS* curve will move to the right and higher output occurs, but with no additional inflationary pressures. Until such improvements occur, movements of aggregate demand will only cause the price level to rise without increasing the level of employment or economic activity.

Figure 13.9 shows how non-inflationary economic growth is intended to occur in a perfect world.

Here we have economic growth but without price movements. Technological improvement, innovation and higher investment cause the short-run aggregate supply curve (*SRAS*) to move outwards, as does the long-run aggregate supply curve (*LRAS*). Income earners at the same time receive higher payments and this pushes the aggregate demand curve (*AD*) to the right as well. But since aggregate supply has also increased, there is no effect on the price level. The price level stays

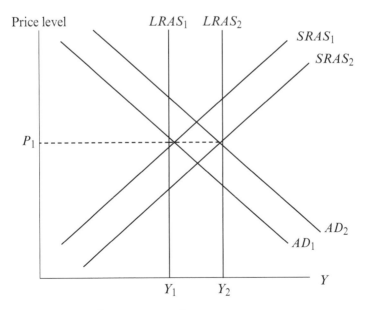

Figure 13.9   Non-inflationary growth

at P_1 the whole time. There is no inflation even while the economy continues to expand.

It is this which is the aim of economic policy, and it is this diagram which explains what policy makers using a Keynesian framework are trying to achieve.

14. The classical theory of the business cycle

To understand the theory of recession as it was understood before Keynes's *General Theory* was published, one must begin with Say's Law. As discussed in Chapter 10, Say's Law is the name popularized by Keynes to describe what he said were the core macroeconomic principles of classical economic theory. It was defined by him as 'supply creates its own demand', by which he meant that classical economic theory had argued that all incomes earned would with certainty be immediately spent on buying everything that had been produced. Therefore, according to Keynes, classical economists had argued that an economy would always be at full employment. Since everything produced would be bought, unemployment so far as classical theory was concerned was, in his view, impossible.

To put this in another way, according to Keynes's interpretation of Say's Law, the incomes received for supplying goods and services to the market would always be spent on demanding the goods and services whose production had allowed those incomes to be earned in the first place. Everything would therefore be bought and no one would become unemployed for long because aggregate demand could always be expected to keep up with aggregate supply.

In terms of the circular flow diagram, the flow of demand into business would always match the flow of payments leaving business at the full employment level of income. In that original Keynesian model, saving would always equal investment at a level of production at which everyone who wanted a job had a job. In relation to the expanded leakages–injections approach, $S + T + M$ would always be equal to $I + G + X$, again at the full employment level of output. Whatever else might happen in an economy, recessions would never occur because demand could never be deficient.

IMPORTANCE OF SAY'S LAW IN CLASSICAL BUSINESS CYCLE THEORY

Classical economists did not, of course, believe they had no explanation for recessions and unemployment. Keynes merely argued that this was the implication of having accepted the validity of Say's Law.

Say himself had pointed out that in an exchange economy, one set of goods is exchanged for other sets of goods with money merely an intermediary that allowed such trade to take place. I work and contribute to the production of some good or service. I am paid money for what I have produced. Others do the same and we each buy from each other using the money we have received for having created something of exchangeable value. Money makes the exchange more efficient but, beneath it all, the actual purchase is made with each person's own productions as represented by the money received as income.

Demand, once the mediating role of money was removed, was made up of the supply of other goods brought to market. Demand is created by supply.

But the existence of money can itself be a cause of instability. What none of this had suggested was that purchasing power in the hands of those who had earned incomes would always be spent at the same pace as in good times if economic conditions became uncertain. Nor did this suggest that there would never be occasions upon which economic conditions became far more uncertain than usual. Nor did the theory suggest that businesses would never make mistakes about what buyers wanted to buy. Nor were there any doubts that innovation and change might well upset previous expectations about what could and could not be produced at a profit. Nor did it suggest that governments would never make major errors in their economic management. Nor did it suggest that the financial system would never create more credit than could be supported by the underlying level of savings in an economy. Nor did it suggest that credit might end up being misdirected or that the flow of finance into an economy might be less than needed.

There were many different sets of problems that were well understood by classical economists as potential sources of instability and recession. What was more often remarked upon by classical economists was how well a market economy worked. It was that the economy operated as well as it did that was recognized as remarkable. That it would from time to time break down, and recessions occur, was just seen as in the nature of things.

THE CLASSICAL THEORY OF RECESSION

Given Say's Law, that demand is created by value-adding supply, the explanation for recessions was invariably found on the supply side of the economy. If production was properly proportioned, so that everything produced met the specific demands of others, everything would find a market.

The classical theory of recession hinged on explaining why production decisions would at different times not match the specific demands of buyers. Moreover, it went beyond the question of why some particular business might have produced the wrong goods or services. There are always firms making bad production decisions. It went beyond that, to asking why producers in large numbers would have ended up producing what could not be sold. The central question was why a large number of firms would end up making these wrong economic decisions at one and the same time.

It is thus one of the strange ironies in the history of economics that Say's Law, the very theory that was once recognized as essential to understanding the causes of recessions and large-scale unemployment, is now said to have been the reason why classical economists could not explain why recessions took place at all.

COORDINATION AND TIME

There are a number of dimensions of an economy's production process that are of major relevance in understanding recession. The first is the immense number of productive activities across an economy which are only coordinated through the price system and market mechanism. Although businesses compete with each other, what is more important is that they are able to cooperate with each other and coordinate their activities so that all are working together as efficiently as possible to create value-adding goods and services across the economy.

Economies are built on specialization and the division of labour. Activity takes place in the myriad of business enterprises scattered across an economy which must somehow coordinate their activities with each other. Most such enterprises produce inputs for sale to other enterprises. Shifts in demand patterns are the rule rather than the exception.

The alternative to markets is central planning, in which government agencies decide in advance, often many years in advance, not just what final goods to produce, but also which inputs need to be produced. Just to state what would be required for central planning to achieve its ends ought to demonstrate how impossible it would be.

No central planning agency could possibly ensure that producers produce exactly what buyers want to buy, never mind all of the various inputs into the production of these final goods and services; and then, even before that, no central agency could possibly ensure that the requisite inputs are produced in just the right amounts, and so on and throughout the whole economy.

To believe that some central agency can plan ahead for an entire economy is one of the major fallacies often associated with economic cranks. No single person, no central body, no government agency can ever know anything remotely like what needs to be known if an economy is to produce the goods and services the community wants, never mind be able to innovate or adjust to new circumstances.

It is only through decentralized decision making of entrepreneurially managed firms, where incomes of the owners and managers of the enterprise are directly dependent on the profitability of the business, that it is possible to have an immediate and concentrated response to changes in the circumstances in which a business finds itself. Only a market economy with entrepreneurial decision making can produce relative costs that mirror relative scarcity and the underlying intensity of demand for the millions of inputs that are used to produce goods and services.

Leaving the decisions that affect incomes and wealth creation in the hands of governments is a certain recipe for poverty and economic decay.

UNCERTAINTY AND ECONOMIC DECISIONS

Uncertainty, indeed radical uncertainty, pervades the business environment. Producers have only a general idea of how much of any product will be sought during the period ahead, normally based on their experience of the past to which are added various considerations about the nature of the market as a whole as they look forward into the future.

Steel producers, to take just one example, make production estimates based on demand over the recent past to which is added their own best guesses about what other circumstances might apply.

Users of steel must depend on the relative accuracy of such forecasts when they are themselves trying to work out their own needs and likely cost structures. And so on across the economy as each and every business independently works out the inputs they will need while others are deciding the level of production of those very inputs.

To say it again, there is no centralized coordination because there never can be, since each of those decisions is based on a vast array of circumstances, many of which will be unknown until the very last moment. Just how much steel will be needed by the construction industry is unlikely to be known with any accuracy at the start of the year but will depend on how many buildings are commissioned once the year has begun.

In the meantime, that same steel might be demanded by the car industry, which may turn out to have either a very good year or a very bad year, which will affect, either upwards or downwards, the demand for that steel. And so on with every other industry that uses steel. And so on with every other product that is used as an input.

The need to adjust production in every single industry as the year unfolds is a straightforward certainty. What others will demand will be different, sometimes extremely different, from what had been predicted when the decisions were made to produce the specific forms of output.

Coordination of the many hundreds and thousands of businesses across even a medium-sized economy is a gigantic operation that can only be determined in real time by businesses which individually react to their own orders and the prices charged by those from which they themselves buy. No one can predict relative prices since no one can know in advance the market conditions for all of the inputs into a production process.

That this coordination process sometimes breaks down should be seen as a fact of economic life. But understanding the nature of the process of economic activity should make it clear not only why such breakdowns occur from time to time but also why, even though recessions are inevitable every so often, there is no other way in which an economy can be organized if higher real incomes and greater personal wealth for an increasingly larger proportion of the population are the aims.

And beyond the economic benefits, personal freedom – not being dependent on governments for anything beyond national defence, the police, the law courts, the administration of justice, sound regulations of economic activities and the provision of welfare for those who may need such assistance from time to time – becomes the additional benefit, possibly the most important benefit, of managing an economy in this way.

PRODUCTION IS IN ANTICIPATION OF DEMAND

The second issue beyond the difficulty of coordination is the recognition that every product that is on the market and available today is the outcome of decisions that were made in the past, often the distant past.

All production is in anticipation of demand. Every product produced for sale has been in preparation for a period of time before it has actually reached the market. And because every production decision comes well before the product is finally put up for sale, it cannot be known in advance with any kind of certainty what economic circumstances will be like when the product is finally put up for sale.

A decision to produce at a profit means that costs must be taken on before revenues can be earned. There is therefore every possibility that when the product is finally brought to market, there may not be enough demand to ensure that sales of the good or service will cover all of their production costs.

This may be because the producer had made a mistake in the decision to sink capital into that particular product. This is an extremely common outcome. There just is not the market that had originally been anticipated. Such businesses lose money and either change their ways or stop production.

In an economy that is performing well, business mistakes are just part of the landscape. There are an endless series of attempts to earn profits through production, and while some fail, others succeed. This is how economies move forward through time.

But so far as the business cycle is concerned, this needs to be understood: the normal coming and going of individual firms is not the cause of recession.

Recessions originate where *systematic* problems in the structure of the economy lead businesses into making production errors across a broad front; it is not just the coming and going of single firms in a competitive economy.

Recessions are caused by wholesale distortions in the structure of the economy, with origins somewhere inside the operation of the economic system. It was to analyse and understand these structural problems that was at the core of the classical theory of the cycle.

RECESSIONS AND THE SUBSEQUENT UPTURN ARE ALMOST ALWAYS UNEXPECTED

Although the business cycle is a regular occurrence, with bad times following good, they are seldom predictable. Most typically, the downturn comes as a surprise as a period of prosperity suddenly turns into a period of recession.

As much as cyclical activity can be predicted to occur at some stage, when the downturn comes it is often greeted as if such events had never previously occurred. And the longer the time between such downturns, the more astonished people seem to be when the inevitable finally shows up.

There appears to be a narrowness and concentration of focus within economies that assume that present conditions, whatever they are, will persist into the future: either that good times will go on forever or, when recessions strike, that the downturn will never end.

In many ways, it is precisely because the downturn is unexpected that it is able to occur at all. If it were generally understood that some particular feature of contemporary economic conditions is about to change, and with major consequences across the economy, then actions to forestall and to take in stride such imminent changes would be factored into decisions being made.

That the unexpected can be expected nevertheless remains outside the perception of most of those engaged in economic activity, since the unexpected can occur in so many different ways. At any moment in time, there are many possibilities that may or may not come to dominate reality.

Business and other economic decisions very seldom can or do take these global issues into account. Businesses just get on with doing business, just as workers and consumers continue to act based on what they know. What they know is seldom related to the economic factors that are bearing down on an economy at some particular moment, especially when their effects are uncertain and may not appear until quite some time into the future. If you are selling shirts, for example, it is hard to know which economic events are going to matter.

RECESSIONS TYPICALLY SPREAD FROM AN INITIAL LOCALIZED DOWNTURN

Recessions do not begin as a full-scale downturn across all industries at one and the same time. A downturn will typically begin in one or two strategic industries and then spread out from there.

But beneath the specific industries first affected is a web of purchase and sale that penetrates deeply into the entire structure of the economy. A downturn in one industry leads to a fall in demand for the production of the industries providing its inputs. These industries in turn begin to contract, with effects on other industries. This continues deeper into the economy until virtually every industry is affected.

The effect on the economy overall is a general recession in which, by the time it is in full swing, the industries where the downturn began may no longer be identifiably more at risk than any others. Enterprises generally feel the effects, and in a major downturn no industry is certain to remain safe.

The most visible part of the downturn is the high level of unemployment. From a national economic point of view, the loss of production is regrettable but can be accommodated. Where the major problems occur, however, are in relation to unemployment. The large number of jobs lost has its massive human dimension.

In retrospect, and looked at from above, the occurrence of a one- or two-year period of recession is embodied in the nature of the modern economy. For the individual experiencing this prolonged period of unemployment, these two years can be a personal and financial catastrophe.

As businesses contract and either refuse to hire new employees or lay off existing ones, a gloom descends that is transmitted into the area of consumer demand. The effects are experienced throughout the retail sector as lower employment leads to lower incomes and makes the jobs of those still working more tentative.

Such tentativeness also spreads to investment decisions. The future becomes more clouded and businesses more pessimistic. Some decisions to invest are cancelled, others are postponed. There is a general fall-off in activity in every branch of the economy irrespective of where the problems might have begun.

The same occurs in reverse as the upturn begins. Industries pick up one by one. There is always an economic logic that can be identified afterwards as to why one area began to grow again, but in the midst of recession determining in advance where the upturn will begin is not possible.

But for all that, the upturn does begin, and with the first shoots of economic improvement come the secondary effects as businesses increase their orders with each other. As some industries begin to pick up, so too do others. The momentum begins to build and eventually a full-scale recovery ends up in place.

Recovery brings with it higher employment. The gloom which had descended begins to lift. New jobs open up and those who had been unemployed return to work, often in industries completely different from the industries where their last jobs had been.

RECESSIONS AND ECONOMIC GROWTH

When the recession has run its course, the very structure of the economy may be quite different from the structure which had existed when the downturn began. The reason for the recession in the first place was that a significant proportion of firms across the economy were incapable of generating profits. They were using the community's resources in ways which were not value-adding, given all of the other aspects of the economy.

The new firms, or those which are expanding, are typically different from those that had existed before. That is, in fact, the very purpose of recession: to ensure that the structure of production is properly related to the structure of demand.

An organic private sector-driven recovery such as this is self-sustaining. The economic momentum will continue to build and conditions will improve until the next downturn occurs, once again surprising everyone when it appears.

THE CONTOURS OF THE BUSINESS CYCLE

That economies regularly go through periodic fluctuations in their level of activity has been well understood amongst economists since the early nineteenth century. Whether the measure used to decide whether an economy is in recession is the level of production, or the level of employment, or some other measure of economic strength, the expectation is that in some periods these will be at a much higher level than in other periods. What models of the cycle do is provide an explanation why these fluctuations occur.

The basic structure of the cycle is shown in Figure 14.1. There are four distinct phases, each one following on the other, and most importantly, each phase leading to its successor because of the ways that businesses, consumers, governments, the employed and the unemployed behave.

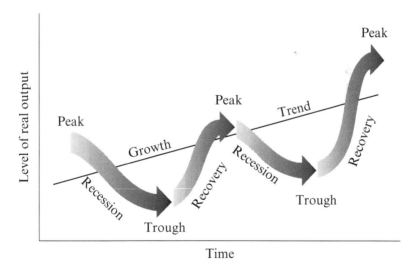

Source: Alan Ellman, 'The blue collar investor blog' (www.bluecollarinvestor.com).

Figure 14.1   Business cycle

In looking at Figure 14.1 it is important to bear in mind that although typically drawn in this way, it contains two very important misrepresentations. In the diagram both the length of time for each phase of the cycle and the amplitude in the level of activity during the phases of the cycle are shown as identical. The time between one trough and the next is shown as more or less unchanging, as is the depth of the recession or the height of the recovery reached.

In actual fact the length between each phase (such as the period of time from one peak to the next), and both the height and the depth to which activity may reach (that is, how deep or shallow the recession happens to be), will differ in each and every cycle. No two are alike: neither in their amplitude nor in the length of time that each phase may last.

The down-phase of the Great Depression, for example, was the deepest that had ever occurred until that time, and it lasted far longer than had any previous depression. No other recession has shown so large a downturn although there have been many others since the 1930s.

All that one can know with any certitude is that wherever one happens to be in terms of the cycle, it will be succeeded, at some moment in time, by the next phase. Every downturn, sooner or later, is followed by an upturn and vice versa. Every period of growth, no matter how sustained it may be, eventually turns into a recession.

THE PHASES OF THE CYCLE

Figure 14.1 thus shows the stylized structure of the cycle. Begin, first, with the trough, the lowest point in the cyclical movements of the economy. It is here that the rate of growth of Gross Domestic Product (GDP) will be at its lowest, will in fact typically be negative, while the unemployment rate will have reached its highest level. Here the old proverb, that 'it's always darkest before the dawn', shows its meaning. There is general despondency in the community, workers are fearful for their jobs, and depressed profits and high levels of bankruptcy are common.

Yet economic conditions are about to change, and the next phase of the cycle is about to begin. This is the recovery phase, the phase during which economic activity flattens before beginning its upwards turn. Recovery often occurs only slowly at first, but once the corner has been turned, economic conditions improve, and improve on a broadening front. This is, overwhelmingly, the result of various spontaneous actions by businesses to find their way out of difficult economic conditions. But once commenced, the upturn then continues, usually for a number of years, until the next phase of the cycle is reached.

This next phase is normally referred to as the peak of the cycle and is usually experienced as an economic 'crisis' of some sort. It is the top of the roller-coaster from which point economic conditions start to unravel. It usually occurs without much prior notice, but at some moment during which everything seems to be going rather well. There is then a sudden realization that conditions are instead about to turn down. It is that bleak moment, lasting for a few months, that heralds the arrival of the next downwards phase. It is during this phase of the cycle that a widespread belief that everything is unravelling becomes general.

This final phase is the downturn or recessionary phase, characterized by a slowdown in economic growth – frequently an actual contraction in national output – and a sharp rise in unemployment along with a fall in employment. It is a phase of the cycle that can come with varying degrees of severity and will be accompanied by high levels of personal distress. In the classical theory of the cycle, the downturn is an inevitable part of the rhythm of economic activity. Its eventual arrival is a certainty; only its length and depth will vary between cycles.

It should also be noted that during classical times right through to the Great Depression in the 1930s, with the downward movement of economic activity there was also a parallel downwards movement in the level of prices. As the economy went into recession, there was typically a fall in the price level which was reflected in the use of the term 'deflation'. Similarly, with the recovery in the level of activity, there was typically a recovery in the level of prices as well.

Finally, what Figure 14.1 also makes clear is that although there are periods of prosperity followed by periods of recession, the general trend is upwards. Over time our economies become more wealthy and the average standard of living has continued to grow. To the extent that history can be a guide to the future, there is no reason that this pattern should not continue for as long as economies remain open and markets are allowed to allocate resources to where they will receive their highest return.

CONTRAST WITH MACROECONOMICS

Study of the theory of the cycle all but disappeared with the advent of Keynesian economics and macroeconomic theory in the 1930s. What did not disappear, however, was the cycle itself.

The certainty is this. Cyclical economic activity can be expected irrespective of the kind of economic system put in place.

Even an entirely agricultural-based economy will experience good years and bad as a result of changes in weather patterns between one year and another. But the theory of the cycle was designed to explain their occurrence in market-based industrialized economies, that is, in modern economies where individual businesses were affected by economic conditions in other firms or government decisions.

Yet even while cyclical activity remained a certainty, with an upturn inevitably following each downturn, Keynesian economics was sold on the basis that an upturn could not be expected without large increases in government expenditure since an underemployment equilibrium would hold an economy rigidly in place for an extended period of time. In the original Keynesian model, there was no guaranteed up-phase of the cycle even though every recession, both before and since the publication of the *General Theory*, has ended with an upturn.

High levels of public spending during recessions were looked upon by classical economists as likely to cause a recession to deepen rather than to generate a recovery sooner than it otherwise would have done. Given that GDP statistics record public spending as value-adding by definition, GDP has been typically a misleading indicator. But the data on employment and unemployment have been stubbornly difficult to budge with higher levels of public spending in every instance where a Keynesian response to an economic downturn has been tried.

To a classical economist, the only spending that can contribute to faster growth and higher employment is growth associated with increased value added. Since most forms of government spending are unlikely to lead to increases in value-adding production, not only is there no actual momentum offered by such increases in government outlays, but the effect is actually negative, slowing real growth rather than adding to its momentum, irrespective of what the national accounting data may say.

Yet even with the virtual dominance of Keynesian economics, theories of cyclical activity are accepted by many, while other theories have been devised based on recognition that systematic errors in production decisions are inevitable. To understand the nature of recession, their inevitability and the steps that need to be taken when recessions occur, it is essential to understand the theories of the cycle that had once dominated economic theory. Keynesian theory, although it may dominate virtually every textbook of the modern era, is nevertheless a dead end so far as being able to understand the causes of recession and the policies needed when they occur.

PROSPERITY AND DEPRESSION

The most useful compendium of classical models of the cycle may be found in a book published in 1937, the year following the publication of

Keynes's *General Theory*. Gottfried Haberler's *Prosperity and Depression: A Theoretical Analysis of Cyclical Movements* was commissioned by the League of Nations (the predecessor to the United Nations) at the start of the Great Depression in 1930 but not published until the Great Depression was well and truly over.

Its aim was to 'examine existing theories with a view to ascertaining what they had in common, the points at which differences of opinion arose, and, in so far as possible, the causes of those differences'. The various models of the cycle discussed below will follow Haberler's analysis. All quotations are from Haberler's first edition.

One observation should, however, be made first. All classical theories of the recession were based on explaining why a large proportion of those who had produced had, for one reason or another, produced what did not end up being bought. The most obvious aspect of recessions is that goods and services have been produced but are not being bought. Keynes had argued, as does modern economic theory, that the reason for the absence of sales is because those who might have bought preferred to save. Classical economists had instead argued that the absence of spending was a symptom of the recession, not its cause. What, then, was the actual cause?

STRUCTURE OF PRODUCTION

Classical theories of the cycle were *structural* in nature. They explained why those who bought were unwilling to buy the products of those who had produced. The economic system was understood to depend on reasonably accurate sales forecasts by businesses who would design their production processes in conformity with their expectations of which products would find a market – and this included not just consumer goods but the production of inputs as well.

And the need to keep in mind the inputs into the production process is crucial. In buying some consumer good one is also buying all of the inputs that went into its production. And each of those inputs also had a series of inputs that went into their production. And so throughout the whole economy. This is what is meant by the structure of production. All of the inputs into every form of output must fit into the entire scheme of things in just such a way that what needs to be produced gets produced.

For an economy to work smoothly, all of the elements that go into producing each of the products sold must be produced in the right proportions. It is the price mechanism that rations whatever exists amongst potential buyers, but also encourages more production where there are shortages and discourages production where too much has been produced.

But the actually existing supply at any moment in time is the result of past decisions that have been based on nothing more substantial than forecasts of what would be bought if the products were produced.

When these forecasts are generally right, the economy continues to grow and no one notices a thing. But when business gets it wrong and too much of particular products is produced and production has to be cut down, not only does the original business feel the contraction but so too do all of its suppliers. The structure of production is the economy trying to balance itself, which most of the times it does but sometimes it does not. When it does not, recessions are often the result.

It was to explain why business forecasts of the demand for the products they sell might have turned out to be wrong that the theory of the cycle was designed. Wrong not for an individual business, since that would occur on a daily basis everywhere across an economy, but wrong on a system-wide basis so that the economy would find a large proportion of its productive efforts had been channelled into producing what could not be sold at prices which covered costs.

CLASSICAL THEORIES OF THE CYCLE

What follows below are the various theories of the cycle discussed by Haberler under the following headings:

- purely monetary theories;
- over-investment theories;
- entrepreneurial error and creative destruction;
- psychological theories;
- under-consumption theories.

Each of these, in one way or another, tries to explain the nature of the misjudgments and errors made by entrepreneurs. Only the last of these, under-consumption theories, is in any way similar to the standard macro models found in most economic texts today.

Purely Monetary Theories

Purely monetary theories of the cycle are related solely to the flow of credit with downturns seen to originate in the banking sector. To quote Haberler: 'Changes in "the flow of money" are the sole and sufficient cause of changes in economic activity, or the alternation of prosperity and depression, of good and bad trade' (1937: 14).

As the flow of money turns up, the economy picks up. When the flow of money slows, the economy contracts. In explaining the occurrence of recession, it is necessary to understand the source of the money supply itself, which for the most part consists of bank credit:

> Bank credit is the principal means of payment ... It is the banking system which creates credit and regulates its quantity ... A single bank cannot go very far in expanding credit on its own account; but the banking system as a whole can, and there is a tendency to make the whole system move along step by step in the same direction. If one bank or group of banks expands credit, other banks will find their reserves strengthened and will be induced, sometimes almost forced, to expand too. (1937: 16)

The upswing in the cycle occurs through an expansion of credit and lasts as long as the credit expansion goes on. An increase in the supply of money, that is credit, will have an expansionary effect on economic activity. Start with an economy in recession and follow the effects of an expansion in credit: 'Demand exceeds anticipations, stocks decrease, dealers give large orders to producers, and prices rise. Production increases and unemployed factors of production are gradually absorbed' (1937: 15).

The principal means of such expansions is a decline in the discount rate and other factors which lead to a decline in the cost of credit; that is, interest rates are made to fall through increases in the supply of credit.

But at some stage capacity constraints are reached and are possibly exceeded if credit growth is not restrained early enough and hard enough. These are the classic symptoms of what is now commonly referred to as a 'credit bubble'. Prices of particular assets rise at rates well beyond the underlying productivity of the economy.

Eventually, as concerns with inflation increase and banks become concerned about the viability of their loans, credit growth is diminished as interest rates are pushed up. The economy then reaches a crisis point and the down phase of the cycle begins.

> If the quantity of money diminishes, demand falls off, and producers who have produced in anticipation of the usual demand will find that they cannot sell the usual output at the anticipated prices. Stocks will accumulate; losses will be incurred; production will fall; unemployment will be rife; and a painful process in which wages and other incomes are reduced will be necessary before equilibrium can be restored. (1937: 15)

This is the very common face of recession which has occurred through a contraction in credit. With the flow of credit diminished, and the related rise in rates of interest, some investment projects become non-viable. The result is a slowdown in investment, a fall in economic activity and a rise in unemployment. The downturn continues until there is a revival in credit markets, at which point the fall in economic activity is reversed and the recovery begins anew.

What is important to recognize in such theories is that they are purely credit-driven. Savings and availability of resources do not affect the cycle which is entirely a monetary phenomenon. In theory the economy could expand forever were it not for the contractions in credit that are brought about by the banking system.

But as Haberler notes, 'that prosperity could be prolonged and depression staved off indefinitely, if the money supply were inexhaustible, would certainly be challenged by most economists' (1937: 28). Other theories of the cycle certainly accepted a good deal from the pure monetary approach, but added in real considerations about the nature of the economy itself.

Over-Investment Theories

Over-investment theories explained the cycle in terms of disharmonies between, on the one hand, production of consumption goods and on the other hand, production of investment goods. These were the most common theories of the cycle. Such theories were based on the occurrence of serious maladjustments which developed during the up phase of the cycle. These were often related to monetary factors but were not exclusively caused by such monetary factors.

Equilibrium across the economy was seen to depend on:

1. the decisions of the population on how much to spend and how much to save;
2. the decisions by consumers on how to allocate their expenditures between different kinds of consumer goods; and
3. the decisions by producers on how to allocate their own expenditures between different forms of inputs and capital goods.

In this analysis, the economy is represented by the always present series of decisions that are constantly being changed. Both consumers and businesses are continuously shifting their patterns of expenditure, continually revising their plans.

If the decisions do not mesh, so that there is an inconsistency amongst all of the independent decisions being made across the economy, there is an eventual breaking down of the economy into recession. Production decisions are revealed to have been incompatible with concurrently made decisions either to save or to buy.

Why might such incompatible decisions be made? There were three broad categories of theory. Each will be discussed in turn below.

1. Money and the structure of production

There are, firstly, theories which were related to dislocations in the structure of production.

These theories argue that the interaction of the monetary and real economies causes the breakdown. The economy simply does not generate enough real saving to finance all of the investment decisions that have been made during the upturn. More investment projects are commenced than can be completed given the level of savings (that is, resources) available. There is, therefore, a breakdown in the financing of activity that causes a series of production decisions to fail.

The process may be made all the worse through the ability of the banking system to create credit beyond the community's willingness to save. The resulting distortions in the structure of production, along with increases in inflation, cause the economy to become even more misshapen.

Once the downturn has begun irrespective of which corner of the economy the downturn had commenced, the effect on activity is cumulative. The falling-away of activity, as investment projects are abandoned through lack of finance, causes the roll-back in production in each of the firms and industries affected in the initial stage. The effect on the banking system, in which more and more loans become 'non-performing', only adds to the depth of the subsequent downturn. The downturn continues until at last the trough is reached, the balance between the demand and supply for saving is restored and an upturn can commence.

2. Non-monetary over-investment theories

Here, too, the problem originates in the production of capital goods but money plays virtually no part in the process until the very end. The concept is based on a shortage of the physical resources needed to complete investment projects. The problem is based on there being too little saving.

Moreover, the various inputs are seen as *complementary goods*, that is, they are used in conjunction with each other, often in more or less fixed proportions. As the economy expands, there are differential rates of growth in various industries until a situation is reached where some industries find they cannot find a market because the complementary goods, which are used in conjunction with the more abundant good, are unavailable. Haberler describes these circumstances in this way:

> The result is a situation in which there is shortage and plenty at the same time. As these categories of goods are complementary, a shortage of one category

means *ipso facto* over-production of the others. It is as if one glove of a pair were lost. The one that remains constitutes a useless and unsaleable surplus stock; the missing one represents an actual deficiency. (1937: 71–2)

At this point, the downwards turn in the economy is accelerated by both psychological and monetary effects as confidence disappears and credit dries up. Both consumers and investors become more reluctant to spend. Meanwhile various rigidities become more apparent, such as a reluctance on the part of some businesses to adjust their prices to take account of the fall-off in demand and a similar reluctance on the part of wage earners to allow their wages to fall even as unemployment goes up.

3. Over-investment due to changes in the demand for consumer goods
The basic concept is usually referred to as the *acceleration principle* and has been grafted onto Keynesian theory.

The theory builds on the notion that a change in the demand for goods and services bought by consumers leads to a proportionately much larger change in demand in the same direction for the inputs needed for their production. As soon as the growth in the demand for consumer goods slows, there is an exaggerated fall-off in the demand for inputs. Such inputs are referred to as 'higher-order' goods. The farther from a consumer in the production chain an input is, the 'higher' that input is seen to be. (A shirt, for example, is a consumer good, cloth production is of a higher order, and the growing of cotton is of a higher order still. No actual hierarchy is implied by the word 'higher'.) Haberler describes the theory in this way:

Slight changes in the demand for consumers' goods may thus be converted into violent changes in goods of a higher order; and, as this intensification tends to work through all stages of production, it is quite natural that fluctuations should be most violent in those stages of production which are farthest removed from the sphere of consumption. In certain circumstances, it may even happen that a slackening in the rate of growth of demand in one stage is converted into an actual decline in the demand for the product of the preceding stage. (1937: 83)

Thus, according to this theory, the cycle is driven by large changes upwards or downwards in the market for inputs which occur even when there are small changes in the demand for consumer goods. In Keynesian models, the accelerator is often paired with the multiplier to generate cyclical movements in activity.

Entrepreneurial Error and Creative Destruction

Theories based on systematic errors in the decision-making process were put forward by some as the basis for understanding the cycle. They are based on an understanding that the entire downwards movement in an economy can be started by mistaken decisions in some particular sector which then spread outwards from that initial fall.

According to such theories, businesses might, for example, be misled about the likelihood of generating a positive return on investment. This makes little difference at the trough of the cycle but becomes more apparent as the economy gathers strength.

Take as an example two businesses which identify an increase in the demand for steel so that each begins to build a plant that will fill 60 per cent of the expanded market. In the end, adding 120 per cent of needed capacity to the economy means that when such businesses are finally in a position to produce, the size of the market is too small to repay both sets of investment. The problems involved were well described by Haberler:

> Error theories stress the great complexity of our economic system, the lack of knowledge, the difficulties in foreseeing correctly the future demand for various products. One producer does not know what the other is doing. A given demand cannot be satisfied by producer A; producers B, C, D, etc., are accordingly called upon to satisfy it, and this creates an exaggerated impression of its volume and urgency. This leads to competitive duplication of plant and equipment, involving errors in the estimation of future wants. (1937: 104)

At the top of the cycle, there can be a wide variety of redundant investments. These are not due to an insufficiency of saving to complete the various projects but occur because the decentralized decision making of the economy causes over-investment in particular forms of production to occur.

To compound the problem, business decision making is often by its nature secretive. Business-in-confidence is a norm in the commercial world. One must therefore expect such errors in the commercial world, with the result that there may often be more capital sunk in some areas of production than is warranted by the eventual level of demand.

The subsequent recession has the role of rationalizing the economy's capital structure. Resources are redeployed into areas where a greater return on investment can be earned. Misreading the future and maladjustments in production are inevitable when the future is unknowable. (Allowing for government planning would be infinitely worse since governments know far less than any market participant and there are literally tens of thousands of markets in a modern economy.) Moreover, many such investments must be made many years before they are required to earn the revenues which justified their construction in the first place.

Beyond this, mistaken investments occur because of innovation and technological advance. No one can be expected to know what will be invented at some stage in the future or which inventions will lead to a commercial application. But they will occur and regularly do, causing adjustment problems for existing firms employing old technologies or producing goods or services that are no longer sought.

New products, industrial techniques and forms of capital equipment are introduced with increasing frequency. Such innovation and technical change make previous forms of output or production processes less competitive and often totally uncompetitive. *Creative destruction* is the phrase often used in describing this process, as the new pushes out the old.

Everything about an existing business may in such circumstances be perfectly fine except that demand for the goods or services it produces has fallen away because some new form of output or some improved form of production technique has been discovered which has consequently either lowered the costs of production or caused the demand for the older product to disappear.

Out-and-out error or innovation and creative destruction, so far as a business is concerned, amount to the same thing. They lead to firms finding that they cannot earn the profits they originally believed they would because the level of sales does not reach their original expectations. The result is a downturn in activity as the economy goes through its processes of adjustment.

The economy may end up stronger, and living standards may end up higher, but the transition is experienced as a downwards turn in the level of economic activity in which recessionary conditions may occur.

Psychological Theories

The fundamental concepts that surrounded psychological theories of the cycle were related to the level of business confidence and expectations. Haberler discusses the crucial significance of the inability to see the future other than as a form of conjecture:

> With the introduction of the element of expectation, uncertainty enters the field. Future events cannot be forecast with absolute precision; and the farther they are distant in the future, the greater the uncertainty, and the greater the possibility of unforeseen and unforeseeable disturbances. Every economic decision is part of an economic plan which extends into the more or less distant

future. In principle, there is therefore always an element of uncertainty in every activity. There are, however, certain cases where the elements of uncertainty is especially great and conspicuous, such as the case of investment of resources in long processes and durable plant and the provision of funds for these purposes. The longer the processes in which capital is to be sunk, and the more durable the instruments and equipment to be constructed, the greater the element of uncertainty and risk of loss. (1937: 136)

Because all economic decisions aside from the most trivial are associated with a degree of uncertainty, economic outcomes are affected by swings of optimism and pessimism. During periods when confidence is high, economic conditions are self-reinforcing as expansion in one industry promotes the expansion of others. When, however, pessimism begins to rule, the process is reversed and the downturn become cumulative.

Whether or not such psychological theories can stand on their own as an explanation for the cycle, there is no question that the level of confidence would add momentum to whichever direction an economy was heading at any particular moment in time. In combination with other factors driving an economy upwards or down, business confidence plays a significant role in exaggerating whichever direction an economy happens to be moving at the time.

Under-Consumption Theories

There were many varieties of under-consumption theory going back almost to the beginning of economics. Malthus's theories were one example, but all were based on some flaw in the economic system which meant that for one reason or another, not everything produced would be bought.

These, rather than being theories of the cycle as such, were more in the way of being explanations for recession. Such theories, in fact, had no means to explain an economic upturn since the circumstances that had caused the downturn would operate even when the economy was going well.

Under-consumption theories argued that the downturn was either due to the failure of consumers to spend all of their incomes or was because purchasing power had for some reason not been distributed at the same time as production had taken place. The basic assumption in all such theories of recession was that production would increase more rapidly than the willingness or ability of consumers to spend.

Theories of under-consumption had the least credibility amongst mainstream classical economists. They were seen as unable to shed light on most aspects of the cycle. Nevertheless, such theories existed in great number and had a great appeal amongst those without formal education in economics.

The form of the theory which was rejected for its incoherence by the vast majority of economists argued that purchasing power was lost to wage earners because of the ways in which incomes were transferred between businesses and their employees. There was some flaw in the economic system that prevented producers from receiving the incomes that would have allowed them to purchase what they had produced.

In this version, purchasing power is somehow lost. Incomes do not rise by a sufficient amount to permit everything produced to find a market. In regard to such theories, the conclusion that was reached at that time remains the conclusion amongst economists to this day. Whatever else might be the cause of recession, it would not be because purchasing power is insufficient. Those with the purchasing power might not use the incomes they have received, but that purchasing power had been distributed was and is universally accepted.

Logically possible but also universally rejected by the mainstream was the possibility that purchasing power received might not be spent. This was the most common form of explanation for under-consumption, typically based on theories of over-saving. It was the voluntary decisions to save, with the resulting failure of potential buyers to buy everything produced, that led to a disequilibrium between production and sales. If money saved is not invested, then a process of slowdown and contraction takes place.

Haberler found this a very unconvincing explanation for cyclical activity. Savings may rise relative to investment once the recession has commenced and business confidence has fallen. But as he makes clear, it cannot be seen as a cause of the downturn, only as a consequence:

> During the depression, when the spirit of enterprise runs low and pessimism prevails, it is probably true to a large extent that saving engenders deflation [i.e. a fall-off in demand and lower prices] rather than new investments, and that the slump is to that extent prolonged and intensified. But the breakdown of the boom can hardly be explained in this way. There is no evidence that an absorption of savings occurs during the boom or before the crisis; on the contrary, there invariably exists a brisk demand for new capital, signalized by high interest rates. There is an excess of investment over saving and not the contrary. The situation changes, of course, completely after the turning point, when the depression has set in. Then there is an excess of savings over investment. (1937: 116)

In addition, Haberler points out the important role that saving plays as the feedstock for investment. Nevertheless, he notes that 'if the money saved is not invested, a cumulative process of deflation will start and saving may thus defeat its own end' (1937: 119). He points out that there is no evidence of a rise in saving taking place at the end of a boom, but as pure theory it is possible. It just never happens in practice.

SUMMING UP

The business cycle is built into the structure of a market economy. Economic downturns can never be avoided. Careful economic management can perhaps reduce their frequency and most certainly can minimize the depth to which economies descend, but will never prevent recessions from occurring.

The problem lies in the belief that the natural state for an economy is for it to be growing with unemployment low, when the reality is that the natural state for an economy is that it is adjusting to new circumstances during every moment of every day. Those new circumstances often come from outside the economy itself but more often than not are generated by the way the economy is evolving.

Businesses do things. They change what and how they produce. Every change in products and productive technique leads to shifts of some sort in the rest of the economy to accommodate each change made. The result is that each and every business is under constant pressure to be the one producing what buyers want at the lowest price.

The classical theory of the cycle recognized that there were problems in the nature of economic activity that cause businesses to mistake what others will want to buy or to make decisions to do particular things that turn out not to have been profitable. Sometimes they are the actions of other businesses that cause those calculations to turn out wrong; sometimes problems occur because the decisions that have been made are inconsistent with economic realities that could not be divined when the decisions were made.

In the end, an economy can avoid recession only when all of the following conditions are present:

- every decision made by every business is consistent with every decision made by every other business;
- producers produce exactly what buyers want to buy, and this includes not only producers of final consumer goods and services but also producers of every input used in the production processes of all other firms;
- savers save enough to finance all of the investment decisions being made;
- new innovations are always expected and never disrupt markets;

- the future provides no surprises so that everything turns out just as everyone thought it would – no one involved in economic activity is ever disappointed.

It need hardly be said that these conditions can never exist. And when these conditions are not met, recession and high rates of unemployment can be the result.

Their absence causes production and sales to become dislocated. There is a maladjustment in the structure of production. There is a failure of coordination within the economy as a whole.

Classical theories of the cycle typically examined reasons why an economy might fall into recession because of factors internal to its own operation. They thus failed to analyse what was even then a major cause of such dislocation, but one which since classical times has become ever more common and widespread. And this is the disruption that takes place because of the actions taken by governments. It is the ways in which governments foster recessions and create unemployment that will be looked at in Chapter 16. First, however, we will examine the classical theory of growth and recession and contrast these with the modern macroeconomic approach.

15. The classical theory of growth and recession

This chapter bring Keynesian macroeconomics together with the classical theory of recession to allow them to be compared within a single framework. It is an undeniable fact that no peace-time economic recovery anywhere in the world can be attributed to a Keynesian public spending stimulus. But even going beyond the reality of the actual economic history since 1936 is the equally undeniable fact that classical economic theory had clearly explained why recovery would never follow upon a Keynesian-type stimulus.

By the end of the 1820s, demand deficiency had been thoroughly rejected by the mainstream of the economics profession with the theoretical explanation bundled into the series of propositions now referred to as Say's Law (and outlined in Chapter 11). John Stuart Mill's fourth fundamental proposition on capital (discussed in Chapter 5) – that 'demand for commodities is not demand for labour' – summarized this universally-held conclusion in 1848. It was a conclusion that remained embedded in both economic theory and policy until the publication of *The General Theory* in 1936. The practical reality of this conclusion was restated by Sir Winston Churchill when, as England's Chancellor of the Exchequer, he brought down his budget in 1929.

> Churchill pointed to recent government expenditure on public works such as housing, roads, telephones, electricity supply, and agricultural development, and concluded that, although expenditure for these purposes had been justified:
>
> > 'for the purposes of curing unemployment the results have certainly been disappointing. They are, in fact, so meagre as to lend considerable colour to the orthodox Treasury doctrine which has been steadfastly held that, whatever might be the political or social advantages, very little additional employment and no permanent additional employment can in fact and as a general rule be created by State borrowing and State expenditure.' (Peden, 1996: 69–70)

These were, moreover, genuine value-adding forms of spending and in no sense of the make-work variety. Yet even so, little if any additional employment had been created as a result. The same may be said of every stimulus package that has ever been adopted across the world. No recovery has ever occurred as a result. The aim of this chapter, therefore, is to provide an understanding from a classical perspective of what has been the inevitable result of a Keynesian stimulus to demand.

THE CLASSICAL PERSPECTIVE

Of fundamental importance in seeing the economy as classical economists would have seen it, is to understand that a classical economist thought of the entire economy as one vast store of wealth that could be used either to produce for present enjoyment or else used to generate additional productive capital. A classical economist was, moreover, continuously aware of an economy's legacy from the past. Nothing bought in the present was the instantaneous result of some immediate decision to buy, but was, instead, the end point of some long drawn-out process that went back in time, encompassing the entire array of labour and inputs that had been essential so that the particular good or service could become available to purchase.

A freshly baked loaf of bread may have come into existence at some moment in time. But its coming into existence just then was the result of a combination of the work of the baker that morning; the milling of the grain, possibly months before; the farmers who had grown and harvested the grain, possibly a year earlier; the various transport networks that had been built over many years; the electricity-generating capacity of long standing that had been needed to mix the ingredients; and so on and so forth. This vast capital structure, as well as the skilled labour that had conceived, designed and built the capital, who were then capable of using this capital productively, all of these were essential so that those final touches could be added at the bakery that particular morning.

Since the publication of *The General Theory*, almost none of this is considered in examining the way an economy works. Since job numbers are, according to Keynesian theory, related to the level of demand for final goods and services, the interest is in the latest set of activities and not the density and composition of the infrastructure that lies behind. The nature of the economy taken as a whole is virtually ignored. Irrespective of the level of real incomes, an economy with ten per cent growth is seen as, in some important sense, doing better than an economy with two per cent growth since the larger the economy's growth rate, the faster the growth in employment is expected to be.

To help explain the core difference between the classical and modern frameworks, the most basic of all diagrams, the production possibility curve, is used below to contrast the nature of classical and modern

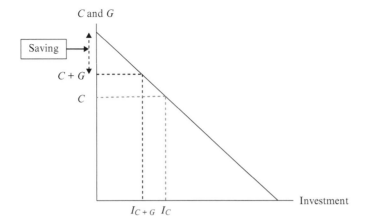

Figure 15.1   Production possibility curve – C, I and G

economics. As discussed in Chapter 4, the two axes of a properly designed diagram must represent two kinds of products whose combined output between them exhausts the entire economy's ability to produce. Examples might include goods on the one hand and services on the other. Or it might show privately-produced products and government-produced products on each of its two axes. But whatever might be chosen, any combination on the line itself cannot be exceeded. To produce more of one necessitates a fall in production of the other.

At the very core of classical thought was the recognition that all production uses up some part of the resource base available. It made no difference whether what was produced was purely for current consumption or whether this was production of new capital goods that were intended to raise productivity levels at some future date. All production drew down on the existing productive capacity of the economy. Most importantly, until the flow of new goods and services could occur, even those activities devoted towards future production were seen as a drawing down with no return until there actually was a return.

In Figure 15.1, the vertical axis shows forms of output that draw down on the resource base with no attempt made to replace what has been drawn down.[1] Shown here are purchases by final users – designated by the standard *C* for consumer demand – and purchases by governments – designated by the traditional *G* for government spending. Their combined production uses up resources but what is produced is not intended to contribute to production at some future date. Resources are drawn down, products are either consumed or services rendered, but the economy is then less capable of producing since the resources have been used up while nothing has been created to replace what has been used up.

The horizontal axis represents all forms of drawing down on the economy's resource base that are directed towards producing forms of output that will add to the economy's productive base in the future. These are referred to as 'investment', shown in the diagram as I_{C+G} which is the investment counterpart of $C+G$ while I_C is the investment counterpart of C on its own. These are products (or services such as education) that are intended to leave the economy able to produce an even greater flow of output at some stage in the future, but also include resource use to replace and maintain productivity worn down during the production process. While public investment is included as part of I, the infrequency that public investment is tested by their market return makes its inclusion problematic, but can be included nowhere else.

In the PPC shown, consumer outlays, government spending plus investment (which is defined to include productive investments by the public sector) exhaust the economy's ability to produce. Either because of institutional limitations, or because the economy cannot produce more than its potential, it is not possible to produce more than some combination on the curve itself.

The value of the PPC diagram is that it brings the interior of the economy into focus, which, in modern theory, is almost entirely ignored. Inside the PPC are the economy's entire array of factors of production that can be used to produce. Some of what is found is used to produce consumer goods (flour and ovens to bake bread) or already are consumer goods (such as actual loaves of bread on a supermarket shelf). And some of those existing resources are being used to produce capital goods that will eventually be used in the production process to produce more capital. But what matters most of all is the structure of production, the interconnected web of productive relationships that exists across the economy. The structure of production is comprised of all of the economy's individual businesses with their capital and employees. There are the purchase and sale between the various firms that produce inputs for the production of other inputs. There is the infrastructure that provides the connecting rods between the various economic entities. There are the various productive inputs provided by governments. And there are the producers of final goods and services.

All of these are what is represented by the interior of the PPC. It is this hinterland of 'factors of production' – a vestigial concept carried over from classical times – whose existence and configuration determine what will be produced and how much of each particular item. Directing resources to their particular uses are entrepreneurs, but also to some extent, the government. These internal relationships between the various inputs are configured according to the price signals that are determined in the market for each of the inputs used, but also, to some extent, by the political signals to which governments respond. The final output produced, that is, the C, I and G shown on the axes, is determined by the decision makers found within the interior of the economy. The outcome of these decisions is shown on the axes in the form of the goods and services bought by consumers, investors and governments: C, I and G.

Modern macroeconomic theory almost entirely ignores the structure of production, focusing only on the production of final goods and services. Macroeconomic theory looks at what is represented by the outer edge of the diagram, but seldom attends to what is represented by the interior. Modern theory argues that the higher the level of C, I and G, the higher will be the level of employment. The causation is seen to go from expenditure to production, that is, from the periphery to the interior.

This is the reverse of the causation as seen by a classical economist. It was the productivity of the economy that determined the flow of consumer and government goods and services, as well as the additions to capital. Jobs were a derived demand that would flow from the need to employ individuals to undertake the required production. During periods not classified as recessionary, individuals would fit themselves out for employment and the wages system would adjust to ensure as many employees as possible were engaged.

SAVING AND INVESTMENT

To a classical economist, the central question was how to increase 'the wealth of nations', that is, how to increase living standards. The answer would be that, in relation to the diagram, it was necessary to increase the area under the PPC by moving it up and to the right. The more net investment there was, the more it might move outwards, but even under the best of circumstances, it would move outwards only very slowly.

The crucial issue was that of saving. In a modern macroeconomic model, saving is enumerated in money terms and is seen as a negative, an absence, a failure to spend. National saving is defined as current money income in total less total money spent on consumption in the current period. Figure 15.1, although conceived in classical terms, can be used to explain modern macroeconomic reasoning. Saving can be seen as the difference between the level of unproductive demand, that is $S = Y-(C+G)$, with Y, as usual, representing total output, which is found where the PPC curve meets the vertical axis. The real level of saving is then equal to the real level of investment, which is here shown as I_{C+G}.

But this does not quite get to the Keynesian conception. First, the PPC is entirely conceived in real terms. The units on the axes are actual products, the billions of items produced in an economy, from bread to bakeries. $C+G$ is made up of actual items of consumer goods and services plus government purchased goods and services. Saving in Keynesian macro is one step further removed from this diagram since it is entirely denominated in money terms. $\$S=\$Y-(\$C+\$G)$ is a near representation of the modern concept. Perhaps complicating these issues further, saving is frequently restricted to $Y-C$, with G net of transfers not entirely defined one way or the other, perhaps intrinsically conceived of as being as productive as business investment.

Saving in classical terms, however, represented the resource base used to produce investment goods while also providing workers with their food and shelter. Saving was not a sum of money. Saving was equal to investment, since saving was by definition resources used to build capital goods. Yet this was more than a tautology, since it emphasized the trade-off between those forms of activity that added nothing to productivity in comparison with those that did, with decisions to save and invest driving the overall outcome.

Understanding the role of saving as the building up of real productive assets, as well as providing the consumer goods that workers buy and use before their own activities result in the production of consumable goods and services, is a necessity if one is to understand how an economy functions. A town in a war zone, or caught short because of some natural disaster, soon discovers how important the real stock of provisions available is.

In sum, the PPC diagram captures with a great deal of subtlety the meaning of saving and investment in classical times. An economy's inheritance from the past can either be used for immediate consumption or as inputs into the creation of a larger capital base. Saving, when understood as a proportion of the productive apparatus of the economy, is then exactly equal to the level of investment. That segment of the entire productive part of the economy not aimed toward improving the future productivity of the economy is used to provide consumer products or government services in the present. All, however, draw down on the economy's existing productive capacity.

In terms of the diagram, classical economic policy was directed at expanding the area under the curve, not raising the level of spending as represented by the final outputs produced. The contrast with modern economic theory could not have been more complete. In modern macroeconomics, it is the total expenditure on C, G and I that supposedly determines the size of the economy, which in turn determines the level of employment. It is the expenditure found on the periphery of the diagram that determines what takes place internally, and most importantly, determines how large the productive triangle is. In a classical model, it was the reverse. The triangular area under the curve determined the economy's potential level of output, with various economic and political circumstances determining the distribution of what was produced among C, I and G.

GDP measures, which are also estimated in terms of C+I+G, could be used as an estimate of the success of the economy so long as the proportion of expenditure on G was a constant. The rate of growth in the triangular area would be roughly reflected in the increases in final demand. It was Keynesian economics that turned this measure of economic activity into a theory of production, so that higher levels of demand would in theory lead to higher levels of output. A classical economist would, however, have understood that the causation was from the interior of the economy to the periphery and not the other way round as modern macroeconomics now argues.

THE BASIS FOR ECONOMIC GROWTH IN A CLASSICAL MODEL

The ability of the economy to produce in a classical model is determined by the stock of existing factors of production, which is represented by the area beneath the production possibility curve. While it might be true to say that some of the inputs used during some period of time are produced during that period of time, overwhelmingly what determines the ability of the economy to produce is the vast array of already-existing capital assets plus the available skilled labour who are deployed in the production process. That some of these productive capabilities are utilized to generate inputs during the period – such as the use of an already-existing electricity generating capacity to produce a flow of power during the period itself – does not distract from the fact that virtually the whole of an economy's productive capacity is in place at the start of a production period. The notion that the various inputs, such as the labour that happens to exist with the skill-set it possesses, is anything besides an inheritance from the past and not some newly sprung productive capacity unrelated to the economy's prior production practices, is to lose sight of the fact that every economy is dependent on its past for its ability to produce in the present. It is also a reminder that future production is importantly determined by what will have occurred when the present became the past.

All production draws down on the existing resource base. All production uses up some of the existing asset base beneath the production possibility

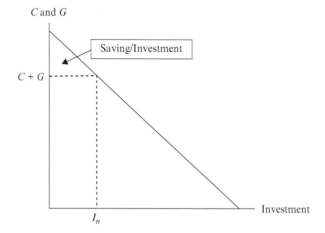

Figure 15.2   The point of steady-state neutral investment

curve. What is produced may then be classified into two branches, output that is used by its buyers without any expectation that it will add to the future flow of goods and services, and output that is intended to increase the future flow of goods and services. This second set of production is referred to as *investment*. The resources that have been used to produce this investment are the proportion of the nation's resources that have been saved and are the nation's *savings*. If one recognizes that the combined asset base plus labour time that have been applied to produce for the future is that proportion of the nation's resources which have been saved (that is, not used to produce consumption goods for present purposes), it will be seen that saving and investment are identical, without this equality being a truism.

In Figure 15.2, saving and investment are not calculated as a proportion of total output, and therefore found on the vertical axis. Saving is an area of the total available productivity of the entire economy. It is represented by an area beneath the production possibility curve showing the proportion of the economy's entire productive capabilities devoted to increasing its future ability to produce.

In the diagram, it appears that it is exactly the proportion of the economy above $C+G$, but that is just an approximation. It is whatever it is and could be more or less than the area shown. It is the conception that is crucial. It is recognition that the amount of saving is that proportion of the entire economy's resource base that is devoted to increasing the future productivity of the economy. It is, moreover, made up of bricks and mortar, food and clothing, capital assets and labour time. The more successful an economy is, the farther that the production possibility curve will move away from the origin. The greater the area under the production possibility curve, the greater the capacity of the economy to produce.

The level of investment on the horizontal axis is not replicated in the modern statistical measure of investment in GDP. It is the sum total of economic activities that not only are intended to raise future productivity but will actually achieve that end. Some of that expenditure is replacement investment for the capital used up during the period. Consumer demand (C) and government spending (G) both require a drawing down of the economy's productive base, as does investment (I). Maintaining the capital base is a necessary element in merely allowing an economy to stay where it is. C and G merely draw down without replacement.

Beyond replacement, there is then the development of the economy's capital base, which is made up of additions to capital, conceived as a stock of newly-produced capital assets, plus the improved technology that is built into new capital that has been deepened by innovation and the application of new knowledge to the capital stock. Within such expenditure there are forms of investment that will never lead to an overall improvement in the economy's productivity. Mistakes are common and ultimately draw down on the economy's existing capacity without completely replacing what has been drawn down. At the same time, some of this improvement in the underlying capacity of the economy is provided by governments, whether in such investments as building drainage systems or providing new roads. Many such government projects, however, though offered up as investment projects never lead to an increase in the ability of the economy to produce larger volumes of output. The distinction made here is thus conceptual in that all that are classified as forms of investment are projects that actually succeed in achieving future improvements in output. The stress in this conception is in the outcome rather than in attempting to find some objective measure that can separate investments that do eventually cause the production possibility curve to move outwards versus those that do not. It might just be noted that investment expenditures that are wholly funded by private entrepreneurs rather than in part or in whole by governments are more likely to cause the economy to expand.

Somewhere on the division between $C+G$ and the level of capital expenditure there is a point, here designated as I_n, which is the point of neutrality between a level of capital investment that will shift the production possibility curve outward and where it will instead shift the curve inwards. A sufficiently rapid level of capital investment will shift the curve out. Too little investment, that does not even allow sufficient investment to replace what has been used up, will cause the curve to shift inwards. At

I_n, the level of investment will leave the economy exactly as productive as it previously was.

It has been only since the eighteenth century, with the advent of the market economy and entrepreneurial decision making, that our economies have been able to improve living standards on an almost annual basis. Year by year the additions to the capital stock and its improvement have more than balanced the level of productivity that has been drawn down during production. From a classical perspective, economic growth is an entirely supply-side phenomenon, driven by the provision, year by year, of a more productive capital stock along with a more highly skilled workforce. There is no necessity for it to continue, but the broad framework of what must occur if growth is to occur was made plain by classical economists who had conceived the mechanism in an entirely different way from those who believe that the underlying drivers are increases in aggregate demand.

THE CLASSICAL THEORY OF THE CYCLE

The classical theory of the cycle was built around an understanding that the individual actions of a large number of producers, especially in an environment in which money and credit were the intermediary between buyers and seller, would from time to time lead to economic crises and a downturn in activity. Business decisions, being made typically in advance of the circumstances in which those decisions would be expected to earn a return, could not be perfectly meshed with the economic outcomes that would actually occur.

Monetary and financial disruption was seen as a major potential for instability. Disruptions in the market for credit were of surpassing importance. Misdirected credit, and problems in the credit-creation process, where ultimately unprofitable enterprises end up being funded by the financial system, were the cornerstone of the downwards phase of the classical theory of the cycle. But other forces might also add to the instability. These might include cataclysmic events such as natural disasters and wars (or even the ending of wars). Just as important were government decisions that themselves disrupted markets (as, for example, the OPEC oil boycott of the 1970s). But whatever might be the cause, a large number of business decisions turning out badly, even where no one in business could have been expected to have foreseen these events, would lead to a downturn in activity. The classical theory of the cycle was a well-developed feature of economics prior to the publication of Keynes's *General Theory*. Let us therefore use the PPC diagram to explain the nature of recession and the recovery process in classical theory.

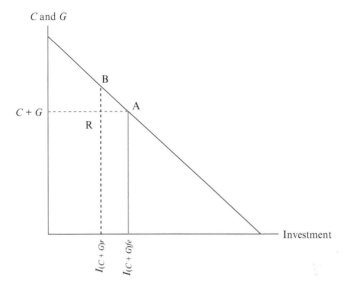

Figure 15.3   An economy in recession

Figure 15.3 shows an economy in non-recessionary times with the economy at Point 'A' on the PPC. There is therefore as much as possible being produced, there is full employment (that is, no cyclical unemployment) and all resources are being used as efficiently as possible. The level of consumption plus public spending is $C+G$ while the level of investment is $I_{(C+G)fe}$, the subscript '*fe*' indicating full employment.

The economy goes into recession for any number of possible reasons, none of which are related to a deficiency of demand. This being a classical model, the economy did not slow because consumers suddenly out of nowhere decided to save and not spend. The coming of recession is shown by the shift of the economy from Point A to Point R. There may perhaps be some inwards movement of the curve itself due to some of the economy's capital base having become unemployable. But since the PPP curve represents the economy's potential and not the actual circumstances of the recession, the inwards movement is generally of little significance at the earliest stage of the recession.

The fall in output is understood as a consequence of some major distortion in the structure of production. There may be a period in which the actual circumstances are disguised by on-going levels of loss-making economic activity. But with the structure of supply no longer conforming to the structure of demand, and therefore with some of the capital stock now uneconomic, a crisis had finally occurred that has revealed the fact that the existing economic structure could no longer support the level of incomes being distributed. A significant proportion of the economy may have appeared to be financially sound until that moment because there are financial assets that can be drawn down, and individual personal economies that can be undertaken to allow the situation to limp along.

The clearest sign of recession is the large drop in investment, shown in the diagram by the fall from $I_{(C+G)_{fe}}$ to $I_{(C+G)_r}$, with the subscript 'r' indicating recession. With the onset of recession, there are higher than normal levels of unemployment. The level of consumption and government expenditure typically remain the same, with a fall in C perhaps even compensated by a rise in G. The economy therefore moves to Point 'R', at a point showing a fall in investment but no significant change in total consumer and government spending (and it would make no difference to the analysis if $C+G$ rose or fell). The policy question then becomes, what can be done to return economic activity and the economy's rate of growth to its former level and reduce the level of unemployment as quickly as possible?

The Keynesian macroeconomic perspective is to assume that the problem has been an increase in saving. That is, the downturn has been caused by a sudden falloff in aggregate demand. The assumption is that the underlying structure of demand for both consumer and capital goods is of no concern so that the community need only increase its expenditures and the economy will return to full employment. No problem with the underlying structure of production is brought into the story. There is a fall in expenditure but the specific goods and services, as well as the investment goods that the economy would produce at full employment, have not changed. So far as the desired composition of output is concerned, or in terms of the actual structure of supply, nothing of significance is different. The assumption would be that the major problem was a fall in confidence ('animal spirits'). No consideration would be given to the possibility that the economy is in need of major readjustment, and more importantly, that increasing public spending to absorb these supposedly unspent savings would impede the return to full employment and the economy's prior rate of growth. Whatever might be the underlying set of considerations, the policy response would be an increase in public spending, increasing the level of G. The economy would be directed towards outcome B, as shown on Figure 15.3. A successful policy, at least according to modern macroeconomic theory, would thus return the economy to full employment but with a reduced level of investment and a higher level of $C+G$. The fall in investment would not necessarily diminish living standards at that particular moment although it might. More long term, however, the fall in productive investment would inevitably reduce the economy's long-term potential rate of growth and could easily lead it into a decline.

In contrast to modern forms of policy, given the importance of value-adding investment in creating economic growth, classical policy was aimed at shifting the economy from R back to A. There would be a number of policy changes that might be adopted, such as seeking to lower real wages, reducing taxation or bringing rates of interest down. But the overall approach was to allow the structure of the economy to adjust to the new circumstances so that wages and prices could move to their full employment market-clearing levels while the economy adjusted to a more productive structure of production that the recession had itself indicated was needed.

The policy that would not be adopted would be to raise public spending (G) to shift the economy from R to B. The crucial imperative would be the restoration of the level of productive investment. Even if the shift from R to B could be effected, the longer-term consequences would have been recognized as a reduction in the economy's long-term rate of growth. At Point B relative to Point A, C+G is greater while productive investment is lower. A smaller proportion of the nation's resources are being used in growth-creating ways.

But more importantly, for a classical economist the economy was in recession because the structure of production had become maladjusted to the underlying realities. The structure of supply no longer matched the structure of demand, and this referred to more than just final demand. The entire structure of production across the economy, which incorporated the structure of value adding supply from the most basic inputs through to final output, was not properly aligned.

Any effort to reward businesses for producing in markets in which they could not earn a profitable return without either direct or indirect government subsidies only meant that the economy would continue to underperform. All production would continue to draw down on the resource base. Subsidizing wasteful forms of output would mean that the recovery process would be increasingly dominated by forms of production that would never repay their costs in further growth. The capital structure of the economy would therefore not improve as rapidly as it might have, and the economy might well end up in a situation in which there was not even sufficient investment to restore the capital that had been used up in production. The production possibility curve could even move inwards towards the origin. The economy would no longer be as productive as it had previously been. Living standards would fall while even the labour market might stagnate. Recovery would be postponed rather than hastened.

The inevitable outcome of such misdirected production would be a fall in real earnings. If the economy does end up at Point B and full employment, it will only have occurred if real wages had contracted since the economy will have become less productive than it had previously been.

SUMMING UP

Classical economic theory focused on the whole economy, its structure, relative prices and its ability to adjust to accommodate new circumstances. Given the unpredictability of events, recessions were recognized as inevitable and sure to occur every so often. The recovery process was therefore also recognized as an occasional necessity. Given how they understood the nature and causes of recession, the efforts made by governments were concentrated on hastening the readjustment, and also on providing temporary work for those who could not find work in a depressed economy. But the long-term benefit of leaving the adjustment process almost entirely to the market was understood as far preferable to governments attempting to provide a short-term fix.

In particular, public spending as a means to hasten recovery was seen as not just useless but counterproductive. Not only would such expenditures not bring about recovery, they would be expected to make things worse. A 'Keynesian' solution was not rejected because of some belief in the virtues of '*laissez-faire*'. Such solutions were rejected because they were recognized as mistaken, with the theory of demand deficiency explicitly rejected as fallacious.

The causes of recession among pre-Keynesian economists were understood as a consequence of disorganization in the structure of production, which would occur from time to time in any dynamic and innovative economy. In particular, it was the recognition that the system of finance and credit creation, in an environment overseen by political decision making, must go through such recessionary periods. There was a classical theory of recession that came with a detailed explanation for involuntary unemployment along with policy recommendations that could be used to bring such recessions to an end. This chapter has outlined what that theory was, a theory unknown to virtually every economist today, the vast majority of whom continue to believe that deficient aggregate demand is central to understanding why recessions occur and provides the correct approach to work out how recessions can be ended, even though no Keynesian stimulus has ever succeeded in bringing an economy from recession into recovery.

NOTE

1. The PPC shown is a straight line since there is no reason to presume resources are more productive in one form of production than in any other. This is all the more so since in classical theory whether some asset is an item of capital is not intrinsic to the object itself, but is dependent on the decision of its owner. Providing a bowed PPC would not change the argument in any way.

16. Cyclical activity and governments

The classical theory of the cycle explained the periodic upwards and downwards movement in the level of economic activity with reference to changes brought about by circumstances prevailing during the previous phase. The seeds of the subsequent recession are sown during the upturn. The factors that will lead to revival come into play as the economy moves into deeper recession.

At the centre of the response to existing circumstance are entrepreneurial decisions made in one business after another. The owners and managers of every business are intensely interested in the state of the economy, the level of demand for the products they sell and the cost of buying the inputs they use. They are mindful of the actions of their competitors. They are aware that no competitor will inform its competition ahead of time of any changes that it plans to make. The unexpected happens all the time. And all the while, each business continuously seeks new and better products and new and better (and not just cheaper) ways to produce.

Beyond all of this there is the unknown future about which all economic decisions are made, but about which no facts can be known. There are therefore tremendous risks experienced by every business as it decides what to do.

But entrepreneurs are not the only ones who react to circumstances. Both workers and the owners of land and capital are also always aware of other opportunities that happen to exist at any moment in time. Both during upturns and recessions, everyone in control of resources which can earn an income on the market continually consider their options. Markets are not static. They are filled with people, many of whom can be guaranteed to take whatever steps they can to improve their economic circumstances as the opportunities arise.

The notion that an economy in recession will just stagnate, time period after time period, is a picture that cannot be sustained by any reference to the way that people actually behave. The reality is that people will make huge efforts to salvage what they can in extreme situations. The recovery, when it comes, is forged out of these individual actions, and if recovery is to be sustainable, can occur in no other way.

GOVERNMENT ACTIONS

But then, behind the natural ebb and flow of the market, are the actions taken by governments and government agencies. Governments everywhere are a major agent in the way in which economies operate and can never be left out of the picture if a complete understanding is sought.

So far as the economy is concerned, governments do four things. They of course do much more than this, but in looking only at the economy, what governments do is spend, tax, regulate and make adjustments to the market for credit.

Each of these can and does have major effects on economic outcomes, but no one can predict other than in a general way what these effects will be. And certainly no business can be expected to forecast with perfect accuracy the effect of some government action on its own business given how large and extensive an economy is.

But what is most apparent from the history of economies is that the actions taken by governments will frequently do great harm to the economies being managed. Unless one brings in the role of government and its effects on production and employment, understanding the causes of the cycle will remain incomplete.

It is governments that are now, and may always have been, the single most important cause of recession. It is their actions, rather than the market itself, that are far more likely to cause instability, recession and unemployment.

Yet what is notable from examining Haberler's *Prosperity and Depression*, which was published in 1937, the year after Keynes published his *General Theory*, is that none of the discussions of the causes of the cycle discuss the possibility that the actions of government may themselves be a major factor in causing economies to enter recession and in then prolonging recessions when they occur. All of the theories discussed are theories of how economies enter recession and then recover without the involvement of governments, either as a cause or as a cure.

THE GREAT DEPRESSION

How realistic this was even during the 1930s is questionable. The Great Depression may have been initiated by decisions of the Federal Reserve in the US and the Bank of England in London to raise interest rates in 1928 and 1929 to slow what were seen as economies which had expanded beyond their potential.

These effects on activity were then heightened by the American decision to implement the highest tariff levels in US history, a decision which then led to similar actions being taken across the world. The subsequent fall in international trade created a depression that would become the deepest ever experienced, and one which would take a world war to bring it finally to a complete end.

If one, in fact, looks at what made the recessionary phase of the Great Depression last as long as it did and reach the depths that were reached, it is quite clear that whatever may have started the downwards process in the first place, it was government action, particularly in the United States, which accelerated and deepened the process. These were some of the actions taken in the US:

- central bank actions to raise interest rates in 1928 and 1929 to contain inflationary pressures (when the recorded growth in the price level showed no economy-wide price increases at all);
- the largest tariff increase in US history in 1930 to protect domestic industry from foreign competition;
- deliberate policy to maintain real wages even as the recession commenced in order to maintain the level of demand;
- mandated limits on some areas of production to allow producer prices to rise;
- major new government regulations to prevent businesses following their most productive paths to growth, aimed at limiting the effects of competitive forces.

Each of these would be seen today as inappropriate if the aim were to create growth and employment. Indeed, all would be recognized by economists as likely to worsen employment and slow activity.

No discussion of the cycle can therefore be complete unless it is also understood that governments themselves are a major contributor to economic instability, and may well have themselves become the major cause. But first, a detour on how economic theory is now taught.

HOW ECONOMIC THEORY IS USUALLY TAUGHT

The approach taken to teaching economics has become one in which the market mechanism is in many ways taught only so that there is a basis for explaining why markets might in some circumstances not operate properly. The market mechanism is seldom explained as what it is: the sole means to achieve prosperity and the basis for a continuing improvement in living standards for an entire population.

And even where the role of the entrepreneurially driven market is taught, it is a minor issue with the entrepreneur, if not actually left out of the story, reduced to a minor figure of little if any importance.

Supply and Demand

In a standard introductory text, somewhere at the very start is the theory of supply and demand. An explanation is given of how the economic system will generate a price for each item sold through the anonymous forces of the market. There is then a discussion of how such prices change through changes in various *ceteris paribus* conditions.

Little will be said about the price system in its entirety. Little will be said about the role of relative prices in causing the economy to adjust. Little if anything will be said about the market system generally, nor about individual decentralized decision-making and the role of innovation and the entrepreneur. There will merely be a discussion of how supply curves and demand curves intersect at a a particular price and volume, with no sense of the dynamics of a world in which everyone is a demander and most adults below the retirement age are producers. There is no sense of a world unfolding as individuals lead their lives, in the midst of which are actions taken to produce, earn incomes and buy.

Marginal Analysis and the Theory of the Firm

A firm is a commercial organization run by an entrepreneur overseeing the production of many different types of products in many different markets. To leave out the entrepreneurial role and then reduce the complexity of such organizations to decisions to increase or reduce the production of a single item sold and then further concentrate on the effect on relative revenues and costs of trying to sell one extra unit narrows the focus to a point virtually empty of economic content.

Marginal analysis makes it appear that decision making within business is not much more than a mechanical analysis of the effect on revenues as against the effect on costs of producing additional units of some product. What is left out at just the first hurdle is that most of the information needed to make the kinds of calculation that it is assumed businesses make is simply unavailable and could never be known in time for such decisions to be made even in any single instance, never mind across the entire business world.

Perfect Competition

From there on, the rest of a typical text will discuss how things are apt to go wrong. There is a micro model described as 'perfect' competition. It is a model that describes how in some markets each individual firm is so small relative to the entire level of sales that it faces a completely elastic demand curve at the price determined by the overall supply and demand for the product.

This is a market that, at most, represents a handful of situations, mostly in the agricultural sector and where the specific conditions for such 'perfection' could not possibly exist in reality (as, for example, the need for complete knowledge about the future), making it absolutely clear that no such market could ever exist.

Imperfect Competition

Beyond perfect competition, every other market type is understood as representing some form of 'imperfect' competition. That is, by the very words used within economics, the implication is that every other market type is inherently flawed in some way. If only perfect competition could prevail in every market, it is generally implied and sometimes said, the economy would be operating as efficiently as possible. Given that this is not the case, inefficiency must abound.

And the worst of all possibilities is monopoly. Where monopolies exist, the effect, as shown in text after text, is to restrict output and raise prices above the levels that would have occurred had a perfect market existed. If the point is made that it is only through the various forms of imperfect market that innovation and novelty occur, it is hardly emphasized and generally downplayed.

Price Discrimination

There is then the use of the phrase 'price discrimination' to describe the completely legitimate practice of businesses selling the same product to different people at different prices as a means of increasing their own profitability. Since 'discrimination' is a word loaded with negative connotations, the implication is that there is something improper about the practice when what it is referring to is, to choose just one example, the lowering of prices on public transport for students.

Having shown that markets are likely to lead to excessive prices and lower levels of production, the stage is set for a discussion of 'market failure' and 'externalities'.

Market Failure

Market failure is an important theme in introductory economics as normally taught, and in its original form meant an inefficient allocation of resources. The economy did not produce as much value added as it might have done, leaving us inside the production possibility curve. The notion has expanded in its general usage amongst non-economists to encompass any outcome that is different from the outcome that policy makers would prefer.

But the major difficulty is that we now embed the notion of market failure in how we teach before we have made sure that there is an understanding of what market success actually means. And what is certainly almost never taught is government failure, which is the departures from an efficient allocation of resources caused by governments.

Externalities

Amongst the most important examples of market failure is what are referred to as externalities. An externality is a cost imposed on some third party not associated with the purchase and sale of the particular product. The typical example is some form of pollution where the market will produce more pollution than is socially optimal.

If some resource has no owner – the air we breathe, say, or some body of water – then businesses will be more likely to dump waste products without regard to the effects on others. Business is thus associated with negative outcomes for the environment.

And while it is perfectly sensible to point such problems out, attention is then given to conceptual solutions so useless in practice that it is a wonder that they are ever introduced at this level. The core concept is something called 'marginal social costs', which are the additional costs to society as a whole caused by some change in activity.

Seldom is there a presentation that points out that as wealth has increased across a community, a reduction in polluting forms of activity has arisen naturally in the political response to such problems. Certainly problems abound, but it is not the normal practice to stress that the benefits of a market economy are massive in comparison with the problems that production of itself might cause.

Absence of the Entrepreneur

Nor is it common practice to stress that it is only because there is private ownership and a price mechanism that realistic solutions to such problems not only can be, but have been developed. Given production techniques in the modern world – where the nature of the production process is driven by technological specifications – every economy faces the same problems in dealing with such externalities.

But given the origins of such problems, how often is it pointed out that no genuine solution is possible without economies organized around entrepreneurial decision making and the pursuit of a profitable return, unless we are prepared to sacrifice massive amounts of our productive potential?

Macroeconomics and the Theory of the Cycle

Then, with the introduction of macroeconomics, the entire economy is seen as continually teetering on the brink of recession, inflation and high rates of unemployment. These are economies that, so far as these theories are concerned, could not possibly be left to themselves, as entrepreneurs go about their business producing for others within the regulatory environment set by governments.

As typically presented, an economy, if left to its own devices, will spin out of control into high rates of inflation, or instead fall into an underemployment equilibrium in which high levels of involuntary unemployment abound.

Macroeconomics as now taught is the direct descendant of Keynes. It is sometimes urged that Keynes is a relic of the past whose views have now been transcended. The reality is that Keynesian theory and concepts are embedded, rock solid, into modern theory. Deficiency of demand is a constant concern in just the same way that excess demand beyond an economy's potential is itself a major concern in dealing with inflation.

The result is that few are any longer taught that economies have major properties for self-adjustment and are able to recuperate on their own without major government involvement. The notion that the cycle is cyclical and can be counted on to provide most of the momentum towards recovery is unknown and untaught. It is a notion foreign to the ways in which economics is presented.

NOT TAUGHT ABOUT MARKETS

By the time students have emerged from an introductory course, they know next to nothing about the market process itself but have been presented with massive evidence that an economy left on its own (which no economy ever is) will create major problems at every turn.

They will not come away with an understanding that the market economy is one of the most beneficial social inventions ever developed by human societies. They will have no concept that an economy in which entrepreneurial decision making is the basis for economic activity cannot be improved upon by any other set of social arrangements. They will not be instructed that a heavy-handed government response aimed at reversing the down-phase of the cycle is possibly unnecessary, and there will certainly be little inkling given that such policies may be positively harmful.

The market does need regulation, but it needs regulation that allows market processes to work. What is not needed are government actions that take the place of the market by determining by directive what can and ought to be the outcome of entrepreneurial actions by businesses trying to find a market.

To believe there is any other set of arrangements outside the market that will lead to personal prosperity across a society is to be left in complete ignorance about how living standards and the good life can be created in our world of scarcity, shortages and radical uncertainties about the future.

And over and above all, it will not be pointed out, let alone stressed, that the market economy is the only set of economic arrangements consistent with personal freedom and individual liberty. The political benefits of a market economy may themselves be the greatest benefits that such arrangements bestow.

None of this is generally taught, and of these matters, most students of introductory economics typically know next to nothing at all.

THE CONSTANT INVOLVEMENT OF GOVERNMENTS

What the typical approach to economic theory now does is to underscore the belief that an economy must have government involvement at virtually every turn in order to rectify and adjust the outcomes the market would itself produce.

Rather than understanding that a functioning market economy for the most part needs government involvement to provide a regulatory framework, the message now being given, whether overt or tacit, is that governments are a constant necessity to correct at every turn the major failings of an entrepreneurially managed market economy.

And this is not just minor adjustments here or there. The way that economics is presented is that governments must become a constant presence, time and again altering the circumstances in the field to head off major instability or to rectify high levels of social injustice.

Economic texts at the introductory level are designed as user's manuals for government action to remedy all manner of problems. Such texts typically and almost exclusively deal with what may go wrong, so that it can be understood how governments can be used to put matters right.

GOVERNMENT POLICY AND RECESSION

Until the Great Depression, governments were largely hands-off. The approaches taken by governments were generally straightforward. Regulations were introduced where problems were recognized, and protection for workers, consumers and the public in general were needed. But for the most part there was a recognition that the economy could be expected to manage itself. The following were amongst the more important limitations that governments placed on their own involvement in economic matters:

- there were strict limits on protectionist measures designed to impede trade;
- the gold standard was maintained as the means to determine the value of each currency in relation to all other currencies;
- budgets were balanced;
- taxation was kept low;
- public spending was kept at a small proportion of total national production.

This is not to suggest that social legislation played no part. The regulation of industry – the introduction of child labour laws, the restrictions on the working week, mandated safety legislation – grew out of the recognition that there had to be standards imposed to ensure the health, safety and welfare of the community and of its working population.

But the assumption was that economic activity was largely the realm of entrepreneurial activity and private ownership. Whatever a government might be capable of, running a business and directing the economy were not skills in its possession.

Since the start of the twentieth century the approach has been increasingly different. This has in many ways been brought on by the two world wars, where government activity became more and more entrenched. Adding to the pressures towards more government involvement and direction was the Russian Revolution in 1917 which made central planning appear to some to be the wave of the future.

Keynesian economics was, in effect, a watered-down version of central planning mixed with private ownership. But what had become clear long before World War II was that governments were taking on more and more of the role of economic managers. It did not require Keynes to write the *General Theory* for governments to feel themselves adequate to the task of direct management of the economies they oversaw.

It is now quite possible that the classical theory of the cycle has been superseded by the actions of governments as a cause of recession. It is even possible that the cycles, even as they were experienced during classical times, were driven by the actions of governments.

But since the early years of the twentieth century, as governments have taken on a greater and greater role as managers of our economic affairs, so they have increased their intrusions into the economy with the specific intent of changing macroeconomic outcomes. This is a role that governments more and more see themselves as capable of assuming for themselves, however little evidence there may actually be in practice, that they are capable of achieving the outcomes they seek, or of doing so without causing serious damage often to the very people they are supposedly trying to help.

RECESSIONS AND POLITICAL DECISIONS

Today there is no aspect of an economy's structure that governments do not believe themselves capable of making positive contributions towards. Governments believe themselves able to make adjustments in the widest array of economic circumstances with little concern about potential collateral damage.

Such actions are not undertaken with a sense of dread at the possible unintended consequences. They are undertaken with a confidence that is simply unwarranted by our level of knowledge about the effects that government-induced changes will cause. It is economic expertise that is often the single most important promise those in governments offer, and there is an enormous self-belief in political leaders that they can change things for the better.

A partial list of the various areas where governments and the bureaucracy are actively involved in crafting outcomes and dictating policy includes all of the following:

- monetary and banking policy;
- interest rates adjustment;
- taxation – involving both tax rates and the structure of the taxation system;

- spending – dealing with both the level of spending and its direction;
- regulation – combining both overall rules of conduct as well as specific directives to take particular actions at particular times;
- exchange rate adjustments – with even a floating exchange rate subject to actions from time to time to shift the value of the currency;
- tariffs and other protectionist measures;
- income redistribution as a conscious policy aim;
- higher and higher welfare payments to an increasing proportion of the population;
- wages and industrial relations.

That so many policies are also driven by the public's demand for greater public services and increased protection from the vicissitudes of life means that governments find themselves offering more because there is a political market for what they do. The demand by the public for governments to take greater command over the resources of the community may bring some kind of explanation for the actions that follow, but shows little appreciation of how poorly done these tasks are or how costly they have become.

APPLYING THE THEORY OF THE CYCLE TO POLITICAL DECISIONS

The theory of the cycle was built around an appreciation that production takes place in anticipation of demand. And why things do not always work out is often because of decisions taken by governments to change the contours of the economies which invalidate the previous decisions made by business.

An entrepreneur thinks about production and sale in an economy which can be imagined in many different ways. But large-scale actions by governments in any single one of the areas in that list of potential policy decision can create major shifts in the economic circumstances in which a business trades.

Decisions to increase levels of liquidity (that is, money and credit) into the economy or then, later on, to remove this added liquidity can have major effects in both instances. Higher inflation or slower growth make the present significantly different from how it was imagined when it was only the future.

In classical times, the pushing up of demand through the creation of credit by the central government was the very meaning of the term 'inflation'. The term that has come back into fashion has been the discussion of a 'bubble'. There is liquidity poured into the economy which has a massive impact on some specific areas of activity which grow well beyond their relative contribution to the economy because of the effect on prices. The bursting of the bubble thereafter has an effect on the overall level of activity, not just in that sector but also elsewhere.

And to the extent that such bubbles affect the banking industry and the availability of finance, so much the worse for the economy overall.

Changes in tax rates or the level of public spending will have consequences which are dependent on the effects they have on after-tax revenues or on the kinds of goods or services eventually bought.

Poorly designed regulations can have a devastating impact on the activities of many firms at one and the same time. And as emphasized by business cycle theory, it does not matter where a downturn starts, but where it finishes.

In the end, it is pulling the rug out from under business through the actions taken by governments that can often be the cause of recession. Businesses have imagined a future based on what they then knew, but that particular future did not eventuate because of the policies that were adopted by government. Repeat this same circumstance over and again, and the result is a recessionary downturn that would not have occurred had the government not acted in the way it did.

Were governments to make their decisions based on an understanding that it is entrepreneurially managed firms that must carry the weight of economic activity, the decisions made would be more consistent with economic growth. Were such decisions made with greater sensitivity to the needs of business, there might be fewer fluctuations in economic activity.

Instead, the attitude too often taken by government is that they are able to stabilize economies, create growth and promote lower unemployment through their own actions and decisions.

COUNTER-CYCLICAL POLICIES IN RECESSION

Yet for all that, a government does not have to just sit still and wait for a recession to end and recovery begin. There are actions a government can take to limit the damage caused by recession and to hasten recovery.

An appropriate counter-cyclical policy should be based on harnessing entrepreneurial activities and market forces to achieve restoration of strong rates of growth. There are things that can be done, some of which are related to ensuring that business costs are brought down as quickly as possible while others are aimed at ensuring market adjustments take place as rapidly as possible.

Lower Taxes

A priority would be lower taxes, especially taxes on business. Increases in after-tax cash flows in healthy firms will provide the momentum for an upturn. Lowering tax levels will assist in the expansion of profitable sectors of the economy.

Keep Wages under Control

The containment of real wages should also be a priority, with efforts made to ensure that as few employees as possible price themselves out of a job and as many others as possible are priced into jobs. Whatever might have been the real level of wages that could be supported by an economy before recessionary conditions set in, as conditions begin to contract, real wages should come down to allow as many jobs as possible to be preserved. This, too, will contribute to putting industry on a more profitable foundation.

Ease Government Regulation

Rolling back some of the restrictions placed by governments on business and business development would also assist in the recovery process. A more market-oriented perspective on regulation and business incentives would foster expansion where it might not otherwise take place.

Reduce Unproductive Forms of Public Spending

There should also be containment in the level of unproductive forms of public spending. As the private sector contracts, there is even less ability for the economy to support the size of the public sector. Limiting the growth in *non-value-adding* forms of public spending, and if possible lowering such spending, will reduce the pressure on private industry.

Perhaps Increase Productive Forms of Public Spending

There may, however, be some benefit in a limited series of increases in public sector infrastructure programmes that genuinely create value. The problem is always to get the timing right, since the various lags between actually recognizing that such programmes are needed and actually putting such programmes into motion may well be too long to do much good. The danger is that the spending will occur after the trough has been reached and recovery is in place. Then, rather than softening the downturn, such outlays will diminish the private sector's ability to grow.

Perhaps Introduce Temporary Work Programmes

There may also be some very limited opportunities for temporary work programmes with employees paid at or near the minimum wage. Such work programmes should not be seen, either by those who run them or by those who are employed, as anything more than a stopgap between genuinely productive jobs.

Maintain Commitment to Fiscal Balance

But as an absolute rudder to help governments to determine what actions they should or should not take, there should be a commitment to a return to fiscal balance at the earliest possible date. Recessions come with lower tax revenue and higher welfare payments. A budget in surplus can be expected to fall into deficit, and where there is already a deficit, the likelihood is that its size will increase. Living with such deficits is the only alternative.

Avoid Increases in Public Debt

As the economy recovers, the deficits will diminish. Keeping in mind that recessions will pass, but the debts accumulated to finance recovery will be very long-lasting, ought to be an important antidote to the rush to higher expenditure as the economy slows down.

Avoid Increases in Taxation

Tax increases in the midst of recession to lower the deficit are especially counterproductive to the needs of the moment. If the deficit is to be deliberately increased, cutting taxes, particularly taxes on business, will at least have the practical value of raising cash flow just when it is needed most. This is the most direct way to preserve jobs.

Reduce Interest Rates

Interest rate reductions should be part of the process. Lower rates are not a solution to a recession but can assist when uncertainty is at its height. While conditions are uncertain there will be a reluctance to venture one's capital in new forms of production. And if the crisis is due to a shortage of credit there should be efforts made to accommodate otherwise solvent borrowers. Reductions in production costs, wages, taxes and public sector demand for resources will themselves induce a fall in rates, as would the existence in the first instance of a recessionary fall in economic activity. Lower interest rates will not only not by themselves generate recovery, pushing rates too low will actually prolong recession as they will reduce the flow of savings back into the market after the crisis has passed.

Summing Up

An economic environment in which businesses find reduced production costs, lower real wages, a reduction in taxes, less regulation and falling rates of interest would be one in which the downturn would be arrested and an upturn would be expected to occur within a reasonable period of time. Once in the grip of recession, the expectation is that the economy will be in a relatively depressed condition for upwards of a year. Governments will, however, feel the pressure both from the community and from those who take a Keynesian approach to macroeconomic issues.

What has been discussed is what ought to be done from an economic point of view. What a government will actually do depends on the circumstances it is faced with at the time and the judgements it then makes. The above framework does, however, provide a template against which policy can be judged from a classical perspective.

The use of Keynesian policies with the coming of recession following the Global Financial Crisis in 2008–09 entrenched a worldwide slowdown. The financial crisis itself evaporated within months. Subdued economic conditions, following the stimulus that was applied by one country after another, became a lasting legacy that should help us to appreciate what should and should not be done when recessions occur, and underscore the kinds of outcome that a Keynesian policy creates.

ACTIONS THAT SHOULD NOT BE TAKEN

For many, leaving things to the market would not appear direct enough, nor would there be a general willingness to generate recovery by raising the profitability of business. These are political issues, and where such attitudes prevail, recovery will be slower and more uncertain. Yet there are popular solutions that are themselves part of the problem. Three are discussed:

1. Public spending to restore growth causes output to be built on a false platform. Public sector construction projects, without an increase in value relative to their costs, is a loss-making enterprise, just as it would be in the private sector.

Keynesian-based macroeconomic theory tells you that there are multiplier effects. Even if the original outlay loses money, it is said, all of the secondary expenditures on various goods and services bought by those working on government-funded projects do their part to keep the economy growing. But if the initial expenditure loses money, then all of the secondary expenditures funded by increases generated by those projects are contributions to an overall loss-making series of activities.

If every one of the related expenditures had been part of a single enterprise, this would be easier to understand. The fact that this spending is divided into individual payments to individual enterprises disguises the fact that whatever is being produced is not leading to the creation of enough value to repay all of the costs.

The economy is not creating enough additional value to validate the increase in the total level of spending. In the end, there will either be inflation, or cuts in other forms of public spending to finance repayment of the debts incurred when the deficits were run up, or there will be large increases in taxation to fund the expenditure. Nothing in an economy comes free.

To believe that deliberately increasing deficits through higher levels of public spending is the road to recovery is the Keynesian fallacy and should be avoided at all costs. Some public works are useful. But the belief that the single most important requirement to pull an economy from recession is a high level of public spending and a vastly increased deficit is a danger.

2. Trade protection is a cure infinitely worse than the disease. Protecting local jobs against imports is a common response to recession. The question is asked: why should domestic sales go to producers in foreign lands when there is already a high rate of unemployment at home?

    Yet it should be obvious that raising domestic production costs during a downturn, which is what taxing imports amounts to, is the reverse of the policy needed to regenerate growth. It is also counterproductive to long-term growth to be depriving domestic industry of the often superior products that can be sourced in other countries, which is part of the reason that such imports have been sought out in the first place.

    But the strongest reason why import restrictions should not be introduced is because of the certain retaliatory actions that will be taken by other countries against the initiating country's own exports. If the home country shuts out imports from others, the certainty is that others will shut out imports from them.

In dealing with recession, maintaining the most efficient least-cost forms of production should be a principle that should not be breached.

3. Attempts to direct economies from the centre are the worst of all possible solutions to recession. The belief that an answer to our economic problems may be found in handing over the management of our economic affairs to politicians and public servants is to lose all understanding of what is required to turn resources into value-adding output.

    A politician will, perhaps, allocate money for schools, roads, hospitals or whatever else comes to mind because it makes good politics. But in so doing, nothing is known of what needs to be done next by those who allocate the funds.

    The various projects each require inputs of all kinds, numbering in the tens of thousands. Each of those inputs requires an intricate hinterland of other firms supplying inputs. It is beyond the competence of governments to organize in any detail the entire network of production that would be required. The only way to create the required inputs, in the required amounts, to be available just when they are needed, is to rely on markets and the price mechanism.

    Governments can perhaps fund a handful of projects. They cannot hope to direct the economy overall. Nor in most instances do they believe they can. A government can provide funds to build schools, and can even build schools using its own employees. But it cannot provide the lumber, hammers or nails, nor the bricks and mortar.

    Government direction of industry has been attempted at one time or another in the past and has in every case been a tremendous failure. The information requirements alone are beyond all possibility of collection. The very concept of a centrally directed economy is a dystopian nightmare that can never be made to work.

17. Savings and the financial system

In making sense of the financial system it is crucial to understand that there is a profound difference between individual saving and a nation saving. Personal saving, which is done by setting aside money, is an entirely different concept from national saving, which is the use of resources that will strengthen the productive capabilities of the economy in the future.

When a person saves, the saving is almost invariably in the form of money. Money has been received and is stored in some financial institution for later use. It is the commonsense everyday meaning of the word and is clearly comprehended by everyone.

National saving is something else again. A country does not save by putting money in the bank. National saving is about the use made of the factors of production. Our existing resources can either be used for present purposes with no productive residue for the future, or those same resources can be used in ways that will allow the economy at some stage in the future to produce more than it otherwise would have been able to produce.

Using our existing resource base to build a more productive future is called investment. But the only way that such investment can occur is if there is saving taking place. Saving in this case means making use of existing resources in ways specifically intended to increase the economy's productive capabilities, not immediately, but in the future.

Failure to distinguish saving in the form of individuals putting money into a financial institution as against saving as investment will mean that you will have very great difficulty making sense of what is going on in an economy.

THE FINANCIAL SYSTEM

The financial system is about money and credit. It is designed to provide a haven for savers who wish to place their financial resources in a safe place while also allowing these financial resources to be transferred to investors. It therefore offers, or at least attempts to offer, a safe harbour for that part of each person's income whose expenditure is to be postponed. Postponed present consumption of income already earned constitutes personal saving.

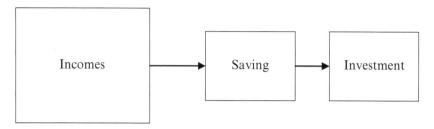

Figure 17.1   Basic framework of saving and investment

Notice that saving occurs out of incomes already earned. Something had to have already been produced so that this income could have been received. Saving is thus not an absence of production, some kind of void. Saving is a transfer of the ability to purchase from one person to another.

Irrespective of how it appears to those persons who are saving, postponement of present consumption by individuals who save allows part of the productive apparatus of an economy to be used to produce capital goods. If all incomes were immediately spent on buying goods and services for immediate consumption, no part of the productive structure of an economy would be available to produce additional capital.

All funds saved are intended to be used to buy goods and services at some stage in the future. The aim of saving by an individual is to postpone until a later date the decision to purchase. During each period, there are therefore individuals adding to the savings pool by not buying as much as their incomes would have allowed them to. At the same time, there are others who are using those funds to allow them to purchase inputs of various kinds even though they do not personally have the financial resources to do so.

In miniature, the process is shown in Figure 17.1. Incomes are earned, some of which are channelled into various forms of saving. Savings are incomes earned but not spent by those who have earned those incomes. The funds are instead placed into a savings institution (bank, pension fund, and so on) which then lends those funds to others.

Importantly, it should be seen that from a national perspective what is saved are real goods and services. Those individuals who are doing the saving see only the money side of it.

TO SAVE IS TO SPEND

Everyone receives money for their productions, but the money represents a share of the goods and services that had been produced for purchase.

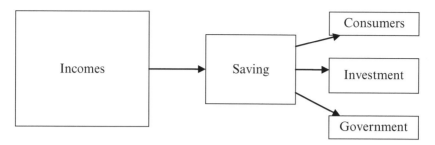

Figure 17.2   Flow of saving to all potential users

In exactly the same way, while the act of individual saving appears to be nothing other than placing money into a financial institution, from an economy-wide perspective, saving means putting to use whatever resources have been purchased by those who borrowed the funds. To save is to spend, but spending on a different set of goods and services chosen by someone other than the person who had originally earned the income.

Where savings are borrowed by business, those savings are actually made up of the capital goods, the machinery, the factories and buildings that the existence of savings has allowed business firms either to rent or to buy. The savings are also used to employ labour and purchase every kind of input needed by the business.

It is, of course, true that savings can also be borrowed by others besides business firms, and these others include those who wish to borrow to buy consumer goods and governments who may wish to use available savings for their own purposes. A more complete picture is thus shown in Figure 17.2, using the familiar $C + I + G$.

The money borrowed by consumers, to buy a car let us say, or to finance the purchase of an overseas trip, does not add to the productive potential of the economy. It is a drawing down of productivity without the intention of adding anything back in.

This is not a criticism, only a statement of fact. Borrowing to finance personal consumption, so long as the money can be repaid through other sources of income, is how economies typically operate. It brings forward in time the ability to purchase some good or service. Rather than having to accumulate the full purchase price of products, they can be bought at an earlier date, with income earned at a later date used to repay the debt incurred.

So be aware of this. Although what is borrowed may in the first instance be money, what is actually taking place is a transfer of the ability to buy real goods and services from savers to those who borrow the available funds.

SAVINGS ARE RESOURCES USED FOR PRODUCTIVE INVESTMENT

These points are so difficult to understand that it is worth repeating one more time using a different approach.

What is all too common in thinking about economic issues is that only the flow of money is noticed while the flow of resources into the hands of producers is ignored. Most of what is used in production in any single year had already existed before the year began. Virtually all of the capital, the factories and office buildings, was already in existence.

It is these resources that are sought. It is the finite and limited amount of such resources that is the major factor in constraining growth and the rise in incomes.

There is then the workforce, with most workers already skilled in the tasks they undertake through their education and then on-the-job training.

And to complete the story of the private sector, there are the entrepreneurs who have built businesses, brought labour and capital together and have been responsible for most of the wealth creation.

These resources are represented by the large box on the left of Figure 17.3. The economy's resource base is made up of every possible input available for use in production. Almost none of the inputs have been newly produced. Most have origins before the current period, often well before.[1]

This vast array of productive inputs is used to produce the output that is created with the usual timeframe seen as a single year. The three small boxes on the right show the kinds of goods and services that the resource

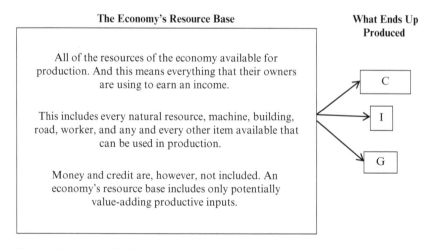

Figure 17.3   Available resources for use in production

base on the left allows the economy to produce. These represent the traditional macroeconomic division between consumption (C), investment (I) and government spending (G).

Also, the relative scale of the box on the left in comparison with the boxes on the right is trying to point out that our living standards depend on the massive stock of assets already in existence. Annual production is small in comparison with the huge endowment most economies bring with them from the past. Our living standards depend on that stock of already accumulated assets. The flow of output in any one year can only occur because of the stock of productive assets accumulated over the many years before.

Economic activity of every kind draws down on productivity. Consumer demand is purely a drawing down on the stock of productive assets. Whether resources are fully used up in producing those consumer goods, or merely create wear and tear on the capital employed, the effect is to lower the future ability of the economy to produce. Consumption is, of course, the ultimate aim of productive activity. But the sole reason we are able to consume at the high standards we are able to relative to the past is only understandable in relation to that stock of factors of production that already exists. If you were abandoned on a desert island you would soon see the difference it makes.

Government spending is mostly a drawing down although there are also important elements of value adding activities as well. Governments hire, use up resources and, in most instances, their activities diminish the capital that the economy has at its disposal. It is a drawing down, paid for in large measure by taxation.

The third form of resource use is investment. This too draws down on the economy's resource base but does so with the intention of adding to the economy's ability to produce in the future. There is, just to start, the maintenance of the existing capital. A major effort goes into merely replacing what has been worn down through use and age. Beyond that, there is the production of new capital, some just adding to what had been there already, while others are new innovations that produce the same goods more cheaply or, often enough, entirely new goods that had never previously existed.

It is this investment that allows the capital stock to grow.

MONEY, CREDIT AND SAVING

The question then is how does the saving that takes place in money become the actual physical resources that are transferred into investment. If you focus only on the money, you will never understand what is going on.

Those who engage in production receive an income in money. Some of that income is spent, some is taken by governments in taxation and some is saved. To the income earner, the money not spent is their savings, usually put away in some financial institution. To the economy, the money not spent represents output produced and available to others. It is at this point that borrowing and credit come into the story if one is to understand the transition from saving as money to saving as real productive investment.

The question any economy must answer is: who will have access to those resources? In an economy that is intending to grow and prosper, they must be channelled in the direction of those who will use them in the most productive way. As our future standard of living depends on the productive use of resources, the great difficulty is in choosing who will be allowed to put those resources to use.

This is what the financial system is designed to do. It provides a channel between those who save and those who intend to invest. The financial system lends out money, but what it is actually providing to others is the ability to buy productive inputs.

The financial institutions also want to get their money back, as do the people whose savings they are lending out. Financial institutions make a very intense effort to ensure, as best they can, that the people to whom the money is lent will repay what they borrowed along with the interest. And the money will only be repaid if those investments are value adding. Not every investment is, which is the challenge financial institutions face. Which of the many potential borrowers of funds will earn a positive return and repay their loans? That is the very essence of uncertainty and risk.

Figure 17.4 on output and the structure of production shows the relationship between that vast stock of productive assets and the flow of output that these inputs produce. The box on the left is the structure of production that exists across the economy that allows the particular output produced to be produced.

The Keynesian model reduces the elaborate and fantastically complex series of relationships that make up the structure of production to the three highly aggregated domestic sources of demand, $C + I + G$, removing in this way almost everything of economic interest. There are not just three blocks of domestic final demand. What is missing in the Keynesian approach is that most of the activity in an economy are sales from one input producer to another.

A miniature version of the actual structure of production looks something like Figure 17.5. Each arrow shows the direction of sales from one business to another.

The figure on the structure of production is not intended to represent anything at all other than the complexity of an economy. Even with a mere seven businesses selling to each other, there is a fantastically complex network of relationships that is entirely beyond the capacity of anyone to

Structure of Production **Produced**

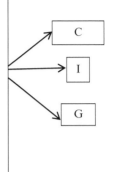

Most of the economy is made up of a series of inputs into the production of other inputs.

Only a small proportion emerges in the form of final goods and services, either bought by consumers, investors or governments.

This network of purchase and sale of inputs is always undergoing change. It is these inputs, directed by entrepreneurs, that determine what gets produced and how.

For more detail on the structure of production and the contents of this box see Figure 17.5 below.

Figure 17.4   Output and the structure of production

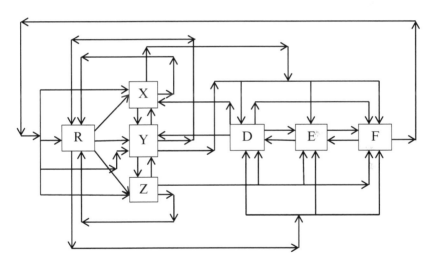

Figure 17.5   Structure of production – a mini example. The actual world is infinitely more complex

map, understand or predict. In an actual economy, there are hundreds of thousands, and, in larger economies, millions of such producers who buy and sell from each other. Each of these businesses makes its own arrangements through the normal processes of the market.

It is this complex set of arrangements that a central planner would have to work out in advance and would need to do so without any consideration of relative prices, future changes in supply conditions, or any of the countless things that might shift in the future. And while in a market economy the adjustment takes place automatically, in a centrally planned economy, for which there is no feedback mechanism through the price system, until new instructions are given, the original plan continues as before.

Recessions are a breakdown in the structure of production. Actual sales have not matched expected sales for at least some of these firms. With buyers not buying what had been produced, sellers cut back on the input purchases they had been making as well. Reconfigurations of the structure of production – the supply chain – are what the recovery process is about, as new firms replace the existing firms, and new products replace the old.

It is the structure that matters, not aggregates. As an economy expands and innovation occurs, the structure becomes more complex and the different elements either expand or contract and sometimes entirely disappear, as virtually every business eventually does. Meanwhile new businesses are created. No one can plan this. No one can even predict what will happen. It is just a free-form structure in which each individual firm tries to ensure that what they are producing matches what their customers want to buy. In the world in which we live, there is no other way that production could possibly be arranged.

THE NATURAL RATE AND THE MONEY RATE

In making sense of the processes of an economy, and more importantly perhaps, in following the waves of recession, unemployment and inflation, it is necessary to recognize the existence of two parallel sets of determinations for the price of borrowed national savings.

There is first the *natural rate of interest*. It is a rate that is, in fact, invisible, almost undiscoverable within the flow of economic events. It is price of savings as determined by the forces of supply and demand for the actual resources that the economy has available for use in productive activities. The natural rate of interest is thus the price of that part of an economy's productive structure that is available for use by others to invest.

And here it is important to recognize that the resources available for investment are almost entirely a stock of existing capital assets; the buildings, factories and machinery that are already in place; the labour force skills embedded in actual labourers; the entrepreneurial talents that are possessed by those who do or perhaps might choose to run a business.

The flow of newly produced capital assets, or newly-trained workers who have just joined the workforce, are a tiny proportion of all that is available in an economy that might be applied to productive purposes.

Although most are, not all resources potentially available for use are made available for use by investors. People often retire and only return to the workforce when a particularly good opportunity arises. People with spare bedrooms do not feel like renting these out until rents begin to climb. Capital equipment seldom gets used to its fullest extent, is often unused on weekends or late at night, but that can change if demand really heats up.

How many resources there are or how much would become available if the returns were higher is unknown. What is not, however, the equivalent to the flow of real savings in an economy is the flow of money and credit made available through the financial system.

The interest rate we do see, the *market* or *nominal* rate of interest, often called the *money* rate of interest, is the interest rate charged by financial institutions or other providers of credit. Credit may come in the form of money, bank accounts or other formats using domestic currency. Or it may simply be a form of permission to take goods or services upon a promise to pay a specific amount of money at a later date. It is therefore a known rate, almost always expressed in so many percentage points per year.

Such interest rates are often described as the price of money, but that is not quite right. More generally, they are the price of market credit. They are the sums paid to gain access to available national savings.

The market rate of interest is a rate directly and often deliberately manipulated by the monetary authorities of every economy. It is the manipulation of this rate that widens the difference between market interest rates and the natural rate.

Such manipulation, as can be imagined, has major effects on the state of an economy for good and very often for bad. The role of governments in the market for credit may be the single most difficult area of economic policy. It is also the area that creates more havoc within market economies than any other, even when the aim is to leave markets to sort themselves out on their own.

THE ROLE OF THE RATE OF INTEREST

Interest rates have had a bad reputation going back at least 2500 years. Yet for all that, interest rates have a function that cannot be dispensed with and will show up in one form or another in every economy even where the aim is to suppress their role in allocating resources.

What must first be understood is this: interest rates are a natural form of payment. Since there are differences between the time individuals receive their incomes and when they would like to spend what they have earned, a market for access to a nation's savings will always exist side by side with a desire by those who have earned incomes to spread across a period of time when those incomes will be put to use by themselves.

Such savings will not be made available to anyone else unless those who borrow pay for the privilege of having use of some portion of a community's available resources. When interest is paid to the lender, it comes as a payment for the use of someone else's purchasing power and deserves a price paid just as if it were any other item of property being used by someone other than its owner.

There was for almost 2000 years a prohibition on the charging of interest that did not largely disappear within the advanced economies of the West until the middle of the nineteenth century, and even now such sentiments have by no means completely gone. Yet without a market for a nation's savings and the charging of interest that must come with it, an economy cannot grow and prosper since it cannot determine who would be likely to make the most productive use of the resources available.

Interest Rates as a Form of Rental

Interest rates are similar to rental payments, except the particular items that the borrower has chosen to use the funds to purchase are not items owned by the lender. Lending money at interest is a more abstract means of giving others access to the goods and services they would not otherwise be able to make use of themselves.

Part of the value given up in lending money out is the loss of immediate use of the funds. There is a need to pay for the postponement. A dollar today is worth more to its owner than even the certainty of a dollar in 12 months' time even where the purchasing power has not changed. Interest rates are the payments that must be made to compensate for whatever psychological reasons there are to prefer spending in the present rather than at some moment in the future.

Interest as a Means to Identify More Productive Investments

But even beyond the requirement to pay interest, there is the need for the economy to ensure that those who use borrowed funds are the optimal users of those funds from an economy-wide perspective. The willingness to pay higher interest in a business context, if it is matched against a proper assessment of the uses for which the funds will be put (which is what financial institutions do), will tend to allow money and capital to flow to those who will make the greatest economic return.

Since a nation's savings are scarce, there is a return to the owners of available capital just as there is on the renting to others of any scarce resource.

If one bought a house and rented it out to others, the rental payments would be the return on the ownership of the house. Lending money is the same process without having first sunk one's savings into a particular form of capital. It is in many ways actually better, since borrowing the savings of others allows lenders to shape the realized form of those savings in any way they please.

Adjustment for Risk

But those who lend money out have as their first criterion a desire to have the money repaid. There is an enormous variety of risks associated with different lending possibilities. Lending money to governments will have a lower risk than lending money to a business which must deal with the endless uncertainties before it. Governments can print their own money, so however the resources they use may be wasted, there is little likelihood in most circumstances that the money will not be returned. This can never be said about a business.

Lending money for a short period will tend to be less risky than lending money for longer stretches of time. Lending money for 12 months has an appreciably lower risk than lending the same sum of money for 12 years. It is much easier to assess the likelihood for success of a venture over the coming year than over the coming decade. So many things can change that beyond a relatively short period of time there is almost nothing that can really be known about borrowers, however large and substantial they may be on the day the loan is made.

There is therefore embedded into each interest rate charged a risk premium. This risk premium takes into account the likelihood that the money will be repaid, which builds into such considerations the length of time over which the money is to be borrowed.

The less risky the project for which the borrower intends to use the funds, or the shorter the period of time, the lower the interest rate will tend to be, all other things being equal.

Moreover, there is not just one interest rate in an economy but a great many. There is, in fact, a different process of interest rate setting for just about every form of borrowing that takes place.

There is therefore within the money market the usual jostling that goes on in any market as those who buy, in this case the borrowers, look for the cheapest price (that is, the lowest interest rates) while those who sell, the lenders, look for the highest price (that is, the highest interest rate). But each, and particularly the lenders, look to balance the risk against the interest rate charged.

Many will choose a lower rate of return for the comfort of greater security. And in the money market, there is no perfect certainty anywhere. Even governments have been known to default on their loans.

The existence of a risk premium is therefore intrinsic to the market for available funds. The greater the risk, *ceteris paribus*, the higher the money rate of interest will be.

Inflation and the Willingness to Lend

But finally, there is the relation between interest rates and the inflation rate. Since savings are transferred by lending money, the aim is to receive in return at least as much in purchasing power as was lent out, plus the additional purchasing power accrued through the interest payment received which itself will contain a risk premium.

Inflation reduces the purchasing power of money. If inflation is running at 5 per cent per year, the value of a unit of currency one year later will buy only 95 per cent of what it did the year before. Therefore, when inflation is running at 5 per cent, for those lending their money to others, if they are to receive in return at least as much in purchasing power as was lent out, the interest rate must include that 5 per cent inflation premium.

Moreover, it is the *expected* rate of inflation that matters. If inflation turns out to be higher than expected, borrowers come out ahead since they pay their debts in a devalued currency since the inflation premium will have been less than necessary to compensate for the actual growth in prices.

Similarly when inflation is falling. If a fall in inflation is not expected, borrowers will be willing to pay a premium consistent with the prevailing expectation while lenders will not accept anything less. The outcome works to the advantage of lenders, but who was to know?

It is for this reason that in attempting to contain inflation, part of the process is to lower inflationary expectations. If a lower inflation rate is expected, interest rates will be lower than they otherwise would have been.

Summary

In summary, the factors that go into the determination of money rates of interest are dependent on a variety of factors which include, but are by no means restricted to:

- the scarcity of available funds;
- the intensity of competing demands for those funds;
- the time period during which the funds are to be borrowed;
- the risks involved and the probability of being repaid in full;
- the expected rate of inflation.

Again, there is no such thing as *the* rate of interest. But every rate actually charged will be determined by these factors.

However, for convenience's sake, and at classroom level to simplify the analysis, the assumption of there being a single rate of interest is made. The rate can be seen as the representative rate, but always bearing in mind that any particular rate will be shaped by risk, the time period involved and the expected rate of inflation as well as a host of other factors that influence the willingness of borrowers to borrow and of lenders to lend.

DETERMINATION OF THE MONEY SUPPLY

But how much money and credit is there in an economy, and what causes the amount of money and credit to vary? In the past, when metallic money was all there was, money was almost entirely in the form of coins. But we are a long way from that now with most forms of money a highly abstract quantum embedded within a worldwide financial system, most of it comprised of electronic forms of payment in one form or another. In these circumstances it does not necessarily make sense to discuss the supply of money, but that is where we must begin.

The supply of money, and the amount of credit available, within an economy are determined jointly by an economy's central bank in collaboration with the economy's banking system. There are two elements that determine the full extent that an economy's money supply may grow:

- the amount of *base money* in that economy;
- the *reserve ratio* imposed on the banks by either law or central bank regulation.

A bank will be compelled by law to maintain a particular proportion of its funds in liquid form; that is, in a form that is either easily convertible into the medium of exchange or is in fact the medium of exchange itself. These extremely liquid forms are the base money of an economy.

The most important parts of the base money are:

- notes and coins in the local currency and
- deposits by the individual trading banks with the central bank.

Both can be used at a moment's notice to meet the demands of depositors should they wish to withdraw their money.

Banks, however, are in the business of lending money. And while it has been a practice that has taken centuries to develop, it is now the case universally within banking systems across the world that each individual bank holds only a small fraction of the value of its deposits in highly liquid form. Most of the assets of a bank are in the form of loans. That is why it is described as a *fractional* reserve system. The *reserve ratio* is the minimum proportion of bank deposits that banks are legally required to hold in the form of base money.

Suppose banks are required to hold 10 per cent of their total bank deposits as liquid assets. That would mean that for every $100 of deposits, they would be compelled to hold $10 in cash or other reserve assets. If every depositor showed up on the doorstep of a bank, no bank in the world could, without assistance from its central bank, meet the demand from depositors for their money.

The total supply of money then consists of base money plus components of the bank deposits of the financial system. Since the focus is seldom on the volume of money *per se*, but is instead on the rate of growth of the amount of money, the particular list of deposits included in definitions of the supply of money are largely arbitrary.

VARYING THE MONEY SUPPLY

Given the relationship between base money, the reserve ratio, the level of deposits and the willingness of others to borrow, it can be seen that raising the supply of money can be effected in any of the following ways:

- an increase in base money;
- an increase in bank deposits;
- a fall in the reserve ratio;
- an increase in the amount of money borrowers seek to borrow;
- an increase in the willingness of banks to lend.

These are the *ceteris paribus* conditions for the money supply. They are the underlying factors that cause the supply of money to increase. And while these are loosely related to the level of production and national saving, they are also in important ways independent of anything going on in the real economy.

Open Market Operations

Much of the variation in the money supply is determined by the central bank itself. Central banks can manipulate the flow of base money through what are called *open market operations*. These are efforts made to increase the level of base money by putting more cash into the hands of the public through buying bonds.

If the central bank buys bonds from the public, the public has more money but fewer bonds. The money supply has in that way increased.

If, however, the central bank wishes to reduce the amount of money in the hands of the public, money is withdrawn from the hands of the public by selling bonds. The public has more bonds but less money. The aim in either case is to change the amount of base money in an economy.

Budget Deficits and Public Spending

The amount of base money is also affected by government spending and tax policy. High public spending, low taxes and budget deficits increase the amount of base money within the economy. Less public spending, higher taxes and a budget surplus will pull money out.

Once base money enters the economy it will find its way to the banking system, where more money is deposited within individual banks. More deposits lead to more loans and a further increase in the level of spending.

Variations in the Deposit Ratio

The central bank can influence the level of loans through variations in the deposit ratio. If it wishes to increase the money supply, the ratio can be lowered. If it wishes to diminish the money supply, the ratio can be raised.

Raising the ratio will compel banks to hold onto more money as a proportion of deposits, and lend out less. The less that is lent by individual banks, the less that the entire banking system can lend in total. And the same process works in reverse, so that if the aim is to raise the money supply, the deposit ratio can be brought down.

Willingness to Borrow and Lend

Finally, the amount of money within an economy can depend on the willingness of borrowers to borrow or the banks to lend. These can both be affected by the state of the economy and the relative optimism or pessimism of those who might be inclined to borrow or lend.

As an economy slows and pessimism spreads, the banks invariably become more reluctant to lend, although at such times borrowers, many of whom are finding themselves in a difficult financial situation, are often desperate to get their hands on liquidity to cover their debts as they come due. That said, in difficult economic circumstances there is generally an increased reluctance to borrow and take on debt on behalf of new projects.

Times improve, and banks become more willing to lend out their funds out just as borrowers also begin to increase their own desire to borrow

Summing Up

The notion that there is some amount of money that is 'the' money supply is untenable, although sometimes argued. The money supply within an economy changes continuously, either through design or simply through the ebb and flow of economic events.

But it is disturbances within the financial system that are often the single most important cause of economic fluctuations, and while such disturbances are often the cause of a downturn they can act to reinforce downwards pressures that have begun elsewhere.

But in the modern economy, it is often the deliberate manipulation of the amount of money with the aim of varying interest rates which is amongst the most important causes of economic instability, and has been since the early years of the nineteenth century.

How to bring stability into the financial system, and how to discipline the monetary authorities, are questions to which the answers have thus far remained elusive. This is one of the reasons why the business cycle is certain to remain a feature of the economic system as far into the future as one might care to look.

We now turn to the interrelationship between the market and natural rates of interest in the functioning of the economy.

MARKET RATE OF INTEREST

In understanding the nature of recessions and inflation, as well as prosperity and growth, examining the overlap in the financial system between money and credit on the one side and the real economy on the other is essential. Being aware of each separately and then jointly as they coexist brings you closer to an appreciation of what is taking place beneath.

The market rate of interest, the money or nominal rate, is determined by the financial system. No one trying to borrow is unaware of what this rate is. Every lender makes a point of informing borrowers how much they will have to repay in return for any of the funds they receive.

But what is directly received is not the actual physical savings of the community, but sums of money which can be used to buy whatever the borrower may wish.

Banks create money. They do not have an ability to limitlessly increase the availability of money, but in collaboration with the monetary authorities of the country they have an ability to increase the supply of money and credit well beyond the increase in the actual level of national savings. Banks have the ability to create an account where none had existed before, or add a sum of money into an existing account whose elastic nature is determined by the monetary authorities using its controls over the money supply.

And what is in that account is not an actual 'physical' sum of money, as there would have been in the days of the gold standard. The sum of money entered to someone's credit is no more than a data entry in the records held by the bank.

The determination of interest rates in the market for credit and money (designated by *i*) is shown in Figure 17.6.

The demand curve may not be much different either in shape or concept from the demand for real savings generally. But the supply curve is different, and more importantly, the *ceteris paribus* conditions of the supply

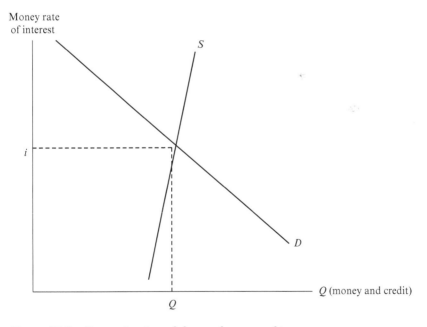

Figure 17.6   Determination of the market rate of interest

of real resources in comparison with the supply of money and credit are potentially very different.

THE NATURAL RATE OF INTEREST

The natural rate of interest refers to the supply and demand for all of the resources being made available for use in productive investment. There is some unknown rate of interest embedded within every economy at which the level of real savings is equal to the demand for those savings. This is how the natural rate of interest (represented by *r*) is determined. Its determination is shown in Figure 17.7.

There we find the supply curve of real savings. Each point on the curve is the answer to an 'if–then' statement which begins from the vertical axis. *If* the rate of interest were at this particular rate, *then* the level of savings would be at the volume shown on the horizontal axis.

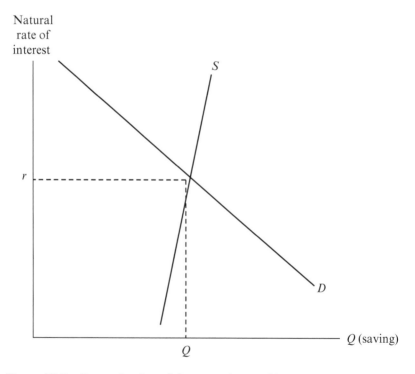

Figure 17.7   Determination of the natural rate of interest

The demand curve for savings is also an if–then statement. *If* interest rates are at this particular rate *then* we know from the horizontal axis that this will be the demand for available savings.

Each of the curves has its underlying *ceteris paribus* conditions. The supply of those savings depends on the quantum of factors of production available for use. The demand for these factors is determined by the aims of investors in working out the projects they would like to complete.

And while the curves are shown as supply and demand, they do not represent sums of money but are constructed entirely in real terms. They are comprised of the fantastically varied array of all of the individual factors of production that might be used as part of a typical investment project. These are bricks and mortar, hours of labour time, factories and shop fronts, and every other possible resource that might be used to increase the future productivity of the economy.

Where the two curves meet is the natural rate of interest, r, which is intrinsically undiscoverable. But the horizontal axis presents a reality of major importance. This is the volume of resources available for use in productive purposes.

The greater the volume of such savings, the more investment is possible. But whatever the volume of savings might be, that is all there is. How much savings there are limits how much investment there can be. The availability of capital is a major limiting factor in every economy.

THE MARKET RATE AND THE NATURAL RATE TOGETHER

In Figure 17.8 we see the supply and demand curves for the market for money and credit side by side with the supply and demand curves in the market for real savings. On the left is the determination of the market rate of interest, i. On the right is the determination of the natural rate of interest, r. In equilibrium, as shown here, $i = r$, the market rate and the natural rate are the same. There is therefore balance in both the supply of money and credit and the supply of the real resources that the money and credit would be used to buy.

That is, what is shown here is where the interest rate for money and credit is identical to the interest rate that allows the supply of savings, thought of in real terms, to exactly match the demand for those savings by investors.

We also see that, given the rate of interest, the level of investment is determined by the point on the 'Invest' curve at that rate of interest. There

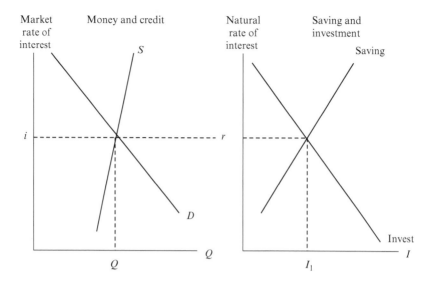

Figure 17.8 Market and natural rates of interest

is a level of investment equal to I_1 which is just equal to the amount of savings available.

INCREASING THE SUPPLY OF MONEY

Into this situation we can introduce an increase in the supply of money and credit (see Figure 17.9). Governments and central banks often take actions to lower interest rates in the belief that lower interest rates will encourage investment, which leads the central bank to increase the supply of money. Open market operations are the normal means by which this is done, and the effect is to move the supply curve of money to the right.

With this increase in the supply of money, changes take place in the financial structure of the economy that will have subsequent effects. Credit is cheaper and easier to get. Nominal interest rates are lower, so the amount of credit sought has increased from Cr to Cr_2.

In following the dynamics of the changes, however, the limitations of the flat timeless nature of supply and demand curves needs to be recognized in thinking through all of the subsequent effects. So far as savers are concerned, nothing happens instantaneously. Therefore, in following the logic of these changes, it is necessary to bear in mind that what will take place will take place through time. Nothing much happens

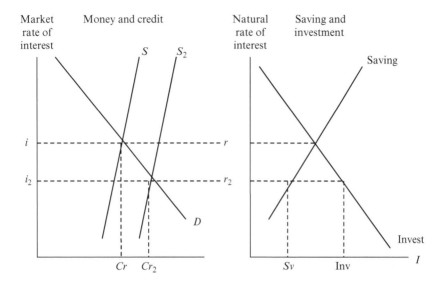

Figure 17.9   An increase in the supply of money

immediately, but across the weeks and months, there are changes taking place as individuals across the economy react to the new circumstances they face.

With the fall in the market rate of interest, conditions have altered over on the real side of the economy. There we find a sudden excess demand for available savings, but at the same time the return for putting those savings into the market falls. The level of real savings therefore falls just as the level of demand for such savings goes up.

In reality, with expectations of all sorts having shifted with the fall in market rates of interest there are possibly no end of changes that might well take place. Here we assume no further shifts in the position of either curve.

With the lower market rate of interest, there is a lower return for the savings made available. As shown in the diagram for the natural rate, the amount of available savings falls back from the former equilibrium level to a lower figure, shown on the figure as Sv. There are fewer real resources being made available to investors.

Meanwhile on the demand side, lower interest rates have brought additional numbers into the market looking for what savings there are. At the lower below-equilibrium interest rate, r_2, which is equal to i_2, there is a demand for investment goods at the level marked, *Inv*. But the amount of saving available, Sv, has diminished. There are, as a result, more potential borrowers in the market looking for savings than there are savings available, which would occur even if the supply curve for real savings was perfectly inelastic. The result, so far as the economy is concerned, is only harmful, irrespective of how much apparent demand there is for the available savings.

CONSEQUENCES WHEN THE MARKET RATE IS BELOW THE NATURAL RATE

And what are these harmful consequences? Here is a list of some of them, after which they will be explained:

- slower economic growth;
- inefficient investments;
- higher inflation;
- inflation of asset prices (the 'bubble' economy).

Slower Growth

The belief that artificially low interest rates are good for an economy, that they will encourage higher rates of investment, is a notion that dies hard. It is a notion that is nevertheless deeply flawed.

Artificially low rates of interest will reduce the supply of savings However much demand there might be – there would be even more 'demand' if we just gave as much credit as was wanted to anyone who asked – lower interest rates reduce the amount of real savings brought to market. There is just not as much capital for investment available as there had previously been.

Less investment means less growth. It is only the availability and utilization of additional supplies of capital that permit higher rates of investment to occur.

The actual level of investment in relation to the natural rate of interest is shown in Figure 17.10. The downward-sloping section in the figure is the relevant section of the demand curve. Starting at an interest rate above the equilibrium, the lower the interest rate, all of the capital demanded will be supplied. But once the equilibrium point is reached, as interest rates fall it is only the supply curve which is relevant to the amount of investment since no matter how many resources are demanded, only the amount supplied will find its way into the economy since that is all there is.

Below the equilibrium point, whatever may happen to the level of demand, the amount of savings supplied falls away. The lower the level of interest, the less capital will be supplied and therefore the less investment there can be.

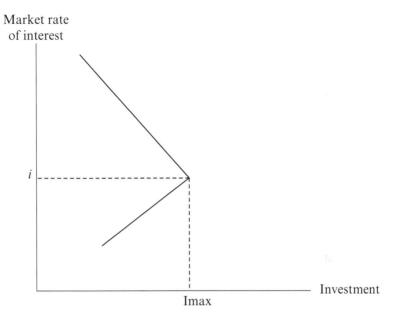

Figure 17.10   Actual level of investment at different rates of interest

Lowering interest rates beyond some point does not increase investment, it slows it down.

Inefficient Investments

The excess demand for available savings means that lenders get to choose amongst the many additional demanders of funds for those with the lowest associated risks attached. There are more seeking the available savings than there are savings available.

The result is that many projects are undertaken that would not have been considered had rates been higher. The sorting mechanism of the price system is diluted. There are many less risky, less productive projects that will earn a positive return at the lower cost of funds. They get the funding while other, more difficult, less certain projects do not.

There are also many projects with a potentially higher return that are not undertaken since the price mechanism does not ensure that they are funded in preference to other projects with a lower real return. With interest rates no longer being used at the cutting edge to discriminate between projects, other criteria come into play, such as friendship with those in control of funds.

The consequence is that the actual investments that are undertaken are suboptimal. There is a lower real return with, therefore, a lesser contribution to growth.

Higher Inflation

If interest rates are below the equilibrium rate, there is more demand for resources to undertake investment projects than there is supply. Excess supply is the market condition out of which prices can be expected to rise.

It goes further. The classic definition of inflation is where there is too much money chasing too few goods. This is the precise condition that is put in place with the fall in natural interest rates below their equilibrium level. Money and credit are being created at a faster rate than the rate at which output is being produced.

For every dollar's worth of goods and services produced, there is more than a dollar's worth of purchasing power inside the economy. Loose credit markets add to inflationary pressures, and in this case 'loose' refers to allowing interest rates to fall below the natural rate of interest.

Loose monetary policy is the most common cause of inflation. It is demand-driven due to the growth in purchasing power allowed by credit conditions relative to the growth in available savings. Hyperinflation is most obviously driven by the rapid growth in money and credit, but even slow, creeping inflation can often be traced back to loosening of the credit conditions.

Whether due to budget deficits or open market operations by the central bank, the effect is similar. There is more money demand than there is real supply. The pressure on the price level is upwards.

Asset Price Inflation

There are, in addition, particular areas that can experience rapid increases in prices through loosening credit conditions. These are in the market for various fixed assets.

House prices, share prices, the prices of paintings and other works of art, tend to rise disproportionately to other goods and services in such an inflationary environment. These are typically the kinds of products with highly inelastic supply conditions over the medium term. Gold is often a refuge when inflationary pressures grow.

Money demand works its way through the economy, pushing up all prices generally, but some rise more rapidly than others. Where supply is inelastic, their prices will show rates of increase above the general average change in the price level.

Whether these assets hold their relative increase in value depends on supply conditions generally over the longer term. But the early stages of an increase in prices can cause a 'bubble' to emerge that is likely to be deflated to at least some extent as the economy moves through the various phases of the cycle.

MORE GOVERNMENT SPENDING MEANS LESS PRIVATE SPENDING

But it is not just business that seeks available savings. So too does government. And the more of a nation's savings that that ends up in the hands of governments to be used for their purposes, the less is available to business.

A production possibility curve is shown in Figure 17.11, with consumption on the vertical axis and investment on the horizontal axis. It is also a straight-line production possibility curve indicating that resources are equally capable of producing consumption goods or investment goods.

In every economy some of its resources are used to provide goods and services for consumers, while some are used to build the economy's productive capabilities. But also in every economy there is only so much that can be produced given the available technology, capital stock, labour, skill levels and general productivity.

In this economy, the level of production for consumption is equal to *C* while the level of investment is equal to *I*.

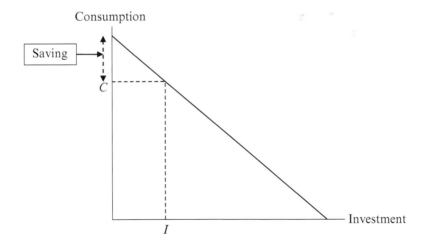

Figure 17.11   Production possibility curve with consumption and investment

But note: the level of investment is dependent on there being saving. If everything produced were consumed, the level of consumption would occur where the production possibility curve reached the vertical axis. The actual level of consumption is less than the total level of consumption possible. The difference between the maximum possible level of consumption and the actual level of consumption is the amount of saving. And because this is a *production* possibility curve, savings must be thought of in real terms. It is actual resources that are being made available for use by investors.

This saving allows investment to take place. The resources released from consuming are directed into the production of investment goods that improve the productive capabilities of the economy. Various entrepreneurs borrow funds and use those funds to purchase and produce capital assets. These are added to the productive base of the economy. The more such investments there are, the faster the economy will grow.

GOVERNMENT SPENDING AND NATIONAL SAVING

But it is not just businesses which use a nation's savings. Governments too take their share of available savings. Consumers save as before but, as shown in Figure 17.12, we bring in government. Governments can take up part of national income through taxation and are also able to borrow,

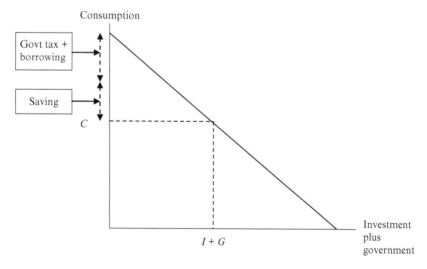

Figure 17.12   Production possibility curve with C, I *and* G

should they wish, additional funds beyond what the power to tax will deliver.

Governments use part of the productive resources of the economy for their own purpose, which if used properly will have a social communal purpose. But in whatever way the government uses these resources, if it does make use of those resources, the rest of the community cannot. There is only so much available, and the more the government has, the less there is for anyone else. When governments borrow, the effect is to limit the amount of savings available for business purposes.

CROWDING OUT

The production possibility curve in Figure 17.13 shows the trade-off between private investment and government expenditures. There are only so many resources, and the more that is available to one, the less is available to the other.

This pushing business out of the way through increased government borrowing of available savings is referred to as *crowding out*. It is said that governments 'crowd out' business where their borrowings come at the

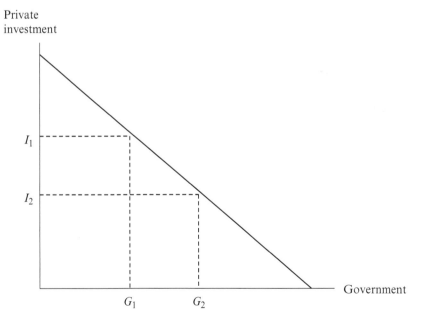

Figure 17.13   Private investment versus government spending

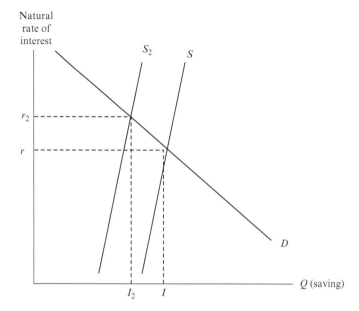

Figure 17.14   Crowding out

expense of private sector borrowings. The private sector is said to have
been crowded by public spending.

In Figure 17.13, we begin with I_1 and G_1. If there is an increase in the
level of government spending, it can only come at the expense of less
private investment. There is nowhere else for it to come from. Where governments are competing with business for resources to be used for investment purposes, the only way for governments to be able to absorb more of
the economy's productive potential is for businesses to absorb less.

This same effect can be shown more formally in Figure 17.14 showing
the supply and demand for savings in the determination of the natural rate
of interest. The figure shows the supply and demand for savings as experienced by the private sector. The supply curve shows how much saving will
be provided at different rates of interest.

Here the initial interest rate is shown as r and the level of investment
in equilibrium is equal to I. With government entering the market for
such savings, the supply curve, as experienced by the private sector,
has moved to the left. There are fewer savings available at every rate of
interest.

In a world of diminished availability of savings, the natural rate of
interest rises to r_2 while the level of investment falls from I to I_2. There is

less private sector investment, which has had to give way in the face of the government's decision to compete for the available resource base.

Were the government's chosen investments as productive for the economy as those of the private sector it would make no difference whether it was business or government undertaking the investment.

The reality is, however, that government spending is less productive than private sector investment. Government spending is, in fact, often unproductive, wasting the resources under its control and creating less value than it has used up in its productions.

It is a serious error to treat public spending as an equivalent to private. It is not. Not only is public spending less productive, but with its lack of productivity the increase in the number of jobs will be lower unless real wages are allowed to fall to accommodate the limited additions to value of public sector activity, assuming any value is created at all.

MONEY, DEBT AND RECESSION

There should, finally, be some appreciation of the dangers that are inherent in an economy that is dependent on credit and debt. Mistakes are regularly made by those who lend because they misjudge the risks. Economies will from time to time enter recession because of failings in the financial system that have led to savings being systematically placed with borrowers who cannot repay their debts.

Money and finance are odd products. Money values are an abstract measure of a quantum of goods and services. Money and credit in the modern world can, moreover, be created at the touch of a keyboard. Keeping the growth in the nominal amount of expenditure at or near the growth in the quantum of goods and services available for purchase is one of the most difficult, but crucially important issues for the management of an economy. If the amount of money and finance increases more rapidly than the quantum of goods and services, the effect is a rise in the price level. If, on the other hand, the amount of money increases more slowly than the flow of goods and services is increasing, there is a potential for prices to fall and for the economy to slow.

But in the situation of a typical financial crisis, there is an actual fall in the flow of credit in comparison with the past. And if the sense of danger increases, so that trust in the banking and financial system as a repository for their savings falls, or financial institutions lose trust in each other, a contraction in the system of credit creation can pull the entire economy down. Without credit to mediate transactions between buyers and sellers, the real economy will invariably go into reverse.

Savings and debt are the glue that holds the economy together. Finance was listed as the fifth factor of production. Without it, virtually no enterprise can succeed. Businesses borrow and the financial system designs various forms of debt that are intended to mediate between those who save and those who seek to use productive resources that these savings have made available.

But the system of credit and debt depends on there being a strong level of trust between those who lend and those who borrow. Where such trust disappears for whatever reason, credit will be withdrawn and the economy will slow or even contract. Such financial crises are the most destabilizing form of economic dislocation and are the most difficult to prevent.

The financial system by its very nature will on occasion be driven towards major dislocation by an unexpected unfolding of events. The future is never perfectly foreseen and financial disasters must be an expectation. An economic system must therefore make contingent arrangements for such events, which usually require the financial authorities taking action to stabilize the financial system by providing liquidity for markets in which credit has for some reason dried up. Liquidity is an essential component of the financial system and in an economy where liquidity is rapidly falling there is an imperative on the financial authorities to act.

A successful free market economy is not one in which the government disappears and does nothing in the face of major financial dislocation. It is one in which those in government understand how a market economy works and take appropriate steps when necessary to ensure that the financial system will continue to function when it is in danger of collapse. Governments are not in this way running the economy; they should be seen as managing it.

Yet even in saying this, the moral hazard in a system where those who manage private sector financial institutions become convinced that the government will bail them out becomes in itself a problem. The more often financial institutions are rescued from the consequences of their own mistakes, the more often financial crises are likely to occur, and the deeper they are likely to be. A properly regulated financial system where fraud and illegality are punished is of course a necessity. And financial institutions should themselves be designed in ways that ensure that those who make the wrong decisions are heavily penalized by their misjudgements. But at the end of the day, there will be honest mistakes in lending decisions, and financial panics will occur. Institutional arrangements to deal with such problems as they arise are all that can ever be hoped for, since there is no means to structure a financial system to ensure that only those who repay their debts on time will ever be allowed to borrow. Risk and uncertainty are in the nature of things, which is why recessions and financial panics are an inevitable part of economic life.

NOTE

1. Some inputs are, of course, imported. But to pay for imports, exports are required. To gain access to these imported inputs thus requires domestic production.

18. Controlling inflation

The explanation of inflation as too much money chasing too few goods, as clichéd as it might be, remains the most accurate short-form description we have, if what it says is properly understood. Since inflation is about the purchasing power of each unit of money in relation to the volume of goods and services sold, somewhere in all of that are the rudiments of what is required to understand the fall in the value of money relative to the prices charged for products bought and sold.

But where is that relationship? And even if it is understood, what tools does it give for creating conditions for rapid rates of long-term non-inflationary growth, the nirvana of economic policy? On this there are no settled conclusions.

QUANTITY THEORY OF MONEY

The oldest theory of inflation is still the best place to start, and is still known by its original nineteenth century name as the 'quantity theory of money'. But as venerable as this theory is, it is deeply flawed. No sensible policy has ever been developed from it because of what it ignores and what cannot be known. It does contain an essential kernel of truth, but it leaves out too much of what needs to be understood to be of much direct use.

So what is this theory? Start with a unit of currency and a period of time, say a year. Each unit of currency will move from hand to hand as goods are bought and sold. The unit of currency received by one person is then used to buy something else. The average number of times a unit of currency changes hands during a period of time is known as its 'velocity of circulation'.

Thus the total currency value of transactions during a period can be calculated as the number of currency units (M for money) times its velocity of circulation (V). Or as a calculation:

$$M \times V$$

It is also possible to see the entire turnover of the economy as the average price (P) of all of the transactions (T) that take place during that period of time. This is not the same as Gross Domestic Product (GDP) since it includes all transactions and not just final sales. Money changes hands for all of the inputs as well.

The total money value of all transactions is therefore calculated as:

$$P \times T$$

The two expressions come to the same outcome, the nominal level of total economy-wide transactions. The quantity theory of money is therefore shown by this identity:

$$M \times V \equiv P \times T$$

Notice that the two sides are not balanced by an equals sign (=) but by something else, a triple bar which is referred to as an identity sign ($\equiv$). As with the expenditure approach to calculating GDP, using the identity sign states that the two sides are equal because each of them has been defined in just such a way that they will always be equal, no matter what. The quantity expression is often shown simply as:

$$MV \equiv PT$$

However, while conceptually true, the underlying numbers to calculate any single part of this expression are intrinsically unknowable. Therefore, because the number of transactions in an economy can never be known but is likely to be closely related to the level of nominal GDP, in the usual way this expression is now shown, transactions is replaced by real GDP (Y). Thus, in its simplest modern form, the quantity theory of money is shown as:

$$MV = PY$$

Y now replaces T. That is, we replace the number of transactions with the level of national output represented by GDP. Since there is no possible way to calculate the number of transactions that take place in an economy during any period of time, and also because we could also never find out the prices charged for every transaction across the economy, GDP is used as a proxy. But what has also occurred is that the purity of the concept has been muddied so that the expression is no longer certain to be true and therefore the identity sign has been replace by the equals sign.

And when it comes to that, there is no means to calculate the velocity of circulation since there is no possible way to determine how often each unit of currency passes from hand to hand during any period of time. And for that matter, determining just what money consists of – notes and coins, bank cheques, credit cards – there is again an imprecision that goes right to the heart of this calculation.

But assuming one could work these things out – which, let it be emphasized, cannot be done – what this expression then states is that the number of units of currency in existence times the frequency with which each unit is used is equal to the number of units of output produced times the average price paid for each unit of output.

Much effort has gone into making this equation into a useful economic construct even with all of the imprecisions that must of necessity surround its use. There are proxies for the price level and the money supply, and the velocity can be estimated from past data, so there are calculations that can be done. The real question has always been whether, once these calculations have been made, the quantity equation provides any useful policy advice.[1]

And the fact is that while economists have been manipulating this equation since at least the middle of the eighteenth century, there is so far precious little evidence that it actually provides any useful guidance for economic management whatsoever.

There is, as already noted, no single definition of even something as simple as the stock of money (there are many such definitions). Definitions of money have proliferated over the years, largely because of the attempts to find some definition of money that can be used to show a regular relationship between the growth in the stock of money as defined and the growth in the price level. No such simple relationship has been found, irrespective of which definition of money one has chosen to use.

The velocity of circulation, the measure of the number of transactions within an economy during some period of time, has turned out to be, as every classical economist once knew, anything but a constant. Not only does velocity vary, it varies in unpredictable ways. Partly it varies depending on the phase of the cycle. Partly it is the development of different forms of payment (for example, credit cards) that causes the relationship between some measure of money and some measure of output to be unstable. And partly it is the introduction of new forms of financial communication (for example, the internet) which has changed velocity into an almost meaningless term. There are many other factors as well. Such changes are ongoing and continuous.

It is in fact next to impossible to conceive of a definition of money that would provide a reliable base for all exchanges that take place within an economic system. Using the quantity theory of money is useful as a rough explanatory guide to economic events, but in spite of all the efforts made, has proven a poor guide to anti-inflationary policy. No policy that has focused on containing the growth of any particular definition of the stock of money has been successful in containing inflation. Economists have more or less given up trying to find one.

THE MODERN KEYNESIAN ROAD TO INFLATION CONTROL

Yet since there can be no denying that inflation is a loss of purchasing power per unit of currency, inflation must in some way be related to money.

Anti-inflation policy therefore remains focused on using the monetary system to maintain low rates of inflation. The classical theory of inflation, structured around the quantity theory, has therefore developed into an approach that now heavily relies on Keynesian aggregate demand. The approach to analysing output and employment is also used to analyse inflation and the inflationary process.

And while it will be noted only in passing, *monetary policy* should be clearly distinguished from *monetarism*. Monetarism is the theory that inflation can be controlled by controlling the growth in the money supply. It links two of the four elements in the quantity theory to achieve price stability. Control the growth in the money stock, it is argued, and the rate of growth in prices is itself controlled.

Monetary policy is the use not only of monetary aggregates but also of interest rate and credit creation policies to effect chosen economic outcomes. And not just inflation, but any aspect of economic policy which now importantly includes policies to affect employment, economic growth or movements in the exchange rate.

Moreover, monetary policy does not necessarily assume a close relationship between growth in monetary aggregates and the rate of inflation, nor does it necessarily assume that controlling inflation is the most important step in achieving economic stability. It is the use of money, interest rates and credit creation to improve economic conditions.

The following are the familiar ingredients around which modern monetary policy is conceived:

- estimates of the natural rate of unemployment and potential GDP;
- aggregate demand and the upwards sloping short-run aggregate supply curve;
- the vertical long-run aggregate supply curve;
- the Phillips curve; and
- interest rate adjustments.

There is probably more fashion in the area of monetary policy than any other area of economics, but these are the basic ingredients that go into the framing of monetary policy at the present time. Each of these was discussed at greater length earlier in the book. They are revisited here to see how they are combined into an anti-inflation policy.

The Natural Rate of Unemployment

The *natural rate of unemployment* is a particular rate of unemployment related to the rate of inflation. It is the unemployment rate which will leave the rate of inflation unchanged.

If the actual unemployment rate is below the natural rate, the inflation rate would be expected to accelerate. If, on the other hand, the actual unemployment rate is above the natural rate, then the inflation rate would be expected to fall. If, finally, the actual unemployment rate is equal to the natural rate, then the inflation rate would be expected to remain at whatever the inflation rate happened to be.

The natural rate is not constant but changes through time. It is estimated by those who are responsible for managing the economy, and in particular by the monetary authorities, and is derived from estimates related to the Phillips curve.

Why do they use this concept for monetary policy? Because since no one can know the future, by positing a relationship that states that an unemployment rate below the natural rate will lead to an acceleration of inflation, at least there is something one can know in the present that relates to that unknown future.

That this relationship is almost completely speculative – with almost no hard and fast relationship between today's unemployment rate and tomorrow's inflation – is, so far as policy makers are concerned, almost totally beside the point. It provides a framework for government action and is widely understood within markets.

Without this relationship, of course, since we have given up using money supply growth as an indicator of future inflation, there would be almost nothing that could be used as a guide to policy. Better even a shaky framework, it is thought, than having no framework at all.

Short-Run Aggregate Supply

Short-run aggregate supply (SRAS) is the relationship between the amount that will be produced at different price levels when all other factors in the economy are held constant. A higher price level means higher profitability since wages and other costs are frozen along the length of the curve, which is what is meant by holding all other things equal.

But as an economy tries to push beyond its natural limits through increases in aggregate demand, it begins to strain against its various resource constraints and at some stage costs begin to rise. And with rising costs the underlying conditions no longer remain equal and we move from the short run to the long run.

Long-Run Aggregate Supply

Long-run aggregate supply (LRAS) is the boundary between what is possible in an economy and what is not possible given its resource base, technical skills, labour force numbers and known technologies. It is the level of output towards which an economy gravitates when the unemployment rate is equal to the natural rate, its potential level of GDP.

Trying to move beyond this level of production will in the long run only add to inflation with no additional output possible. Only changes that make an economy more productive can allow economic growth to move beyond this level of output without creating inflationary pressures.

The *LRAS* is shown in Figure 18.1. Increased aggregate demand only increases the price level. Y_n is the full employment level of output, which is the output at which the unemployment rate is equal to the natural rate. The only unemployment is frictional or structural. As shown, in thinking of the longer term, increases in aggregate demand from AD_1 to AD_2 have no effect on the level of output in the long run but cause only an increase in the price level from P_1 to P_2.

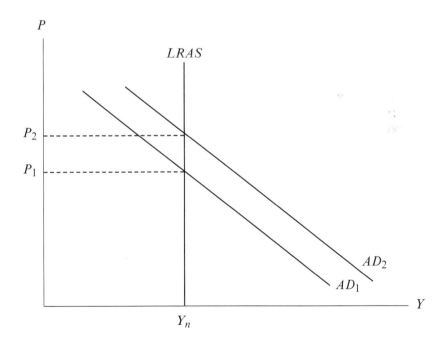

Figure 18.1 Inflation and long-run aggregate supply

Phillips Curve

The Phillips curve is derived from a study conducted during the 1950s on the historical relationship between movements in wages and movements in the unemployment rate in the UK between 1861 and 1957. The lower the level of unemployment, it was shown, the higher was the rate of growth in wage rates.

The relationship was then altered to make the comparison between movements in the price level (that is, the rate of inflation) and the rate of unemployment. Low unemployment, it was concluded, resulted in more rapid inflation. It is a relationship that has been applied in every economy in which central banks have an important role to play in framing policy.

The downward-sloping curve shown in Figure 18.2 is the traditional Phillips curve. The lower the unemployment rate, the higher the rate of inflation.

The vertical line is the long-run Phillips curve which is drawn at the natural rate of unemployment. Whatever trade-off there may be in the short run, in the long run, it is argued, there is no trade-off at all. It is similar to the *LRAS* curve. If the rate of unemployment falls *below* the natural rate of unemployment, *Un*, inflation will accelerate in the same

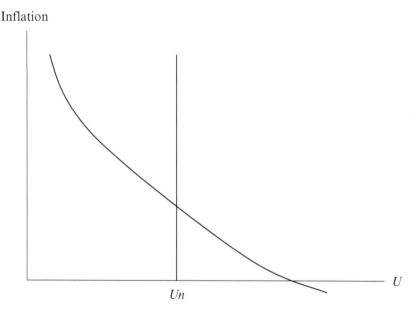

Figure 18.2   Short-run and long-run Phillips curve

way and for the same reason that inflation will accelerate if the level of GDP rises above its potential.

To summarize: the rate of unemployment associated with an economy's potential GDP is its natural rate. There is therefore no point trying to lower the unemployment rate below the natural rate since all that will happen is higher inflation and no actual increases in the level of output or the number of jobs. It is therefore the role of policy to keep the unemployment rate at or near the natural rate to prevent inflation from becoming entrenched. Keeping inflation down is seen as the most important role for governments in providing a platform for long-term sustainable non-inflationary growth.

Interest Rate Adjustments

Given the nature of long-run aggregate demand and the long-run Phillips curve as developed as part of the Keynesian macroeconomic framework, the aim of policy has been to estimate the natural rate of unemployment and thereafter ensure that the actual rate never falls lower than this estimated natural rate.

The basis for policy went even beyond that. The view was that if inflation were kept under control, recessions could be all but eliminated. Manipulation of interest rates became the instrument, with the aim being to keep the actual rate of unemployment above the natural. This was argued to be the key to long-term and generally uninterrupted improvement in production combined with unemployment rates as low as could possibly be achieved.

The variable used to control the unemployment rate was the rate of interest. No longer was it thought that the aim was to keep unemployment as low as possible as a prime aim of policy. Instead an inflation 'target' was often chosen, and interest rates were raised or lowered as needed to ensure that the actual unemployment rate coincided with the natural rate, which would ensure that the inflation rate was stable. Once stable inflation was reached at the natural rate, the aim of policy was to keep the unemployment rate at its natural rate.

If, however, inflation was too high, then interest rate policy would be used to deliberately drive the actual unemployment rate up above the natural rate until inflation was again under control. Rates would then be brought down until the actual rate was the same as the natural rate.

If, on the other hand, an economy was already at the desired inflation rate but the unemployment rate went below the estimated natural rate, then rates would go up again until unemployment went back to its natural rate.

STABILITY

Here then was the answer to the problem of economic stability. Recessions would be brief, assuming that they occurred at all. But unlike with the original Keynesian theory which focused on public spending, it was no longer fiscal policy that would matter but monetary policy. Aggregate demand was still the crucial variable but the difference was the instrument used to vary how much was demanded.

And while it was 'monetary' policy, the instrument was not money itself, but the market rate of interest, the price of money and credit within the financial system, that mattered.

The basic aim of monetary policy was to get the inflation rate to the desired rate and then use interest rate adjustments to keep the unemployment rate at the rate consistent with that target rate of inflation.

Slowing aggregate demand to raise unemployment would require a fall in one of the components of demand. Interest rate adjustments would be aimed at lowering the level of private sector investment. The central bank would raise interest rates arbitrarily, which then led to the situation shown in Figure 18.3.

Bad luck to the economy that the axe must fall on private investment, the part of the economy producing long-term growth. Almost certainly for political reasons, as little as possible of the reduction in demand and employment would be allowed to fall on the public sector.

With the contraction in the stock of money from S to S_1, interest rates rise from i_1 to i_2. Some form of open market operation causes rates to rise. The effect on investment is shown, with the level of investment falling from I_1 to I_2.

The effect transmits across to aggregate demand which itself moves to the left, lowering the price level. The effect of higher rates of interest has been to reduce the level of aggregate demand from the inflationary level beyond the economy's potential to a lower more acceptable rate.

The equilibrium of the AD and $SRAS$ at a level beyond the capacity of the economy to sustain is the problem to be solved. The increase in interest rates therefore lowers aggregate demand until an equilibrium point is established where the $SRAS$, $LRAS$ and AD all meet at a level of production equal to the economy's potential.

As shown in Figure 18.4, this is the convergence of $LRAS$, $SRAS$ and AD_2 where output is at a level of unemployment equal to the natural rate and the price level is P.

The economy is at this point producing as much as can be expected, there is no cyclical unemployment and the price level is stable. It is this

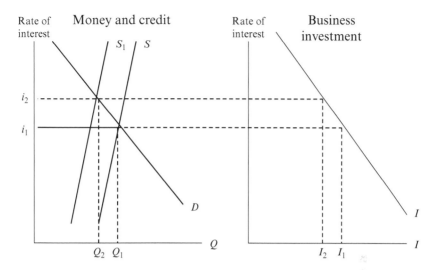

Figure 18.3   Increase in market rate of interest and its effect on investment

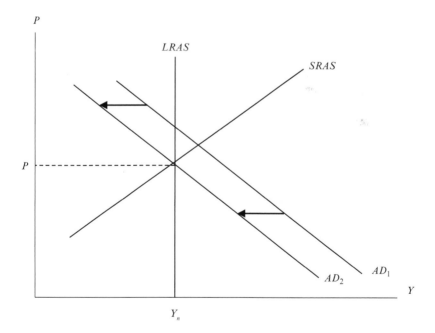

Figure 18.4   Stable equilibrium

outcome that monetary policy and inflation targeting are designed to achieve.

WHAT'S WRONG WITH THE POLICY MODEL

Although there is much to say for this model, it is seriously incomplete. In essence what we find is a model of inflation ultimately based on only a single factor, the rate of unemployment.

It is particularly notable that there is nothing explicit in this approach to inflation directly related to money itself, even though it is changes in the value of money in relation to other goods and services that is the very meaning of an inflationary process. There is a price level in the form of an index, the index being comprised of untold millions of price movements. There are market interest rate adjustments which must presume some kind of subterranean adjustment of the amount of money which caused that rate to shift. But money itself is nowhere to be seen.

What we have is the movement of an aggregate demand curve relative to an aggregate supply curve where the entire world of buyers is buried in one curve while the whole world of entrepreneurial activity is buried in another.

To the aggregate demand and supply curves are then added the notion of a natural rate of unemployment and vertical long-run Phillips curve. Whatever Phillips may have found in the data on the UK between 1861 and 1957, no such smoothly continuous downward relationship is any longer visible in the data that have been collected since. The amount of work that has gone into finding some ongoing relationship between movements in prices and the rate of unemployment has been intensive. No such relationship can be found that reliably stands up across time.

The Phillips curve relationship has nevertheless found its way to the centre of economic theory, because without it there is no Keynesian theory of inflation, there is no inflation forecasting model that can be constructed. And why is such a model needed? So that some event in the present, that we can measure today, can be said to affect price movements in the future over the short to medium term. Because without information of some kind or another available in the present that can foretell what will happen to the price level at some stage in the not-too-distant future, there is no basis on which an anti-inflation policy can be built.

And finally, it is assumed that adjusting interest rates will merely lower the overall growth rate without consideration of the effects on the structure of production that rising rates must inevitably create.

CLASSICAL INFLATION

This last issue may be of particular importance. The approach to inflation control ignores that when interest rates are used to control inflation, the effect is to depress private investment. The space vacated by business can then be filled by increased activity in the public sector. Rising interest rates facilitates crowding-out as governments inflate the money supply.

Indeed, the very meaning of 'inflation' originally meant an excess creation of the medium of exchange beyond the growth in productive output. Inflation meant an inflation of the money supply, one of whose consequences was rapid increases in the price level. The following passage is from a standard text of the time, published in 1932, in a chapter simply titled 'Inflation':

> Strictly speaking, the term 'inflation' is not easily defined. But the phenomenon appears to be distinct and recognizable, and for broad general purposes it will perhaps serve the purpose at present if it is described as an excessive supply of money in relation to the amount of work the money has to do, leading to a general rise in prices. The difficulty is that inflation is often associated with inconvertible paper currencies. (Jack, 1932: 149)

This was written when currencies were directly convertible into a certain weight in gold. The 'gold standard', as the system was called, ensured that a country could not just issue as much currency as it pleased, but was always disciplined by the need to be able to sell gold at the official price. It is a system now long gone, and it is inconceivable that it should ever return.

The problems of a non-convertible currency – that is, the problem associated with 'fiat money', that is, money backed by nothing at all other than the self-discipline of the issuing authority – were well known; an absolute commonplace amongst economists and even the general public in those days. This is William Stanley Jevons, the originator of the marginal revolution in England, writing on these matters in his 1875 text, *Money and the Mechanism of Exchange*.

> It is hardly requisite to tell again the well-worn tale of the over issue of paper money which has almost always followed the removal of the legal necessity of convertibility. Hardly any civilized nation exists ... which has not suffered from the scourge of paper money at one time or another ... Italy, Austria, and the United States, countries where the highest economical intelligence might be expected to guide the governments, endure evils of an inconvertible paper currency. Time after time in the earlier history of New England and some of the other states now forming parts of the American Union, paper money had been issued and had wrought ruin. (Jevons, 1875: 235–6)

Inconvertible paper currency allows the government to spend money by issuing new currency, in this way diverting the resources of the nation to its own purposes. It is a form of taxation by stealth. Jevons discusses this approach to government finance:

> The issue of an inconvertible money has often been recommended as a convenient means of making a forced loan from the people, when the finances of the government are in a desperate condition. It is true that money may be thus easily abstracted from the people, and the government debts are effectually lessened. At the same time, however, every private debtor is enabled to take a forced contribution from his creditor. A government should, indeed, be in a desperate position, which ventures thus to break all social contracts and relations which it was created to preserve. (Jevons, 1875: 236)

And one last reminder of the depth of understanding that was once common but is now almost entirely forgotten. This is from an American text published in 1940 by Lewis Froman and Harlan McCracken. There they wrote:

> The difficulty with using a practically valueless commodity as the principal money of the country is that there is always the temptation to issue more and more of it. The substance of which it is made is easily accessible, and the government can raise money easily by this method. To be sure, it would be a form of taxation, but an indirect one, and indirect taxes are always more popular than direct taxes. Irresponsible governments, therefore, cannot be empowered with the issuance of un-backed paper money. With the pressure which is put upon most modern governments for the raising of revenue, it might be fair to say that most governments would be 'irresponsible' once they began to issue fiat money. For this reason, therefore, it is desirable that money have an intrinsic value or at least a conversion privilege. (Froman and McCracken, 1940: 513–14)

Without some kind of discipline on spending, governments just keep pouring more money into their economies as a way of financing their own activities. The answer is to chain the domestic currency to some form of conversion, which no government will ever willingly do for long. The consequence is that governments will continue to add to inflationary pressures without abatement.

Here all that can be done is to explain. But the attempt to saddle the problems of inflation onto the market economy and the system of exchange will also be an ever-present temptation for governments. To try to stop inflation by pretending that the fault lies with entrepreneurial activity, as if the solution is simply to get businesses to stop raising prices, is an enormous folly that only adds to unemployment and does nothing about inflation: too much money spent chasing too few goods produced.

The fact remains that with the government in charge of the issuance of money, no other entity in an economy can cause inflation other than the government and no other entity but government can ever bring an inflation to an end.

SOME FINAL CONSIDERATIONS ON INFLATION

Inflation is the result of too much money chasing too few goods. If money is recognized as what it is, purchasing power in the hands of buyers with governments included amongst those buyers, and if those with money to spend are attempting to buy more than 100 per cent of all available goods and services, then these circumstances properly represent the nature of inflation.

The question then is: how does this purchasing power get into the hands of buyers? There are three main ways, which are often closely related.

Liquidity

There is firstly an excess supply of liquidity, that is, of spendable money. Although interest rates are determined by the supply and demand for savings, there is also an inflationary component that can be embedded in lending rates.

The financial system, and in particular banks, create money. Money is often no more than a line entry in the balance sheet of a bank.

Since banks hold only a small proportion of the total value of their loans in the form of cash and other reserves, banks can increase the total volume of money on loan by simply increasing the amount of money they create within bank deposits.

The *money multiplier* is an estimate of the change in the total amount of money in circulation in response to a change in the amount of reserves held by financial institutions. An increase in liquidity beyond the actual available real savings of the economy in general will put upwards pressures on the price level.

Government Spending and Deficit Finance

The great inflations of the past have been due to large increases in liquidity caused by increases in public spending unfunded either by taxation or by borrowing from the public.

The financial system generally and the banking system in particular are typically prudential lenders which aim to lend only to those who are seen as likely to repay their loans. To the extent that financial institutions behave prudently, there is little likelihood that a serious inflation can arise from a rapid increase in lending to those unable to repay. Where this occurs, bank failure is a brutal cure that nevertheless brings this excess into line.

Governments, however, can spend monies they do not have, since a cheque written by the government will be accepted at face value. Other than in very unstable regimes, it is certain to cash for the amount stated.

Governments can therefore create inflation, firstly, through their own spending and then, secondly, through their ability to create the liquidity that such inflations are dependent on. It is very difficult to sustain an inflation without deficit finance as the prime instigator and driving force behind the process.

Wages Growth

A crucially important element in the process of inflation is the certain demands that will come from wage earners for compensation for the loss of purchasing power that rising prices are certain to bring. Wage increases do not normally initiate the processes of inflation, but once inflation begins, the role of wage earners becomes increasingly important.

The processes involved are a sequence:

- The sequence begins with higher prices caused by increased liquidity and deficit finance.
- A growing resentment follows at the loss of real incomes, which is translated into industrial militancy to restore lost purchasing power.
- Higher wage increases then fuel increases in business costs which push prices upwards and add to the demands for higher wages by workers.
- The wage–price spiral becomes embedded with both wage earners and business attempting to maintain their own relative economic positions.
- Where business fails to keep prices high enough to cover costs, business activity contracts and unemployment goes up.
- The higher unemployment eventually puts a break on worker militancy and the demand for higher wages. But higher unemployment is almost certainly a necessary part in the process of eventually bringing inflation to an end. Extraordinarily costly in wealth and personal welfare, which is why inflation should be avoided at all costs.

It is a very intense struggle all round. But the central problems remain with public sector deficits and the growth in liquidity. Only a restoration of some kind of balance between the growth in the amount of purchasing power and a growth in the level of production can allow for the simultaneous occurrence of low unemployment, rapid growth and stable prices.

SUPPRESSED INFLATION

By shifting the meaning of the term 'inflation' from a focus on public spending towards movements in the price level, it has become less easy to understand the nature of the problem or to recognize the dangers being created by excessive increases in public spending and money supply growth.

Most of what is bought during any period of time is based on production using the pre-existing stock of capital and other assets that an economy already possesses. Once those assets exist, their original production costs are no longer a cost of production in the usual sense. Their owner, when an inflationary process has commenced, may well go bankrupt, but the assets will be sold on at 'fire-sale' prices and continue to be available for use in production.

The return may compensate the buyer of those assets but does not create a sufficiently large return to finance their replacement and renewal. They can be maintained, since keeping assets running is cheaper than replacement, but over time even these assets wear out and must be replaced. But the time before replacement can be a long time coming, possibly many years. In the meantime, businesses get by as their capital stock wears down.

Inflation therefore does not have to occur as a rise in prices. It can also occur as a depreciation of the asset base of the economy. Just as the average age of all of the cars in an economy can increase, so too can the average age of all of the capital equipment in an economy. The economy becomes less productive, people make do with less, but the price level does not accelerate to the extent that it might otherwise have done. If inflation is seen in terms of both higher prices and also an ageing and decaying capital stock, the effects on the economy of an inflation of the money supply will be more completely understood.

CAUSES OF INFLATION AND ITS CONTROL

Here we once again return to the more complete model of the inflationary process presented in the previous chapter. What was shown was a process

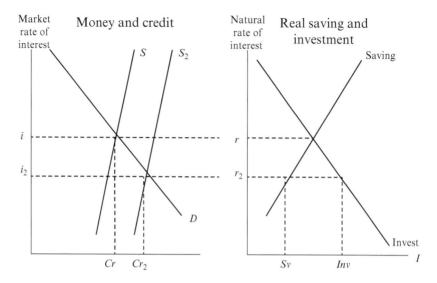

Figure 18.5   The inflationary process

in which the growth in the amount of money and credit exceeded the growth in the underlying level of real savings relative to the demand for such savings. This is shown once again in Figure 18.5.

The crucial element is where the growth in the supply of money and credit exceed the growth in the supply of physical capital and other resources needed for investment.

The increase in the supply of credit will either have been a deliberate act by government to lower interest rates to encourage investment or a consequence of deficit financing where the amount of base money and bank reserves rise because public spending exceeds the level of taxation.

The result is less investment, investment on less productive assets, less value-adding production overall, but more money and credit available. This is the classic situation of too much money chasing too few goods.

And the place to focus attention is on the right-hand side diagram showing the natural rate of interest. Lower interest rates increase the amount of national saving demanded, but lead to a falling-away in the supply of those savings.

What to do is basically to reverse the process:

- allow interest rates to rise;
- end deficit financing;
- reduce the level of unproductive public expenditure;

- contain the growth in money and credit;
- encourage higher levels of national saving;
- encourage higher rates of private investment;
- encourage higher levels of entrepreneurial activity.

Raising interest rates and keeping them above some rock-bottom rate may be the crucial policy need, given how counter-intuitive such advice now seems. But interest rates remain singularly the most important price within the economy, allowing resources to be distributed to where they will earn their highest return.

And at the end of the day, it may be of the highest social value to let financial institutions fail where they have lent to borrowers who cannot repay their debts. Ways should be found to protect depositors, always of course bearing in mind considerations of moral hazard, but the financial institutions should be allowed to fail and their assets sold off if those to whom they lend cannot repay their debts. It may be the only way in the modern world to ensure that money lent out is a proper reflection of the amount of real savings that actually exist.

In essence, use the market. Prosperity can only come from market activity. Unless policy makers understand that, nothing they do will lead to the economic outcomes they are looking to create, or will encourage the prosperity they are seeking to achieve.

NOTE

1. The way in which the equation has been used is to try to construct a relationship in form of: $\Delta P = k \Delta M$. Delta (Δ) is the sign that means 'the change in'. The change in the price level is equal to some constant proportion (k) of the growth in the stock of money. This was the central equation in an economic set of theories that sought to control inflation by controlling the growth in the stock of money.

Afterword

There are a number of people to whom I owe a great deal in getting this book into print. I began it at the height of the Global Financial Crisis at the end of 2008, at a moment when I could no longer bear teaching Keynesian economics. I had put up with it when things were going reasonably well, but the descent into recession, followed by the worldwide adoption of Keynesian stimulus policies, meant that I could no longer in good conscience continue teaching in the way I had.

I am therefore endlessly grateful to my colleague Bronwyn Coate who allowed me to write the book as the basis for the course we taught together. Her support, encouragement and sensible advice meant a good deal to me, as the book was being carved out of nothing more than my own ideas which had been developing in my mind over a goodly number of years. Neither she nor I knew what would come out during any given week. Her willingness to allow me to put onto paper my views on economics, and to use these as the basis for our classroom instruction, was essential for this project even to have commenced.

I am also grateful to my Head of School at the time, Tony Naughton, now sadly deceased, who not only agreed to allow me to write my own text but also supported the transformation of this course from beginning to end.

I am also grateful to my students in Economic Analysis for Business, especially the first tranche back at the start of 2009 who had no set text but had to wait each week for me to finish the chapter in time for distribution in class. Each group of students until the first edition was published – and there were four – also had to put up with further iterations as I moved towards the completed work, and I am grateful for their indulgence and frequent commentary.

I would also like to thank Edward Elgar at Edward Elgar Publishing, and Phillip Booth at the Institute of Economic Affairs in London. Both had seen the potential merit in this book and I appreciate their indispensable support. I must also mention the work team at Edward Elgar Publishing who are unfailingly skilled and helpful and for whose professionalism I am deeply indebted.

Let me also mention the early twentieth-century economist Henry Clay from whom I have learned a great deal. In my view, his *Economics: An Introduction for the General Reader* (Clay, 1916) was the best introductory book on economics written during the whole of the twentieth century. Clay had the advantage of having written before economic theory was affected by Keynes, and thus could write a compact and coherent text which perfectly summed up classical thought. It is as readable today as it was when first published in 1916 and it lasted long enough through many reprints for a second edition to be published in 1942. What of course spelled its demise was the advent of Keynesian economics which rendered the classical view obsolete inside the classroom, although it remained entirely relevant for understanding the economics of the real world. An article of mine commemorating the hundredth anniversary of the publication of Clay's *Economics* sets all of this out in much more detail (Kates, 2016).

Lastly in order of mention, but first in my feeling of gratitude, are my sons Benjamin and Joshua but especially their mother and my wife, Zuzanna, without whom nothing would ever get done. They make all the difference in my life. The book is dedicated to Zuzanna who has made the greatest difference of all.

References

Bagehot, Walter ([1873] 1919), *Lombard Street: A Description of the Money Market*, London: John Murray.

Becker, Gary and William J. Baumol (1952), 'The classical economic theory: the outcome of the discussion', *Economica*, **19**, 355–76.

Clay, Henry (1916), *Economics: An Introduction for the General Reader*, 1st edn, London: Macmillan and Co.

Davis, Tracy C. (2007), *The Economics of the British Stage 1860–1914*, Cambridge: Cambridge University Press.

Froman, Lewis A. and Harlan L. McCracken (1940), *Principles of Economics*, Chicago, IL: Richard D. Irwin.

Gellner, E. (1994), *Conditions of Liberty: Civil Society and its Rivals*, New York: Viking

Haberler, Gottfried (1937), *Prosperity and Depression: A Theoretical Analysis of Cyclical Movements*, 1st edn, Geneva: League of Nations.

Hayek, Friedrich A. (1931), 'The "paradox" of saving', *Economica*, **11** (Old Series), 125–69.

Hicks, John R. (1937), 'Mr Keynes and the "classics": a suggested interpretation', *Econometrica*, **5**, 147–59.

Jack, D.T. (1932), *Currency and Banking*, London: Sir Isaac Pitman and Sons.

Jevons, W. Stanley (1875), *Money and the Mechanism of Exchange*, New York: D. Appleton and Co.

Kates, Steven (2016), 'The hundredth anniversary of Clay's *Economics*: the best introduction to economics ever written', *History of Economics Review*, **64**,1.

Keynes, John Maynard (1920), *The Economic Consequences of the Peace*, London: Macmillan.

Keynes, John Maynard ([1936] 1987), *The General Theory of Employment, Interest and Money*, Vol. VII of *The Collected Writings of John Maynard Keynes*, London and Basingstoke: Macmillan.

Knight, Frank ([1921] 1933), *Risk, Uncertainty and Profit*, London: London School of Economics and Political Science.

Malthus, Thomas Robert (1986), *The Works of Thomas Robert Malthus*, edited by E.A. Wrigley and David Souden, London: William Pickering.

Vol. 1: *An Essay on the Principles of Population* (1798); Vol. 5: *Principles of Political Economy*, 2nd edn (1836) with variant readings from the 1st edn (1820), Part I; Vol. 6: *Principles of Political Economy*, 2nd edn (1836) with variant readings from the 1st edn (1820), Part II.

Marshall, Alfred ([1920] 1947), *Principles of Economics: An Introductory Volume*, 8th edn, London: Macmillan and Co.

Marshall, Alfred ([1920] 1961), *Principles of Economics*, 9th (variorum) edn, with annotations by C.W. Guillebrand, Vol. I Text, Vol. II Notes, London: Macmillan for Royal Economic Society.

Marshall, Alfred and Mary Paley Marshall ([1879] 1881), *The Economics of Industry*, 2nd edn, London: Macmillan and Co.

Marx, Karl ([1867] 1918), *Capital: A Critique of Political Economy*, translated from the German by Samuel Moore and Edward Aveling and edited by Fredrich Engels. Revised and amplified according to the 4th German edn by Ernest Untermann, Chicago, IL: Charles H. Kerr.

Marx, Karl and Friedrich Engels ([1848] 1977), *Manifesto of the Communist Party*, Moscow: Progress Publishers

McCracken, Harlan Linneus (1933), *Value Theory and Business Cycles*, Binghampton, NY: Falcon Press.

Mill, James ([1808] 1966), *Commerce Defended*, 2nd edn, in Donald Winch (ed.), *James Mill: Selected Economic Writings*, Edinburgh: Oliver and Boyd, pp. 85–159.

Mill, John Stuart ([1871] 1921), *Principles of Political Economy with Some of Their Applications to Social Philosophy*, 7th edn, edited with an introduction by Sir W.J. Ashley, London: Longmans, Green, & Co. First edition published in 1848.

Mill, John Stuart ([1874] 1974), 'Of the influence of consumption on production', in *Essays on Some Unsettled Questions of Political Economy*, 2nd edn, Clifton, NJ: Augustus M. Kelley, pp. 47–74. Originally published in 1844.

Mises, Ludwig von ([1950] 1980), 'Lord Keynes and Say's Law', in *Planning for Freedom: And Sixteen Other Essays and Addresses*, 4th edn, South Holland, IL: Libertarian Press, pp. 64–71.

Peden, George (1996), 'The treasury view in the interwar period: an example of political economy?', in Bernard Corry (ed.), *Unemployment and the Economists*, Cheltenham, UK: Edward Elgar Publishing.

Ricardo, David ([1817] 1951–73), *Principles of Political Economy and Taxation*, Vol. I of *The Works and Correspondence of David Ricardo*, edited by P. Sraffa with the collaboration of M.H. Dobb, Cambridge: Cambridge University Press.

Ricardo, David (1951–73), *Correspondence 1819–1821*, Vol. VIII of *The Works and Correspondence of David Ricardo*, edited by P. Sraffa with the collaboration of M.H. Dobb, Cambridge: Cambridge University Press.

Robbins, Lionel ([1935] 1945), *An Essay on the Nature and Significance of Economic Science*, 2nd edn, London: Macmillan.

Say, Jean-Baptiste ([1803] 1821), *A Treatise on Political Economy; Or the Production, Distribution, and Consumption of Wealth*, translated from the 4th edn of the French by C.R. Prinsep with notes by the translator, 2 vols, London: Longman, Hurst, Rees, Orme, and Brown.

Sloman, John and Keith Norris (2002), *Macroeconomics*, 2nd edn, Frenchs Forest, NSW: Pearson.

Smart, William (1906), *The Return to Protection: Being a Re-Statement of the Case for Free Trade*, London: Macmillan.

Smith, Adam ([1776] 1976), *An Inquiry into the Nature and Causes of the Wealth of Nations*, Chicago, IL: University of Chicago Press.

Taylor, F.M. (1925), *Principles of Economics*, 9th edn, New York: Ronald Press.

Torrens, Robert ([1821] 1965), *An Essay on the Production of Wealth*, New York: Augustus M. Kelley.

Index

45-degree line model 292, 294–6,
   298–9, 300, 304, 309–10

acceleration principle 346
aggregate demand 6, 30, 47, 268, 310,
   311–13
   and aggregate supply 309–28
   anti-inflationary policy on 323
   classical theory of cycle 279–80
   decrease leads to recession 305
   deficiency 282
   exports and imports 301
   inflation control 419, 426
   inventory adjustments 292
   Keynesian Cross 294, 296
   Keynesian equation 292
   Keynesian macroeconomic model
      281, 283, 284
   Keynesian policy 304–5
   leakages and injections 288
   long-run non-inflationary growth
      327
   National Accounts 208
   recession 306
   Say's Law and related propositions
      271, 273
   stability 424
aggregate supply 30–31, 268, 310,
   311–13
   and aggregate demand 309–28
   inflation control 426
   Keynesian equation 292
   Say's Law and related propositions
      273
   see also long-run aggregate supply
      (LRAS); short-run aggregate
      supply (SRAS)
agricultural price supports 169
anarchy 96
'animal spirits' (business confidence)
   272, 364

anti-competitive practices 193
anti-inflationary policy 319, 323–7, 418
anticipation of demand 46, 73–4,
   333–4, 378
asset price inflation 408–9
average annual growth rates 239
average cost 202–4
average revenue 202–4
axioms of a free market economy 32–8

Bagehot, Walter 277
   Lombard Street 278
balance of payments 60, 206, 236–8
Bank of England 369
banks 123, 265, 286, 343, 397–8,
   399–401, 404, 429
   central banks 26, 237, 324, 369, 399,
      422
base money 397
basic rules of market economy 38–53
basket of goods and services 28–9,
   226–8, 288, 289–90
Baumol, William J. 278
Becker, Gary 278
benefits 178
   costs and 177–8, 257
   expected 178, 190
borrowing 124, 353, 387, 390, 395,
   410–12, 429
   government 124
   willingness to borrow and lend 396,
      399–400
   see also credit; finance
bubbles 265, 343, 379
budget deficits 51, 399
business confidence 272, 364
business cycle 6–7, 78–9, 260–61
   classical theories 342–51
   contours 337–8
   coordination and time 331–2
   creative destruction 347–8

economics teaching 374
error theories 347–8
macroeconomics, contrast with 60,
    339–40
monetary theories 342–4
over-investment theories 344–6
peaks 78–9, 337–9
phases 338–9
and political decisions 378–9
production in anticipation of
    demand 333–4
prosperity and depression 340–41
psychological theories 348–9
recessionary phase 339
recovery phase 338
Say's Law, importance of 330
structure of production 341–2
troughs of cycle 78, 337–8, 345, 347,
    380
uncertainty and economic decisions
    332–3
under-consumption theories 349–51
see also recession
business loans 123
businesses 40–41, 98–100
buyers 156–7

capital 15, 110–11, 113, 118–19, 207,
    285
see also human capital
capital account 236
capital flows, international 79–80
capital goods versus consumption
    goods 215
Capital (Marx) 255
capitalist system 16
central banks 26, 237, 324, 399, 422
centrally planned economies 35, 90,
    94, 392
an impossibility 90
ceteris paribus – all other things being
    equal 18, 91
demand curve movement 149
exchange rates 237
horizontal and downward-sloping
    supply 161
interest rates 396
market demand 146
market rate of interest 401
market supply 141

money supply 398
natural rate of interest 403
price increase 135–6
price movements 165
production and sale 131
supply curve movement 144
supply and demand 371
change
accommodating 34–5
reacting to 92
character of a population 58–9
charity 1
Churchill, Sir Winston 353
cinemas 119
circular flow of income 285–6, 290
diagram 290–91, 329
classical economics 241–7, 259
business cycle theory 260
and economic growth 353–66
recession 311, 331, 353–66
saving 286–7
structure of production 12
Classical School 256–8
classical theory of the cycle 31, 279–80,
    351–2, 362–6
Clay, Henry 273
command economies *see* centrally
    planned economies
commercial relationships 38
commercially useful knowledge 32,
    35–6
Communist Manifesto (Marx) 255
comparative advantage 80–81, 248–9
competition 19, 120–21, 138–9, 193–4,
    372
complementary goods 345
concentration, industry 192
Consumer Price Index (CPI) 28–9,
    226–30, 239, 311
basket of goods and services 226–7
construction of 227–9
real movements in economic
    indicators 229–30
consumption 16, 27, 300
crowding out 409
fundamental propositions on capital
    (Mill) 114–16
government 300–301
government spending and national
    saving 410

Keynesian Cross 294, 296
Keynesian macroeconomic model
    272, 283
Keynesian policy 304–5
leakages and injections 288, 303
and personal satisfaction 40
recession 305–6
savings and financial system 387–91
consumption goods 220
    versus capital goods 215
coordination 61, 66–7, 127, 331–2, 333
corruption 58–9
cost curve 189
cost–benefit analysis (CBA) 22–3,
    186–7
costs 178
    average 202–4
    expected 178, 188, 190
    fixed 177, 196–7
    future 191
    marginal social 373
    and market prices 36–7
    opportunity 14–15, 103, 178–9, 191
    production 197
    relative 177
    sunk 177
    total 196–7, 198–200
    variable 197
    weighing up potential costs against
        benefits 177, 201
    see also marginal cost (*MC*)
counter-cyclical policies in recession
    379–82
creative destruction 34, 347–8
credit 25
    inflation control 432
    market rate and natural rate 404
    money supply 405
    saving, money and 389–92
    stability 425
crises 362
    financial 31, 339
    Global Financial Crisis 382
crowding out 409–10, 411–13
current account 236
cyclical activity and governments
    368–84
    actions 369
    counter-cyclical policies in recession
        379–82

economic theory, teaching 370–74
Great Depression 369–70
involvement 375–6
markets 374–5
policy and recession 376–7
political decision making 378–9
public spending 382–3
recession and political decisions
    377–8
trade protection 383–4
cyclical unemployment 315–16, 322

Darwin, Charles 251
debt 25
    money, recession and 413–15
    public 381
decision making 21, 33, 42–3, 72–3,
    332–3
    at the margin 68–70, 176–7
    and marginal analysis 182, 184–5,
        187, 191
deficit finance 429–30
deficits 236
    budget 51, 399
definitions 8–31
deflation 339
demand 17, 19, 46, 64–5, 151, 163–4,
    222
    aggregate *see* aggregate demand
    analysis 17–18
    anticipation of 46, 73–4, 333–4, 378
    as a barrier 146–8
    circular flow 299
    classical perspective 355–7
    classical theory of the cycle 279–80,
        363–5
    for commodities is not demand for
        labour 116–17, 353
    created by supply 272–3
    deficiency 287
    domestic 284
    economic growth in classical model
        360–61
    economics teaching 371
    effect of changes in demand on
        revenue 173–4
    effective 267
    increase in 155–6
    law of 160
    market 145–6

market adjustment 156
market supply 140
natural rate of interest 402
perfect competition 372
price system 63
production in anticipation of 73–4,
    333–4
savings 299
Say's Law and related propositions
    274, 276–7
shifting 156–7
structure of 31, 75–6
using 164–5
versus quantity demanded 148
see also demand curves; supply and
    demand analysis
demand curves 19, 46–7, 138, 150, 151,
    167
change in supply 159
demand as a barrier 146–7
demand versus quantity demanded
    148
elasticity and inelasticity 173–5
equilibrium 151
horizontal and downward-sloping
    supply 160–62
increase in demand 155
industry supply 159
innovation 162–3
marginal analysis 184
marginal revenue and marginal cost
    183
market activity reduction 163–4
market demand 146
movement of 149–50
price ceiling 169
price increase 135–7
price and volume of individual
    product 134
prices and inflation 166
production and sale 130–31
profit maximization 195–6, 202, 204
structure 132
supply and demand: beyond
    equilibrium 154
supply and demand, using 164–5
demand deficiency 30, 250, 252–3, 261,
    287, 289, 366
Keynesian Revolution and Say's Law
    266–7, 269–70, 276–7, 279

demand elasticity 171–2, 174, 202, 372
deposit ratio 399
depreciation 215–16
depression 26, 271–2, 277, 340–41
    see also Great Depression
diagrams 106–7
diamond–water paradox 258
discouraged workers 235–6
disequilibrium 291
division of labour 246
double counting 214–15
downturns 79, 278, 335–6, 351
downward-sloping supply curves
    160–62

economic activity 82
measures of *see* measures of
    economic activity
*Economic Consequences of the Peace,
    The* (Keynes) 263
economic decisions *see* decision
    making
economic growth 12–13, 103–4
in classical model 359–62
Keynesian macroeconomic model
    283
market rate and natural rate 406–7
and recessions 336–7
and valued added 84
economic indicators, real movements
    in 229–30
economic management 6, 39, 100–101,
    316, 325, 330, 351
economic outcomes 243
economic return and time 179–80
economic theory 8, 259
teaching 370–74
economics
definition 55–6
of free markets 54–81
history of 240–65
teaching approach 370–74
see also classical economics;
    Keynesian economics
economies of scale 160–61, 194
efficiency 24, 80, 106, 163
elastic demand 171–2, 174, 202, 372
elasticity 171, 172–5
employment 230–36
full 282, 305, 306, 316

entrepreneurial error 347–8
entrepreneurs 8, 9, 15, 42–3, 70–71, 117–19, 285
  absence of in teaching of economics 373–4
  competition and 120–21, 139
  examples 118–19
  factors of production 117–21
  finance 121–2
  marginal analysis 191–2
  private sector 34, 41–2, 127
  risk versus uncertainty 119–20
  Say on 249
  technology and innovation 126
equality not an economic principle 49–51
equilibrium 20, 47, 91, 151–3, 158, 313–14, 320
  demand, increase in 155
  income expenditure and saving analysis 298
  inventory adjustments 291
  over-investment theories 344
  price 204
  quantity 204
  stable 425
  supply, change in 157, 159
  where aggregate supply and aggregate demand are equal 313–14
  where consumption and investment equal production 295
  where quantity supplied and quantity demanded are equal 151–2
  where savings and investment are equal 293
error theories of the business cycle 347–8
ethics 37, 58, 251
evolution theory 251
exchange rates 79–80, 237–8
  fixed 236–7
  floating 237
exchange value 29, 129, 254, 258, 316
expectations 141
  and exchange rates 237
expenditure method for calculating GDP 219–21, 283

exports 27, 218–19, 284, 299, 301–2
  net 30, 284, 301, 303
externalities 257, 372, 373

factor markets 163
factors of production 15, 109–28, 162
  capital 15, 108, 110–11, 285
  circular flow 285–6
  classical perspective 356
  economic growth in classical model 359
  entrepreneurs 15, 108, 117–19, 285
  finance 15, 121–2
  interest, nature of 122–4
  knowledge, technology, know-how and skills 15, 125–6
  labour 15, 108, 109–10, 285
  land 15, 108, 109, 285
  risk versus uncertainty 119–20
  stocks and flows 127–8
  technological sophistication of capital 15
  time 15, 126–7
  see also fundamental propositions on capital (Mill)
Federal Reserve (United States) 369
feudal aristocratic societies 257
fiat money 427
film making 119
final goods and services 82, 182, 308, 332, 354, 356–7, 391
  measuring the economy 211, 219–20
finance 15, 24–5, 121–2
  deficit 429–30
financial crises 31, 339
  Global Financial Crisis (2008–09) 382
  see also recessions
financial disruption 362
financial institutions 25, 45, 123, 206, 329–30, 433
  Keynesian macroeconomic model 285–6, 288, 290
  savings and financial system 390, 393, 395, 413–14
  see also banks
financial system 385–6
  see also savings
firm, theory of the 23
firm's supply curve 134, 137, 157

fiscal balance 381
fixed exchange rates 236–7
floating exchange rates 237
flows 14, 65–6, 127–8, 208–9
  international capital 79–80
free markets *see* market economy
free trade 246–7
freedom, personal 4, 8, 10, 333, 375
free-riding 99
frictional unemployment 315, 322
Froman, Lewis 428
full employment 304
fundamental principles of market
  economy 38–53
fundamental propositions on capital
  (Mill) 111–17
  capital is result of saving 113
  demand for commodities is not
    demand for labour 116–17
  industry limited by capital 111–12
  what is saved is spent 113–16

Gellner, E. 256–7
'general glut' (overproduction) 250,
  252, 267, 269–70, 277–8, 280
  see also demand deficiency
General Theory of Employment,
  Interest and Money, The (Keynes)
  6, 11, 30, 250, 253, 263, 281–3
  circular flow 286
  classical perspective 354
  classical theory of the cycle 362
  classical theory of growth and
    recession 353
  government actions 369
  Keynesian Revolution and Say's Law
    266–8, 270, 272, 275, 279
  prosperity and depression 341
Global Financial Crisis (2008–09) 382
gold standard 427
goods and services 300
  capital goods versus consumption
    goods 215
  complementary goods 345
  final 82, 182, 211, 219–20, 308, 332,
    354, 356–7, 391
  government-produced 212
  higher-order goods 346
  home-produced 213
  inferior 154

investment 220, 282
  public 99
  range of 210–12, 217
  see also basket of goods and services
government 93–107
  actions 369
  actual problems 94–5
  administrative side 96
  attitudes towards 244–5
  businesses 98–100
  circular flow 288
  contribution 100–101
  corruption 58–9
  cyclical activity *see* cyclical activity
    and governments
  economic decisions 42
  free markets and 'mixed' economy
    94
  infrastructure 97
  institutional arrangements 52
  involvement, constant 375–6
  justice system 52
  Keynesian macroeconomic model
    300–301
  legal side 96
  market economy, role in 95–100
  and markets 95–100
  permissible actions 52
  policy and recession 376–7
  political decisions 377–9
  price ceilings 167–8
  price floors 169
  production possibility curve 102–6
  productive economic environment
    45–6
  regulation 51–2, 96–7
  regulation in recession 380
  as social institutions run by self-
    interested individuals 52–3
  taxation levels and structure 98
  welfare 97–8
government borrowing 124
government businesses 98–100
government grants 2
government spending 27, 47, 300,
  307–8, 382–3
  and budget deficits 399
  circular flow 299
  classical perspective 355–7
  classical theory of the cycle 363–5

crowding out 413
deficit finance and 429–30
economic growth in classical model
  360–61
foreign sector 289–90
Keynesian macroeconomic model
  284
Keynesian policy 304–5
leakages and injections 287, 302
and national saving 410–11
non value-adding 380
recession 100, 305–6, 380
to restore aggregate demand 306
saving and investment 357–9,
  387–91
versus private investment 411
government-produced goods and
  services 212
Great Depression 211, 253, 282,
  369–70
business cycle 338, 339, 341
National Accounts 207
gross domestic product (GDP) 27,
  209–19, 239
accounting for movements in the
  price level 223–5
annual real growth 225
business cycle 338, 340
calculation 219–21
consumption goods versus capital
  goods 215
depreciation 215–16
double counting 214–15
economic growth in classical model
  361
expenditure calculation versus
  Keynesian macro equation
  221–2
expenditure method 219–21, 283
exports and imports 218–19
goods and services, variety of
  211–12
government 301
government-produced goods and
  services 212
growth rates 225
home-produced goods and services
  213
identity 27, 220–22, 417
income method 223

inflationary policy and short run
  aggregate supply 320–21
interpretation 222–3
Keynesian Cross 294, 296
Keynesian equation 292
Keynesian macroeconomic model
  282, 283
leakages-injections 293
long-run aggregate supply 321–2,
  421
measurement 217–18
multiplier 307
nominal 28, 223
numerical calculation 224–5
Phillips curve 423
potential 316
private and public sector activity,
  adding together 218
production function 297
products, range of 213–14
quantity theory of money 417
real 224
recession 306
saving and investment 359
seasonality 216
trend 216–17
value-added method 222
variety of goods and services 211–12
Gross National Product (GNP) 238
growth 43–4
non-inflationary 327–8
real 28
see also classical theory of growth
  and recession; economic growth
growth rates
average annual 239
GDP 225
percentage movements between any
  two periods 228–9

Haberler, Gottfried
business cycle 342
entrepreneurial error and creative
  destruction 347–8
monetary theories 342–4
over-investment theories 345–6
Prosperity and Depression 275, 277,
  341, 369
psychological theories 348–9
under-consumption theories 350–51

Hayek, Friedrich 272
healthcare 99
Hicks, Sir John 267
higher-order goods 346
highly competitive industry 193
history of economics 240–65
home-produced goods and services 213
honesty 58–9
horizontal supply curves 160–62
housing loan 124
human capital 111, 125

'if-then' statements 107, 141, 146, 294,
    311
imperfect competition 372
imports 218–19, 284, 289–90, 299,
    301–2
income 272, 386–7
    approach to measuring national
        output 219
    see also circular flow of income
income distribution 51, 60, 247, 257,
    259
income method for GDP 223
inconvertible currency 428
individual product, price and volume
    of 134–5
individuals, focus on 241–2
industrial revolution 241, 249, 256–7
industrial societies 256
industry
    concentration of 192
    limited by capital 111–12
industry structure 192–4
inefficiency, meaning of 105–6
inelasticity 172–3
inferior goods 154
inflation 29, 268, 318–19, 416–33
    anti-inflationary policy 319, 323–7,
        418
    asset price 408–9
    causes 431–3
    classical 427–9
    control 431–3
    cyclical activity and governments
        378
    expectations 323
    expected rate 396
    Keynesian approach to control
        419–23

Keynesian macroeconomic model
    283
market rate and natural rate 408
Phillips curve 325, 326, 422
and prices 166
problems caused by 316–18
quantity theory of money
    416–18
rate, optimum 325
stability 424–6
suppressed 431
and willingness to lend 396
inflationary policy 320–21, 426
infrastructure 97
initial localized downturn 335–6
injections *see* leakages-injections
    approach
innovation 13, 125–6, 143, 162–3,
    191–2
    commercialization 48
institutional arrangements 52
intended investment 291
interest, nature of 122–4
interest rates 25
    adjustment for risk 395–6
    and inflation 318, 325, 423
    Keynesian macroeconomic model
        282
    market rate of interest (money rate)
        400–402
    as means to identify more productive
        investments 394–5
    in recession 381–2
    rental as analogy with 123, 394
    role of 393–7
    saving in Keynesian and classical
        models 287
    see also money rate of interest;
        natural rate of interest
international capital flows 79–80
international trade 11, 60, 79–81, 246,
    289–90, 302, 370
inventory adjustments 291–2
investment 16, 27, 222, 298, 300,
    357–9, 386
    circular flow 286, 299
    classical perspective 355–7
    classical theory of the cycle 363–4
    crowding out 409
    curve 294, 296

economic growth in classical model
360–61
foreign sector 289–90
fundamental propositions on capital
(Mill) 115
government 300–301
government spending and national
saving 410
and inflation 317, 432
intended 291
Keynesian macroeconomic model
272, 283
Keynesian policy 304–5
leakages and injections 288, 293–4,
302
market rate and natural rate 404,
406, 407–8
money supply 405
private 411
recession 305–6
savings and financial system 386–91
stability 425
steady-state neutral 360
unintended 291
investment goods 220, 282
invisible hand 241–2
involuntary unemployment 275–6
see also unemployment
iron law of wages 251
IS-LM curves 267

Jack, D.T. 427
Jevons, William Stanley 428
*Money and the Mechanism of
Exchange* 427
Theory of Political Economy 259

Keynes, John Maynard 261, 264,
266–8, 308
circular flow 291
*Economic Consequences of the Peace,
The* 263
Keynesian equation 292
saving 287, 299
Say's Law 30, 269
Say's Law and classical business
cycle theory 330
Say's Law and related propositions
274–5, 276, 278
Treatise on Money 266

*see also General Theory of
Employment, Interest and
Money, The* (Keynes)
'Keynesian Cross' diagram 267, 294–6,
309–10
Keynesian economics 7, 11–12
aggregate demand and aggregate
supply 30, 398
business cycle 339–40
classical perspective 354
equality 51
government policy and recession
376–7
inflation control 419–23
long-run non-inflationary growth
328
over-investment due to changes in
demand for consumer goods
346
saving and investment 359
stability 424
structure of production 12
Keynesian macroeconomic model
281–308
basic Keynesian equation 292–9
business cycle 329, 340
circular flow *see* circular flow
classical theory of the cycle 364
classical theory of growth and
recession 353
cyclical activity and governments
383
explanation of 283–4
exports and imports 301–2
foreign sector 289–90
government 300–301
interest rate adjustments 423
inventory adjustments 291–2
leakages-injections 287–9, 293–4,
302–3
multiplier 307
original model 281–3
over-investment due to changes in
demand for consumer goods
346
policy 304–5
public spending 307–8
recession 305–7
savings and financial system 286–7,
299–300, 390

Keynesian policy 29, 291, 296–7,
304–5, 382
Keynesian Revolution 250, 263
and Say's Law 266–80
Keynesian stimulus 291
Knight, Frank: *Risk, Uncertainty and
Profit* 72–3
know-how 125–6
knowledge 13, 125–6
commercially useful 32, 35–6
diffusion 35–6
skills, know-how and abilities 15

labour 15, 109–10, 118–19, 285
division of 246
marginal productivity of 182
labour force 125, 235
Labour Force Survey 232
labour theory of value (LTV) 254–6,
259
laissez-faire 256, 283, 366
land 15, 109, 118–19, 285
Law, John 265
League of Nations 275, 341
leakages-injections approach 287–94,
302–3, 329
limits to wealth creation 112
liquidity 378–9
inflation and 429
preference 308
liquidity trap 282
living standards 48, 208
loans 395
business 123
housing 124
personal 124
willingness to borrow and lend 396,
399–400
localized downturn 335–6
Lombard Street (Bagehot) 278
long-run aggregate supply (LRAS)
310, 319, 321–2, 327, 421–2, 424–5
long-run non-inflationary growth
327–8

McCracken, Harlan Linneus 428
'supply creates its own demand'
263–4
Value Theory and Business Cycles
263–4

macroeconomic model *see* Keynesian
macroeconomic model
macroeconomics 11, 60–61
and business cycle theory, contrast
with 339–40
economics teaching 374
macroeconomy, nature of 76–7
Malthus, Thomas Robert 250–51, 253,
266–7, 272, 276, 349
'General Glut' 269–70
On Population 250–51, 252, 263
Principles of Political Economy 252,
269, 280
marginal analysis 21, 176–205, 259
all decisions made in the present
186–7
costs and benefits 178
and decision making 184–5
decisions at the margin 176–7
economics teaching 371
graphical representation 187–91,
202–4
industry structure 192–4
innovation, entrepreneurs and 191–2
marginal revenue and marginal cost
183
opportunity cost 178–9
problems with traditional 183–4
profit maximization 180–81, 195–205
summarizing 187
and theory of the firm 185–6
time and economic return 179–80
traditional 21, 181–4
marginal cost (MC) 22, 70, 181, 183–5,
203
graphical representation 187–91
MR equals MC 23–4, 186–7, 191–2,
198, 204–5
profit maximization 201–2, 205
marginal product 182, 259
marginal productivity of labour 182
marginal revenue (MR) 22, 70, 181–5,
203
graphical representation 187–91
MR equals MC 23–4, 186–7, 191–2,
198, 204–5
profit maximization 201–5
marginal revolution 258–60
marginal social costs 373
marginal utility 182, 259

market 129–32
market activity 2–3
market competition 193–4
market cooperation 66–7
market coordination 66–7
market, defining 18
market demand 145–6
market economy 4, 35, 40, 94
  axioms 32–8
  defining 9–10
  economics teaching 375
  fundamental principles 38–53
market failure 372, 373
market forces, obstructing 67–8
market mechanism 62–3
market price 129–30
  and costs 36–7
market rate of interest (money rate) 25,
    392–3, 400–402, 404–6, 425, 432
  below natural rate 406–9
  and natural rate of interest 403–4
market supply curve 140–41
market system 34
Marshall, Alfred 2–3
  Principles of Economics 271
Marshall, Mary Paley 271
Marx, Karl 247–8, 251
  Capital 255
  Communist Manifesto 255
  labour theory of value 254–6, 259
measures of economic activity 206–39
  balance of payments 236–8
  Consumer Price Index 226–30
  employment 230–36
  GDP *see* gross domestic product
    (GDP)
  National Accounts 207–8
  stocks and flows 208–9
  unemployment 230–36
medium of exchange 24, 83, 250, 274,
    397, 427
Menger, Carl 259
merchant class 243–4
microeconomics 10, 61–2
Mill, James 272, 273
Mill, John Stuart 209, 252–3
  fundamental propositions on capital
    111–17, 207, 353
  Principles of Political Economy
    252–3, 269

Say's Law and related propositions
    278–9
minimum wage 169–71
Mises, Ludwig von 274
'mixed' economy 94
monetarism and monetary policy
  distinction 419
monetary factors 278–9
monetary policy 26, 424
  and monetarism distinction 419
money 24, 110
  base 397
  circular flow 285–6
  credit, saving and 389–92
  estimates 28
  fiat 427
  and inflation 317, 432
  market rate and natural rate 404
  quantity theory of 416–18
  recession, debt and 413–15
  Say's Law and related propositions
    273–4
  stability 425
  and structure of production 345
  supply 405
Money and the Mechanism of Exchange
    (Jevons) 427
money multiplier 429
money rate of interest *see* market rate
  of interest
money supply
  determination of 397–8
  increasing 404–6
  varying 398–400
monopolistic competition 193
monopoly 193
  natural monopolies 98, 99, 101
moral hazard 414, 433
MR equals *MC* 23–4, 186–7, 191–2,
    198, 204–5
multiplier 307

National Accounts 27, 207–8, 209, 212
  seasonally adjusted data 234
  see also measures of economic
    activity
national saving 17, 357, 385, 392–3,
    398, 401, 403, 432–3
  government spending and 410–11
natural monopolies 98, 99, 101

natural rate of interest 25–6, 392–3,
    402–5, 412
  and market rate of interest 403–4,
    406–9
natural rate of unemployment 314–17,
    319–20, 325–6, 420, 426
net exports 30, 284, 301, 303
new products/services 126
nominal (definition) 28
nominal movements in economic
    indicators 223–4
nominal rate of interest *see* market rate
    of interest (money rate)
nominal wages 226, 230, 311
non-convertible currency 427
non-inflationary growth 327–8
non-monetary over-investment theories
    345–6
normal goods 153
Norris, Keith 299

oil shock 30
oligopoly 193
On Population (Malthus) 250–51, 252,
    263
open market operations 26, 399, 404
opportunity cost 14–15, 103, 178–9,
    191
optimum rate of inflation 325
over-investment theories 344–6
  non-monetary 345–6
overproduction *see* 'general glut'
    (overproduction)

paper money 428
peaks of the cycle 78–9, 337–9
perfect competition 372
personal loans 124
Phillips, Bill 324, 426
Phillips curve 324–6, 420, 423, 426
political decisions 377–8
  and cycle, theory of 378–9
political economy 3, 4–5
political freedom 4
population growth 250–51
potential GDP 316
price 17, 41, 133–4, 136, 138, 140
  at which unit sold 28
  change in supply 158
  demand as a barrier 147

demand curve movement 149
demand versus quantity demanded
    148, 149
effect 195
elasticity changes along demand
    curve 173–4
equilibrium 152, 153
firm's supply curve 138
horizontal and downward-sloping
    supply 160–61
increase, effect of 135–7
increase in quantity demanded 154
of individual product 134–5
industry supply 159
and inflation 166
market 36–7, 129–30
market adjustment with supply and
    demand 140, 147, 156
movements 165
profit maximization 195–6, 199–200,
    203–4
and quantity relationship 173, 185
relative 24, 44–5, 64, 163–4, 287
sandwich shop example 150
supply 133
supply curve movement 145
supply and demand, using 164–5
supply means whole curve 142
supply versus quantity supplied 144
support programmes (agriculture)
    170
system 63–4
and volume of individual product
    134
see also Consumer Price Index
    (CPI); inflation
price ceilings 167–9
price controls 67
price determination 19–20
price discrimination 372
price floors 169–71
price level
  accounting for movements in 223–5
  aggregate demand and aggregate
    supply 312–13
  average 166
  and inflation 320, 323
  long-run aggregate supply 322
price mechanism 44–5
Principles of Economics (Marshall) 271

Principles of Political Economy
(Malthus) 252
Principles of Political Economy (Mill)
252–3
*Principles of Political Economy and
Taxation* (Ricardo) 247, 254
private sector activity 52, 99, 101, 218,
308
production 46, 130–31
in anticipation of demand 73–4,
333–4
level of 284
and profit 40
total 284
and valued added 84
see also factors of production;
structure of production
production costs 196, 197
production function 296–7
production possibility curve (PPC) 14,
102–6, 107, 355
classical perspective 354–6
classical theory of the cycle 362–3,
365
classical theory of growth and
recession 367
with consumption, investment and
government 409, 410
crowding out 410, 411
economic growth 103–4
economic growth in classical model
359–61
fundamental propositions on capital
(Mill) 115
inefficiency 104, 105–6
market failure 373
opportunity cost 103
saving and investment 357–8
stocks and flows 127–8, 208–9
unemployment 104–5
production process destroys value
while it creates it 85–6
productive economic environment 45–6
products, range of 213–14
profit 40, 199–200
total 198–9
see also profit maximization
profit maximization 23, 180–81, 183,
185
traditional theory of 195–205

where *MC* equals *MR* 204
where *MR* equals *MC* 195–8, 199
property rights 59, 67
prosperity 43–4, 340–41
Prosperity and Depression (Haberler)
275, 277, 341, 369
psychological theories of the business
cycle 348–9
public debt 381
public goods 99
public sector activity 218
public spending *see* government
spending
public utilities 98, 99
purely monetary theories of the
business cycle 342–4

quantity 28, 133–4, 136, 138, 140
demand as a barrier 147
demand curve movement 149
demand, increase in 154
demand versus quantity demanded
149
elasticity along demand curve
173–4
equilibrium 152, 153
exchange rates 238
firm's supply curve 138
horizontal and downward-sloping
supply 160–61
industry supply 159
market adjustment with supply and
demand 156
market demand 147
market supply 140
price ceiling 168
price floors 170
price increase 136
price and volume of individual
product 134
prices and inflation 166
profit maximization 195–7, 199–200,
203–4
sandwich shop example 150
supply 133
supply, change in 158
supply curve movements 145
supply and demand, using 164–5
supply means whole curve 142
quantity demanded 149

quantity supplied 143
quantity theory of money 416–18

range of goods and services 210–11,
    217
rationality 178
real, definition of 28
real GDP 224
real growth 28
real movements in economic indicators
    229–30
real variables 278
real wage 31, 226, 230, 311, 365–6, 370,
    380, 382, 413
recession 26, 305–7, 363
    business cycle theory 260–61
    circular flow 291
    classical theory of cycle 31, 279–80,
        331
    counter-cyclical policies 379–82
    cyclical activity and governments
        368
    downturns 79, 278, 335–6, 351
    and economic growth 336–7
    government actions to be avoided
        383–4
    and government policy 376–7
    government spending 100
    Keynes on 267–8
    Keynesian macroeconomic model
        272
    money, debt and 413–15
    and political decisions 377–8
    Say's Law and related propositions
        263, 270, 272, 275–9
    spreading from downturn 335–6
    and structure of production 77–8
    structure of supply dislocations
        48–9
    and subsequent upturn 334–5
    theory of 12, 79
    under-consumption theories 349
    see also classical theory of growth
        and recession
recovery 26–7
regulation 256, 375–6, 378, 382, 397
    government 39, 51, 95, 96–7, 100,
        380
relative prices 24, 44–5, 64, 163–4, 287
rent controls 167–9

rental, interest rates as form of 123,
    394
reserve ratio 26, 397–8
resource base 16, 44, 113, 121, 321, 421
    classical theory of growth and
        recession 355–6, 358–60, 365
    governments and the market 102,
        106–7
    savings and financial system 385,
        388–9, 413
resources, inefficient use of 105
return, economic 179–80, 307, 395
revenue 196
    average 202–4
    curve 189
    effect 195
    expected 188, 190
    future 191
    see also marginal revenue (*MR*);
        total revenue
Ricardo, David 247–9, 251, 252, 253,
    255–6, 266–7, 280
    *Principles of Political Economy and
        Taxation* 247, 254
risk 21, 71–2
risk adjustment 395–6
risk premium 395
Risk, Uncertainty and Profit (Knight)
    72–3
risk versus uncertainty 119–20
Robbins, Lionel 56
rule of law 57–8
Russian Revolution (1917) 376

Samuelson, Paul 267
saving 17, 122, 286–7, 298–300, 357–9,
    385–415
    business loans 123
    circular flow 286, 299
    classical perspective 355
    crowding out 409–10, 411–13
    economic growth in classical model
        360
    flow to potential users 387
    foreign sector 289–90
    government spending and national
        saving 410–11
    importance of 245–6
    inflation control 432
    interest rate, role of 393–7

and investment 115–16, 357–9
Keynesian macroeconomic model
   272
leakages-injections 288, 293–4,
   302–3
market rate and natural rate 400–
   404, 406–9
money, credit and 389–92
money, debt and recession 413–15
money supply 405
money supply, determination of
   397–8
money supply, increasing 404–6
money supply, varying 398–400
natural rate and money rate 392–3,
   402–3
paradox 272
personal 317
resources used for productive
   investment 388–9
Say's Law and related propositions
   271
as spending 386–7
see also national saving
Say, Jean-Baptiste 249–50, 262, 264,
   270–72, 276
Treatise on Political Economy
   249–50, 274
Say's Identity 278
Say's Law 6–7, 30, 250, 252, 261–3, 264
   aggregate demand and aggregate
      supply 310
   business cycle 329
   classical theory of growth and
      recession 331, 353
   importance of in classical business
      cycle theory 330
   and Keynesian Revolution 266–80
   Malthus and 'General Glut' debate
      269–70
   related propositions 270–79
schools, state-run 98–9
seasonality in production 216
seasonally adjusted data 29, 234
self-interest 37–8, 243
sequence, time and 74
short-run aggregate supply (SRAS)
   311–14, 320–23, 327, 420, 424–5
side agreements (private) 193
skills 125–6

Sloman, John 299
Smart, William 260
Smith, Adam 241–7, 249, 256, 261, 271
   *Inquiry into The Nature and the
      Causes of the Wealth of Nations,
      An* 55, 241
   Wealth of Nations 241, 243, 244,
      247, 254, 258, 265
social conditions 56–9
social costs, marginal 373
specialization 214, 246, 248, 331
Sraffa, Piero 266
stability 424–6
standard of living 48, 208
stimulus package 354
stocks and flows 13–14, 65–6, 127–8,
   208–9
store of value 24
structural problems 278
structural unemployment 315, 322
structure of production 12, 74–5, 88–9,
   164, 341–2
   example 391
   and money 345
   and output 391
   and recessions 77–8
   savings and financial system 390–91
supply 17, 19, 132–4, 139, 151, 159–60,
   163–4
   analysis 17–18
   as a barrier 142–3
   change in 157–9
   classical theory of cycle 279–80
   creates its own demand 263–4, 272,
      329
   dislocations, structure of 48–9
   economics of free market 64–5
   economics teaching 371
   horizontal and downward-sloping
      160–62
   market adjustment 156
   market supply 140
   means whole curve 141–2
   natural rate of interest 402
   perfect competition 372
   price system 63
   Say's Law and related propositions
      274, 276–7
   structure of 31, 75–6
   using 164–5

versus quantity supplied 143–4
see also aggregate supply; supply
    curves; supply and demand
    analysis
supply creates its own demand 263–4,
    272, 329
supply curves 19, 137–8, 141–2, 151,
    167
    change in supply 157
    competition 139
    crowding out 412
    equilibrium 151
    firms 134, 137, 157
    horizontal and downward-sloping
        supply 160–62
    increase in demand 155–6
    industry supply 159
    innovation 162
    market 140–41
    market activity reduction 163–4
    market rate of interest 401, 406
    market supply 140
    money supply 404
    movements of 144–5
    natural rate of interest 402–3
    price ceilings 167, 169
    prices and inflation 166
    production and sale 130–31
    structure 132
    supply as a barrier 142–3
    supply and demand: beyond
        equilibrium 154
    supply and demand, using 164–5
    supply versus quantity supplied 144
supply and demand analysis 129–52
    competition 138–9
    demand 145–6
    demand as a barrier 146–8
    demand curve, movement of 149–50
    demand versus quantity demanded
        148
    equilibrium 151–2
    market 129–30, 131–2
    price increase, effect of 135–7
    price and volume of individual
        product 134–5
    production and sale 130–31
    supply 132–4, 140–41
    supply as a barrier 142–3
    supply curve 137–8, 144–5

supply means the whole curve 141–2
supply versus quantity supplied
    143–4
see also supply and demand analysis
    beyond equilibrium
supply and demand analysis beyond
    equilibrium 153–75
    buyers, effects on 156–7
    demand elasticity and total revenue
        171–2
    demand, increase in 155–6
    elasticity and inelasticity 171,
        172–5
    horizontal and downward-sloping
        supply curves 160
    innovation 162–3
    price ceilings 167–9
    price floors 169–71
    price movements 165
    prices and inflation 166
    supply 159–60
    supply, change in 157–9
    using 164–5
supply-side economics 46–7, 139
suppressed inflation 431
surplus value theory 255
symphony orchestra 118

tariff increase 370
taxation
    circular flow 299
    foreign sector 289–90
    and inflation 317
    leakages-injections 287, 288,
        302–3
    levels and structure 98
    in recession 380, 381
Taylor, Fred 261–2, 263
    invents the term 'Say's Law' 261–3
technology 125–6
    technological sophistication of
        capital 15
temporary work programmes 381
theory of the business cycle *see*
    business cycle theory
theory of the firm
    economics teaching 371
    and marginal analysis 185–6
Theory of Political Economy (Jevons)
    259

time 126–7, 331–2
  and economic return 179–80
  as factor of production 15
Torrens, Robert 276–7
total costs 196–7, 198–200
total profits 198–9
total revenue 171–3, 195–6, 198–200,
    202
trade
  comparative advantage 80–81
  free 246–7
  international 11, 60, 79–81, 246, 290,
    302, 370
trade protection 383–4
trade-offs 102
traditional marginal analysis 21,
    181–4
traditional theory of profit
    maximization 195–205
transactions 416–18
Treatise on Money (Keynes) 266
Treatise on Political Economy (Say)
    249–50, 274
trend data 216–17
troughs of cycle 78, 337–8, 345, 347,
    380

uncertainty 20–21, 42–3, 71–3, 185,
    332–3
  versus risk 119–20
under-consumption theories of the
    business cycle 349–51
underemployment 235–6
unemployment 27, 104–5, 233–4, 235,
    268, 314–16
  aggregate demand and aggregate
    supply 309
  cyclical 315–16
  frictional 315
  and inflation 316, 318, 323
  involuntary 275–6
  Keynesian macroeconomic model
    282, 283
  low 351
  measures of economic activity
    230–36
  natural rate of 314–17, 319–20,
    325–6, 420, 426
  Phillips curve 325, 326, 422
  and recessions 336

structural 315
  see also unemployment rate
unemployment rate 27–8, 231–2, 235,
    322
  below natural rate 321, 324
  calculation 234–5
unintended inventory accumulation
    281
unintended inventory decumulation
    291
unintended investment 291
unit of account 24
United States 30, 283, 370
  Federal Reserve 369
upturns 79, 368
utility 70
  marginal 182, 259
  value added 82, 86, 87–8

value 10–11, 259–60
  exchange 29, 129, 254, 258, 316
  is subjective 86–7
  present 179
  sources of 258–9
  store of 24
  in use 258
  as utility 83
  see also present value; value added
value added 11, 82–92, 222, 223
  centrally planned economies are an
    impossibility 90
  ceteris paribus 91
  change, assisted by entrepreneurs
    reacting to 92
  classical theory of growth and
    recession 353
  and economic growth 86
  equilibrium 91
  forms of production 43–4
  in production 84, 279
  production process destroys value
    while it creates it 85–6
  Say's Law and related propositions
    249, 274
  structure of production 88–9
  and utility 82, 86, 87–8
value added method for GDP
    calculation 219
Value Theory and Business Cycles
    (McCracken) 263–4

values 10, 58, 69, 93
variety of goods and services 211–12
velocity of circulation 416–18
Vietnam War 310
volume of individual product 134–5
volume of production, price and 201

wages 25, 116–17, 166, 247, 255, 257,
    259–60
  aggregate demand and aggregate
      supply 315, 318, 321, 323–4
  classical theory of business cycle
      343, 346
  classical theory of growth and
      recession 357
  cyclical activity and governments
      378, 381–2
  growth 430
  and inflation 317, 420, 422, 430–31
  iron law of 251
  Keynesian macroeconomic model
      285–6, 288, 290

Keynesian Revolution and Say's Law
    271
  marginal analysis 189
  measuring the economy 209, 212,
      223, 229–30
  minimum 169–71
  nominal 226, 230, 311
  real 31, 226, 230, 311, 365–6, 370,
      380, 382, 413
  in recession 380
  supply and demand 145
Wallace, Alfred Russel 251
Walras, Lèon 259
wealth creation, limited by capital
    112
Wealth of Nations (Smith) 55, 241, 243,
    244, 247, 254, 258, 265
wealth, sharing 1–2
welfare 1–2, 95–8, 100
willingness to borrow and lend 396,
    399–400
work programmes, temporary 381

l